TALES FROM
the
BOOM-BOOM
ROOM

TALES FROM
— *the* —
BOOM-BOOM
ROOM

Susan Antilla

HarperBusiness
An Imprint of HarperCollinsPublishers

HarperCollins books may be purchased for educational, business, or sales promotional use. For information please write: Special Markets Department, HarperCollins Publishers Inc., 10 East 53rd Street, New York, NY 10022.

First HarperBusiness edition published 2003
Reprinted by arrangement with Bloomberg Press

Designed by Laurie Lohne / Design It Communications

The Library of Congress has catalogued the hardcover edition as follows:

Antilla, Susan, 1954–
    Tales from the boom-boom room / Susan Antilla.

    p. cm.
    Includes index.
    ISBN 1-57660-078-5
1. Women stockbrokers—New York (State)—New York. 2. Sexual harassment of women—New York (State)—New York. 3. Sexual harassment of women—Law and legislation—United States. 4. Sex discrimination in employment—New York (State)—New York. I. Title.
    HG4928.5 .A585 2002
    331.4'133'097471—dc21   2002011782

ISBN 0-06-056545-4 (pbk.)
03 04 05 06 07 ❖RRD 10 9 8 7 6 5 4 3 2 1

For my son, Matt

Contents

Acknowledgments

JOURNALISTS RESEARCH AND WRITE STORIES, but stories don't reach an audience without editors and others who support an idea to publication. I've been blessed with many such advocates during this project and throughout my career.

This book would never have been published without the backing of Matthew Winkler, editor-in-chief of Bloomberg News. Matt generously allowed me a long break from my newsroom duties so that I could work without other professional obligations. He has had an open mind about covering sex discrimination from the first time I approached him with a story idea on the topic in 1996. That might seem to be exactly what any editor would do. I can attest to the fact, though, that not every editor at every news organization has Matt's courage to face controversy. Matt is unique among his peers in supporting coverage of this topic. My biggest thanks go to him.

In a multimedia news organization, reporters have the chance to work with many editors. Jim Bartimo was a booster of my initial stories about sex discrimination on Wall Street on Bloomberg's print side; Kathleen Campion, Katherine Oliver, Bob Leverone, and Charlie Pellett saw to it that the story was told on radio and television.

Before coming to Bloomberg, I had begun to look into sex discrimination on Wall Street at my job at the *New York Times*. Tom Redburn and Margot Slade were advocates of my stories there.

Denise Marcil, a friend and literary agent, was the earliest believer in this topic as a viable book. Over runny scrambled eggs at a greasy-spoon diner in Stamford, Connecticut, Denise shared my passion for the subject and told me that she believed I could successfully write it.

When it came time to actually write *Tales from the Boom-Boom Room,* I got supremely lucky. Jared Kieling, my editor, turned out to be a reporter's dream. He is smart, funny, and unfrazzled by deadlines; in fact, his jokes got better as the pressure rose. Jared saved me constantly from sins of jargon and convolution. If the reader finds this book well-organized, it is he who is to be credited.

Tracy Tait, associate editor at Bloomberg Press, organized the unwieldy endnotes and uncountable other details of *Tales from the Boom-Boom Room.* Tracy and the rest of the Bloomberg Press group, under Bill Inman, embody a gem of Bloomberg—very smart people from whom I learned a lot.

At the other end of hundreds of my e-mail requests for research were the staff at the Bloomberg Library Department. Thank you to Arlene Goldhammer, Karen Heitz, Anita Kumar, Suzanne Lau, Bill Merk, Leslie Norman, Mike Novatkoski, Amanda Schultz, and Mike Weiss.

Tom Golden, Charles Glasser, and a friend we miss in the newsroom, the late Richard Klein, were valued advisers. So was my friend Diana Henriques, who had the option of relaxing in the Vermont countryside in August 2001 but instead gave up vacation time to read the manuscript. Over coffee on September 10, 2001, Diana spent hours giving me feedback in the lobby of a West Side New York City hotel. Had we put off our meeting by twenty-four hours, we would not have had a chance to meet before publication: the events of the following day would take my reporter friend to coverage of the tragedy of lower Manhattan, which consumed her time day and night for months to come.

There are men and women who spoke to me for this book trusting that I would not reveal who they were. I am grateful for that trust, particularly in light of the job-related risks that some of those people took. Whether on or off the record, though, my sources have been generous with their time, their patience, and often with skills that had to include tedious photocopying and trips to the local Federal Express office as they shared memos, arbitration filings, and company documents.

Margro Long, wife of the late Perrin Long, entrusted me with her only copies of Perrin's historical work on the securities industry in the early 1980s, an important period in the book. At the time, Perrin had but one or two peers covering the industry. His insights were key in understanding how strong a player Shearson Lehman Brothers was at the point when women were becoming brokers in significant numbers for the first time.

In my personal life, my mother, Gloria Claudet, taught me by example that women can be economically and intellectually independent. She also taught by example that a person's social and economic standing should have no bearing on the decency with which they are treated—simple values that have guided my work and my selection of stories to pursue.

My number-one enthusiast through this project has been my husband, Dennis Leibowitz. He has prodded me when I've been in slumps, cheered me on when I've hit milestones (a chapter completed!), and tolerated my messy takeover of our home with files, legal briefs, and depositions. For your cheerleading, love, and abundant patience through the gestation of *Tales from the Boom-Boom Room,* thank you, Denny.

Preface

"I can't tell you who I am. I know you've been calling around to the other women. Call these lawyers in Chicago. I'm gonna give you their number. You ready to write it down? 312-431-_ _ _ _. I shouldn't be talking to you."

Click.

THUS BEGAN THIS BOOK, though I didn't realize it at the time. I was sipping my first cup of coffee of the day at my desk at the *New York Times* in the winter of 1995 when an anonymous caller phoned to give me the names and telephone number of two civil rights lawyers I'd never heard of, Mary Stowell and Linda Friedman, who were pressing a case against Olde Discount Corp.

I had written a story a few days before about abusive sales practices at Olde, a brokerage firm based in Detroit. The day that story ran, February 14, 1995, I arrived at the office to a voice mailbox overloaded with messages from Olde employees telling me something that reporters hate to hear: You missed the story.

Or rather, there was yet another story about Olde crying to be told. Sex discrimination and sexual harassment at Olde was rampant, the callers were telling me. The phone rang with more informants even as I was listening to the backlog of calls that already had come in.

I had written about business and finance for seventeen years, thirteen of which I'd spent exclusively covering the brokerage industry and the stock market. Stories about wrongs done to women on Wall Street no longer struck me as shocking news.

What was news to me was evidence that a brokerage firm would rather forgo profits than keep women on board, which is what I was hearing on my voice mail: Some of these callers had evidence suggesting that Olde wanted women out so badly, it was willing to drive away rainmakers. I had long thought that Wall Street, in its desire to make money, would accept it equably from any source, be it men, women, or the Devil. So I did a second story about Olde, this time focusing on its women, and then got back to my regular assignment writing a weekly column for the *Times* and, subsequently, for Bloomberg News, which hired me in September 1995.

Three months after I joined Bloomberg, I later found out, a stockbroker named Pamela K. Martens dusted off a copy of that second Olde story from her personal files and gave it to one of her former colleagues, Roberta Thomann. She suggested that Thomann call the two lawyers who had represented the Olde women, whom I had mentioned in the article.

Martens and Thomann were preparing to sue Smith Barney, where both had once worked. They wound up hiring Stowell and Friedman. And I wound up talking to Martens, Thomann, and some of their coplaintiffs before they filed their complaint.

I knew that their lawsuit was coming; in fact I'd seen a draft of it. I wanted to break the story of the lawsuit against Smith Barney for Bloomberg, and my editor, Matthew Winkler, approved that story provided I could corroborate with independent reporting that the discriminatory practices described in the lawsuit had occurred.

When I began to discuss the lawsuit's allegations with women who worked or used to work at Smith Barney, I quickly discovered that most of the women were terrified at the idea of talking about their experiences. Some would whisper to me on their office phones that they were afraid to talk to me at work, so I'd arrange to call them at home in the late evening. Many would back out at the last minute.

Some, if they found the courage to get on the phone, would begin to speak but then break down and cry. To a reporter who had spent years on a business beat where regulatory filings, stock market data, and robotic executives with public relations mouthpieces by their sides were the reporting norm, it was an emotional experience to say the least.

The fear and strain the women expressed was also a starting point to my believing them.

In the years that I have been hearing these stories, I have yet to hear a convincing answer to a couple of questions that would make liars of the sources I have come to believe: How could numerous women all over the country who did not know one another have told me such similar stories of discrimination? How could so many have displayed such distress in their interviews without actually having been harmed? The pain about which they spoke was palpable; I was not talking to people trained in acting.

I have heard many a defense lawyer talk about a prototypical gold-digging litigant who contrives her story in order to raid the deep pockets of a big company. If such women exist in significant numbers, it is hard for me to imagine how they would survive in a sex-discrimination dispute against the typical Wall Street firm. There are several reasons.

Once lawsuits or arbitration complaints were filed in such cases, the plaintiffs' problems had just begun. Brokerage firms frequently retaliated, doling out punishments that ranged from subtle social and business exclusions to obvious taking away of privileges. Litigation techniques could be even more ruthless. A woman claiming emotional distress risked having her psychological, marital, and gynecological records subpoenaed and exposed to an arbitration panel. Women who fought on despite such counterattacks were known to suffer emotional problems. In fact, their former employers sometimes pointed to the women's quick tempers, depression, or other manifestations of the stress the women had been under as evidence that they had been unfit for their jobs in the first place.

Why would a woman start down such an ugly avenue if her complaint were not a solid one? The defrauder on a quest for easy money would discover that it wasn't so easy.

I have spoken to women who said they were discriminated against or harassed at firms large and small, in trading rooms and at company conferences, on the West Coast and in Manhattan's financial district, in Midwestern branch offices and at the company picnic, and I have not encountered that gold-digging litigant. If her story is in my notebooks, she is a good actress indeed. I have, however, extensively interviewed one woman who did prove to be unreliable, telling me her story and later changing her version of events. Not surprisingly, she tried without success to find a lawyer to help her sue her firm in the late 1980s. She has never filed any claim. I was therefore particularly skeptical of her leads and her comments.

The most egregious sex discrimination cases settle for generous amounts, with plaintiffs promising in exchange not to disclose what happened to them—or the price they were paid for their silence. Those who do sue rarely get to trial, or even to the process of discovery. To the extent that this book draws on lawsuits, the reader should bear in mind that not one was heard by a jury. This, of course, is of equal disadvantage to the wrongly accused man as it is to the woman who never gets a public hearing. In the case of the lawsuit against Smith Barney, the firm didn't even file a response, and all claims against individual Smith Barney employees were dismissed in the settlement.

People involved in sex discrimination controversies typically do not wish to talk, even in their own defense. Although I sent registered and certified letters to forty-four of the people or entities referred to in the book, twenty-two failed to respond, four threatened legal action, three said they had nothing to contribute, and seven could not be located by the postal service. The remaining eight of the forty-four cooperated with my inquiries; two of the eight were two of the women who had sued Smith Barney, and one of the eight was the Chicago firm representing the plaintiffs. With regard to those who declined to cooperate, I found no evidence contradicting the statements made about them. Ultimately, the reader must form a view of what happened without benefit of some parties' stories. Arguments can be made for an innocent man's choosing to sit by in silence while he is wrongly accused of harassment. Some defense lawyers advise their innocent clients that denials serve to drag out a story in the media even longer.

Over a period of months, as representatives for Smith Barney failed to return telephone calls or respond to queries I made after court sessions in the *Martens* case, it became clear to me that the company did not wish to cooperate with me in my efforts to create a balanced account. I thus decided that I would accumulate my questions over time and send them all to Smith Barney when I was further along with the project. I also contacted key executives on my own, going around the public relations department and getting important information and guidance on an off-the-record basis.

On July 12, 2000, I sent a list of twenty-eight questions to Smith

Barney spokeswoman Arda Nazerian. Seven weeks later, I received a six-page response from the firm's defamation counsel, Martin London. In his response, London answered certain questions that would reflect favorably on Smith Barney; ignored most questions; and warned me to hold on to my notes in case his client should sue me. London said that, in addition to Smith Barney, he also was speaking on behalf of other persons to whom I had sent registered mail, but he didn't name them, leaving me to guess who they might have been. On contacting several recipients of my letters in the months after that, I was told that London had dissuaded them from speaking to me by saying that this book was substantially farther along than it was, which could have suggested to them that I was not really serious about incorporating their version of events.

The firm's lack of cooperation continued. On October 31, 2001, six lawyers representing the firm by then known as Salomon Smith Barney came to Tampa, Florida, for the first arbitration hearing to be held under the settlement of a class-action discrimination lawsuit brought by women at Smith Barney on May 20, 1996. The arbitration was to resolve the claim of coplaintiff Edna Broyles. Under the terms of the settlement, two members of the press were permitted to attend the hearing. Broyles invited me and a reporter from a local newspaper in Florida. When distributing documents at the hearing, Salomon's lawyers declined my requests for copies. I did not know the names of two of the lawyers who represented Smith Barney. Although they actively participated in the hearing, they declined to give me their names.

I was fortunate, however, to have had a long interview on September 8, 1999, with Mark Belnick, the lawyer at Paul, Weiss, Rifkind, Wharton & Garrison who represented Smith Barney through most of the settlement process. Belnick was generous with his time. I also learned much about what the firm was doing from court filings that described the positive aspects of the settlement. Smith Barney became less tolerant of hostile workplace incidents after the women's lawsuit and was not shy about releasing information about firing men who were involved in improper behavior. I have attempted to include in this book the positive changes that Smith Barney made after the lawsuit.

A class-action lawsuit brought against Merrill Lynch in 1997 is also discussed here. Merrill Lynch is a passive minority investor in

Bloomberg L.P., the parent company of Bloomberg News and Bloomberg Press.

—•—

IN THE NOTES SECTION that begins on page 303, the endnotes of several chapters start with a brief summary of the sources I used to research the events described in that chapter. Readers may find it useful to read these summaries before proceeding with each chapter.

Prologue

AT TWENTY-THREE, smart, attractive, with sweeping long dark hair, Lori Hurwitz started with tall ambitions as a rookie at the Garden City, New York, office of Shearson Lehman Brothers, one of the biggest firms on Wall Street.

Her job was to telephone total strangers and persuade them to open accounts and buy securities—known as "cold-calling." She would initially make the pitches on behalf of two brokers in their early thirties who were senior to her. But she hoped to become a broker herself so that one day she could be a partner with her father, who worked at a different Shearson office. He was tickled that his daughter looked to him as a role model. Lori used to get up before sunrise during her summers off from school so that she could ride the train to New York City in the pitch black and spend the day with her dad at his big-time job. Now her childhood dreams of doing what he did were actually coming true.

They could work together in an exciting financial company that had it all: one that provided investment banking services for corporate customers who needed to raise money and retail brokerage services for individuals who had money to invest. But he warned her that his business was a rough place for women.

She should have paid more attention to that. Despite the trappings of Garden City, a pretty New York City suburb where mansions stood down the street from attractive middle-class houses with manicured lawns, the atmosphere inside the Shearson office was not what she had bargained for.

Her coworkers referred to women as "cunts" or "whores," or sometimes "bitches" or "tramps," depending on the label du jour. She sat in a small room with the two senior salesmen and two trainees, all male, all the time. There was no way to tune out their conversations.

The mentor assigned to her had opinions on the uselessness of females as sex partners after they'd borne children. "As soon as a woman squeezes out a kid, you stamp 'A million dollars' on the kid's forehead and 'Stretched goods' on the woman's," he said. In between their calls to clients, the men talked technique—not for selling stocks but for going down on their girlfriends, the sexual tricks and treats their bedmates gave them, the length of time they could keep up their erections. They called their paramours liberally on their work phones. Lori tried to concentrate on her cold calls, which totaled between 300 and 400 a day, and to pretend that none of it bothered her.

"You guys are pigs," she tossed off sometimes during the early months, giving it a dismissive tone that she hoped would come off as tough and detached. Maybe if they don't get a rise out of me, she told herself, they'll stop the raunchy talk and get down to business.

But she had no such luck. Even her branch manager, Nicholas Cuneo, amazed and repulsed her by his ability to fashion the F-word into a noun, adjective, verb, and adverb. He was popular throughout the office for announcing impromptu branch parties and for his basement "Boom-Boom Room," where the guys celebrated happy hour.

Lori learned to hate Monday mornings, when her colleagues tallied their exploits and outdid each other with graphic depictions of their sexual conquests from the weekend. It got to the point that she would feel nauseous the moment she woke up.

Then a new salesman arrived from the competition down the street, and word got around that he had been fired from his previous job for sexually harassing a sales assistant. "I knew there was a reason I liked this guy," said one senior manager. She let her dad know she was unhappy; tearful sessions several nights running led to a confession that it wasn't just the cold-calling getting to her.

She finally decided to complain at work. After that, life became impossible. Her mentor sent a memo to all his charges prohibiting the application of makeup and nail polish at their desks and outlawing phone conversations with boyfriends—"boyfriends," the memo said— on company time. Yet Lori was the only female among them.

Eventually she was told that she had a problem getting along with men, that there was no future for her as a broker. She resigned after fourteen months in the business. Six months later, her father had left Shearson, too. The chief reason for his departure was a change in corporate ownership, but it had been a slap in the face that they didn't do right by his daughter. If he had known everything that went on at the Boom-Boom Room branch, he never would have let her go to work there.

Chapter One

Garden City's Party Spot

Stuff happens on Wall Street and you live with it.

—PATTI, A FORMER BOND TRADER

WALL STREET NEVER COULD help itself when things got good, and in 1982, at the dawn of the greatest bull market in history, it was inevitable that the industry would be gearing up to repeat old mistakes: firms would be hiring too many people, building too many offices, putting on too many fancy parties, and leasing too many stretch limousines.

In the midst of this rush to expand, though, was a brokerage firm known for an adroit management that could grow its number of offices while somehow controlling its expenses per employee. It was Shearson/American Express, an empire of investment banking and brokerage operations that was constantly bucking the trends of excess despite a payroll that stood at 14,480 employees by the end of 1982.

Essential to the profitability of this standout among spendthrifts was its nationwide 352-branch network of retail stock brokerages that fed commissions back to New York headquarters. Investors all over the nation knew the name Shearson and entrusted their money to the company's brokers, who sold them stocks, bonds, commodities, and mutual funds. And a half-hour train ride to the east of New York City, amid a row of brokerage houses in the Long Island town of Garden City, was one celebrity office whose output was among the highest in the system. Lori Hurwitz and Pamela Martens were to receive their harsh introductions to the world of women on Wall Street in the Garden City branch.

The leading man in Garden City was branch manager Nicholas F. Cuneo. He was from the old guard of Wall Street's retail sales: loud, direct, demanding, and frequently crude in the office, he was accustomed to managing men like himself. Cuneo, five foot nine and slightly overweight, with a little potbelly, had a salt-and-pepper beard to match the salt-and-pepper hair that had largely remained atop his head even as middle age—he was fifty years old in 1982—had bared the pates of his peers. He wore a suit and white shirt each day, removing his jacket as soon as he arrived and not replacing it unless a VIP visited the office or he was leaving for lunch.

When it came to women, Cuneo possessed a combination of personas. Cuneo the old-fashioned gentleman might show deference to someone who stayed home to tend to her house and her children—roles he sometimes described approvingly to a male broker who reported to him. But Cuneo the manager, suddenly faced with the arrival of women in his workplace, was not so anxious to be deferential.

Even the setting of the Garden City office seemed to mock the handful of females who worked there, at 901 Franklin Avenue. They came and went each day across the street from a discount ladies' dress store whose sign read "Pay Half." Cuneo had been known to tell women, with more than a little bravado, that they should not expect to be paid as much as the men, some of whom made significantly more than they. Further, they should not even consider trying to sue him. Many had tried and failed, he once bellowed.

Considering the industry's record, Cuneo could hardly be singled out for underpaying women. Shearson's rival Merrill Lynch had settled a lawsuit in 1976 brought by a woman who'd graduated with honors from Wellesley and had an M.A. in economics from Stanford.[1] Helen O'Bannon, a former college economics instructor whose résumé leading up to her application at Merrill included jobs at the House Banking and Currency Committee, the Treasury Department, and the Comptroller of the Currency, was rejected from the broker training program. O'Bannon took a personality test as part of the application process, answering questions that assumed the applicants would be male.

"Which quality in a woman do you consider most important?" it asked: "1) beauty 2) intelligence 3) dependency 4) independence or 5) affectionateness?" O'Bannon, who answered "2," got it wrong, because no points were given for intelligence or independence, while two points were given for dependency or affectionateness, and one for beauty. "Dear Mr. O'Bannon," a subsequent letter from Merrill began. "We regret we are unable to take more of the men who apply."[2] Another woman applicant, who also was rejected, had a master's degree, had been director of a business school, and had significant sales experience.

The four applicants who did make the cut all were male. None of them had earned more than a bachelor's degree. One had dropped out of college because of his poor academic performance. Another previously had worked as a gas station attendant. And two of the four had flunked Merrill's aptitude test.[3]

So Nicholas Cuneo of Shearson was not alone in thinking that men needed the jobs to cover their big mortgages, or that women should be home with their children. Brokers who worked for him said that Cuneo—like many other Wall Street managers—probably wouldn't have hired women as brokers at all if he had had his way.[4]

He did, however, distinguish himself by his tendency to be a little louder, a little more vulgar, and even a little more arrogant than his peers in an industry already long on hubris.[5] And he clung to ancient dress codes for women—no pantsuits—even as First Lady Nancy Reagan was wearing knicker pants to the American Embassy in Paris.[6]

Cuneo was, in short, the king of his branch of Shearson/American Express. Settled on the western end of Long Island, just seventeen miles from Manhattan, Cuneo's office regularly ranked among the top 40 branches out of the more than 400 that Shearson had in those days. With profits fat, his brokers were living the good life, with luxury homes and country club memberships. Cuneo, who hailed from the far more modest Jersey City, New Jersey, now had houses in Port Washington, New York, and Stuart, Florida, an ocean community on Florida's "Treasure Coast."[7]

Many of the branch's male employees seemed to appreciate the atmosphere he fostered. He would roll up his sleeves and flip burgers in the back parking lot during lunch hour or on a Friday afternoon. Even the clique of women sales assistants with whom he was least popular would join those festivities for a beer and a snack. He once pulled up to the branch at the wheel of a flashy (albeit sputtering and backfiring) red fire engine for a pre–Memorial Day party. And he happily approved the minor expense of T-shirts for the branch softball team, which challenged local brokerage firms and other companies to games at nearby fields. The blue-and-white T-shirts read "Shearson, Etc.," a playful reference to the fact that the acquisitive firm changed names too often to keep up with.

In the days of the three-martini lunch—and with stocks on an upswing—Nicholas Cuneo was the perfect good-times boss, an inspiration to the partying types working for him. More important, though, Cuneo was a favorite with top management, commanding access as high up as the chairman of the company, Sanford I. "Sandy" Weill, when he needed it. That kind of entrée was valued by Cuneo's staff, who benefited when he used his powerful chits on their behalf.

A broker who came to Cuneo in the early 1980s with a complaint that his client's huge trade had been mishandled got to watch Cuneo's clout from a front-row seat. While the broker sat in the branch manager's office, Cuneo called Weill for his approval on big expenses that would help smooth things out with the angry customer. Cuneo's finesse and rapport with Weill resulted in an OK for the funds, and he signed off in his classic locker-room style. "Sandy, you're the nicest guy, but fuck you anyway," he said in vulgar but apparently fraternal thanks. The broker was dazzled. If Nick can talk that way to Weill, the broker thought, then Nick and Sandy must be very tight.[8]

Cuneo had come to Wall Street in 1962, the emergence of an earlier golden age that saw the Dow Jones Industrial Average shoot from a low of 539 in June 1962 to nearly double that by February 1966. He started at the 14 Wall Street office of what was then called Shearson, Hammill & Co., and in 1974 became part of the empire that Sandy Weill was building when Weill's brokerage firm Hayden Stone acquired Shearson Hammill.[9] Cuneo ultimately was named manager of the Garden City office, and it didn't take long for his branch to rise to the top. Year after year, Cuneo's office ranked in the top 10 percent of all the company branches in profits.[10] By many measures, Garden City deserved its favored status.

It was a hardworking and hard-partying office surrounded by the trappings of wealth. Cuneo started there when the branch was located at 975 Franklin Avenue, amid a row of competing brokerage house branches that included Prudential Securities, Merrill Lynch, and Charles Schwab & Co. Garden City's little Wall Street was just down the way from Saks Fifth Avenue, along a lane that included Arista Furs and the fine-art store Garden City Galleries. Around the corner, landscape artists carved whimsical animal figures and happy-faces into the shrubs in the town square. It was an affluent location, all right.

But not so affluent that it was impossible to impress people a little. When word got around the office one day in the early 1980s that Cuneo's newly acquired (albeit secondhand) silver Bentley was parked on the sidewalk outside, even the jaded brokers who owned new Mercedeses came out to lean over and look in.

Inside the office there was an easygoing dormitory atmosphere; several men jogged to work in the days before running shoes were the stuff of chain stores, and Nick Cuneo put a shower in the basement because, as one of his lieutenants put it, the guys "smelled like billy goats" when they got to the office.[11]

With Cuneo's encouragement and on their own, his brokers were big revelers. Ducking out for lunch and a drink was not frowned upon in the early 1980s; nor was the idea of decompressing at a local saloon after-hours. Cuneo encouraged a merry atmosphere, ordering in White Castle hamburgers and a keg of beer one afternoon, and barbecuing behind the building on another. Though of Italian heritage, he liked to arrive at the office with corned beef and cabbage to celebrate St. Patrick's Day. (He was said to have cooked the unwieldy feasts at home himself.) And he would occasionally return from an expansive Italian lunch with extra mini-loaves of his favorite garlic bread to pass out to his friends. Cuneo kept an assortment of candies in his office in case someone stopped by; if the visitor was a favorite, he'd break out the booze he kept on hand.

Just about everybody loved Cuneo, because he believed in fun and he believed in having his staff, mostly male heads of households, make money. Big money was spent on entertainment, too. Cuneo's lavish Christmas gathering was considered the hot ticket of the season even by the sophisticates at Shearson headquarters in New York. For his Halloween parties, even he would dress up: once Cuneo came as a piece of gold bullion.

With the reveling, though, came the outrageous, and Cuneo's old-school, boys-will-be-boys approach abetted an environment where things could cross the line. Male brokers howled as a strip-o-gram was delivered for all in the branch to see. Female brokers—always in the minority—were quickly dubbed with degrading nicknames: "Slits and Tits" was one that especially irked the female staff.[12] Cuneo's shouting, his crass language, and his anti-Semitic remarks made all but the most hardened brokers cringe.[13] There were decent men in Cuneo's office who wanted to work hard and get the job done. Some were conflicted about what they heard. Others didn't like Cuneo's language in front of women but agreed with him that women should be at home. It was a time when men in branch offices of brokerage firms were encountering significant numbers of female colleagues for the first time. For some of them, it was unsettling.

Leslie Frutkin, one of the first women to work as a broker in Garden City, was inclined to like the boss's wild style when she arrived at age twenty-five in 1982. As far as she was concerned, Nick was a lot of fun, providing opportunities for staff to let off steam at a high-stress job. Frutkin, though, was a protected species relative to the handful of other women, having known Cuneo—a family friend—since she was a child. But even she was shocked to see Cuneo slam things, throw things, scream, and curse. That behavior was apparently contagious. In the early 1980s, the office was encouraging small investors to get into commodities trading, and one broker who was there at the time remembers that visiting clients sometimes got into fistfights with one another over their strategies.

For all the atmosphere of madness he established at the office, Cuneo was appreciated for a softer side. His workdays ended with a ten-mile ride home to attend to his wheelchair-bound wife, Caroline, who had for years suffered from multiple sclerosis. (In later years, he would be on the receiving end of compassion when he developed heart problems.) Caroline was well-liked even by the boss's fiercest enemies, praised for her gentle demeanor and her grace in the face of a debilitating illness. Hospice of Long Island depended heavily on Cuneo's personal and financial support. Employees knew that Cuneo would lend an ear—and perhaps even a desk—if a relative desperately needed work.[14]

The brokers watched Cuneo dote on Caroline when she came for company parties, though he made no effort to censor his salty tongue in front of her. One employee was aghast when, at the first office Christmas party she attended, Cuneo with microphone in hand told the gathered staff that one of the male brokers was a "faggot."[15] Another year, he told employees at a holiday party at Zachary's Disco in East Meadow that the previous twelve months' success had gained them notoriety as "the biggest whorehouse in Garden City."[16] Still, his Dr. Jekyll aspect also could be seen: He bought the house in Florida so that Caroline would have a more comfortable place to spend the cold Northeastern winters, one of his supporters said.[17] When he bought a van and the silver Bentley, the supporter speculated that he did so in order to allow Caroline to get in and out of the vehicles as easily as possible when she had to travel.

As a larger-than-life local dignitary, Cuneo reaped the rewards of his position in Garden City circles. When he parked the Bentley on the sidewalk behind the branch, staffers never saw a parking ticket on it.[18] When smoke billowed above the Franklin Avenue parking lot during Cuneo's barbecues, nobody complained to the fire department. In fact, the police occasionally stopped by for a hamburger.[19]

Nicholas Cuneo usually got his way, and had the bottom-line results to justify it. He didn't need any pushy females trying to tell him how to run his office.

Cuneo was known for his practice of personally passing out paychecks each month, flinging them in the direction of employees who were not his favorites. A broker with whom he had a particular rub said that on delivering her first check he quipped, "Well, which Jewish charity are you going to give it to?" as if to say that she was so rich she didn't need the money.[20] She complained to the higher-ups about Cuneo at one point, but New York headquarters told her that "Everybody loves Nick" and that there were no problems in Garden City.[21]

Depending upon one's point of view, it was possible to see Cuneo as a critic who never meant his insults personally. Even one of his detractors admitted that Cuneo was capable of putting down *everyone*, not just the people he disliked. He was an equal-opportunity basher, this former Garden City broker said.[22]

In 1982, the Garden City office moved down the street to a flashier new site that formerly had been a furniture store. The sparkling new office with its glass atrium lifted the spirits of Cuneo's troops, who shared a chuckle early on when two elderly ladies ambled in and began to lift the cushions off the new sectional sofa in the lobby, apparently looking for a price tag.

Downstairs in the basement, in a large space that housed the furnace, brokers were busy using what spare time they had to set up a party room. They brought in a cheap plywood bar and hung a rusted bicycle and a toilet bowl from the ceiling. The latter, a remnant from the old office, was there for nostalgia's sake. The party room had a huge plastic garbage pail, too—something to keep beer or Bloody Marys cold, depending upon the occasion. And there was a boom box, of course, to provide the requisite party music.

They called it the Boom-Boom Room. And when a phone was installed there, the Shearson telephone book listed the extension under the Bs.

Now Cuneo had two rooms on the basement level where he could hold court: the elegant, oak-paneled conference room where the brokers gathered to hear him hold forth each Tuesday afternoon when the stock market closed, and the adjacent Boom-Boom Room, where everybody could unwind afterward, typically over beer and potato chips.

Cuneo's staff of brokers, which included his two sons, Nicholas Jr. and Leslie, didn't have to show up in the Boom-Boom Room, though most of the men popped in at one time or another. But attendance at the Tuesday-afternoon meetings was mandatory. It was there that they would be praised or, more likely, chewed out if commissions were down or if other branches were showing them up.

One thing Cuneo was not known to expound on was the percolating problem of customers complaining about the way some of his brokers did business.[23] He employed his share of brokers who had arrived with questionable entries on their regulatory records. Those records, filed with the National Association of Securities Dealers, are known as the Central Registration Depository, or CRD. Cuneo hired those brokers with the knowledge of his own bosses, whose New York compliance department ultimately processed a broker's paperwork, which always included records of any regulatory problems.[24]

Cuneo hired Edgar M. Fitzsimons in 1983,[25] fresh out of a dispute with a customer who had charged him with a series of unauthorized options trades while he was a broker at E. F. Hutton.[26] Information about the complaint was filed with the New York Stock Exchange on May 9, 1983, with a notation that the dispute was settled for $25,000 and that "Fitzsimons was terminated."

Once at Shearson, Fitzsimons had problems with other customers. Arbitrators at the New York Stock Exchange awarded one of them $12,400 related to a complaint that an $18,000 error took place when Fitzsimons executed a trade. New York Stock Exchange arbitrators told Shearson to reimburse another customer $16,541 related to charges of misrepresentation by Fitzsimons. He eventually would be cited in a proceeding in which drugstore magnate Leonard Genovese named him and others at the branch in a misrepresentation case that sought $17.8 million in actual, punitive, and RICO damages. According to the "current status" listing of Fitzsimons's CRD, that "case is closed, settled."[27] But there is no listing of a settlement amount; NASD at the time required that brokers who settled cases for amounts of $5,000 and greater list those settlements in their regulatory records. Although it is of course possible, it would seem unlikely that a multimillion-dollar case was settled for less than $5,000, leaving open the question of exactly how the case had been resolved.[28]

Others hired in Cuneo's Garden City office despite a record of customer problems included Taihwa "Terry" Ho, who, like Cuneo, had flunked the Series 63 state regulators' exam the first time he took it.[29] Ho had four customer settlements related to the massive Prudential Securities limited partnership fraud of the 1980s that put black marks on the records of many brokers who didn't realize the inferior level of what Prudential was directing them to sell.[30] Ho, though, also earned a few customer complaints without the assistance of those shoddy limited partnership products.

Although his records say he had a "voluntary" termination from Prudential-Bache Securities Inc. in April 1988, the citation made reference to a charge one month before his departure by a customer who said Ho had churned his portfolio of stock index products, making unnecessary transactions in order to generate commissions. (A year later, on May 3, 1989, the National Futures Association dismissed the churning claim.) He had been involved in a case two years before in which he personally contributed $4,000 of a $7,000 settlement shared by the company to an investor who charged him with unauthorized trading.[31] Contributions by individual brokers to arbitration awards are the exception, not the rule. Records show that he settled "for economic reasons."

Under Cuneo, Ho was a target of further accusations by customers, contributing $20,000 of a $175,000 settlement of charges of misrepresentation and unauthorized trading in one case, and watching the firm contribute all of a $21,500 settlement in another.[32] (The latter, also a case brought for misrepresentation and unauthorized trading, was settled "for business reasons," according to Ho's CRD.)[33]

Glenn H. Fischer, who began as Cuneo's sales manager, arrived in the Garden City office in 1984, likewise having worked at Prudential Securities. In August of that year, a case brought by two of Fischer's former clients was settled for $12,500 after they claimed that they had not been made aware of the risks involved in buying Ginnie Mae securities with borrowed money.[34]

Stockbroker Jerry Alampi also joined the Garden City branch in 1984. He had been discharged from Prudential-Bache Securities in March of that year after Prudential alleged that he had violated company policy, according to his regulatory file.[35]

Brokering was a rough-and-tumble business, and some of Cuneo's hires had marks on their records that were perhaps benign enough to ignore in making a hiring decision. Gary W. Owens had been charged with petty larceny—reduced to disorderly conduct—when he was twenty years old for taking a used tire from an abandoned van, his broker records say.[36] Three years later, while working as an insurance investigator, he pleaded guilty to reckless endangerment.[37] In his NASD files, he gave the explanation that he was assigned to photograph certain people who had claimed a disability from a car accident. "The plaintiff spotted the investigators taking pictures and called the police which charged Owens with wreckless [*sic*] endangerment," Owens's file says, offering no further assistance in understanding the infraction.[38]

As it happens, though, Owens as a broker got into more altercations, albeit relatively inexpensive ones. Shearson paid one investor $1,800 to settle a case in which the investor claimed $1,994 in losses related to a dispute over options pricing. Owens said in his file that Shearson did not require that he participate in paying the settlement and that he "strongly disputed" the investor's charge.[39] In another case, the firm paid $2,000 to settle a $3,050 case related to a charge of unsuitable investments. Owens noted in his CRD records that he did not join in that payment either and that an internal investigation by Shearson "found no wrongdoing on my part."[40]

"He is my model broker," said Nick Cuneo at a morning meeting of the bullpen brokers, horrifying Kathleen Keegan, a broker who was repelled by Owens's dirty jokes.[41]

Cuneo hired plenty of brokers who started off with clean records. Yet many of them got on the wrong side of customers once they were working on Cuneo's watch. John C. Gatto was charged with breach of fiduciary duty, negligence, and breach of contract by two customers, who got $70,000 in a settlement. (In his regulatory record, Gatto denies the allegations, says his lawyers "have agreed to the compromise and settlement," and says he doesn't believe the complaint was warranted.)[42] Another customer charge—this one alleging excessive and unsuitable trading, negligent misrepresentation, negligent supervision, and breach of fiduciary duty—was settled for $24,000.[43] In the latter case, the claims against Gatto were dropped; brokerage houses frequently settle on the condition that the individual broker's name be removed from the list of defendants despite the broker's involvement.[44]

Kenneth A. Gatto, brother of John, lost a case that went to New York Stock Exchange arbitration; the customer was awarded $11,027 after telling arbitrators that Gatto had assured him that the North Side Savings Bank was a great buy because it was going to be taken over.[45] The takeover never happened, but brokers who assure clients of an impending takeover are breaking regulatory rules in any event. Kenneth Gatto said in his regulatory file that the customer was an officer in a publicly held company at the time of the complaint, and that the customer was familiar with "types of investments." His regulatory file also said that two other customer complaints against him were "denied" by Smith Barney, which merged with Shearson's brokerage branches, including the Garden City office, in 1994.[46]

Charles J. Slicklen, Jr., another Cuneo hire, arrived with a clean record but was named as a defendant along with Edgar Fitzsimons in the multimillion-dollar Genovese complaint that ultimately was settled for unknown terms.[47] Slicklen's records also state that he was cited in an earlier case where Shearson settled for $45,000 on charges that he had made unsuitable investments for a customer.[48] He says in his regulatory file that he settled the case "in order to avoid the time, expense, and uncertainty involved with litigation."

Finally, there were Cuneo's progeny, Nicholas Jr. and Leslie Cuneo. Fortunately for the two, who were criticized behind their backs for alleged favored treatment at a firm that had a written policy forbidding "direct or indirect supervision of relatives,"[49] their records were without scandal. They had only two small customer complaints between them, one of which was won in arbitration by Nicholas Jr., the other of which—a correction of an administrative error—was settled for less than $200 by Leslie.[50] Nicholas Jr. failed the Series 3 exam for a commodities license twice in 1991; his records show no subsequent attempt at taking the exam.[51]

———

CUNEO'S FLOCK of hard-charging brokers worked the phones each day in their highly competitive jobs. They fought over clients. They curried favor with the boss to get accounts that were left behind when a broker retired, was fired, or quit without taking of all his customers. Stockbrokering was a scrappy business that suited aggressive and persistent salespeople. It took a personality that could cope with rejection, because brokers—particularly at the start of their careers—had to make hundreds of cold calls a day.

In Cuneo's branch, the big-shot brokers often had women doing their cold calls for them. Men made cold calls, too. For some reason, though, Shearson in general had more women filling the cold-calling jobs.

It could get raunchy in Cuneo's office—more so than in the typical branch. But scuffling for accounts and pitching a firm's investment wares was a high-pressure venture, particularly with excitement mounting over a stock market that seemed to be picking up steam. The records of the brokers might not all be pristine. Their deportment, and the branch manager's own example, might not win any awards for political correctness. But in the nerve center of Shearson/American Express in lower Manhattan, the bosses looked at Cuneo's bottom line and saw that it was good. Whatever he was doing was fine by them.

Chapter **2** *Two*

From Appalachia
to Wall Street

I felt like a worthless piece of dog meat when I left work every day.

—SURVEY RESPONDENT QUOTED IN THE PLAINTIFFS'
EXPERT REPORT ON SMITH BARNEY WOMEN

IN 1982, WHILE NICK CUNEO'S CREW at the Garden City branch of Shearson/American Express was making big profits and blowing off steam, Pamela Martens was becoming increasingly preoccupied with finding new ways to make money. On September 15, she walked into the Merrill Lynch & Co. office on Franklin Avenue in Garden City, just a few doors down from the Shearson office, and told the receptionist she wanted to buy some stock. Martens had just moved to Garden City. She had never bought a stock before, didn't have a broker, and wasn't sure how to go about getting one. It was the first time in her life that she'd been able to accumulate a little money that she could invest. She had flexible hours at her publicist job just ten minutes away at the Rehabilitation Institute, a center for emotionally disturbed children, so she was able to duck out of the office to swing by the Merrill branch. The receptionist assigned her to the "broker of the day"—a rotating assignment in a retail office in which a designated person takes care of walk-in business.

On call that day was Roberta Schwartz, who greeted her and asked what she had in mind. Something conservative, said Martens. I'm very conservative. Schwartz suggested that Pam invest the $6,000 she'd allocated for the stock market in Long Island Lighting Company, the local utility. Schwartz took care to be cautious with this first-time investor, putting her not only into an electric company but into its ultra-safe preferred shares. Pam invested $5,992.50 in all and said she wanted to take possession of the shares rather than leave them in Merrill Lynch's custody. When the document arrived in the mail, she put it in the locked metal box where she kept her marriage certificate.

It never occurred to Pam Martens how unusual it was that her stockbroker was a woman. In those days, not a single woman ranked among the managing directors or general partners at Salomon Brothers, Bear, Stearns & Co., Morgan Stanley & Co., or Goldman, Sachs & Co.[1] At Goldman, only 8.6 percent of the 643 vice presidents were women.[2]

Scared off by a slight decline in the LILCO stock, Pam's first venture as a capitalist became a false start: she sold less than three months later at a loss. She never had occasion to talk to the Merrill Lynch broker again. She did have occasion, though, to keep thinking about ways to make better money, whether by investing or some other way. She had a new obligation in her life.

Her two-year-old son, Sean, had been born on January 2, 1980. Pam and her husband, Russ, had put off becoming parents for seven years, until they were satisfied they were financially secure. They'd met back in 1970 when both of them were working at *Executive Business Media,* a trade magazine in the Long Island town of Lynbrook. Russ was printing production assistant. She was editor-in-chief. Pam had been taken by this tall fellow with sandy brown hair, whom she got to know over lunches with office friends at McQuade's Pub in Rockville Center. He seemed wholesome. He was very laid-back. He talked about family and his work with the Boy Scouts. It wasn't long before they were dating.

Pam had been in the New York area for six years by the time she met Russ, having fled the confines of Appalachia soon after she graduated from high school in 1964. She lived with her sister on Long Island and worked as a bookkeeper, an editorial assistant, and ultimately an editor of submarine manuals before she got the job at *Executive Business Media.*

Now, though, in 1982, despite the savings they had managed, it was nagging at her that what they had wasn't going to be enough. The Rehabilitation Institute didn't pay much. The job before that had been running publicity at Woodward Mental Health Center, another center for children with emotional problems. That position had had a troubled ending, and equally low pay. Yet up to now, she had not had sufficient drive to make a dramatic change and enter the real business world.

—

MAKING THE BREAK took two more years. In 1984, the summer before Sean was to begin kindergarten, she quit her job at the Rehabilitation Institute, hoping to find something promising by the time he started school. That summer off with Sean marked her complete split with the not-for-profit world. While she was sunning with him at the Garden City Municipal Pool, another mom showed her a magazine with a horrifying story: *Money* had just published a treatise about the cost of sending a child to college. Pam was tens of thousands of dollars short of the nest egg the magazine advised having by Sean's tender age of four. I've got to do something, Pam decided. There had to be a way to make decent money and fulfill her dreams for her son. But it wasn't likely it would be by working for someone else again.

Pam was ready to take a big step, and already she had come a long way. She was the product of a West Virginia town that offered two lines of work: the glass factory and the coal mines. Neither was acceptable to Pam, who sprinted for New York right out of Lost Creek High School, just like her sister, Diana, had. No prima donna about her living accommodations, she had launched her New York life the way many hopeful working girls start out, first as her sister's roommate and then, when Diana got married, setting up housekeeping in the basement of Diana's Long Island home. Pam's quirky combination of qualities made her in some ways a quintessential transplant to Manhattan. Her brown hair and gentle brown eyes, her disarming accent, and her genteel, sometimes righteous Southern values exposed her soft side at first blush. Indeed, with her tiny five-foot-three frame, she appeared most unthreatening, someone more likely to spend her free time talking with her sister over a cup of coffee and a cigarette than engaging in any of New York City's more dramatic or sophisticated pastimes. But Pam also had a contentious side: she quarreled easily, and it jolted new acquaintances that so soft-spoken a person also could be so strident or uncompromising. She racked up one too many speeding tickets during her early New York years and got her driver's license suspended in the mid-1970s—not the last time she would be pulled over for a moving violation. Now, after nearly a decade in New York, she had put a toe into the stock market, taken it quickly out, and was ready to push into a new career. The dilemma was, how could she be more her own boss yet still have somebody showing her the ropes in a new line of work?

She had learned a good deal about the risks and rewards of entrepreneurial control at the knee of her maternal grandmother, Carrie Virginia Rowe. Grandma Carrie was a matriarch of their rural hometown of Mt. Claire, in central West Virginia; as a newborn Pam was carried home to Grandma Carrie's house from the local hospital twenty minutes away, St. Mary's in Clarksburg. Pam's father, Frank J. Convertine, was away in the Army Air Force.[3] Her parents had been high school sweethearts at Lost Creek High but were divorced by the time Pam was in grade school.

Pam's mother, Lola Ellen Rowe Smith, frequently relied on Grandma Carrie to take care of her two daughters—Pamela Kay and Diana, who was two years Pam's senior. To help support the family, Lola often took out-of-town jobs, from subscription clerk at the Washington, D.C., *Evening Star* to telegraph operator at the Alexandria, Virginia, Western Union office.

The Rowes were heroes in the eyes of most locals, a legacy of admiration rooted in the family's kindnesses to neighbors during hard times in the late 1920s. Her great-grandfather's Rowe General Store was a bustling core of the community, a place where just about everyone dropped in eventually during the course of a week. The store was a success until the tail end of the Great Depression coincided with a mining strike that financially crippled many in the town. William Louis Rowe extended credit to his suffering customers, and his largesse ultimately brought him down. But the townsfolk never forgot the generosity he showed them: Two generations later in Mt. Claire, Pam, despite her family's poverty, enjoyed special respect reserved for the Rowes, who continued to be viewed with deference.

She thus grew up with the confidence of having come from a venerable family. Apart from the Rowes' praiseworthy history, though, people in tiny Mt. Claire made few distinctions about status or class, because everyone was poor. To be an aristocrat was to have indoor plumbing. If she were to venture someday into the world beyond Mt. Claire, maybe her lack of familiarity with class structure would be some kind of handicap. But here in town, her rural-bred naïveté about pecking orders and social distinctions was harmless and irrelevant.

She was hardly favored to find gainful employment where she was, though. Available jobs were out on farms, in the local glass factory, or in the unhealthy, black-lung-inducing pits of the region's coal mines. Pam was uncomfortable with the town history of workers who once received part of their salary in scrip that could be used only at the company store. And she couldn't help noticing the deaths around her, as miners succumbed to a pulmonary disease that in those days had no name. The constant job-related fatalities planted seeds of outrage in her.

Mining is how Pam's grandfather, Frank Rowe, Grandma Carrie's husband, had made a living. Frank Rowe, though, was never a part of Pam's upbringing. Pam never did get a conclusive answer as to why her granddad had left his family. One of Pam's aunts, bitter at her father, maintained that Frank walked off and lit out for California because he couldn't take the stress of six children. Another aunt and an uncle said that their father had vanished because he was too heavily beholden to his employer. He had run up a $400 debt at the mining company store, they explained, a sum he could not pay back while supporting a wife and six children on his modest miner's salary. The only way he could relieve his family of the liability was to disappear.

Beyond the mystery about Frank Rowe, Pam grew up in an environment suspicious of big employers. Her grandfather had been virtually indentured to the mining company, which, for all practical purposes, was printing its own currency for the miners. She didn't like to see the relatively weak position of the working people of her town.

Frank's abandoned wife carried on stoically without her husband, never divorcing him. Divorce was simply not something one did in that part of West Virginia. Carrie was Baptist, though she did not attend church regularly. The Lost Creek Baptist Church had lost its roof in a tornado before Pam was born, making it a good thing that Carrie was content to pursue the Bible at home. On Sunday nights, Pam would hear the impassioned sermons of the Reverend Billy Graham on the radio—a fixture of her grandmother's spirituality. For the most part, though, Grandma Carrie would read Scripture and interpret it on her own, quoting to her children and grandchildren regularly. She took from the Bible certain precepts: she never cut her hair, never drank alcohol, and never wore a trace of makeup. Pam didn't mind the homespun catechisms, and their poverty didn't bother her much, either. In fact, life in Mt. Claire was idyllic, in her youthful view.

There were annual Firemen's Carnivals at the Lost Creek Fire Department, ice cream socials at church, and a sunrise breakfast at the Mt. Claire Methodist Church on Easter Morning (everyone brought a covered dish). It was the stuff of a Norman Rockwell painting. And, though she never studied finance—home economics, not math, was pushed on Mt. Claire's girls—she at least got an early introduction to trade through a self-taught barter system.

Armed with a galvanized bucket in each hand for their booty, Pam and her best friend and cousin, Ginger Rowe, would labor in the berry field next door, called Grace Grove's. It was owned by Irving and Grace Grove, but Irving was so quiet that the whole town referred to the plot of land by only his wife's name. Its fat raspberries and blackberries made a lush centerpiece for breakfasts at Grandma Carrie's. The children looked forward especially to the mornings that Carrie sent them off on a deal-making venture: to swap eggs from their chicken farm for bottles of milk from Grace and Irving's dairy. Armed with the berries and the milk, the cousins would return home to Grandma Carrie's kitchen, where they would pour the sweet cream from the top of the bottles over their harvest while the milk was still warm from the udders of the cows.

By the time they returned, Carrie already would have dressed and swept the house. Her work ethic required that no one should lolligag, so chores were done before breakfast was served. Once the house was swept, she would join the girls and delight them with stories of her childhood on a farm in Braxton County, West Virginia, and of the work she did later in a clothespin factory and as a substitute teacher.

As the girls ate their berries, they also heard about Carrie's family's mineral rights on the farm in Braxton County. For generations, the family had received minuscule checks that averaged $100 a year—to be divided among six siblings—for the oil and gas that came from the land. Carrie couldn't figure out why the family wasn't getting more than that.

Carrie saved her Bible lectures for nighttime, footnoting them the next day with righteous stories about the proper way to live one's life. "It's a lie, and it's a black one," she would bellow to the girls whenever the moral of her story touched some defilement of truth that particularly offended her. Pam loved her grandmother, whose ethics had an indelible impact. Carrie taught her to be a purist, to hold out for "the greater good," and to be wary of making easy compromises.

In Mt. Claire, Pam developed a sense that doing the right thing would lead to more right things. She was named Outstanding Student in Home Economics at Lost Creek High School when she was fifteen, claiming a brass-plated trophy coveted by her peers. The so-called Crisco Award was a thin-waisted, Barbie-doll-like figurine draped with a cape and holding a brass wreath over her head.

Pam excelled at nearly everything she did. She earned a senior life-saving license at sixteen, enduring a rigorous test that required swimming thirty laps with a struggling "drowning" man twice her weight. The swim coach trained Pam never to fight back when the drowning man was thrashing, but instead to simply go under temporarily with him. She took away the lesson that she should work to make a little headway all the time, particularly when things looked bleak.

She finished her senior year with the highest grade-point average in her class and wrote out her valedictorian speech carefully on note cards. Though Pamela K. Martens surely had been a big winner at Lost Creek, she sounded more restless than content as she addressed her class of ninety with a call to keep moving and to plow ahead through life. "What we have achieved is simply a small weapon we shall need in battling the forces of nature and man," she told them, adding that she and her classmates had learned "to take a box on the ear and come up again fighting"— an approach she took to heart as she set out on her own. She warned that slouches "would rust from idleness" and ended with a quote from Robert Louis Stevenson that "to travel hopefully is a better thing than to arrive." Pam Martens was a seventeen-year-old who didn't want to sit still.

———

NOR DID SHE at thirty-five. By the end of the summer of 1984, after four months of uninterrupted time with Sean, she'd had enough of the good life, enough of anxiety over bills, and enough of working for others. She opened the want ads of the Sunday *New York Times*, the paper that had supplied her with three of her previous four jobs. Her eyes jumped to a rectangular solicitation bearing the familiar American Express logo.

"Be Your Own Boss," it said. Shearson/American Express was looking for new stockbrokers—entrepreneurs, it appeared—who would be trained by the quality company with the well-known "Blue Box" logo to sell investments and make big bucks.

Pam never looked at another ad. She sent her résumé to Shearson/American Express the next day.

Shearson answered and said they'd like her to go to Manhattan to take psychological tests that would determine whether she had the right stuff to be a broker. In November 1984, Pam took the test in a dingy Manhattan work space that looked to her like the back office of a low-ranking civil service bureau. One question read:

If you were at a dinner party and an individual made an obnoxious remark, you would

(A) challenge it

(B) ignore it

(C) try to change the subject

It would be terrible to upset a hostess by furthering a disturbance at a dinner party, Pam thought. All that time that a hostess invests in cleaning the house, putting the monogrammed hand towels in the bathroom, getting out the crystal and china. What decent person would contribute to making things worse? She circled B.

Then Pam, an ace math student in high school, went to another Manhattan building—this one an impressive high-rise in the financial district—to take the math test in a room with a sweeping view of New York City. She was very impressed. She settled in at a sleek conference-room table and breezed through Shearson's examination of her quantitative abilities.

Shearson was interested in this numbers whiz who came off in the psychological test like a peacemaker who would not rock the boat. They tried to steer her to their Long Island offices in Bay Shore or Patchogue—towns much farther away—but Pam persisted in pushing for a job in the Garden City branch, which was just four blocks from where she lived. She couldn't imagine why she should drive for an hour to try to sell stocks in a market she didn't know when she could drive for five minutes to sell stocks in an affluent town. Besides, why would she work so far from her son just as he was starting school at age five? No way, she told Shearson.

They reluctantly set up an interview for her with the manager in Garden City, Nicholas F. Cuneo.

ABOUT A WEEK after she'd taken the tests in New York City, Pam arose on a late fall morning, said goodbye to Russ as he headed out to work, and readied Sean for his nursery school, which was five miles north of Garden City, in New Hyde Park. She was relieved to know that it would be a calm morning now that Sean was happy with school; the first few days in September, he had cried and clung to her leg when she dropped him off.

The drop-off was uneventful, and she drove back home to relax for the rest of the morning. She had been working part-time lately on free-lance projects for the Nassau Symphony Orchestra but had nothing pressing that day. So she ate lunch and got ready for her early-afternoon interview with Mr. Cuneo. She drove off in her light blue Mazda RX-7, excited over the prospect of a new career.

Pam was wowed when she walked into the impressive new quarters of 901 Franklin Avenue with its overarching glass atrium. She felt confident in her standard dark blue suit and white blouse. She would be sure that Mr. Cuneo saw the best of her: polite, charming, sincere, and smart. She was determined to get this job.

Chapter 3 Three

Wild Times
for Wall Street

*He made it clear that I would be able to do all his trades and keep
his commissions if I slept with him.*

—DONNA, A FORMER STOCKBROKER

N INETEEN EIGHTY-FOUR was a portentous year to be considering a career in the brokerage business. As Pam walked into the
Garden City office of Shearson for the first time, ethics were
sinking to a new low even by the investment world's standards. Stockbrokers at big firms like Shearson were dining out on their Madison
Avenue–produced image as professionals who imparted to favored
clients the wisdom of crack research departments. But the fact was that
some brokers were little more than salespeople who hit the phones each
day with a list of products to push, answering to a manager preoccupied
with commissions, not customers. It was not unheard-of to find high-
producing stockbrokers drafted from the ranks of used-car salesmen, to
say nothing of their colleagues who hailed from cashier jobs at the local
department store. The nation's 52,000 stockbrokers were no assemblage
of pedigreed MBAs.

The public was rarely aware of it when their phones rang with a pitch for the latest miracle investment, but the industry was awash in barely disclosed caveats and hidden fees that lined the pockets of brokers at the customers' expense. The products investors bought most—mutual funds—were touted in pervasive advertising that exaggerated or simply masked their past returns. Never had so many funds been "Number One."

Goings-on in the mergers-and-acquisitions business also benefited more powerful folk at the expense of the naïve small investor. Illegal insider trading was so rampant in the M&A industry that the chairman of the Securities and Exchange Commission—the federal regulators of the financial world—threatened in 1981 to come down on the crooks "with hobnail boots."[1] The attendant loss of faith in the system was a blow to the legitimate capital-raising function for which the markets existed. Yet three years after chairman John S. R. Shad's warning, it had become standard operating procedure for a stock, or options on the stock, to move up briskly in the days before a merger or hostile takeover deal was announced, as cheaters with inside knowledge bought shares of about-to-be hot companies. So standard, in fact, that it was noteworthy when a stock didn't rise before such an announcement. Law firms and investment banks would, from time to time, suffer a bout of bad publicity when one of their employees was accused in civil or criminal proceedings. The frequent private reaction of legal and financial professionals to such censures, though, was that it was a pity that a lawbreaker had been caught.

The preannouncement stock run-ups got bad enough that securities regulators could no longer ignore what was happening. Concerned that the public was losing confidence in U.S. stock exchanges as a level playing field for investors big and small, the SEC decided that the insider shenanigans had to be stopped, and Shad's warning gained some strength.

Up to 1984, the year that Pam Martens set her sights on Wall Street, not much punishment had been meted out for stock transgressions, which were done with a strong dash of arrogance—that is, with a wink, a nod, and a quick call to a Swiss bank. The famous arbitrageur Ivan F. Boesky was riding high in this era of blatant illegal trading. To the delight and admiration of plenty of people in the business, Boesky gave what became known as his "greed is good" speech to students at the

University of California, Berkeley, in 1986. "Greed is all right, by the way," he told the commencement crowd, prompting a spontaneous round of applause.[2] "I want you to know that. I think greed is healthy. You can be greedy and still feel good about yourself." This proclamation by an industry superstar was music to the ears of students fresh out of business school: it's OK to care about money above all else. The ethics professor was becoming the campus dinosaur while the investment banking professor was lecturing to packed classes.

Boesky was considered a brilliant speculator who placed colossal bets on the outcome of proposed—and anticipated—mergers. He was a big bettor who scattered his buy-and-sell orders to firms all over the Street in an effort to keep word from spreading that he was behind the trading. The public did not know that Boesky the far-seeing merger speculator was the kingpin of a massive insider trading ring.

While Boesky wheeled and dealed, a thirty-two-year-old banker at Shearson Lehman/American Express, Dennis B. Levine, was effortlessly raking in millions of dollars by swapping illegal tips with his banker and lawyer buddies. (Levine's initial $40,000 investment would grow to a balance of $10 million over a six-year period. About $9 million of that belonged to Levine, the rest to his cohorts.)[3] In fact, Levine was laying the groundwork to enfold Boesky in his operations, oblivious to the fact that Boesky's own circle of illegal tipsters could put to shame the relatively small network Levine had set up. Not to say, of course, that Boesky spurned Levine's advances as too puny for him. He happily set up an arrangement with the young Shearson banker.[4] Both men, meanwhile, were much pursued by financial reporters, who too frequently treated the powerful sources with a deference that an impartial journalist has no business showing anybody.[5] The rogues, abetted by a wide-eyed press, were becoming luminaries.

In fact, celebrities were popping up all over as the dollar value of financial deals mounted. Martin Siegel, a movie-star-handsome investment banker at Kidder, Peabody & Co., had become a standout among deal makers, sought after by the managements of blue-chip companies to advise them on their strategies and to defend them when raiders tried to take them over. All the while Siegel was secretly scurrying about as a mole in Boesky's network, even as America's corporate leaders endorsed him.[6] Little did they imagine that their trusted adviser would be the protagonist in a James Bond–style scene in which a Boesky operative handed

Siegel a briefcase full of cash in payment for illegal tips just inside the revolving door of New York City's Plaza Hotel.[7] Siegel used the $150,000 stash—bundled in stacks of $100 bills—to dole out weekly wages to his nanny and other servants.[8]

While undetected crooks cleaned up in the mergers and acquisitions arena, a new generation of corporate raiders was commanding a high profile. Takeover artists stocked up on enough shares of a public company to frighten management, then got paid to go away. These so-called greenmailers—Saul Steinberg and T. Boone Pickens among them— were by some accounts no better than the golden-parachute-packing top brass of the companies they preyed upon. Among the companies whose managements paid off predators were the would-be squeaky-clean bosses of the Walt Disney Corporation, which on June 11, 1984, paid Saul Steinberg $31.7 million—plus $28 million in "expenses"—to exit the scene and leave management in place.[9]

Shareholder-rights activists cried foul over the payoffs with shareholder money. That planted seeds of discontent in the minds of investors and eventually made the term "entrenched management" a household expression.

As the raiding and merging raged on, once-anonymous upstarts were becoming Wall Street forces overnight. Despite the fact that the stock market was in the doldrums in 1984, Drexel Burnham Lambert Inc. drew 800 titans of finance to its annual power huddle at the Beverly Wilshire Hotel. The confab formerly had been a backwater gathering of financial types interested in bond funding for companies that had trouble raising money. The attendance roster of the following year's "Predators' Ball" would turn out to be a road map for securities regulators looking to crack a coast-to-coast illegal trading conspiracy. At the time, though, the fact that Drexel could pay for all this in a down market was simply ascribed to its investing genius.

Pam Martens could not have been looking to join the brokerage industry in a year more noted for scandal in every quarter. Along with investment bankers, a few nominally unprejudiced financial journalists earned their own disrepute. R. Foster Winans, a former columnist at the *Wall Street Journal*, admitted in 1984 that he had taken payments in exchange for providing inside information to two stockbrokers. Winans had tipped the brokers to what he would be saying in his influential "Heard on the Street" column a day or more before the newspaper came off the presses. The well-informed brokers pocketed an easy $600,000 in four months as a result of Winans's information, buying stocks he was praising before the paper made its way onto the delivery trucks.

Winans's competitors covered the shocking story and figuratively shook their heads in disgust, but many members of the financial press had little to feel superior about. Reporting standards were getting lower by the day as journalists, desperate for a scoop in the accelerating merger-mania, published reports that one big player or another had amassed a low-single-digit position in a stock. "So-and-so has purchased 3 percent of the shares of such-and-such company, this newspaper/magazine/channel has learned," the stories would typically report. These news accounts, which would be based on information from unidentified sources, frequently sent the stock flying, perhaps just in time for the story's source to sell out near the top and take the rest of the day off.

After a lengthy bear market that had kept the Dow Jones Industrial Average languishing between 600 and 1,000 since 1974, stocks had taken off in August 1982, staging a welcome rally that actually included the investing public at first, and spreading significant cheer through the financial community. By 1984, partisans of the theory that a prescient stock market predicts the direction of the economy were having their day. The Gross National Product was up 7 percent, an increase not seen since 1951. Civilian unemployment dropped to 7.5 percent from 9.6 percent in 1983, and inflation appeared to be under control, with prices rising only 3.9 percent in 1984. Four years before, in 1980, inflation had been at 12.5 percent, and the only one smiling then was the conservative retiree with a hoard of Certificates of Deposit.

All things considered, the stock market had every reason to be perking up, and trading volumes also were booming. From average daily volume of 46.9 million shares in 1981, daily trading on the New York Stock Exchange exploded to 85.3 million shares by 1983, and to nearly double the 1981 level by 1984, with 91.2 million shares changing hands in a six-hour trading day. Smaller stocks, which traded in the over-the-counter market, had even greater levels of volume growth. Volume on Nasdaq nearly doubled from 1982 to 1983.

The new bustle in the stock market began to pique the interest of publishers who were looking to cash in on the new good times. *Manhattan Inc.*, a slick monthly magazine that chronicled the movers and shakers of business, was launched in 1984. So was *Investor's Daily*, a newspaper whose claim to fame was page after page of charts depicting movement in individual stocks.

Times were good all over, and along with legitimate securities, some dicey products were being pitched to the newly interested public by a persuasive new wave of industry hucksters. In 1984 lawsuits were already flying against some large brokerage firms that had peddled the now-worthless securities of the Washington Public Power Supply System and Baldwin-United to retail customers.[10] Merrill Lynch brokers had been selling Baldwin-United to unsuspecting customers until just before the company filed to reorganize under Chapter 11 bankruptcy protection.[11] Class-action lawyers were licking their lips at such grievous treatment of investors.

In dribs and drabs, word was starting to get out that the small investor had better watch his or her wallet. In 1982 *Forbes* magazine had published a groundbreaking story about Robert E. Brennan, president of a small-stock brokerage called First Jersey Securities. To the astonishment of innocents who were caught up in Brennan's flashy television ads (in which he invited investors to "Come grow with us" as he stepped into his private helicopter), *Forbes* said Brennan was running a crooked boiler room—a hard-sell telemarketing operation with little regard for the products it sold.[12] *Forbes* continued to write about Brennan, but investors lost millions on First Jersey's frequently worthless stocks nonetheless. Brennan, epitomizing the era, attacked *Forbes* for suggesting that his operation was less than aboveboard.

Over the short term, Brennan stayed largely untouched by the bad publicity, bilking a public who wanted to believe they could profit by sharing in a piece of "something exciting," as Brennan's brokers described their companies in a scripted pitch.[13] For more than a decade, Brennan fought securities regulators, even asking the United States Supreme Court to hear his appeal of a Securities and Exchange Commission action against him. The Supreme Court declined to hear the case, and a Federal judge in 1997 told Brennan to pay $22 million in ill-gotten gains plus $53 million in interest for his schemes from 1982 to 1985.[14] He ultimately was barred from the industry,[15] settled with the state of New Jersey for $100 million, and was convicted of bankruptcy fraud and money laundering on April 16, 2001.[16] On July 26, 2001, he was sentenced to nine years and two months in prison.[17]

Stockbrokers less flamboyant than Brennan were still easily able to find investors whom they could swindle, buying lists of prospects most likely to be suckers (subscription lists to get-rich-quick magazines were a good source) and persistently wooing them. It was a time, in fact, when many brokers were perfecting a three-step "kill" for selling stocks to strangers over the telephone. Lehman Brothers, which became part of Shearson in 1984, had a downtown Manhattan office that was famous for its aggressive, script-reading cold-callers. Call Number One was to introduce oneself to the target—with a promise to let them know if something "special" came along. Call Number Two was a pitch for a solid-sounding blue-chip stock—a strategy to establish a veneer of respectability. (Bad brokers knew that investors all over were making money by working with the legions of legitimate people selling stocks and bonds. So they disarmed their prospects by suggesting a more customary sale.) And Call Number Three was the big loser: the "opportunity" to buy shares in what might turn out to be a profitless company whose underwriting would bring bonus commissions to the broker.

The public was largely oblivious to the boiler-room tactics, which included creatively named companies that sounded like established investment firms. The names Morgan, Goldmen (misspelled), Prudential, and Solomon (misspelled) made their way onto the front doors of firms utterly unrelated to the big names they mimicked.

Big-firm brokers looked down their noses at their telemarketing cousins of ill repute but were not necessarily of perfect scruples; among them were some who simply used different and more elegantly wrapped tricks. Investors fell for touts from big firms, too, taking the bait, for example, when brokers endorsed deceptive limited partnerships that they claimed to understand thoroughly during their table-pounding endorsements.

Many major firms were distributing their own prepackaged scripts, full of lies and exaggeration, for their people to read (with feeling) to prospects on the phone, almost the way the boiler rooms did. Their slightly more polished approach could actually do more damage when trusting customers followed the advice of their brand-name broker and ended up owning a dud. As always was the case when people were feeling flush, an exposé of these scams was as likely greeted with a shrug as with a gasp of horror.

When customers occasionally caught on and went to the regulators, the big firms had a handy advantage. Their huge legal staffs already had protected the companies in the fine print of customer agreements, prospectuses, and sales literature. Brokerage firms also had the where-withal to fight long legal battles that would deplete most customers' resources long before a day in court ever came. Firms had fought hard to force customers to forgo court and settle for arbitration in the event of any business dispute. When arbitrators ruled in favor of the customer, though, it was not unheard-of to see the same firms that had fought to keep the customer away from judges and juries race to the courthouse to complain that the arbitrators had erred.

With stocks, bonds, funds, and partnerships, brokers had plenty of merchandise on hand. But to keep commissions flowing, the exchanges devised new financial vehicles to woo investors large and small. Thirteen new derivative instruments—such as options or futures that played off the prices of underlying securities—were introduced in the surge of euphoria in 1983, up from only three such unveilings in the previous year. Stock-brokers got busy extolling to the small investor the virtues of options trad-ing. Sales forces that once offered just stocks and bonds were now hawk-ing insurance, real estate investment trusts, research and development partnerships, futures, Certificates of Deposit, options, and commodi-ties. Any recruits who had answered the Shearson want-ad along with Pam Martens were going to have no shortage of products to pitch.

NEW YORK CITY, the Money Capital of the World, was churning out profits for bankers, traders, even financial journalists. The restaurant scene was hot, from the old standards uptown—Christ Cella and The 21 Club—to brash new entries right in the financial district. Even spots like the Pussycat Lounge, a men's bar on Greenwich Street just north of the financial district, were watching business pick up.[18] Wall Street firms were in many cases allowing brokers to claim strip lounges as entertain-ment expenses as long as they brought clients. Landmarks such as Harry's Bar at Hanover Square and its cousin, Harry's at the American Stock Exchange, were filling their tables within minutes after the 4 P.M. closing bell was rung.

Some of the new boom was attributable to politics. The Reagan administration had fostered an atmosphere of deregulation that pleased the Street, both because deals were easier to get done and because the brokerage firms themselves could now take on new forms. The financial supermarket—one-stop financial shopping for everything from checking accounts to options trading—was rolled out as the answer to investors' dreams. Whether it actually served investors is an open question, but there was no doubt that it rewarded the lawyers and bankers who concocted the deals.

The firm Pam was interested in joining was a good example. After buying Shearson Loeb Rhodes in 1981, American Express had bought the regional brokerage firms Robinson-Humphrey and Davis Skaggs and the insurance company Foster & Marshall. With its acquisition of Lehman Brothers in April of 1984, Shearson Lehman/American Express became the number-two financial services firm in the United States, second only to Merrill Lynch. As firms like American Express branched out in the kinds of businesses they acquired, their sales forces hurriedly studied up on a longer list of lucrative products.

At this festival of moneymaking, the public often was either left at the door or invited in only when the booby prize was being awarded.

THE BROKERAGE INDUSTRY is drawn to excess as toddlers are drawn to bruises on the head, and it didn't take long for the expansion to go too far too fast. Although the bull market that began in August 1982 would barely take a breath on its upward climb until the 1987 stock market crash, 1984 was a tough year, one in which stocks pulled back and firms had to pay for some of their overbuilding. Aggressive hiring of new brokers by firms that did business with the retail public meant that expenses went through the roof starting in 1983. By the first quarter of 1984, profits at the big brokerage firms that are known as "wire houses" —Merrill, Shearson, Dean Witter, and the like—were 70 percent below what they'd been a year earlier. By the end of the second quarter, 200 of the 397 New York Stock Exchange member firms doing a public business were operating at a loss before taxes.

For the full year 1984, mutual fund sales were down 29 percent, to $550 million. The investors who had put a toe in the water in the heady market of 1983 were getting frightened that the stock market was too risky.

Worse yet for the brokerage firms, commission sales were down 15 percent by the end of 1984, to only $7.1 billion. Proof positive that the small investor was scared could be seen in the portion of commission revenues coming from the retail public: only 35 percent, down from 40 percent in 1983. So not only was the "pie" of total commissions smaller, but the portion attributable to business from small investors had shrunk even more than the pullback by professional investors.

Curiously, as management at securities firms agitated over out-of-control expenses in the face of declining profits, one company was not only expanding but also getting praise for its proven ability to keep costs down. Shearson/American Express had the highest pretax profit margins of all the national firms tracked by Lipper Analytical Securities Corp. in the twelve months that ended June 1984. Perrin H. Long, who at that time was the only Wall Street analyst devoting himself to full-time coverage of brokerage companies, pointed out in report after report during 1984 that no competitor came close to Shearson.

Long looked at the five big firms that dealt with the public—Prudential-Bache, E. F. Hutton, Merrill Lynch, PaineWebber, and Shearson/American Express—for the five years that ended in December 1983 and found that Shearson's dollar expenses per employee were the lowest. Shearson's expenses were only $64,169 per employee, compared to $75,737 for Hutton and $69,945 for PaineWebber. And Shearson accomplished this feat despite rapid growth: total employees at Shearson had grown from 14,480 in December 1982 to 16,871 a year later. The number of branch offices had grown from 352 to 365 during that time.

By June 1984, with the addition of Lehman Brothers, which it had acquired in April, Shearson had 380 branch offices and 20,489 employees, including the highly profitable Dennis B. Levine.

The well-managed brokerage firm thus found itself in terrific shape when the dreary market of 1984 appeared finally to be reviving. After what could most generously be called a sloppy stock market in the last two months of 1984, the Dow Jones Industrial Average lost thirty points in the first three trading days of 1985 but then began to rally by the second week of the year.

Shearson's competitors perked up, too, having taken draconian steps to get expenses under control. After-tax return on equity for brokerage firms as a group rose 16 percent in the first half of 1985, up from 7 percent in 1984. And after a depressing showing by mutual funds in 1984, fund sales by July 1985 were at record levels, showing that small investors were getting confident about the market again. Americans were about to take $5.4 billion out of their money market accounts during 1985 while adding $73 billion to stock and bond funds, beginning a movement into stocks that would take household stock investment from $1.1 trillion in 1985 to $6.3 trillion by 1998.

Thus, although Pam didn't know it, this was a perfect time to make a run at the recruiters of a brokerage firm looking for new salespeople. Should she land this job, she would be at a firm that stood out among the Wall Street competition. She would also be at a local branch that was a standout profit maker for Shearson. She could learn a lot about the industry, about Shearson, and about how to be a successful broker, right here close to her home. She was a self-starter. She wanted to be her own boss. And she certainly considered herself an uncompromising person who could carry the American Express banner with integrity and grace. Pam figured this was the right place for her, and she valued the reassurance that came with a big and well-respected company like American Express. And it would be a bonus not to be working under the rule of a single boss at a tiny employer, as she had at the ill-fated job at Woodward.

Indeed, never had there been such a perfect time to be starting out as a stockbroker at Shearson/American Express.

If only she hadn't been a woman.

Chapter Four

Nick's Way with Women

It was worse than vulgar.

—A FORMER BROKER IN SHEARSON'S GARDEN CITY OFFICE,
ON THE ATMOSPHERE SHE ENCOUNTERED

HE'S GOT TO BE KIDDING.
The branch manager, the pudgy man who was lecturing
Pam about the way things worked around here, could have
been a demented Santa Claus with his cropped white beard and his
loud, dictatorial style.

Pam considered whether Nicholas F. Cuneo might be putting her on.
She listened politely, acting as professionally as she could in the face of
the strange oration. As she sat attentively, she stole glances around
Cuneo's grand new second-floor office with its huge oak desk, matching
built-in cupboards, and elaborate round coffee table with containers of
Hershey's Kisses. The leather chairs were colored gold.

"What makes you think you can make it as a stockbroker?" Cuneo
barked. He was waving his hands with each point he made. "I'll spill
more liquor than you're gonna earn in your first year."[1]

Sensing that the question was rhetorical, Pam remained silent. This guy can't be serious, she thought. Maybe it's a test.

"Don't expect me to pay you the same stipend as the men," he added, as Pam would later allege in federal court.[2]

It was not quite what she had expected. Shearson was, after all, a high-profile piece of American Express, one of corporate America's crown jewels. American Express was one of the best-managed companies in the nation. He's checking me out, she concluded. He's trying to see if I'm tough enough. He needs to be sure I'm not too timid for this business.

And if I'm wrong and he's just crazy, I'll make it as a broker here anyway, she thought. She had made it for years in the male-dominated trade publishing business. As for persuading this management enigma that she was worthy, Pam had no doubts. I always get the job, she thought, because I knock myself out at interviews. I'm sincere, and I'll work harder than anyone.

This interview was running the better part of an hour. Pam was able to stay poised despite Cuneo's in-your-face style. She had put no preparation into the meeting, rarely looked at the *Wall Street Journal,* and didn't include business books in her regular reading repertoire, which went more along the lines of *House Beautiful* than *Fortune.* Too bad she hadn't brushed up on recent developments at brokerage firms. Only a month before, *BusinessWeek* had run a story that chronicled fact gathering toward a class-action discrimination complaint against Goldman, Sachs & Co. Readers who got to the end of the article read the projection of the firm's co-chairman John C. Whitehead that Goldman would have women partners "within ten years."

Cuneo finally was winding down.

"I want you to come back, to meet my assistant manager," he said.

"Why, I'd love to," said Pam, rising from her chair and following him out of the office. To herself, she said "This guy can't scare me," figuring the interview was some kind of tough-guy game that people at big companies played.

She was certain that it was the right time to break away from the public relations and publishing positions that she'd been in for sixteen years. With one eye on Sean's future education bills and another on the idea of developing expertise in a new area—finance—where she could help clients make money, she was motivated like never before. If she could get accepted at Shearson, she could in large part be her own boss.

Cuneo had left things up in the air, but Pam figured she had another shot at persuading the assistant manager, Henry Chin, when she came back. As she walked down the stairs under the sunny atrium skylight, past the ficus trees and the posh oak paneling, she resolved to make sure that Mr. Chin would like her.

At home that night, she at first said little to Russ about her meeting with Cuneo. Pam and Russ typically kept their career business to themselves, mostly out of concern that mentioning big changes or problems might cause the other to worry. The session with Cuneo, though, prompted Pam to talk more than she usually did. "He was very boastful," she said of Cuneo. She had never met anyone quite like him.

<hr />

PAM'S SECOND INTERVIEW came less than a week later. This time, a friendly Asian face greeted her. There were no lectures, no barking, and no threats of inferior salaries for women.

Henry Chin clearly was another Garden City big shot. He had a mammoth oak desk, overstuffed light blue chairs, and a matching oak table that stood between them. Chin was on the main floor of the office, behind a big window that showcased his status there.

Unlike Cuneo, Chin was open, approachable, and welcoming. He was wearing a dark, Wall Street–style suit, yet he simply invited Pam to make herself comfortable and observe him doing what brokers do. Chin opened his daily business diary and began dialing the clients he had listed on his calendar. So this is what it's like, Pam thought. She listened as the old pro schmoozed his customers, catching up on their jobs and health and recommending a stock he thought would be just right for their portfolios. He was fastidious about marking down on trade slips exactly what he and the client had agreed upon. Pam could see that the job demanded concentration as well as personality. It looked like fun.

Chin finished a few calls, then swiveled in his chair to face Pam. That's when she saw the gun emerge from under his pant cuff. Strapped to Chin's ankle was a handgun, not exactly what Pam expected brokers would need in the line of duty. She continued the conversation as though she hadn't noticed it.

I guess they keep a lot of cash around here, she thought. Like a bank or something. That makes sense. They need to protect all this money.

Indeed, the gun was on Chin's ankle for security reasons, though not quite in the way Pam imagined. Every couple of years—almost always during a market downturn—employees at some branch or other would be thrown into a panic when an unstable customer who had lost money in the stock market showed up with a gun. Though such incidents were infrequent, they happened enough to persuade Garden City's brass that someone up top—and near the main entrance—should be armed.

Chin himself seemed not in the least threatening. What he appeared to be was terrifically busy, and Pam appreciated his willingness to give her a straight taste of a broker's workday. She told him she was excited about Shearson, that she'd be a hard worker, and that she was grateful for his time and thoughtfulness. He evidently liked her, too.

They must have set this up as one of those good-cop/bad-cop things, Pam thought. First Cuneo, then this guy. Chin escorted her to the door and later told Cuneo that he thought she'd be a great addition to the branch.

———

SHEARSON CALLED PAM TO TELL HER she'd start in the training program at $24,000 a year. It would be two months later that she would overhear gossip in the office that men in the same class as she were making $30,000.[3] Still, Pam must have been considered something of a catch compared to several of her female peers in the training class, who later told her they were making $200 a month less than she was.

To say it was a time of flux for women in finance would be an understatement. By some measures, it was an era of hope, with business schools reporting increasing numbers of women landing spots in their MBA programs. The Anderson School at the University of California in Los Angeles registered an all-time high of 40 percent female enrollment in 1985. Women were beginning to be frustrated, though, when they entered jobs in finance and failed to be paid at the level the men were paid.[4]

Not only did women in finance—particularly its Wall Street arm—make less, they also occupied fewer of the positions available at securities firms. In 1974, women held 33.8 percent of all securities industry jobs but only 6.5 percent of management positions.[5] By comparison, women were at the same time filling more than half of all clerical jobs.[6]

It is not only the statistics that tell how little the power elite did to bring women in. The predecessor organization to today's Financial Women's Association was formed in 1956 because the all-male Bond Club wouldn't allow women members. Muriel Siebert succeeded in being the first woman to buy a seat on the New York Stock Exchange in 1967, but her membership was anything but smooth. Siebert raged in the mid-1970s when, while hosting a group of French women executives at the Stock Exchange Luncheon Club, she was forced to traipse her guests down the stairs to get them to a ladies' room. Siebert subsequently threatened to have a Port-O-San delivered to the board of directors if they did not see to it that a ladies' rest room was opened on the luncheon club floor.

She got her bathroom. It was an early clue that change was most likely to come when complaints were made loudly and publicly.

———

FEW THINGS CAME EASILY to the women who worked on the Street—something Pam had thought little about in her zeal to become a broker. It was not just the pay disparity or the gender-specific nuisances such as Siebert's long treks to the latrine. Those who invaded male bastions frequently suffered other disadvantages beyond unequal pay and bulging bladders.

Sometimes the inequities had to do with the cost of becoming qualified for the job. When Patricia Clemente joined the Los Angeles office of Shearson in 1981 as a sales assistant, she learned about some of the benefits that assisted only the men. In a statement later entered in court, Clemente said that while her male counterparts were given time off to study for the Series 7 test, she had to use one week of her vacation time for her cramming.[7] Brokers must pass the Series 7 test in order to get a license to sell stocks to the public. Little wonder that when the men in the office learned that a woman was scheduled to take the test, they laid bets on whether she would flunk.[8]

Forty percent of the women who took the test during a period studied by the EEOC in late 1994 and early 1995 failed, compared to only a 27 percent failure rate by the men.[9] The EEOC took the opportunity to suggest that gender-based biases might exist in the test questions, but the fact that men got more support and study time may provide a better clue.[10]

Although the system did not tend to support its female test-takers, many studied and excelled nonetheless. Lacking equal support, however, it could be a struggle.

Court filings asserted that Clemente worked in an atmosphere where brokers gave bonuses to sales assistants who were willing to give men neck massages.[11] She complained that her manager once arranged a career advancement seminar whose agenda was instruction in hair styling and makeup application.[12] After Clemente protested about the hair-styling confab, the meeting was canceled.[13]

Years after Clemente received her invitation to attend the hair-styling seminar, Jennifer Alvarez joined the company that by then had merged with Smith Barney in Berkeley, California, and experienced still other injustices related to getting her broker's license. She said later in court documents that the men got study time, but she squeezed in her studying for the Series 7 after she got home from work. The documents said the men got study books for free from the company, but she paid for hers. At an "appreciation lunch" for sales assistants, the branch manager said he didn't hire men for sales assistant positions because men are too ambitious. "That's what I like about you women," he said. "You're lapdogs. You're content to stay put."[14]

Alvarez said in a 1999 Statement of Claim against Smith Barney that, before she quit in 1995, she routinely endured workplace confrontations in which one of her male bosses spread his legs and told her to "get on your knees and give me what I want." The statement of claim said that the same broker tried to convince her that there was a tradition at office Christmas parties she should know about: sales assistants like Alvarez were supposed to flash their breasts to him. Alvarez complained to the female operations manager, but the manager responded that the broker was "just flirting." In fact, the woman added, he'd treated her the same way.[15]

Lydia Klein, who began as the assistant to the branch manager at a Shearson office in Manhattan in 1981, advanced farther than many of her peers, working her way up the ladder to portfolio adviser to high-net-worth clients.[16] She got there, though, at a high price, and would tell the story of a demeaning environment in her 1999 Statement of Claim against Smith Barney, which merged with Shearson's brokerage operations in 1994.[17]

In 1982, two men—a trader and an officer in the municipal bond department—sent her a calzone shaped like a penis, with ricotta cheese seeping from a hole in the pastry. The harassment Klein says she experienced was constant and public. The same trader would stare at her breasts and ask "How they hanging?" He approached her at a business dinner making lewd remarks as he hung a banana outside his pants zipper. Another man—a supervisor—would stare at her breasts and say "Oooh, I love them, booby booby boo."[18] A male coworker once bit her ankles at work, tearing out patches of her nylons.[19]

A wire operator in Walnut Creek, California, was told she couldn't become a broker because "Your dick isn't hard enough."[20] According to court documents, a broker in Colorado grumbled about discrimination only to hear her branch manager respond that she couldn't quit "because you are my token bitch."[21] A broker in New Jersey would arrive at work to a male broker's query as to whether she masturbated in the morning and then washed "that thing" before she got to the office.[22] The same broker took his penis out of his pants in front of female colleagues, put it in his drink at a party, and told them "It's thirsty."[23] Another male broker at an office in California cornered a wire operator against the wall, placed his right hand against the wall, his left hand up her skirt and on her buttocks, and told her "This is going to be so good, I've wanted to do this for such a long time." He then rubbed his erect penis, through his pants, up and down her buttocks. When the branch manager learned of the conduct, he said the broker should be left alone because he was "going through a mid-life crisis."[24] In the late 1990s, when a psychologist surveyed women who said they had been harassed at the firm, seven out of ten said they feared retaliation and that filing a complaint would hurt their chances of advancement. Of those who complained, only 2 percent said the person about whom they complained was punished. Courts would later say that employees who failed to use the company's complaint system didn't have a valid case.

These incidents and allegations of discrimination and harassment, from Pam's Garden City office to Patricia Clemente's in Los Angeles, were legion at the time Pam was training for the job, yet the women were unaware of the similarities in ill treatment from one branch to the next. It was thus with utter ignorance of this side of the brokerage business that Pam Martens signed on as a trainee in the Class of 1985 at Shearson/American Express.

SHEARSON GAVE HER the indispensable Golle & Holmes study guide for the Series 7 test, a white tome with a blue spine packed with instructions and practice tests on everything from securities regulation and account management to the nuts and bolts of how securities work. Pam began to devour the information. Management gave her the option of studying at home, but Pam preferred the discipline of traveling the four blocks to the Franklin Avenue branch, where she holed up each day in an empty office on the second floor. With her paid study time and free study guide, Pam was at least more fortunate than female trainees like Clemente and Alvarez had been at their branches.

On January 18, 1985, while Pam was still cramming for the test she would take that spring, she and Nicholas F. Cuneo signed a regulatory document known as the U-4, which officially put her on file with securities regulators. Both signers of the ostensibly routine document overlooked caveats that should have been red flags to each.

What Pam never noticed was a minuscule waiver that forever excluded her from the nation's courts should she have a dispute with Shearson or any other brokerage firm she might work for.

What Cuneo apparently paid no attention to was a hint that Pam Martens could be a boss's worst nightmare. Question 27 A of her regulatory form asked "Have you ever been the subject of a major complaint or legal proceeding." Pam checked the "yes" box. She attached a sheet that annotated a hellish period in her life—a time when she'd tried to do the right thing but had triggered the wrath of a former boss. She had moved on from that episode, which could have derailed her financially. But she had not forgotten the way it began, early one day in October 1976....

WHEN THE DOORBELL HAD RUNG that Monday morning, Pamela Kay Martens perked up to see a messenger on the other side of her storm door. Maybe it's something nice, she thought. That would be welcome, considering that she was, for the moment, unemployed and worrying about life as a one-paycheck couple. The cost of living was always a worry these days, President Ford's "Whip Inflation Now" initiative notwithstanding.

She opened the door of her two-story colonial, letting in brisk October air. But there was no box with ribbons, and no smile on the face of the messenger.

"Are you Pamela Martens?"

"Yes, I am."

He shoved a plain manila envelope into her hand and turned wordlessly to retrace his path down the driveway, past the shrubs she and Russ had manicured, past what was left of the Indian corn that unexpectedly cross-germinated with the regular corn that season.

Baffled, she shut the front door, opened the envelope, and stared at a formal, ominous-looking legal document. She could barely believe what she saw.

"You are hereby summoned to answer the complaint in this action," it began. She turned to the next page and saw the name of her former boss. "Gertrude K. Berman, Plaintiff, against Pamela Kay Martens, Defendant," it read.

Defendant? I'm a defendant in something? She flipped through the document, past the allegations of her "false, defamatory, and malicious" statements about Berman, and found the demand in the last paragraph of Page Ten. "Wherefore, plaintiff demands judgment against the defendant for the sum of Five Hundred Thousand ($500,000.00) Dollars, together with the costs and disbursements of this action."[25]

Five hundred thousand dollars? The figure was mind-boggling. She was an unemployed woman with $6,000 in savings. She and Russ, married only three years, had bought their pretty brown house in Smithtown, Long Island, with its robin's-egg-blue shutters, for $55,000 only two years before, and the mortgage had become a burden since Pam had quit her job at Gertrude Berman's organization six weeks before.

Frightened, she hurried to the telephone in the kitchen, clutching the papers in one hand and dialing her husband's Manhattan office with the other. He was a manager at United Artists Corp.

"Russ, Gert sued me," she blurted out. "For half a million dollars."

Russ Martens switched gears from his work and tried to focus on what his wife was telling him. His first instinct was that Berman's lawsuit was a stratagem to divert attention from controversies that had been swirling around Berman herself. But he knew Pam could not ignore the salvo. "You need a lawyer," he said, not mentioning, for the moment, that they barely had the financial wherewithal for small claims court, much less a serious legal battle. In fact, at a time when legal connections would be vital, there was only one lawyer whom Russ Martens even knew.

It would have to be Michael Coco, Russ's longtime buddy and fellow assistant scoutmaster at Wauwepex Boy Scout Camp, out in Wading River, New York. Mike had run the commissary during summer camp when Russ was younger, and he admired the Martens family. Russ, his brothers, and their father all had been drafted into the Order of the Arrow, scouting's honor society. Mike considered the Martens clan solid family men who were devoted to kids. A telephone call from Russ's wife would be a priority.

Russ trusted Coco, but he didn't immediately understand the unevenness of the match in pitting his camping buddy against the big guns of Long Island's business and health care communities. Pam and her lawyer by most measures would be out of their league in a legal battle with Gertrude Berman, the well-thought-of head of the Woodward Mental Health Center, where Pam had been director of community relations. The Woodward Center was a respected not-for-profit agency, and Berman was the local Florence Nightingale of mental health, with a stellar career launched in 1957 when she began caring for emotionally disturbed children in the basement of her home.[26] That kind of munificence would be a natural to pull at the heartstrings of a jury.

Yet there was a lot Russ didn't know. Pam tended to leave the minutiae of office life at the office. She had told him practically nothing about any rumblings around Berman until this past Labor Day weekend. That was the weekend Russ watched his ordinarily mild-mannered bride turn into a combative whistle-blower, holing up to write a fifteen-page treatise about her boss's alleged misdeeds. Now Pam was getting sued for the explosive contents of that letter, which she had shot off on September 7 to twenty-seven members of the Woodward board of directors and to the Nassau County Mental Health Department. On the day the letters were distributed, Russ had called Berman to say that his wife would not be returning to work.[27]

Even if the lawsuit was a ploy, it would have to be dealt with. Russ told his wife to call Michael Coco and set up an appointment. Pam said she would begin to pull together the papers she would need.

Pam actually had resigned on August 9, 1976, but had agreed to remain for at least a month to see through a big project before she walked out the center's doors for the last time.[28] She had been uncomfortable with goings-on at the center, having heard gossip of doctored enrollment numbers and padded billing of agencies.

On September 3, though, Pam had decided to go back on her

promise and leave a week early. Staffers at Woodward were reeling over an explosive story in *Newsday,* the biggest Long Island newspaper, with the headline "School Accused of Illegal Billing" across three of the page's four columns. The Nassau County Department of Mental Health, the story said, was investigating charges "that the school illegally triple-billed agencies for services provided to students." The deputy mental health commissioner confirmed to *Newsday* that an investigation was in the works, though no conclusions had been drawn.[29] Berman told *Newsday* that there had been no irregularities in the billing.[30]

Pam might have stuck it out until a replacement was found for her public relations slot if not for a job demand she was unwilling to meet: several board members had approached Pam to write a rebuttal letter to *Newsday* that Friday afternoon. Write a rebuttal letter when she wasn't certain that the rebuttal was true? Pam at that point had no hard evidence that her boss had doctored enrollment numbers.[31] But she wasn't certain that it wasn't true, either. She decided she would not put her name on a letter that defended Berman. She instead gathered copies of old board minutes to take home over the long Labor Day weekend.

That night, on her fifty-mile drive home, she began composing a memorandum in her head. It would go to every board member. Plus the county Department of Mental Health. Some problems she had herself observed, such as high turnover at the center.[32] Other charges had come to her only secondhand. One piece of office scuttlebutt had it that Berman was pushing out teachers who had the most seniority, an unsubstantiated accusation based on a theory that Berman wanted to reduce the number of people with whom she would share a pension pool. Active union members had complained to Pam that their every move was being scrutinized by the boss.

Mentally outlining the letter took her back over events since she'd come to the center. Woodward's program, which helped severely disturbed children get jobs or get back into mainstream schools, was by its nature made up of a community of students who put tough demands on the faculty and staff. That she knew firsthand. She had been relaxing over coffee with colleagues in the cafeteria one day when a student menaced them with a knife. On another day, while she was making her way through the cafeteria line, a student working behind the counter told her "I recommend the spaghetti." Pam looked down at the entree in time to hear him add, "I just spit in it."

Incidents like those made it a strain to get too involved with the children. She had focused her energy on the job, which had been specifically designed for her: to drum up publicity for the center and to attract celebrities who would brighten the days of the children and contribute to the publicity push.

Pam had been a success as a promoter. She knew how to play the publicity game, setting up a Community Advisory Board of celebrities. Screen star Cliff Robertson was on it, as was basketball great Dave DeBusschere of the New York Knickerbockers, who lived in Garden City. Jimmy Piersall, the Boston Red Sox star, was a natural recruit in Pam's view because of his candid disclosures about his own mental illness in his book *Fear Strikes Out: The Jim Piersall Story*. With Piersall in tow, Pam made the rounds to local television and radio stations. When the New York Jets were practicing at nearby Hofstra University, Pam talked quarterback Joe Namath into stopping by to sign footballs for the children. The New York Yankees signed baseballs for kids who had a paucity of happy memories.

The local newspaper, *The Freeport Leader*, chronicled the celebs' visits to Woodward, and the *Long Island Graphic* carried stories about accreditation renewals that reflected the high standards the center maintained. Pam had written rah-rah stories that ran in the in-house publication *The Woodward News*. "Governor Cites Woodward as Model Center" had been the lead headline in the May/June 1976 issue. Actually, Governor Hugh L. Carey sent a replacement to accept Woodward's Humanitarian Award—and his speech praising the center was written by Pam herself.

That had been barely two months ago. Now she would be writing her own material. And distributing her denunciation of Berman to the full board.

———

MICHAEL COCO WAS SIZING UP the new client who had called him only a couple of hours ago. His first impression of Pam Martens was that she was very sure that she was right. His second impression: she was extremely intelligent.

It was remarkable, he thought, that she could remember things as well as she did. If her reports to him were accurate, hers was the closest thing to a photographic memory that he'd ever seen.

Pam had showed up five minutes late for her 2 P.M. meeting at Coco's offices on Glen Street, in the tony Long Island suburb of Glen Cove. Coco took her to the conference room down the hall from his own modest office. His building had old-fashioned, high, stamped-tin ceilings. Coco was happy at his new job at Crowe, Deegan, which had hired him fourteen months before to help with real estate closings. He was new to the firm and new to the legal profession, having been admitted to the New York State Bar three-and-a-half years before.

He had never defended a libel case but felt comfort in observing that Pam had the makings of a good witness: believable, certain of her position, and loaded with documents she thought would back up her claims. Because Pam was Russ's wife, he'd made time for her the same day she called. It was October 20, 1976, two days after she'd been served with the summons and complaint.

Coco took notes as she described herself and her predicament: 29, married in April 1973, no children. She was worried about losing her home, but Coco assured her that she and Russ were safe: the two owned their house as "tenants by entirety," and unless Russ died, Berman could not touch their only significant asset.

Pam told Coco that she wanted to make a separate claim against the board of directors, charging that Woodward and its board were responsible for her actions in writing the letter because she wrote it in the line of duty. Once sued, the board might pressure Berman to drop the suit against Pam, or so her thinking went. Coco thought a counterpunch like that was a good idea and scribbled some notes about what he'd say in such a complaint. At 3:20, he accompanied Pam to the elevator and then walked back to his office, jotting a notation to bill her for 1.3 hours.

———

PAM TRIED TO GET ON WITH HER LIFE despite the looming legal threat, and by January she had settled in at a publicity job at the Rehabilitation Institute, another center for emotionally disturbed children. The ongoing lawsuit, however, gave her little rest. Berman opposed Pam's motion to dismiss the suit and filed an affidavit in support of that opposition on April 20, 1977, taking a personal shot at Pam. "Defendant is in public relations," Berman swore to the court. The letter Pam sent to the board was "the cold, calculated work product of a professional."[33] On June 6, the court dismissed Pam's third-party lawsuit against the board of directors.[34]

Despite that setback, Mike Coco became increasingly comfortable with the claims of his client. He would get his hands on a document Pam had mentioned only to find that it matched nearly verbatim the notes he'd taken from Pam's memory.

Berman filed more papers in July complaining that Pam's whistle-blowing had turned her into a pariah in the mental health industry. She said that she was "bogged down in trivia" at her job as a result of Pam's actions.[35] Berman said that her relationship with the staff at the center had become tense, and that both she and the center were under investigation by the board of directors and by three county agencies as a result of Pam's alleged libel.[36] As a result of Pam's libel, the center also lost a contract for a program that would have secured additional staff, Berman said.[37] And "an important committee" of the Nassau County Mental Health Department had recently shunned her.[38]

A day later, Berman's lawyers urged the court to make the *Berman v. Martens* trial a priority because Pam was persisting in dragging Berman's name through the mud. Pam had sent a letter to *Newsday* that was published on June 28, 1977, opining that a flattering article about Woodward two weeks before was not deserved. She said in her letter that investigations were pending against Berman,[39] who'd been accused by former staff of illegal billing and expelling students without making arrangements to place them elsewhere.[40] But it was understandable that the reporter was "used" by Berman, Pam's letter said. "I, as the former public relations director of Woodward, was used just as he was used," she wrote. Rarely shy about admitting her talents, she added, "I now must fight the very legend I helped to create through feature articles in the newspapers, TV bookings, and press releases."[41]

Lawyers for Berman said they'd had enough. In order to prevent the "continuing barrage of defamation," the court should give precedence to the Berman case. But then, as suddenly as the suit had emerged, it evaporated. The trickle of subsequent court filings concerned clerical requests for the consolidation of Berman's actions against Martens, and a trial never occurred.

Berman dropped the lawsuit[42] against Pam and left the center in 1979. Board members differ about the circumstances of Berman's departure. One board member later said that Berman had been fired;

another said that Berman had quit because of stress related to the accusations and the death of her husband. The latter board member also said the board liked Berman and had never wanted to deal with the accusations against her in the first place. A Nassau County official said that a fire had destroyed many county records, apparently including those relating to the investigation of Berman. Twenty-four years later, Berman would say only that it was a "very unpleasant period" in her life, and that she could not remember details about the episode, which "was investigated by the proper agencies in the government" and had "no substance."[43]

———

THE $500,000 LIBEL LAWSUIT had come to nothing. As a result of the Berman drama, however, Pam was armed with combat experience, and the knowledge that threatening legal situations could be confronted and survived....

And now that she worked at Shearson, tucked away in the firm's files was a document with her signature on it, explaining how she had gone public with allegations of "serious improprieties" on the part of her boss, who had "filed a libel suit against me" in response. It would gather dust along with the other paperwork collected for her regulatory files. The episode was never brought up by anyone at Shearson. She was a trainee at the firm now, and there was much to learn.

Chapter **5** Five

Martens's Disorienting Orientation

I was the head of Human Resources for a year ... I would ask them to remove their pornographic items and they would laugh ... One of the gropers was the owner.

—CONFIDENTIAL COMPLAINANT #3, FORMER EMPLOYEE OF A SMALL FIRM

Hearings before the New York State
Attorney General, January 22, 1998

I T WAS A DISTRACTION to hear so much hollering when she was trying to study.

Pam was incredulous that the salesman around the corner from her office would scream at paying customers. But he did, almost every morning for days at a time, telling clients that they were wrong or stupid or both if they suggested he'd been the cause of their losses. Pam had gained an appreciation for his wisdom about the markets; he had had a long career on Wall Street. She actually liked him. But it struck her as she sipped her morning coffee and crammed for her Series 7 test that something was amiss in an environment where the people who were paying the bills got yelled at by their brokers.

She plugged along despite the clamor, getting 99s and 100s in the weekly practice tests she took. Gladys Lawson, Cuneo's secretary, would collect the tests after Pam self-scored them. Lawson also administered a midterm and a final, which Pam took under supervision and without study materials. She was giddy at the notion of getting paid to learn and having her company spring for the books she needed.

It was a tad disconcerting, though, the first time she received a paycheck. Nicholas Cuneo walked into her little study-office and flung the check in her direction. It was a habit he would stick to each month, sometimes missing her desk altogether. One day, Lawson stopped by to instruct Pam on the policy that women must wear skirts or dresses to the office—no pantsuits. That didn't affect Pam—she wore suits with skirts each day anyway—but what was this thing about mandating that women show their legs?

Preoccupied with doing well on the Series 7, Pam did her best to ignore these quirks. She went beyond the already voluminous texts that Shearson had given her to study. She trekked to the Garden City library and read up on what's known as the '34 Act, legislation passed in 1934 that, among other things, required broker-dealers to register with the SEC. She devoured books about the 1929 stock market crash. She learned about Joseph P. Kennedy, the first chairman of the Securities and Exchange Commission, whose experience doing insider trading perversely fitted him to oversee the new regulatory system that banned the practice.

She kept up with the business news and developed strong opinions about the world she was discovering. When she didn't agree with what she read in the February 24, 1985, issue of the *New York Times Magazine,* she wrote a letter to the editor taking issue with the conclusion that the multimillionaires at Lehman Brothers were villains. The story was about the infighting at Lehman that led to its April 1984 sale to Shearson, and in Pam's view it had depicted the Lehman partners as greedy and cowardly. Pam took a decidedly free-market stance, crediting the seventeen Lehman senior partners who pocketed $134 million with using "just good business acumen." The *Times* published her letter in the Sunday magazine five weeks later, on March 31, 1985, prompting an unexpected visit to her study room from Nick Cuneo on Monday, April 1.

"Do you know someone at the *New York Times*?" he asked her. He had a copy of the magazine in his hand.

"No, I just mailed them the letter."

Cuneo turned and walked out of the office, leaving the impression that he didn't like seeing his brand-new broker's name in the paper.

But someone else must have. By day's end, a colleague had posted her letter on the office bulletin board that hung just inside the parking lot entrance.

———

IN APRIL, PAM TOOK the six-hour Series 7 test with its 250 multiple-choice questions. When she returned home that night, Russ had a dinner of champagne and lobster waiting. They toasted her new career. Even though the grueling exam had yet to be shipped off to be scored, Russ had no doubt that Pam would pass.

When the results were in, Russ Martens was correct, and Pam joined thirty-seven other applicants who would advance to the final training class. She was irritated to have gotten an 86 out of a possible 100; the section on options had been more demanding and time-consuming than she had expected. But she had made the cut on her first try. When she reported for a six-week training session at Two World Trade Center in downtown Manhattan, her nit-picking of the less-than-perfect score was swept away by praise from instructors: They announced to the class of thirty-eight trainees that they were the only ones chosen from a massive pool of 800 applicants. Pam had the third-highest score, and only three of the thirty-eight had passed the commodities exam. Two of those three were women.

Pam loved the training program. They were up on the 103rd floor of what was then still Manhattan's tallest skyscraper. She and the other trainees caught an occasional glimpse of Shearson CEO Peter A. Cohen, who rode the same elevator all the way up. (Both the training class and the executive offices were in the five highest floors of the building, and thus were served by the same elevator bank.) Her new career was starting out to be all she'd hoped, with an exciting atmosphere, a chance to learn and get paid for it, and the opportunity to rub shoulders occasionally with the financial world's stars.

Days were long, with a noisy train commute at each end, but rich with information that Pam soaked up. Instructors taught the group how to cold-call—telephone potential customers they didn't know in the hope they'd open an account. The trainers explained how Wall Street works, from underwriting to trading to selling to the public. They even instructed the new brokers on how they should go about reading the

Wall Street Journal as it was formatted at the time. First, read the news strip on Page One—the second column from the left. Then read the influential "Heard on the Street" column, which frequently moves a stock price when the market opens. After that, read the "Credit Markets" column to get a handle on interest rates and the economy. With all that done, it was then OK to peruse the rest of the paper, the teachers said. Fifteen years later, Pam would still be following those instructions.

Pam stood out as an anomaly in the profession. In the first few sessions, the instructor asked the trainees to go around the room and explain why each had decided to become a stockbroker. Most gave variations of a single answer: they did it for the money. Then came Pam's turn. "I thought I could help people," she said, explaining that finance was something the average person really needed assistance with in order not to lose what they'd earned. Of course, she was there to fund her son's future, too—and in fact the desire for more money had propelled her out of the not-for-profit world. Already she was coming across as an outsider in an industry that attracted people highly motivated by money for money's sake. Like many other women, she had not been brought up to consider brokers, executives, or most other wielders of power as role models.

She was "graduated" in May 1985 and attended an elegant dinner at a lower Manhattan hotel on her last day of training. Pam was now a "financial consultant," better known as an "FC" in Shearson-speak. The lead trainer addressed the class from the podium. Don't expect life to be fair, she told them. Pam wondered how that pertained to her working future at Shearson. She's warning us that the brokerage business is tough, Pam figured. Well, I'm tough, so no matter.

What the trainer knew and Pam did not was a fact of life in branch offices, whether in Garden City or East Anywhere: the retail brokerage business could be ruthless, with managers acting as office policemen over a group that included angry, egotistical competitors capable of shouting and pounding fists over the privileges they demanded and the clients they coveted. Staff at a branch were prone to gossip, and it took little to stir up jealousy if one of them landed a great account from a retiring broker and another received a dud. As if that weren't enough, a jittery stock market and nervous clients could turn a perfectly calm day into a disaster. It was an environment difficult for an outsider to imagine.[1]

"Girls Just Want to Have Fun."

The Cyndi Lauper song title on a glossy poster was one of the first things Pam noticed when she walked into the basement bullpen in Garden City. It was a visual shock after the elegant Manhattan offices where Shearson's training program had been conducted.

The bullpen was a crowded, windowless, frequently noisy place where new brokers made cold calls for the more experienced staff on the floors above them. Just around the corner and down two steps was a room that was getting set up as a party spot. Pam didn't find out about it until later, but in-the-know veteran brokers on the two floors above her had designs on this space and were slowly stocking it with party supplies. It had the same name as a West Coast gay strip joint and a 1972 David Rabe play that had been set in part in a go-go bar. Asked about the name years later, a lawyer for the firm said it was derived from the Rabe play, *In the Boom Boom Room*.[2]

Pam set about making friends with the two other women in the bullpen. Jackie Bacon, a blonde woman who sat across from her, was a rookie broker from Mineola who had two small children at home. Leslie Frutkin, a commodities trader, was a young, single, outgoing Long Island woman who amused Pam to no end with her shouting over the uncooperative price movements of oil and other products. "We're getting violated in the pit," Leslie would shout. Pam hadn't a clue what that meant, but she liked her spirit.

One day during her first months there, she looked up to see Nick Cuneo standing over her as she dialed the phone to pitch strangers from a cold-call list. "Well, look at Little Miss Goody Two Shoes," he said. As with the flying paycheck business, she was mystified. She had no idea that she was among a small circle of women for whom Cuneo had special names. Not long afterward, he took to calling her "the Stepford Wife."

A few days later Cuneo stopped by again. He wanted Pam to attend a special presentation for partnerships in Balcor Films the following week. Bring clients, he said. She did what the boss asked her to, inviting a local politician and his wife whose business she was trying to cultivate. As she sat with the couple in the Garden City conference room, the lights dimmed and a buxom, 300-pound Mexican woman appeared on the screen. The title of the newly released Balcor creation, a B-movie western spoof, was *Lust in the Dust*. Then, to howls of laughter from the other brokers in the room, the "woman," a drag queen who went by the screen name Divine, emerged from the desert slowly dropping her blouse for Tab Hunter, the aging 1950s pop singer and star who had just ridden in on a horse. Pam's would-be clients walked out, horrified, and she vowed never again to invite a prospect to a Shearson pitch.

That Balcor partnership—and other Balcor deals pushed by Shearson, as it happened—would end up in bankruptcy. And Pam never did do business with the local dignitary and his spouse.

<hr/>

DESPITE THE ACCUMULATING WARNING SIGNS, Pam adopted a "glass half-full" attitude, leaving her house gung ho by 8:15 each morning, parking in the back lot of 901 Franklin Avenue, then ducking in to Jimmy's newsstand for a *Wall Street Journal*.

Quarters were tight and privacy nonexistent, but she didn't mind the bullpen, where having a couple of woman friends among eight male brokers made work bearable and even enjoyable. By October, she, Jackie Bacon, and Leslie Frutkin were joined by Kathleen Keegan, a former schoolteacher. Keegan had developed a miracle-working music therapy method for mentally retarded children, only to have her program bumped and the kids moved to another school. She figured that if a "helping" profession was going to be that ruthless, she might as well put up with ruthlessness in a place where she could make money.

Much of Pam's early time at the Garden City branch was pleasant—in part because Cuneo, difficult as he could be, was also a big promoter of office partying. Women happily joined in the annual Halloween fun of coming to work in costume. That year, Leslie donned a curly wig as a character from the Little Rascals, and Pam dressed up as a goofy Raggedy Ann doll.

The bullpen camaraderie helped, but the overriding culture was that of the men, who, after all, dominated the branch and the industry. Pam was uncomfortable when one of them went on tirades about African Americans and various ethnic groups, bellowing out derogatory opinions that anyone on the floor could hear. Some of the other brokers, though, held back, apparently unsure of how to act around a woman they saw as, well, prissy.

Any manager in any branch would have to confront and change some old customs these days, no matter who the women were in the increasingly mixed new professional staffs. Fishing trips, golf games, shaving kits, even size XL T-shirts were long-established rewards for sales teams that had included only men. Now, managers like Cuneo faced challenges that they could rise to or flub. The traditionally all-male golf games, for example, were not considered off-limits to the women by every man in the branch: one of them, Bill Gordon, told his wife he was impressed by the golf skills of one of his female colleagues during an outing when a woman made a fuss and was allowed to join. But another male broker said in frustration that women in the branch who did not play failed to understand a code of the game: that it is discourteous to entertain guests who are clumsy beginners and thereby hold up the players behind you.[3] With women apparently unaware of the etiquette attached to the sport—or of some male colleagues' assessment of their skills—and management unwilling to find outings more compatible with both sexes, the hostility only heightened.

In fact, gender issues were often handled in a brusque manner. Lorraine Parker had given Cuneo an out when she offered to join the group for dinner only after a golf jaunt, but Cuneo turned her down. Given the inflow of women into the business, it was not an easy time to be a manager. But reactions like the one Cuneo gave to Parker were oil on an already smoldering fire.

And then there was that locker room environment. The retail brokerage segment of Wall Street was bedeviled by its custom of allowing untoward behavior to go unpunished and—from headquarters' point of view—undetected. Some days it seemed as if everything by definition had to be taken a step too far. On the birthday of Garden City broker Jerry Alampi one year, Pam noticed a commotion and went over to where a bunch of her colleagues had gathered. Alampi had just received a surprise strip-o-gram and was smirking as his "present" took a seat on his lap.[4] No sooner had she gotten comfortable in Alampi's lap than "she" stripped off her shirt to reveal the hairy chest of a man.[5] Alampi looked mortified. His male colleagues watching outside his door burst into laughter. Pam turned away, resolving not to be so curious next time a party was on.

A few men in the office disdained the tone that was set. Two in particular—both veterans of the branch—shuddered at Cuneo's vulgarity.

"I was the only person in that office that women with a grievance would talk to," said one of them. "But the powers that be didn't listen to me. And Nick Cuneo's style was despicable. He was a bully."[6]

Most bizarre for the women who knew about it was the thought that somewhere along the line while they were rookie brokers, Cuneo might find reason to have them in his office and casually pull his gun out of a desk drawer.[7] He never pointed it at anyone. But the message they got, however casually he handled his weapon, was that Cuneo was no one to mess with. Pam, who had already seen Henry Chin's ankle holster, once asked Glenn Fischer whether he was concerned that Cuneo kept a gun. He told her that it was nothing to worry about. Nick just does that to get the attention of trainees, he told her.

Managers of highly profitable branches such as Garden City could condone or be part of questionable decorum because, like the nanny whose boss is away at the office every day, they rarely are observed by anyone in authority while they're doing their jobs. And even if they were, there's no guaranteeing that an unruly manager would be sanctioned, particularly if his shop was a big contributor to the firm's bottom line. This made retail branches a petri dish for discrimination and, most of all, open sexual harassment.

Elaine Garzarelli, now a money manager and CEO of her own firm, Garzarelli Investment Management, was a Shearson superstar in the 1980s. She would brace herself each time she visited a retail office. On one cross-country trek to promote a mutual fund she was launching in late 1986, a retail broker suggested she unbutton her blouse a bit further when she made television appearances. In another city, a branch manager introduced her by boasting "This is no dog-meat fund." At a sales meeting at New York's Waldorf Astoria, a cocky broker with a thick Bronx accent walked up to her and said, "You looked like shit on TV last week."

The retail system has no class, Garzarelli would tell herself, moving on to give another of the presentations that had her on the A-list for retail branches and the media.

KATHLEEN KEEGAN WAS INITIALLY SHOCKED at the way coworkers comported themselves in a work setting.[8] In her initial months, Keegan endured a broker who railed about blacks, Jews, women, and anyone else he didn't like or felt superior to. In the summer of 1986, when Pam graduated out of her rookie status and moved from the bullpen to her own private office, the boisterousness went into overdrive. At that point, Keegan and a secretary were the only women in the bullpen. It was not unusual for Keegan to return from lunch and walk in on a belching contest. Typically, that would deteriorate into a session in which the men challenged one another to competitive rounds of flatulence. The air frequently became so unpleasant that Keegan would have to leave the room, amid howls of laughter. She prayed for the day her production would be high enough to earn her a private office.

Early on in her bullpen tenure, she heard Cuneo's voice over the office loudspeaker system on a Friday afternoon just before the 4 P.M. close of trading. "The Boom-Boom Room is now open," he said. "We are now serving cocktails."[9] On other occasions, the merrymaking would begin as early as 10 A.M.[10] Keegan thought it was a nice idea that office camaraderie would bring the gang together after a tough workweek. That image dissolved as she crossed the threshold of the room. The toilet seat and bicycle were hanging from the ceiling, and massive garbage pails were lined with plastic for drink mixing.[11] It was noisy; the brokers were strutting their business success. She had a feeling that it wasn't a good place for her to be and resolved not to come back.

Keegan worked in the bullpen longer than most rookies, harangued by Cuneo that she was not meeting his standards and was not steering customers to the highest-commission products. She was anxious to get out of the pen but seemed never able to satisfy the boss.

She left mid-morning one day in the summer of 1987 to attend the funeral of one of her friends and returned during lunch hour to a mostly empty bullpen. One of her male colleagues had written in bold black letters on the bullpen whiteboard "KATHLEEN GIVES GOOD HEAD." In a rage, she went to Cuneo's office and demanded that he get her a private office. "I'm sick and tired of this shit that goes on day in and day out," she said. "They think it's funny. *You* think it's funny. I come back from lunch and they're belching and farting, and now I'm just back from a funeral and they've written obscenities on the board." Cuneo said he was surprised and that he would talk to the violators.

"Don't tell me you're surprised," she told him, thinking of times Cuneo told lewd stories of his own and said he didn't care who heard him because he would never be sanctioned. Keegan stood her ground. "I want out of there."

He did move her to an office but made her keep coming to morning meetings in the bullpen, meaning that she was still subjected to the men's jokes. Women are no good in bed after they've had a baby, one would say. Yeah, I got laid with a mother and know what you mean, another said, adding vulgar details to buttress his story.

When she was in more public forums, Keegan was a target of constant ridicule by the boss. One Tuesday afternoon, as she came through the door of the basement conference room for the staff sales meeting, Cuneo shouted from the podium, "Oh God, here comes Keegan—she's not even gonna make $50,000 this year." Keegan would say nothing and slip into a chair next to the other female brokers, who sat together. When Cuneo made his monthly rounds to fling paychecks, he would begin a speech directed at Keegan from several doors down the hall: "Oh God, Keegan, you're not gonna amount to anything. What are you wasting your time for here?" Cuneo was sending the message that women should not be stockbrokers, Keegan thought.[12]

On October 19, 1987, Cuneo threw a party to celebrate the high commissions generated by panic selling during that day's stock market crash. He invited a local television news crew into the branch to get footage for that evening's broadcast; they stopped Keegan and asked her for a comment on her way out at the end of an exhausting day.[13] Pam, from her perch on the second floor, was horrified by the sight of Cuneo below in the atrium popping champagne corks on a day when some clients had lost their life savings.[14]

Not long after that, he told Pam that it would be a good idea for her to go on a $40,000 a year salary.[15] (She had earned $80,000 in commissions the previous year.) After Pam refused, she had the distinction of being the first woman in the Garden City office to earn three Cuneo nicknames. To "Miss Goody Two Shoes" and "The Stepford Wife" was added "Peppy Henin II." That was a reference to his least favorite female broker, a veteran in the Garden City office.

Henin had suffered mightily at Cuneo's hand. The boss drew from a repertoire of anti-Semitic barbs he had at the ready,[16] going so far as chastising the staff at one Tuesday afternoon meeting for letting the "Jewish bitch" beat them out.[17] (By early 1988, Henin, who had come to Shearson from Merrill Lynch, would be told to leave in a forced retirement.[18] Then they would be down another woman at the nearly all-male Tuesday afternoon assemblages.)

Usually, nobody challenged Cuneo at the weekly meetings. The idea was to let him vent and then end the weekly obligation as early as possible. Everybody's eagerness to leave made a talkative broker like Pam Martens unpopular. Even women colleagues bristled to hear Pam carry on with follow-up questions and explanations that they considered show-offy. One afternoon, when Pam began to comment on recent actions by the Federal Reserve, one of the bullpen men screamed "That is the stupidest thing I ever heard." Pam knew that he was hostile to the women in the office. What she didn't pick up on was that even the women were pleased that someone could turn off Pam's commentary. For all her competence, Pam was viewed by many as a Bible-thumping know-it-all who offered too many opinions and kept meetings going too long.

Among those who became irritated with Pam was Lorraine Parker, a tall, attractive woman with wavy auburn hair who had most recently been a senior auditor with the accounting firm Touche Ross. When Cuneo had hired her in September 1986, he had boasted tongue-in-cheek that he'd hired a Playboy bunny. Parker signed on for the Garden City office despite efforts by Steve Fields, the regional manager, to steer her to a different office—the same effort that was made when Pam came to Shearson. Fields told Parker, who had an honors degree in accounting and a refined manner, that she was too classy for Nick.[19] Parker was not put off. She was certain she could make it in a man's world, with hard work and profits at the bottom line.

The so-called Playboy bunny's honeymoon was soon over. The final divorce, though, was a long time in coming. Though she fought back more than most, it took four years for the lightbulb to go on in Parker's head that the men were getting critical business assistance that she wasn't.

She became worn down by repeatedly hiring and training new sales assistants only to see them, once trained, passed on to male brokers. Ultimately, she hired a cold-caller whom she paid herself. She requested that Cuneo pay for her to attend a Dale Carnegie course—something he was willing to underwrite for the men. He declined. (Years later, Paine-Webber would pay for her to attend the seminar, and she did so well that she was asked to return as an instructor.)

Parker persisted in pushing for her fair share of office perks, pointing out to Cuneo that he lunched regularly with his brokers but didn't invite the females. Cuneo's response shed light on the segregation that women experienced: he agreed to have lunch with her but did not include any other brokers. On their way out the door at noon, she heard men snicker at seeing the boss departing with one of the women.

Parker endured catcalls and suggestive whispers as she walked through the office; at an outing once, a colleague pinched her buttocks. She watched as her male colleagues were given leads to rich clients; as they got preference when customers walked in cold from the street; and as they received first shot when someone telephoned to open an account. When hot new companies offered shares to the public, she wasn't in the loop to get allocations for her customers. While male broker trainees received mentors, she went without one.[20]

Pam observed much of what went on in silence, opting to stay out of the fray and plug away at work. Pam had let it pass when, in the summer of 1987, Cuneo had invited all the brokers to a golf and dinner outing, then said it was a "mistake" when Parker accepted the invitation. Women are not invited, he told her. "No one ever said I wasn't a male chauvinist pig." When Shearson superstar Elaine Garzarelli came to the branch to pitch her new mutual fund later in 1987, Cuneo's introduction was "Here comes the queen."

"I don't think you like me—I don't think you like women," Garzarelli said to Cuneo.

He invited her back, though, and then told her that his brokers had just finished pushing a fund for rival Mario Gabelli and had no time to push hers.

Pam began paying more attention, though, in the spring of 1988, when Kathleen Keegan told her that Cuneo had made it impossible for her to do business anymore, taking away her broker number that identified her on clients' statements and telling her that her business would be routed through a male colleague, Joseph Scotto. Without her name on the statements reminding clients of their allegiance, Keegan knew that it would be only a matter of time before Scotto was in charge of all her accounts, and she would be out of business. In spring of 1988, Keegan quit.

By July 2, 1988, Pam took her first bold stance, writing a two-page letter to Hardwick Simmons, Shearson's CEO.[21]

Dear Mr. Simmons:

I am a graduate of the May 1985 Shearson training class. At that time you offered each of the graduates an "open door" should we need your assistance.

Women have never had it easy in this branch but at least my efforts have enabled me to move forward. About a month ago, our branch manager—speaking loudly outside my office—asked the operations manager if he was working on a way to get rid of me.

At first, I assumed this was a joke....

Unfortunately, the facts do support the premise that women are not wanted in this branch: the branch is about 20 years old. I have been in production 3 years. I am the senior female FC in this branch. Peppy Henin, an FC for about 8 years, was recently let go. Kathleen Keegan, a Shearson trainee of about 2½ years in production, was asked to merge her book with a male FC. She left this week rather than lose control of her book. Cheryl Cox, a female FC in the Manhasset office, came to visit a month or so ago. She asked me in front of another male FC, Gene Trudden, how many women FCs we had in this office. Mr. Trudden remarked, "We're getting rid of all of them, they're not working out."

She told Simmons that she knew she could move her clients to some other firm but that she lived only four blocks away and had a client base that was heavily local. She did not want to leave, and she told him so. She additionally described serious operational errors occurring on her accounts. Unbeknownst to Pam, Edna Broyles, a broker in the Tampa branch of Shearson, was complaining to management about problems with operations, too. Broyles was wondering if in her case it had something to do with her gender.

Pam did not get what she was hoping for after drumming up the courage to write to the boss's boss's boss.[22] In response, a representative of the New York Human Resources office was sent as a gesture toward appeasing the women. After an hour-and-a-half lunch at Devons, a local Garden City restaurant, with the corporate emissary, Jodie-Beth Galos, the women figured Galos couldn't help but come through with assistance. They were stunned at Galos's reaction, though. Just "try to get along with Nick," she told them, even after getting an earful about the oppressive working conditions.[23] Lorraine Parker wound up picking up the check.

And Cuneo, apparently misreading what the women were complaining about, later treated his female staff members to a free aerobics class.

Pam found her solace in a husband who supported what she was doing and a son, now eight, whose activities took her from managing the Mother's Day plant sales for her Cub Scout den to a succession of scout field trips. But her distress at the office came from more than the mistreatment of workers. The Garden City office was a place where rules in general seemed to be flouted—and not just the ones that applied to the women.

She grew weary of the memos that went out before internal audits, telling brokers which accounts they could officially say they had "discretion" over—that is, the accounts for which they could make trades without first consulting with the client.[24] Brokers are permitted to trade in a customer's account without calling the customer ahead of time provided the customer has given the broker sweeping permission to use what is known as "discretion." So when Pam saw the memos about discretionary accounts, the message she took away was that some brokers were making trades that way even though the customer had not given them that level of authority.

Pam also was distressed that Cuneo had joked to the staff that they'd better not be dumb enough to leave cash receipts in their desk drawers—documentation that the broker had accepted cash from customers to put into their brokerage accounts.[25] Cuneo warned that the audit team might go through their desks; Pam figured that the boss was worried that the auditors might conclude—rightly or wrongly—that money laundering could be going on. As she brooded over what she considered suspicious practices, the settlements of complaints brought by unhappy customers continued apace.

She looked around the office at the male brokers: she was uncomfortable watching several of the big stars, whose conduct raised red flags to her from time to time. She also knew that among the staff were brokers who had been terminated from their previous jobs. Apart from what Pam was observing on her own, the regulatory files of at least eight of her colleagues showed a problem of one sort or another—anything from a customer complaint to a violation of company policy. Only one woman among those Pam knew—Peppy Henin—had a blotch on her record.[26] And Henin's complaint involved a customer who filed a request for a stock exchange arbitration five days after the October 1987 stock market crash.

Pam had seen how the system worked when principles got in the way of profits. In February 1987, when new assistant manager Glenn Fischer had called Keegan in to suggest changing Keegan's strategy for the proceeds of the recently sold home of an elderly client, Keegan was insubordinate. The assistant manager urged her to put the woman's $300,000 into a government securities fund.[27] Keegan refused, citing the $12,000—4 percent—commission that her client would have to pay. It was the following year that Cuneo merged her accounts with those of another broker, effectively driving her out.

To Pam, it was a lesson as important as any she had memorized for her license exam. Watching out for the customer was no way to get ahead in this place.

Some customers thought they were getting special treatment, only to find out years later that they actually were getting fleeced. One of Pam's colleagues, Stanley J. Feminella, was a big star in the office. She heard from her buddies that on occasion Feminella could pick up $100,000 in commissions in a single day. But neither Pam nor any of her peers had a clue that Feminella was pulling off a scam right under management's nose. And that he was able to afford to do it because of the exorbitant commissions that Cuneo had been willing to charge Feminella's biggest customer. It would be a prime example to Pam of how bad things could get at Cuneo's shop without Cuneo's being held accountable.

———

FEMINELLA WAS AN ARISTOCRAT by Long Island standards, owner of a comfortable home on Valley Avenue in Locust Valley, a town whose residents' self-consciously patrician speech—delivered through barely moving mouths—has been dubbed "Locust Valley lockjaw." Feminella had been a member of the Creek Club in Locust Valley since 1975. It was so exclusive that it bore no street address.

During the winter, Feminella was a regular at the skeet range, and he struck up a friendship with David Granston, an executive at the *New York Times,* whom he met in the late 1970s.[28] When Feminella became a broker in 1983, Granston also made a career change, becoming chief financial officer of Consumers Union, owner of the influential magazine *Consumer Reports.*

Feminella had landed his new job by reconnecting with David Sobocinski, a stockbroker he'd met on the golf course during a vacation in the Bahamas the year before.[29] Come in and meet the boss, suggested Sobocinski, who worked at David Lerner Associates, a financial firm in the Long Island town of Lake Success. Within several months, Feminella had a desk at Lerner, selling municipal bonds, insurance, and government securities while reporting to Sobocinski.

When he got settled in, one of his first calls was to Granston. Feminella asked if Granston could think of him if he had any business for a broker in his areas, which at the time did not include stocks. A few months later, he got a call. As a matter of fact, Granston did have some money to invest on behalf of Consumers Union in Ginnie Maes—the government securities that Feminella specialized in.

Granston became Feminella's biggest client and his regular dinner guest at the poshest Long Island restaurants.[30] The men racked up bills approaching $300 when they dined with their wives, and nearly always, Feminella picked up the tab. Apart from the gastronomical rendezvous, the two men also enjoyed several gala sporting dinners at New York's Waldorf Astoria.[31] But sometime in 1985, as Pam was getting her wings as a broker nine miles away, Feminella had to give Granston some bad news. He told his client that he had family problems—health concerns over the hearing disability of one of his sons and the second heart attack of his mother. The developing new demands would mean less time to wine and dine Granston and his wife.

It was not an altogether disastrous scenario to Granston. "Look, if it's so difficult for you to entertain, which I can understand with your family problems, why don't you just give me cash?"[32] Thus it was in 1985, a year in which Feminella earned $100,000 at Lerner, that he began to give kickbacks to his skeet buddy from Consumers Union.

———

THE PAYMENTS CAME IN CLOSE PROXIMITY to the trades, working out to about one-tenth of a percent of each transaction's size. Almost always, they would be in cash.[33] One or the other of the men would communicate a code—"Isn't it time we got together?"—and they would meet at Granston's house, less than a mile from Feminella's place on Valley Avenue.

Her name was on the joint checking account at Norstar Bank, but Jo Ann Feminella had no idea that her husband was taking money out of their account to hand over to Granston. With his payment in hand, Feminella would stand in the garage, the den, or a room the Granstons called the study room. Feminella would hand over amounts as small as $1,000 and as large as $5,000. Typically, he would write checks to himself for an amount, cash them, and, within a week or so, the same amount would be deposited into Granston's checking account.[34]

Feminella at thirty-eight years old became a hotter ticket in the eyes of brokerage houses, none of whom would necessarily have any reason to know about his schemes at that point. He heard from Glenn Rudy, branch manager of the Roosevelt Field, New York, office of Paine-Webber in 1986.[35] PaineWebber was giving signing bonuses of $100,000 to new brokers. Feminella took the job and took the Consumers Union account with him.

His former boss Sobocinski called Feminella in 1988. Sobocinski by then had moved to Shearson in Garden City and was alerting Feminella that there was a recruiting push on with great incentives for brokers.[36] This time, there was no big one-time signing bonus, as there had been when Feminella bolted from Lerner to PaineWebber. But what was being offered was very attractive to a broker with large trades like the ones Feminella now had. Shearson was paying experienced stockbrokers 80 percent of the total commissions paid by a customer—a portion known as "payout." The high commissions would go on for a minimum of a year, Sobocinski said. Sobocinski would benefit, too, he revealed to Feminella, because Shearson would pay him a recruiting fee.[37]

Feminella met Nicholas Cuneo in September 1988.

Cuneo confirmed what Sobocinski had said about the 80 percent payouts for one year, adding that at the end of the year, Feminella could pick his two best months of the twelve and get 100 percent of the commissions for those months.[38] Glenn Fischer, Cuneo's second-in-command at the office, stopped by. Feminella told the two bosses that he did big trades for a client whose name he would not disclose. Was Shearson equipped to handle the business? Cuneo said it would be no problem. What sort of markup is charged? Feminella asked, looking to see what his take would be on a trade of $1,000. Cuneo made several telephone calls, mouthing to Feminella that he was hearing "three to four points" were paid on Ginnie Maes.[39] That meant that Shearson could charge Consumers Union between $3,000 and $4,000—4 percent of the trade amount—on a $100,000 trade.

That would be a very high markup indeed.

At a subsequent meeting, Cuneo said he would stretch the 80 percent payout to fourteen or fifteen months. To reassure his recruit that Shearson could handle the still-unnamed Ginnie Mae client, Cuneo put Feminella on the telephone with the national manager for retail government securities.

Cuneo and Feminella met yet again, and the branch manager fiddled with his computer and showed his recruit actual examples of Shearson's selling Ginnie Maes at markups of three to four points on the size trade Feminella would typically have.[40] By his final meeting in the Garden City office, even Alan Rhein, the regional division manager, stopped in to meet the superbroker recruit.[41]

In November, $40 million in securities were transferred from the PaineWebber account of Consumers Union to a new account at Shearson Lehman Brothers in Garden City. David Sobocinski received a bonus for wooing Feminella. And, with Nicholas Cuneo standing by his side, Feminella executed his first trade at Shearson for Consumers Union.[42]

At a time when his previous employer, PaineWebber, was charging a sales credit of $78 on every million-dollar trade of Ginnie Maes, Shearson's trading desks were taking commissions for themselves as well as the "credit" provided Feminella. Consumers Union at one point bought $2.3 million in Ginnie Mae mortgage-backed securities, and the trade was done in several steps that profited Shearson. In one, the institutional trading desk sold bonds to the retail desk, which added its own markup plus Feminella's take. The cost for that: $53,262. For the remaining securities, the retail desk got the bonds from another broker, again adding a markup both for itself and Feminella, at a cost of $21,674. If one includes the markups at each desk, plus the 3 percent sales credit for Feminella, Shearson and its broker shared $81,768 on a $2.3 million trade.[43]

Staff was always buzzing about Feminella's account with Consumers Union: Cuneo posted all the brokers' commissions in a public spot, so it was obvious not only that Feminella was making lots of money but also that he was making it mostly on one client. Controversy seemed to swirl around his name. In late 1990, talk went around the office that Feminella was asking colleagues to write him personal checks in exchange for cash. It was never clear why the transactions took place. For whatever reason, Feminella's checking account suddenly was credited with deposits from his Garden City coworkers. On October 3, 1990, Feminella received a $2,000 check written on the account of Jerry Alampi, another broker in the office. That was followed by four others written on Alampi's personal account for a total of $16,000 in the final three months of the year.[44]

At the same time, Feminella also was depositing checks in his joint account with Jo Ann, checks that were drawn on the account of one of the Garden City sales assistants. The sales assistant wrote him checks on October 10, October 16, October 30, December 8, and December 18, 1990. They ranged in size from $4,000 to $5,000.

The trail of checks went all the way to the top of the branch. On November 16, a $6,000 check to Feminella was drawn on the account of Nicholas F. and Caroline Cuneo, and signed by Nicholas Cuneo.[45]

By then, there was no pretense around the fact that Consumers Union was his bread and butter: in the first two months of 1991, all of his $100,000 in compensation came from that account. On the last day of February, though, a distressed Granston called Feminella at home to say they'd better meet the next morning before work. Consumers Union had just told Granston that he was suspended pending an internal investigation.

They met in Granston's study room. Feminella was shocked to hear that Granston had been asked to take a leave of absence.[46]

Despite the ominous morning meeting, Feminella was not prepared for what happened when he arrived at the Franklin Avenue office on March 1, 1991. The moment he arrived, Glenn Fischer told him that he would like Feminella to read a letter from Consumers Union to Shearson. "Dear Mr. Clark," it began. They had sent their correspondence to Howard Clark, chief executive officer of Shearson Lehman/American Express. Only then did Feminella understand the gravity of the situation. Consumers Union wanted its securities returned immediately and its account at Shearson closed.

Fischer was in and out of Feminella's office with questions throughout the day; he also had contacted Cuneo, who was not in the office that

Friday. Feminella was relieved when his phone rang with Cuneo on the other end, sounding concerned for his top broker and expressing his worry over the impact the stress might have on Feminella's health. When the long day was over, Feminella returned to Granston's house and sat in the study room with him for over an hour. Feminella told him about the contents of the letter to Howard Clark, which said Shearson should transfer all its funds back to Consumers Union immediately.

For the moment it seemed that the crisis might end with Feminella suffering only the loss of a critical account, but the investigators at Consumers Union were on to him. In late March, Consumers Union approached Shearson and told management about the payments.[47] Still, Cuneo was reassuring. In a half-hour meeting in his office, he told Feminella that Consumers Union was looking into all aspects of Granston and the vendors and others he dealt with in his role as an executive at the company. Feminella denied having made any payments to Granston.[48] Cuneo then told him that Consumers Union had another complaint: that Shearson had been overcharging the account. Shearson would take a strong stance on the issue of commissions, Cuneo told Feminella, assuring him that there was nothing wrong with the charges their former client had paid. Management at Shearson's New York headquarters called Cuneo and Feminella in for a meeting in lower Manhattan in April.[49] Granston was fired by Consumers Union on April 11.[50] Feminella was suspended by Shearson on April 17[51] and fired in June.[52]

By July, Feminella was transferring ownership of his Locust Valley home to his wife and beginning the process of moving a half-million dollars from their joint money market account at Fidelity to a money market account in her name only at Vanguard.[53] In Feminella's view, Jo Ann was managing the Vanguard money, although Feminella filled out checks on that account, which Jo Ann would subsequently sign.[54] Feminella told regulators that he considered the change of asset ownership to be part of his overall estate plan.[55]

Meanwhile, another of the unexplained deposits from what was now a former colleague went into Feminella's account. On December 5, 1991, a check drawn on the account of Nicholas Cuneo and his wife, signed by Cuneo, was made out to Feminella and cashed for $900.[56]

A year later, Granston settled a lawsuit brought against him by Consumers Union. The year after that, 1993, Feminella was interrogated by lawyers for the Securities and Exchange Commission and the United States Attorney's office in Manhattan. He pleaded the Fifth Amendment when asked about the checks from Cuneo, Alampi, and the sales assistant. (In an interview nearly a decade later, he would proclaim his innocence in the Consumers Union matter, noting that there is never credit given for the fact that Consumers Union made $26 million in profits during the period he managed its money, by his account. Feminella was a broken man, he said, and had barely survived the ordeal, which was "worse than going to prison.")[57]

The government backed off in light of word from Feminella's lawyers that his health was bad and his financial situation was dire. Then, in March 1994, he, his wife, and their two sons went to the Mirage Hotel and Casino in Las Vegas, where the self-described bankrupt[58] man spent more than $10,000 at the casinos. On April 1, apparently in need of extra funds, he twice used his AT&T Universal Card to borrow money to gamble, taking out $1,562.99 each time. He also used his Chase Manhattan Visa Gold Card at the Mirage for cash advances for gambling and spending money.[59] In July 1994, he and his family vacationed at the Omni Sagamore hotel, where he charged $2,399.57 to his American Express Card. A month later, the family vacationed for a week at the White Face Inn Resort in New York. The same month, he wrote to his lawyer that he was trying to rent his home so that it could provide enough income for his family to survive.[60]

So far, the government had accumulated a great deal of information about the two men who had lost their jobs, Granston and Feminella. And now Feminella, who was getting leniency from the government as a result of his supposed financial straits, was living the high life, taking a string of family vacations.

Although he was not suffering a life of poverty, he had been disgraced and banished from his industry. His supervisors, though, so far had felt no consequences.

In August 1994, the Securities and Exchange Commission spoke to Feminella's lawyer, Robert Costello and said it indeed would not make sense to levy some huge fine on Feminella—believing, as the agency did, that he was destitute. Although Feminella seemed to be off the hook for a fine, the investigation into the conduct of Feminella and Shearson continued. Two key matters pertained to Shearson and to its Garden City office: What was its culpability as the manager of this broker who made payoffs for business? And what should be the punishment for the firm and its managers for the excessive commissions, if it were determined that the commissions were indeed illegally high? Those questions had yet to be answered. On paper, at least, Cuneo was at high risk of regulatory trouble.

———

OVER THE FEMINELLA YEARS, Pam had heard about his six-figure-commission days but knew little more about what her coworker was doing or who his customer was. There were rumors that Stan had asked many of the brokers to write him checks in exchange for large amounts of cash. Stan had told them that his mother had died and left him a safe-deposit box stuffed with money, the story went.[61] Pam remembered stories about Stan asking his assistant to take the cash next door to the American Express Travel Services office and exchange it for traveler's checks. Later, at a retirement party for Gladys Lawson, Cuneo's assistant, Pam was stunned when Cuneo said the Federal Bureau of Investigation would be coming to the branch for an investigation of Feminella. Given all the stories about writing checks for cash, Pam figured it had something to do with money laundering.

But once the news was out about Feminella, Granston, and the government's allegations about excessive commission charges by Shearson, for Pam, the Feminella scandal was one more sign that things were out of control in Garden City, and one more indication to her that her branch manager was made of Teflon.

If Cuneo's bosses didn't see fit to make some public gesture to demonstrate their disapproval of his supervision of Feminella, how could Pam expect Cuneo to be held accountable for other management problems, such as gender discrimination in the office? She had tried writing to Simmons. It had gotten her nowhere. As she looked around the Garden City office, she increasingly was finding every reason to pursue an insular existence at work. From then on, Pam was cordial to her coworkers but kept her office door shut and stuck to business during the workday. There was enough to keep her busy just fighting for herself.

Chapter Six

Martens Snaps

I witnessed quite a few cases of brokers coming on to sales assistants, verbally and by actions.

—SURVEY RESPONDENT QUOTED IN THE PLAINTIFFS'
EXPERT REPORT ON SMITH BARNEY WOMEN

U SUALLY IT IS NOT THE BIG EVENT that causes a person to go over the edge. The divorce doesn't do it, but meeting the new girlfriend does. Getting fired fails to sap the spirit, but a remark about your abundant free time unleashes a torrent of anger. In a similar way, the incident that caused Pam Martens to snap paled in comparison to much of what preceded it at the branch.

Pam awoke with a jolt at 6 A.M. on August 31, 1994, to the blare of 1010 WINS, an all-news station, on Russ's clock radio. "Turn that off," she murmured. The station's crime-heavy coverage bothered her, especially first thing in the morning.

After a quick shower, she put a pitcher of orange juice on the table for Sean in the hope he would take some sort of nourishment before he left for Garden City High. Russ had brewed the Folgers, a mug of which Pam carried with her from room to room, making the bed; packing her maroon "good luck" briefcase, a going-away gift from the Rehabilitation Institute; and feeding Fritzy, their noisy calico, her can of Alpo and some fresh Poland Spring water. She didn't trust the water that came from the tap in Garden City.

By the time Pam was into her standard linen skirt suit and white blouse, Russ had left for the job he'd begun only a couple of weeks earlier, at Commercial Envelope Corp. Pam gathered up her keys and briefcase, locked the door behind her, and climbed up into "Bluey," a 1988 Jeep Cherokee named by the Martens clan for its now-chipping midnight-blue paint.

She did the commute in five minutes, driving down Wyatt and past Bloomingdales, then turning into the back parking lot. Her six-year-old Jeep didn't add much to the status of the opulent cars alongside it—the humbling late-model Mercedeses, BMWs, Porsches, and Jaguars that belonged to the male brokers. Cuneo's silver Bentley was there, too. Shearson's brokerage offices had merged with Smith Barney in May 1994, but not much had changed except the name here at the Garden City branch. Pam picked up a *Wall Street Journal* at the Hallmark Card store and walked past the rear entrances of Merrill Lynch and Charles Schwab before ducking in the back door of what was now Smith Barney and checking her cubbyhole for mail. There would be a staff meeting after the close of the stock market, a memo advised. Something about employee benefits. She tucked her mail into her newspaper and took the elevator to her second-floor office, closing the door as she did most days.

Pam scanned the business news summary on the *Journal's* front page first, the way she'd been taught in Shearson's training program. Today the summaries were more a reflection of summer doldrums than any critical news she would need on the job. She turned to the "Heard on the Street" column and rolled her eyes when she saw the topic: a divergence of opinion between two of her own firm's female superstars. Elaine Garzarelli, the million-dollar-a-year quantitative analyst, was telling investors that the stock market was through with its correction. Katherine Hensel, the stock market strategist, was saying that the market would go down another 10 to 15 percent. Isn't it just like the good old boys to turn this into a catfight, Pam mused. Men on Wall Street dispute each other every day, but when women disagree, the *Wall Street Journal* makes a special fuss. (The *Journal*, in fact, frequently made sport of such differences of opinion in the same investment house—typically disagreements between two men. Pam, though, was particularly attuned to barbs against Garzarelli, whom Cuneo had mocked at a sales meeting one afternoon.)

Time was that the moment-by-moment stock market strategies of these two high-profile women would have been critically important to Pam at her job. In her early days as a stockbroker, she had been aggressive in suggesting stocks for short-term gains. But that was in 1985 and 1986, when she believed that stocks were cheap. Nowadays, Pam couldn't justify the high prices of stocks relative to earnings and steered her clients to more conservative investment strategies.

She scanned her desk calendar just before the 9:30 opening to see which clients were slated for an office visit and whether any were expecting checks to be cut from their accounts that day. Before starting her calls, she looked to see how the market opened and whether any of her customers' stocks were in the news. Then she hit the phones, suggesting replacements for bonds that were maturing and passing on news that affected her investors' holdings.

Life in the Garden City branch had continued to be a strain that reflected the boss's mixture of characteristics. Pam and her female coworkers had difficulty getting equal footing with the men, and the atmosphere could be demeaning and wearing. At the same time, Nicholas Cuneo was a celebrator of life events big and small, a positive quality that bred solidarity and suited Pam's personality. Over the years she had slid right into this piece of Cuneo's culture, taking charge of her sales group's birthday bagel celebrations—bagels and coffee on the morning of a staff member's birthday—and volunteering if she saw that the birthday captain in another unit would be out of the office and miss someone's celebration. When she worried that a lunch featuring a six-foot-long sandwich would not be adequate to honor the retirement of the wire operator, Pam lobbied the assistant manager and got money for a more elegant catered affair. When her sales assistant was pregnant, Pam threw a baby shower and decorated the ficus trees in the atrium with pink, white, and blue netting. At one point, Pam was worried that nobody would have a wedding shower for the assistant operations manager because the woman was on the outs with her coworkers. Rather than risk that the occasion would go unobserved, Pam took over and handled the event.

So Pam by the early-to-mid 1990s was a fixture in the Garden City branch and a coordinator of many of the office's more gracious celebrations, although she wasn't always appreciated for it and was sometimes resented for her outspokenness at meetings and her frequently closed door. Focused as she was on her customers, Pam did not pick up on that.

By early afternoon, the August rally in the stock market had stalled slightly, a nonevent to a long-term investor like Pam. Finishing her client calls, Pam contemplated an afternoon cup of coffee and figured she'd better take the time to get it while the market was still open. Trading stopped at 4 P.M., and there was this mandatory 4:15 meeting to discuss changes in the firm's benefits package. With the notoriously frugal Sandy Weill having taken over, the news couldn't be good.

Two floors below, on the Boom-Boom Room level, Pam's colleague Judy Mione was about to find out at the second of three benefit sessions that Pam was right. Under the new regime, management's generosity would indeed be scaled back. It would be all Judy could do, though, to concentrate on the benefits spiel, considering the commotion that Nick Cuneo was about to stir up as the meeting began.

———

JUDY MIONE HAD TAKEN AN AISLE SEAT in a middle row, next to her sister, Joan Chasin. It was the sort of gathering that would not usually call for the presence of the branch manager, Cuneo, or his Number Two, Glenn Fischer. Yet there they were by the podium in the elegant, oak-paneled conference room, with a nondescript human resources executive from New York headquarters whom most of the sales assistants had never seen before. The mousy woman in bland corporate garb was named Robin Leopold.

For years, Mione and Chasin, identical twins and very close to one another, had shared their eight-minute morning drive from North Bellmore to 901 Franklin Avenue in Chasin's Pontiac GrandAm. Chasin, who lived next door to Mione, was a savior to her sister in many ways. She had pitched in when Mione's husband had left her days after the youngest of their three children turned three months old. Chasin was also responsible for Mione's employment in the Garden City branch. In 1990, Mione had lost a high-paying job as senior compliance director of a firm that had gone out of business. Mione had sent her résumé to a dozen Wall Street firms; an executive in the human resources department of Shearson called her enthusiastically after reviewing her qualifications.

On the heels of an encouraging two-and-a-half-hour interview with the recruiter from human resources, though, Mione was passed on to a less welcoming company executive. Nick Marinello, manager of the compliance department, left her waiting outside his door for fifteen minutes. When he did see her, he advised her that a woman should not be working in the downtown Manhattan neighborhood where Shearson was headquartered. Mione was perplexed by the attempts to stifle her interest in the job. "What exactly are you looking for?" she quizzed him.

"Some guy with brass balls from Merrill Lynch."[1]

Mione stormed out of the office. On arriving home, she called her sister, who told the story to Cuneo. With Chasin sitting in his office, Cuneo called Marinello's boss and complained that Marinello might have planted the seeds of a lawsuit.

Marinello to this day denies that Mione's version of their meeting is accurate,[2] but Cuneo did find a spot for her in Garden City. The job paid $25,000, a fraction of the $65,000-a-year job she had interviewed for in New York, but she accepted it with the understanding that she would quickly move into management.[3] On opening her first paycheck, however, she learned that she was making only $19,000.[4] And that job, the temporary one, was the same job she had now, four years later, as she sat waiting for Cuneo's meeting to begin.

———•———

THE LAST FEW ASSISTANTS—all women—drifted in as they finished client phone calls. Seated at the back of the room was Claudia Galvin, an assistant who said she was once paraded to various brokers' offices so they could examine her culottes to see if they violated the office dress code. (One broker told her to spread her legs to improve his view.)[5] Roberta Thomann—always a standout in the crowd with her platinum Buster Brown bob—found a spot with two of her sales-assistant allies, and all three braced themselves when they saw the boss. If Cuneo was there, the agenda was bound to include a chiding for some infraction or another. Too many rings before phones are picked up. Too few cold calls. A number of the sales assistants were easily intimidated by the brash, larger-than-life head man, who would stride back and forth in front of them as he spoke. Thomann and her friends dreaded staff meetings when Cuneo was presiding.

Thomann had been complaining to her husband that she didn't know how much longer she could bear her job at the Garden City branch. Six weeks after Emily, their firstborn, had arrived on April 12, 1994, the phone had rung just after 4 P.M. at the home of Thomann's mother, where she and the baby visited frequently during her maternity leave. It was a familiar voice—that of Paula Doll, secretary of the assistant branch manager—but with an edge. When Thomann asked what was up, Doll said "I'm not going to tell you, I'm too upset." Then Doll's boss, Glenn Fischer, picked up. And that Friday afternoon, on the last day of her maternity leave, Roberta heard the stunning news. Her former job as sales assistant to the most successful broker in the office was no longer available.[6] When she returned on Monday, she was to choose between two equally unappealing jobs: office cashier, or sales assistant to eleven young male trainees in the basement bullpen.[7] Thomann, who had thought she was on a track to become a broker in her own right, called human resources in New York and was told that she would not be paid if she did not show up for work on Monday. She picked the spot assisting the male rookies.[8]

She also wrote a letter of complaint to human resources, saying it wasn't fair that a senior sales assistant should be demoted after a six-week maternity leave. Cuneo had been none too pleased when he learned of the letter.[9] In the weeks after Thomann's letter hit, Cuneo sometimes perched at a desk just across from her and glared at her.[10] On other occasions, he would stroll by her desk singing "I don't care ... "[11]

Now, seated for the benefits meeting, Thomann wondered whether she had done something wrong by having a baby. Her career was derailed, nights at home were tearful, and job anxiety had led to frequent arguments with her husband. She had been a Shearson employee for only a month when her boss, Eugene Trudden, had asked her to type up a prank memo saying that charges of sexual harassment would be deliberated in the Boom-Boom Room.[12] It was his idea of a joke amid the national tension of the Clarence Thomas/Anita Hill hearings on Capitol Hill. Thomann didn't get the joke, not yet knowing what the Boom-Boom Room was. Later in her tenure, she watched Trudden put a condom through the pneumatic tube system that was used to shuttle order tickets from the sales floor to the operations staff below.[13] Thomann met up with the two women at the other end of the tube just as they were receiving it. As Thomann remembers the conversation, her colleagues were disgusted. "Your boss," one of them said, "is a pig."[14]

———

CUNEO WAS AT THE PODIUM in shirtsleeves, with his lieutenants from the branch and headquarters at his side. "I don't know if what I'm about to say is legal or not," he began. "But I don't care."[15]

Thomann was instantly attentive.

The branch's sales assistants were to be enlisted in some unpaid work, Cuneo said. Specifically, he expected sales assistants to begin volunteering some personal time each month for Hospice of Long Island, his favorite charity. Not to cooperate with this initiative would be at their peril. Their employment would at best be "tolerated" should they choose not to give time to Hospice of Long Island.[16] And such amenities as raises, sick pay, time off for funerals or medical appointments, and even cigarette breaks would be a thing of the past for anyone who was not cooperative.[17] The brokers can write me checks to further the cause, Cuneo told them. But you can't afford to do that. So you will give me your time.[18]

There were some rumblings, but no one spoke up. Thomann decided she had nothing to lose. Heads turned as her quaking voice rose above the whispers.

"If it is called charity work, shouldn't we *want* to do it?"[19] Through tears, Thomann suggested that her boss's demand was very likely against the law.

If she didn't like it, she could "bring it up with Glenn," Cuneo said, passing the buck to his second-in-command. Then, he gave his standard adieu. "If you don't like it, there's the door. Don't let it hit you in the ass on the way out." And he left, abruptly ending the exchange.[20]

A startled-looking Robin Leopold took the podium and gave an abbreviated version of the prepared benefits talk, but the audience was too distracted to catch much of it. Once Leopold ended the meeting, Thomann, dejected, made her way to the elevator. As the doors were opening at the basement level, a colleague got in alongside her holding a hot coffee. It was Pam Martens, returning to her office after making her coffee run. She studied Thomann's tear-stained face and wondered what had happened.

Pam followed Thomann and some of Thomann's friends to the second floor, where an impromptu meeting of distraught assistants was shaping up. Hearing what Cuneo had demanded the assistants do, Pam seethed. Looking up from the gathering, she saw Karen Sendel, compliance director, standing nearby, and said to her angrily, "You just stood there and did nothing?"

Sendel was not fazed. "You're gonna hear it next."

ROUND THREE OF THE BENEFITS ROAD SHOW, the 4:15 session for the brokers, started on time, with about fifty of them in the room. Pam, rising from her chair beside Denise Elf, the only other woman attending, addressed Cuneo before he could begin.

"Before you get started—." Heads turned. "I've listened to your filthy mouth for ten years, and I should have spoken up sooner." Her voice quavered. Her entire body shook. "What you did here today was nothing short of extortion."

The room was utterly silent. Some of the brokers had been clued in about the previous meetings because their distraught sales assistants had told them about Cuneo's demands. Others in the room, though, were not sure what Pam was talking about. Energized by the sight of Cuneo's face reddening with rage, she kept going.

"You've basically told these women that they are indentured servants who will work for you during their personal time," she said. "You know they need your paychecks. You've destroyed the morale of this office in one afternoon." No one broke the hush in the room as they awaited Cuneo's reaction.

Cuneo came back at her. "You'll be tossed out of this office, and we'll throw a party like we did when Peppy Henin left."

"I don't think so," she said. "This time, there are twenty-four eyewitnesses"—meaning the assistants from the two earlier sessions. Stunned by the encounter, Cuneo walked off the podium and stomped down the aisle and through the sliding oak doors. Robin Leopold took over as she had in the earlier meeting, trying to get the group to calm down and absorb the news about medical coverage. But after a few minutes, she cut the meeting short. She had not said a word during Cuneo's exchange with Pam.

WHEN THE MEETING BROKE UP, Pam followed the crowd outside and into a packed elevator. No one spoke during the short ride to the second floor. As she headed down the hall to get her purse and leave for the day, a hushed voice beckoned her from an office on the left. "Pam, could you come in?" It was Terry Ho, the Chinese-American broker who worked across the atrium from Pam's office. Pam ducked inside with him. Cuneo had once summoned Ho on the intercom system with "Get your yellow ass in here." When Ho advertised for clients in Chinese newspapers, Cuneo would make remarks about the Chinese being excessive gamblers.[21]

"Thank you for speaking our mind," said Ho simply.

"You're welcome." She and Ho regarded each other for a moment, then Pam left for her office. Gathering her things there, she heard a knock and looked up to see Judy Mione. "Pam, I know you are having problems with what's going on here," said Mione. "You have a lot of heart. I want you to know that, whatever you decide to do, I will be with you."

Pam was moved to tears. Though Pam had not exactly been timid during her tenure in the Garden City office, she was no rebel, either. She pondered her eruption and was struck suddenly by the similarity between what she saw as Cuneo's dictatorship and the oppression she'd witnessed growing up in West Virginia. The coal miners were virtual slaves to their employers. Grandma Carrie had talked about it often. Unless you worked your own land, or could get a job at the glass factory, you were indentured.

And here—in a workplace where women heard themselves called "Tits and Slits"; where happy hours kicked off as early as 10 A.M.; where the boss was known to have a gun in his drawer, just in case—coercion, intimidation, and anxiety also reigned. In her gut, Pam had made the connection between Appalachia and Garden City, and she was riled up.

Her new supporter, Judy Mione, had left, and Pam was alone in her office. At the end of a suddenly exhausting day, she picked up her purse and briefcase and headed downstairs to her battered Bluey in the parking lot. Cuneo had provided motivation for an action that was going to blow open the windows of the Old Boys' Club.

Chapter Seven

That Was Happening to You, Too?

I could win any contests that were put in writing, so the manager stopped putting them in writing or would twist them in a way that I/women [sic] would not win them. Some of the prizes were men's shoes.

—FEMALE BROKER QUOTED IN THE PLAINTIFFS' EXPERT REPORT ON MERRILL LYNCH WOMEN

TROUBLE WAS BREWING in branch offices from New York's financial district to the Pacific Coast Highway, but women in the securities industry were in the dark about one another's distress. Not until after the dawn of the new century would social scientists have data to show how uniformly they kept their harassment experiences to themselves.

They had settled in during the late 1980s and early 1990s, when Pam Martens and thousands of others were drawn to brokerage industry jobs, believing that hard work would cut them in on a slice of the bounteous Wall Street pie. The pie, though, was being divvied up with defective cutlery. Women made up 25.9 percent of management jobs on Wall Street by 1994, and that is despite a pipeline full of female MBAs. (The peak year for female MBAs was 1986.)[1] Still, the rookies enrolled with anticipation that they could get ahead.

Susan Jaskowski was one of the hopeful newcomers. She was working in a personnel agency in 1982, intrigued by the excitement she saw at client companies in the brokerage business. The entrepreneurial aspect of Wall Street appealed to her, and financial services looked like a particularly wide-open place for women. During a very slow month at her office, when she had no recruits to offer a Chicago company called Rodman & Renshaw, she decided to take an assignment there herself. Rodman needed a mailroom clerk, so Jaskowski took the temp job they were offering. While there, she heard that the firm was looking for sales assistants. She left the employment agency and took one of those jobs. In 1989, after seven years of working her way up from the initial job as a mailroom clerk, she became one of 16 women among the firm's 146 professionals who ranked vice president or above.[2] Rodman named her director of human resources—a promotion of which she at first felt rightly proud. That soon changed.

Her days became increasingly dedicated to contending with intimidation meted out by a certain highly successful and surpassingly vulgar broker. Once Jaskowski was in place as HR director, women at the firm came to her in increasing numbers with complaints about men in the office, particularly Mark Grant, an executive vice president who was a luminary at Rodman. Grant was forever reminding women that they were objects, according to lawsuits and EEOC complaints against him. He told one woman that her job description was to be "flat on her back," according to a complaint filed by a Rodman sales assistant.[3] He told another that her job was to relieve his sexual stress and tried to kiss her, the same complaint charged.[4]

To another, Jeannine Finley, he said he would take her home and play connect the dots with her freckles to see where the freckles led, according to the complaint Finley eventually filed.[5] Grant told the press that the charges were "totally unfounded."[6] Finley charged that he taunted her with references to a pin in the shape of a cat that she wore one day. "Hey, Jeannine, I like the pussy that you are wearing." And "How is your pussy today?" And "Where has your pussy been?"[7] She charged that once he touched her chest in the spot where the pin usually went. He asked Finley to have dinner and drinks, and she declined. Later, he called her "white trash." She said that he asked her to watch his dog when he went away, but she had heard that two previous dog sitters had quit because he had greeted them at the door without any clothes on. Finley did not take care of the dog.[8]

Susan Jaskowski approached management with reports that the office rainmaker was touching women and staring at their breasts, making them uncomfortable in the workplace. She went to Grant, too, when from time to time a complaint was over the top. She also tried to present job recruits to Grant who were people of color or women who were not attractive. "He would see them across the room and say 'I am not gonna hire her' if the candidate was an unattractive woman," Jaskowski says. "He would not hire anybody who was not pleasing to the eye." She occasionally would try to discuss with Grant that he should not be behaving in that and other ways but found it fruitless. "He basically would not listen," she says. "He'd say, 'Yeah, OK, you did your job, you told me that. Now you're done.' I was basically an annoyance to him."[9] She went as high as the president of the firm, to whom she directly reported, telling him what was going on, but getting a response that the issue was not a priority.[10]

Jaskowski met with the women herself to give them some advice. Try walking in a way that doesn't call attention to your pregnancy, she told the one whom Grant taunted with "Moo, moo, here comes the cow." "It was my job as an officer of the firm to smooth out these things. I could never advocate that somebody should go see a lawyer, so I would counsel them, try to move them into another position, do something to kind of get rid of all that stuff," she says.

And it wasn't just Grant, Jaskowski says. "People would come to my desk, and I'd say, 'What can I do for you?' They'd say, 'Oh, well, you can kneel down and give me a blow job.' If you wanted to work there, you put up with it. I'd tell them, 'Get out of here, I'm busy.'" That happened to her on a regular basis.

As 1991 unfolded, Jaskowski was pregnant and wound up on the entertainment circuit herself. Grant rubbed up against her stomach and made remarks about how large a pregnant woman's breasts become, according to the complaint. Another executive opined that she should have stayed at her desk rather than get pregnant, she would charge eventually in her own complaint: Tell your husband "to keep his penis in his pants," he said.[11]

Jaskowski needed the financial security that came with her job, so she sought and received assurance in June 1991 that after her baby came she would come back to a comparably responsible and lucrative position.[12] Her son Benjamin was born in December. By then, Rodman had hired a man to replace her as director of human resources. They paid him 40 percent more than they had paid Jaskowski.[13]

When it came time for her to return, the promise of a "comparably responsible and lucrative job" proved empty. Rodman offered her a position as a mutual funds clerk at a 50 percent reduction in pay.[14] When she complained, they offered her a spot as assistant director of human resources, but still with a salary cut and reporting to the better-paid man who had replaced her.[15] By February 1992, with her newborn three months old, Jaskowski opened a letter from management telling her she would be reporting to Mark Grant.[16] Now she'd had enough. She found the names of two lawyers in Chicago who came highly recommended. With their help, Jaskowski sued Rodman later that year.

The firm then started to suffer from bad publicity it couldn't get rid of. Three other women filed legal actions against Grant and the firm, and soon Rodman & Renshaw was reeling as reporters got their hands on copies of the women's EEOC complaints and lawsuits. The public disclosures hurt the firm in its pocketbook: by August 1993, Illinois Governor Jim Edgar scratched Rodman from the list of underwriters assigned to a lucrative college savings bond deal designed to appeal to small investors.[17] When customers called Rodman wanting to buy the popular bonds, Rodman's brokers had to apologize that they had no inventory, and send them to the competition.

It didn't seem fair to Rodman, whose general counsel told the *Chicago Tribune* that it intended to protest the decision to remove it from the bond deal. The injustice that was troubling general counsel Gregory Quinlivan, according to the *Tribune* story: among the brokerage firms that remained in the bond deal were firms that had been hit with allegations similar to the ones lodged at Rodman. Thus, it was "totally unfair" to single out Rodman, which merely had had the misfortune of catching some bad publicity.[18] (A federal judge would later sentence Quinlivan to a year in prison on charges related to a plan to defraud Rodman in a phony billing scheme.)[19]

Grant and three other executives were fired from Rodman when new owners took over in early 1994.[20] He landed another job immediately, though, with the Chicago office of Josephthal Lyon & Ross Inc., in February 1994. Six months later, in August 1994, he was gone from Josephthal (and would later find himself involved in an arbitration with that firm in which allegations of harassment played a role).[21] But he was painting himself as a winner nonetheless: on November 1, 1995, Grant was quoted in the *Chicago Tribune* saying that all was well. "I never paid a penny and was never found guilty," he boasted to the reporter, who was writing on the occasion of Grant's new job as president of Access Financial Group Inc.'s Chicago bond division.

Grant's lawyer maintained years later, in August 2000, that Grant had never paid "even one dollar" for any sexual harassment claim. On October 30, 1997, however, a panel of NASD arbitrators had said that Grant was liable to pay Josephthal Lyon & Ross Inc. $22,000 in compensatory damages related to Josephthal's 1994 complaint against Grant that included charges of breach of oral contract, misrepresentation, failure to supervise, and liability for costs and expenses arising out of six separate claims of sexual harassment.[22] The NASD's regulatory arm never received any indication that Grant had failed to pay up. Therefore, if Grant's lawyer is correct that his client never paid "even one dollar" associated with sexual harassment, it could be because Grant either failed to satisfy the $22,000 award or reached some accommodation with Josephthal after the panel's decision. It could also be because the $22,000 award was not related to the six charges of sexual harassment. In fact, since the arbitrators simply rendered a four-sentence award with no explanation of their decision, the record gives no indication of what weight they gave to the various allegations—or even how they arrived at the $22,000 figure. It is the sort of mystery that is a recurring drawback of arbitration. (In the same proceedings, Josephthal was ordered to pay Grant $8,600 related to his partnership interest in a business venture called Skyline Partners. Grant had filed a counterclaim against Josephthal, charging his former employer with breach of employment contract, wrongful termination, and fraudulent misrepresentation.)

Josephthal told the NASD arbitrators that several women had claimed they were harassed by Grant, resulting in settlement agreements in which the firm agreed to give the women annual pay raises in return for their dropping charges. In one case, Josephthal told the arbitrators, Grant agreed to fund a $10,000-a-year annual increase to settle the dispute. The firm said that Grant was responsible for two other such yearly increases, one for $12,000 and another for $16,000. Grant told the arbitrators that he was either not responsible for the payments or that Josephthal was premature in asserting its claims.[23] His lawyer claims that Josephthal produced no evidence to support the underlying harassment claims and that those claims had no merit.

As for Rodman, after losing out on the bond deal, it reached confidential settlements with the women who sued,[24] a then-rare case of economic loss attending what was more typically just some harmful publicity. In most of the stories of the early generations of women ill treated on Wall Street, firms suffered little economic impact—or, like a Long Island firm named Lew Lieberbaum & Co., it took a long time before the public heard anything.

In August 1989, the same year that Jaskowski got her promotion to head of human resources at her firm, Kimberly Casper took an entry-level job at Lieberbaum, a small brokerage around the corner from Shearson's Garden City, New York, office. Casper was nineteen when she started work at the fifth-floor headquarters on Old Country Road.

An affidavit that Casper filed with the U.S. Equal Employment Opportunity Commission revealed that the job became a living nightmare for her.[25] According to that sworn statement, her boss told her she had to remain in the office for a lesbian strip show one April afternoon in 1993 after the stock market closed, purportedly in order to guarantee telephone coverage during a party. She objected but followed instructions to stay, making her the only female employee amid a crowd of clamorous men and hired strippers.[26] The indignity redoubled the next day as men recapped the highlights of the afternoon within Casper's earshot—the way one broker poked one of the strippers in the buttocks with a stick during the show; how the other stripper had an earring in her pierced genitals, and the way she then passed the jewelry around for the men to smell.[27] Casper was nauseated by the talk, and by the realization that these men could say whatever they wanted to her.[28]

Men harassed Casper as she went by their desks. She was at first self-conscious, then afraid to move around the office. A broker who sat in a "quad" of four men once yelled to her, "Casper, how much to blow the quad?"[29] Casper could feel her face flush. Thereafter, she would literally run if she had to pass their area.[30] Her office was a war zone in which the men had the weapons.

Sworn affidavits depicted some of the Lieberbaum men as downright vicious. A senior financial officer told Linette Cinelli, a trading assistant, to bring a copy of a completed trade to his office "without your jacket on," a command she ignored, or tried to.[31] Hours later, he found her in the trading room. As the affidavit describes it, he pinched and twisted the skin on the back of her neck and told her that she had best listen to him next time: "When I tell you to come into my office without your jacket on, I mean it."[32] Cinelli would later be told by the same manager that she could keep her job if she serviced him sexually.[33]

Another woman at Lieberbaum, Deanna Caliendo, received an order from the sales manager, identified as "John Doe" in her EEOC affidavit, to report to his office on a Friday at 4 P.M. When she got there, the manager closed the door behind her, sat on the couch, and leered at her while he unbuttoned his pants and asked for oral sex, Caliendo wrote in her affidavit.[34] She fled from his office.[35] Two months later, another senior manager approached her in the front of the office while she was sorting checks and asked her if she was wearing a G-string that day.[36] As her mouth dropped at the question, he pulled the elastic waist on the back of her pants to look down at her buttocks. When she put her hands on his to stop him, he shifted his weight to get an unobstructed view down the back of her pants despite her efforts to keep her arms in the way.[37] "I can go on all night," he whispered, adding that he was "amazing" at oral sex.[38]

Defenders of the securities industry frequently protest that sexual harassment is an isolated problem at brokerage firms, but the Lieberbaum cases as described in the EEOC complaints were anything but. Lori-Ann Pugliese, a sales assistant, wrote in a sworn affidavit to the EEOC that she went to the office kitchen to pour a cup of coffee one October morning in 1995 only to hear one of the brokers telling a male colleague about the oral sex he had enjoyed the night before.[39] The affidavit says that the broker looked up at Pugliese in the middle of his sexually stimulating conversation and said "She's lucky I don't rape her right now." According to the sworn statement, Pugliese ran out of the kitchen and, barely composing herself, told her sister, another Lieberbaum employee, what had happened. That proved to be a mistake. Later that day, a senior manager (and brother of the man who made the remark) approached her angrily and began yelling at her for making a fuss over nothing. "Who do you think you are, making a fucking federal case out of this?" he shouted. She was a "fucking bitch" to have gotten the broker in trouble, according to Pugliese's account.[40]

Safety became a worry for Pugliese in other ways, according to her sworn statement. She began to change the way she dressed, for example, after a male colleague clued her in on an inside joke among the guys: the men had taken to calling her "Guns," supposedly a reference to her large breasts.[41] She decided she had better downplay her figure if she was to work in relative peace and avoid a groping, or worse.

The problem was that there seemed to be no conversation, no mode of dress, and no occasion that was safe from a sexual connotation or threat. On Cinelli's 25th birthday, a senior manager asked her how many of the men in the office she would like to "slam," according to her sworn affidavit.[42] He said he would line them up for her in his office, the document said. According to the affidavit, the manager, who frequently called her a "whore," requested on a regular basis that she give him oral sex.[43] Cinelli swore in her statement that one stockbroker constantly suggested that she "suck my dick." Another came up behind her in the office and rubbed against her, moaning "Hey baby, hey baby." She turned around. The young man had unbuttoned and unzipped his pants and asked her to "service" him, she wrote in her affidavit to the EEOC.[44] (Lieberbaum and the EEOC reached a $1.75 million settlement on April 8, 1998, with Lieberbaum simultaneously stating that it "strongly disagreed" with many of the agency's claims but that it wished to avoid "years of costly litigation.")

As a small regional firm with only 300 employees, Lieberbaum may have been more prone to extreme behavior than a higher-profile firm with large, established human resources offices. Yet large firms were not immune, and human resources departments often proved to be no help to women suffering harassment on the job. Unbeknownst to Pam Martens, her contemporaries in the Fifth Avenue office of Shearson were subjected regularly to creepy talk and sexual solicitations from managers. Lydia Klein, hired by Shearson in 1981, worked with men who sent gifts of pastry and chocolate in the shape of a penis (Klein received one from a male coworker who was later promoted to manager in her department) and who referred to women as "cunts."[45] Two of her coworkers referred to women's breasts as "bodacious ta-tas."[46] Men in her office played a makeshift basketball game in which tennis balls were shot into a bra that was hooked up over one of their desks.[47]

At the Shearson office in Paramus, New Jersey, a broker named Eileen Valentino was attacked from behind in a stock room in 1992.[48] While Valentino was reaching to get a form for a customer who wanted to open an Individual Retirement Account, she felt a body lunge at her from behind and a pair of hands lock beneath her breasts. At the other end of the same office, a sales assistant had to cope with a boss who would call her from a phone outside the office asking her to "talk dirty to me."[49] The young woman, Betty Escarpenter, felt ill every Sunday night in anticipation of another week at work. So undone was she by the heckling that she hid the humiliating story from her husband for months. Such stifled behavior is not unusual among women who are being harassed, especially by men who have financial power over them. The women frequently are afraid that they have done something to invite it and become ashamed of what they are putting up with. Some find themselves genuinely unsure whether they are overreacting or misreading the situation. Their reticence to immediately report problems often works against them should they later file a claim: Companies inevitably argue that, if something had really happened, a woman certainly would have sought help from her boss or from HR.

Defense lawyers at the extreme suggest that these cases without witnesses can be contrived by money seekers. While it would not seem simple—or with any certainty worthwhile—to fabricate a harassment story, it is entirely possible that a woman could be emotionally disturbed, or that she could embellish a true story, or that a relationship could have been more consensual than she had described. Frances Farber-Walter, a civil rights lawyer in Hackensack, New Jersey, said that ten percent of the cases she has seen over the years involve such dynamics. Typically, though, victims tend to understate rather than overstate their problems.

The troubles arose from the most junior to the most senior levels. Marianne Spraggins, a superstar African American manager in the public finance department of Smith Barney in New York, quit on January 3, 1994, amid compensation and discrimination complaints. Spraggins, who reaped a $1.35 million settlement after the Reverend Jesse L. Jackson Sr. lobbied on her behalf, said she was not paid as much as her male peers.[50] A former male colleague, Michael Lissack, said that he witnessed situations in which Spraggins was mocked for her race and her aggressiveness. Lissack, a former Smith Barney public finance executive with a long history of his own litigation with the firm, used to listen in horror as his colleagues referred to Spraggins as a "nigger." At a company party in 1994, Lissack says he stood by aghast as a top manager speculated about the size of Marianne Spraggins's penis. Lissack wound up ratting on Smith Barney and others for their illegal practices in municipal bond pricing. (While his information brought Wall Street's municipal bond business to its knees, he, too, got in trouble, earning a five-year ban from the industry in 1997 by the Securities and Exchange Commission.[51] Smith Barney executives call Lissack unstable and dangerous; Lissack in return incessantly criticizes management for actions he says he witnessed firsthand.)[52]

Outside of the major cities, women were living with some terrifying personal hells. In the Charlotte, North Carolina, branch of Smith Barney, an ambitious sales assistant said that she had threats on her life. A complaint filed against Smith Barney by Linda Atkins Smoot described allegations that, if true, amounted to a bullying abuse of power by a stockbroker who was a major producer for the firm.[53] Smoot started in the branch in 1987 as a sales assistant working for a boss who would garner formal complaints by other women in the Charlotte office by December 2000. She claimed that she succumbed to his demands for sex in 1988, then broke off the relationship only to undergo years of harassment under his professional control. While refusing to discuss specifics, he categorically denied all her claims. Presumably that included a denial of even a consensual relationship.

Cases like Smoot's are particularly difficult ones. Once a woman has had a sexual relationship with her alleged harasser, those who sit in judgment of the case must ask to what degree the liaison might have continued to be a consensual one. Academics who study harassment and lawyers who have represented women over the years raise a countervailing issue: the power that bosses have over subordinates. "In an employer-employee situation, there is no such thing as consensual sex," says Farber-Walter. "There is always an aspect of coercion." One of her clients, a single mother who was worried about supporting her child, continued in a sexual affair with her boss for years. Another, a woman who performed oral sex on her boss for five years, turned out to be emotionally disturbed—an agoraphobic whose office, and thus her boss, was within her "safe zone." All her one-on-one relationships had to exist within a restricted geographic area. Not every affair is a power grab by the boss. But because of the authority that constantly hovers over a boss in the workplace, it must be considered.

Smoot's complaint says that the boss, Roger Shuster, would grab her breasts and buttocks in front of colleagues; that he regularly barged into the women's rest room while she was there; that he called her "a stupid pig"; and that he said that if she would have sex with him, he would back off on his vitriol and be nice to her. She claimed that Shuster asked questions such as when she had last had sexual intercourse and with whom, whether her breasts were real, and whether her nipples were hard. The complaint said that he would send her e-mail both asking for sex and asking whether she had masturbated the previous night.[54] The e-mails, according to the complaint, additionally asked if she would like to watch him masturbate. The complaint asserted that he once took his clothes off and stroked his penis in front of her in the office while telling her that he dreamed about having intercourse with her. According to the complaint, she experienced more severe mistreatment after she broke off the relationship. She claimed that her boss called her a "lazy slut," once threw a cup of coffee at her, and would hit her in the head if she disagreed with him. "Shuster frequently told claimant, 'You don't cold call and you don't put out. You are no use to me,'" the complaint said.

In her complaint, Smoot claims her boss stepped up his harassment when she entered Smith Barney's broker training program in Atlanta in 1995. He sent e-mails to her and to her sister saying that Smoot was a loser who would fail at the training program, the complaint says. When she returned from her training, his harassment escalated further still: if he saw that she was on a sales call, he would walk over and disconnect the phone. Finally, she said, when an unusually lucrative account was close to becoming hers, he sent a provocative letter to her prospective client that wound up killing the deal.

She complained to her bosses' boss, who took no action, according to Smoot's complaint. When a psychologist finally advised her in 1995 that she was suffering from depression and should quit immediately to get away from the man, she took a low-paying job at a bank but still found no peace. He called at the new job to say that he hated her. And then, despite her record of complaints to Smith Barney about harassment on the job, the firm actually requested her help in responding to a customer complaint against her former boss, Smoot's legal papers say. Her boss subsequently visited her at home, purportedly to discuss the case, but instead began to verbally abuse her again. He said that he hated her for having quit the job, but this time, she alleges, he added an addendum: if she were ever to do anything against him, such as file a lawsuit, he would kill her two-year-old nephew.

The broker, who has since left Smith Barney for Prudential Securities, says that Smoot's charges are entirely fabricated and that she and others who ultimately filed complaints against Smith Barney were enticed by money and "blood-sucking lawyers." He would not respond to any of her specific charges.[55]

Interwoven with the harassment and discrimination was an economic issue: as women rose in qualifications, male incumbents did not want to share the wealth. The women who worked at Olde Discount Corporation, a national firm based in Detroit, Michigan, perhaps best attest to this formidable combination of economic hoarding and personal contempt.

Olde (pronounced old-ee), which began as a classic, no-frills discount broker in the 1980s, hired a lot of women to fill customer service jobs in its early days. Those service staffers needed licenses to function as stockbrokers, but Ernest Olde, founder of the firm, started out with a philosophy that brokers would be order takers who simply followed the instructions of the customers who called to buy or sell.

In 1983, when half of those order takers were women, Mary Graff joined the firm as a broker in the Glenview, Illinois, office.[56] She did very well in a short time and was named manager in 1985, when the three brokers at her tiny branch had only $8 million in collective assets.[57] Graff hustled during a period in which Olde was slowly transforming from a bare-bones discounter to a firm that solicited and serviced customers. By 1994, the Glenview office had $130 million in assets.[58] She was the biggest seller of bonds among all of Olde's 1,000 brokers in April 1994;[59] that year, her office ranked in the top 2 percent of all Olde branches nationally.[60]

In March of that year, though, branch manager Graff had received a visit from Dan Katzman, the new national sales manager.[61] "I just have to ask, how is your daughter?" he wanted to know, not querying Graff on any business matters.[62] He did, however, take the time to mention that *his* wife stayed at home with their child.[63]

She had not been invited when, a few months before, various Olde managers—all male—met in Florida for pep talks and strategy meetings led by CEO Ernest Olde. But according to her complaint, she apparently learned from male colleagues that Olde exhorted the troops to be savvy portfolio managers. Don't fall in love with a stock, he said, because "it is like falling in love with a woman; it falls and falls and all you're left with is a yeast infection."[64] The court papers say that he additionally told the men that he wanted to become more like competitor Charles Schwab & Co., which was known for its technological sophistication. They use computers to answer phones, he said, which meant they didn't have to deal with women who lost time having babies and got moody from menstrual cycles. As described in the complaint, he told his brokers to go out and recruit "young, good-looking, studly males." And not to hire "broads."[65]

Court papers say that in May, Graff got word that Katzman had asked one of her subordinates what Graff's husband did for a living and how much money he made. Which spouse made more money? Katzman wanted to know.[66]

On June 10, Katzman came for another visit to the Glenview office, and the ax came down. "You can't be a manager anymore," he said, commencing a bizarre lecture about Graff's home life. According to court papers, he told her, "You need to be closer to home to spend more time with your daughter. You don't know if anyone is reading to her during the day. You do not know what she is eating. She really needs you." Katzman even told her that her job was better allocated to a young man just starting out. "The twenty-five-year-old guys have goals," he reportedly told her. "They want to drive fancy sports cars so they can pick up the girls and get out of mommy and daddy's house and get married."[67]

Although Graff responded to Katzman that she, too, had goals, she was demoted to broker. Her assistant was taken away. She was transferred to a smaller office and told to report to a less qualified, younger man. Olde only let her take a fraction of her accounts. Her income shrank from $12,000 a month to $1,500 a month. In September, she quit.

In a sworn affidavit, Maura M. Cook, who was director of registered representative recruiting from January 1992 to January 1993, said that she was specifically counseled by her direct supervisor not to hire women, minorities, older persons, or handicapped persons.[68] Her supervisor told her that women were not as ambitious or competitive as men, that he did not want to take on the expenses related to women's pregnancies, that women would let their children take precedence over their work, and that women shouldn't be hired because they would get involved sexually with men at work. Cook would watch him interview candidates he didn't want and use tactics to doom them. He would ask exceptionally difficult questions, she said, or describe the job in very unfavorable terms, or quote a salary below Olde's regular rate. "He frequently told Olde managers in my presence that given fifteen minutes, he could find something not to like about anyone," she wrote.[69] And if the candidate happened to be a woman, that is exactly what would happen.

The winnowing was a tad more difficult, of course, with women who were already in place. As Katzman was preparing to oust Graff, he also was busy reevaluating another star in the Olde broker system. Julia Quintero, hired in 1988 by Olde Discount, had been promoted to manager of the Olympia Fields, Illinois, office in 1990, and, like Graff, had boosted her branch to top-rank status. By November 1993, Quintero ranked 25th among 500 brokers on a list generated by Olde—a so-called Superbroker by Olde standards. (Graff, also a Superbroker, took 17th place).[70]

Quintero advanced despite the policies of the firm's founder, who liked to flaunt his power. During a characteristic visit, Ernest Olde lit up a cigarette, made mention of the firm's no-smoking policy, and said, It's my firm, and I can fire you all if I want."[71]

Katzman's first salvo at Quintero was to give her an assignment: go out to the side of Governor's Highway and shoot photographs of alternate sites for branch offices. Thus, a full-time broker and manager found herself taking Polaroid shots of Burger King restaurants in the middle of the trading day. In April 1994, two months before he demoted Graff, Katzman visited Quintero at the branch and told her he did not want her to be seen working in the manager's office. Get a terminal for the empty desk outside, he said.[72]

Motioning to her wedding ring, he also asked Quintero, who ranked 9th of 1,000 brokers in bond sales, if she really needed to work.[73] By the end of the day, court papers allege that Dan Bryson, a male broker from another office, called to ask Quintero if she had yet moved her things out of the manager's office; he said that she would be terminated if she was seen there. Soon after, Quintero was transferred to a smaller office. There she reported to a man with qualifications inferior to hers. After boosting her income from $20,000 in 1989 to $43,000 in 1991 and $104,000 in 1993, she saw her earnings slump to $65,000.[74] Clients, who liked to stop into the office and visit with Quintero, did not have the option to keep her as their broker. Bryson, the broker who'd called to warn her to get her belongings out of the manager's office, moved to Olympia Fields and took over.

Taking a page from the managements of many a brokerage firm, Olde held its nonmanagement women back by changing the rules about what they would have to accomplish in order to get certain perks that would help them in their jobs. Gina Caposieno, who was hired by Graff in April 1989, was "next in line" to get a sales assistant, only to find out the firm had altered the prerequisites necessary to get an aide. In one of the rule changes, Caposieno learned that brokers were now required to recruit their own assistants rather than get someone hired by management. The only problem was that female brokers weren't allowed to participate in recruiting.[75] Caposieno finished one of her best months ever in April 1994, expecting that, finally, she would be able to have a sales assistant to help with cold-calling and administrative chores.

Instead, she got word that she was being transferred to a smaller office. She could keep $3 million of her $25 million in accounts. She now reported to a twenty-four-year-old man who was so junior to her that she had to sign certain regulatory documents on his behalf.[76]

When her new boss at the smaller office quit less than a year later, he was replaced by a young man from Caposieno's old office. The new manager arrived in charge of many of the accounts she had been forced to leave behind when Olde transferred her.[77]

It had become far more profitable to be a broker than it had been in the old discount days of the 1980s, when brokering amounted to little more than following the market and picking up the telephone. The average Olde broker made $12,000 a year in 1983, a time when half the Illinois sales force was made up of women. By 1994, when it was not unusual for an Olde broker to make $100,000 a year, the representation of women had dropped to one in one hundred. While these jobs were becoming more lucrative, management was aggressively making room for men to take them. It also became the time when Olde Discount Corp. launched into a collection of sales practices that were so abusive of customers that Ernest Olde ultimately would be suspended from the brokerage business for eighteen months and personally pay a $1.5 million fine to the Securities and Exchange Commission for his role in creating an environment that was conducive to fraud.[78] Some of the now-purged women had been scorned for their protective fiduciary approach to dealing with customers. At the new Olde, there was no room for that.

The sorts of humiliations that women suffered at Olde could be found in just about any firm in the securities industry, yet Olde did stand out for one thing: here the pyramid of harassers reached as high as its chairman and founder. Those who were targets of his abuse say that Ernest Olde himself set the tone for his male minions to follow.

Among subjects of Ernest Olde's harassment was Susan Bell, a broker who joined the Phoenix-Camelback branch of Olde in November 1989. Bell had previously worked at both Dean Witter and Merrill

Lynch; Olde wooed her with a lure of $1,400 a month plus a commission rate of 33 percent on particular stocks that Olde was pushing.[79]

According to allegations in legal papers, Bell was there only four months when the harassment began. At a three-week training session run by Ernest Olde at the Detroit headquarters, Olde singled her out for an impromptu quiz on her brokering skills. What sexual enticements might she use in order to close a sale with a customer who was reluctant about buying a stock? Olde asked her. Would she wear a shorter skirt if he were a leg man? Would she wear a low-cut blouse and show a little cleavage to get the deal done?[80]

Bell was shaken by the embarrassing public grilling, her legal filing says. Nevertheless, she focused on her work and did well enough that by the following June, she made "Superbroker," a status that confers special privileges.[81]

It also meant Bell had to attend the Superbroker Conference in Detroit the following month, which put her in harm's way again. Before the formal proceedings, Olde again singled her out in front of others to say how surprised he was that she had attained superbroker status so quickly. She, in particular, was not his idea of someone who would take the securities business seriously, he said. Later, when the meetings began, Olde again asked her what sexual overtures she would use to close a sale, her complaint says.[82]

She was promoted that fall—in October 1991—but it was a hollow victory. The branch manager had left, and Bell got to replace him, but there was no pay raise. In fact, the other licensed broker in the office made more money than she despite her Superbroker status, her branch manager title, and her significantly greater production. He had been hired only eight months before.[83]

With the new job, Bell did get new duties, however. She stocked the supply closet and coordinated a move to a new office, and between November 1992 and February 1993 she even vacuumed the carpets and scrubbed the toilets.[84] She did the latter before office hours in order to be sure that clients would not catch sight of their branch manager performing janitorial duties.

In the meantime, a senior officer made demands of sexual favors during a business meeting. Bell declined. She tried to report that and other problems to management, which brought no satisfaction. Among the higher-ups to whom Bell says she brought her complaints: Susan

Olde, the company's supervisory administrator identified in Bell's complaint as sister-in-law of Ernest Olde and one of four shareholders of the privately owned firm.

Bell attended her second Superbroker Conference on August 13, 1992, a time when she should have been a hero. According to legal papers, she was the highest-producing broker in the room, beating the other brokers' commissions by 40 percent. Her legal filing reveals that Ernest Olde went around the room recognizing one broker after another for their accomplishments. When he came to Bell, he launched a vicious attack and told her to look for another job.[85] Two months later, when she was the top producer in Arizona, a trainee got word that he would be taking over the client book of a "girl" who was "not doing very well."[86] Bell was demoted to broker status in the summer of 1993. She was transferred to the Scottsdale, Arizona, office, where her salary was reduced by 25 percent and she was permitted to take only $3 million of her $20 million in accounts.[87] In late August, the stress built to such a level that she was rushed to the emergency room with chest pains. She quit on September 7, 1993.[88]

During a later hospital stay, though, she had the presence of mind to be sure that she did not let lapse her opportunity to get back at Olde. In January 1994, while recuperating from an emergency appendectomy in an Arizona hospital, Bell realized that the statute of limitations was about to end her ability to file an EEOC complaint against Olde. Barely able to stand, Bell enlisted her sister-in-law to drive her to downtown Phoenix to drop off the paperwork. She later collapsed back into her hospital bed, mulling her theory that harassers turned out two kinds of victims: the ones so beaten down that they are drained of self-esteem and do nothing to fight back, and the ones so fighting mad that they are obsessive about seeing justice done. Bell was the latter.

Susan Bell is no longer permitted to discuss what happened to her at Olde. As part of her settlement, she signed a confidentiality agreement that would yank back the settlement money if she were ever to speak about the treatment she received. She and her lawyer granted interviews to the author in 1995, before the settlement, as did Quintero and Graff, who also have now signed what are known as "shut-up" contracts.

(Olde Discount was sold to H&R Block, whose spokeswoman did not comment and said she could not locate Ernest Olde. Two of his former lawyers said they would not be the appropriate people to comment on his behalf at this time. In 1995, when these accusations were being made about Ernest Olde, he declined through his company's counsel to comment, as did other senior managers at the firm. The firm at the time said it did not engage in discrimination. Certified mail to Ernest Olde's home was sent back to the author.)

Companies pay premiums to settle this way with their disgruntled employees. Shut-up agreements typically mean that the woman vows never to speak about the discrimination or harassment that she experienced and promises never to discuss the amount of money that she was paid for her silence. She also agrees that she will not sue the firm for harassment or discrimination related to those events in the future. The penalty for breach of the agreement is loss of the settlement money.

Gary Schoener, a clinical psychologist based in Minneapolis who is an expert on sexual harassment, says that many of the women who sign shut-up clauses turn out to feel badly frustrated in the end. "Since at least half the reason they sue is to bring about change, it's not only a hollow consequence," he says. "People go away with what I call the Judas Theory about themselves. They come to believe they took their thirty pieces of silver and betrayed other women."

Brokerage firms have the highest incentive to keep egregious cases quiet and offer the most money to those women in exchange for a promise of secrecy, so lawyers working for plaintiffs on a contingency basis might be prone to a bias to get cases over with quickly. As for turning down a settlement altogether, in an unusual case, a lawyer might honor a client's passion to hold out for a public hearing at trial, whether to effect change, to get a story out, or to punish the offenders. But going to court could cost the lawyer hundreds of thousands or millions of dollars out of pocket, and settlement money in hand is a tough motivator to beat.

Frances Farber-Walter, who has represented a woman who won an arbitration against Shearson, says that she tries not to take cases to trial. "The good cases settle, to tell you the truth. The lawyers on the other side are as smart as I am. They will recognize the exposure a client has to liability, and if the case is strong, they're going to recommend that the defendant settle. Their exposure at trial is monumentally higher than what it costs to settle."

In the rare case when Farber-Walter does go to trial or to arbitration, she says the emotional level is high as a result of the personal nature of the charges being made. She tries to keep things cool by doing such things as serving subpoenas through the defendant's lawyer, and she has settled cases through such niceties. "They don't want their wives to know what's going on and have been willing to negotiate a settlement," she says.

When settlements don't come easily, though, harassment cases come down to judgments of credibility in the hearing room, Farber-Walter says. The accused man typically takes an offensive stance, she says, expressing horror that anyone could accuse him of such acts. Defendants can be expected to describe their idyllic marriages and happy families. With the burden of proof on the plaintiff, harassment cases are difficult ones, Farber-Walter explains. "A guy isn't going to walk around the office with a bullhorn screaming discriminatory remarks so that people can hear it," she says. "And he's certainly not going to hit on you in the presence of people unless he's drunk." Almost essential in a case is that the plaintiff immediately reported any egregious single incident to someone in the office. Courts expect that even when employees consider their human resources departments or employee hotlines to be ineffective, the harassed women should have put an incident on the record with one of the two. Or, at the very least, told a friend or colleague in the office right after something happened.

While it benefits from public exposure that tends to minimize abuse, court is no panacea. A plaintiff can draw a judge who has preconceived notions about discrimination cases, seeing her case thrown out early on. And trials, like the arbitration fight, have been known to leave once-vibrant working women emotionally broken down. Courts, though, are more easily challenged than arbitration panels: When the women who worked the iron mines of Eveleth, Minnesota challenged a lower court decision against them after they sued Eveleth Mines for discrimination, the Eighth Circuit Court of Appeals overturned the judge who had ruled from his bench. The Eighth Circuit also spoke out against the unfair way in which the defense pursued details of the women's pasts, exposing information concerning abortions, children given up for adoption, marital disputes, and emotional difficulties related to the plaintiffs' upbringing. Both arbitration and court may be wearing on the plaintiff, but court at least holds out hope for future generations through the appeals process.

Helen E. Fisher, professor of anthropology at Rutgers University, says whether the forum is court or arbitration, some women in civil rights battles may be handicapped by a tendency to see their corporation as a person—one they care for. Women act differently in companies, Fisher says, spending less on their expense accounts than men, thanking people more, apologizing more, and sharing more information. That does not serve them well in a legal fight, where women can become so confident that justice will prevail that they botch the details.

"Men make rules and stick to them no matter what," she says. "For women, rules are much more flexible." Fisher says the woman entering a court fight would figure that if doing the right thing meant changing the rules, that would be fine, "because the point is we have to get to the right place." In a judicial forum, that can lead to a situation in which a woman is unprepared and a man has prepared a careful defense in which every rule is considered, Fisher says. As an anthropologist, she traces the differences to child rearing, where women in charge of infants must do whatever it takes to care for them, casting aside rulebooks or other instructions. The long-term impact, in her view, is a controversial one—a gender difference that leads to enhanced flexibility. In the demanding courtroom setting, though, it could lead to unrealistic expectations from the unprepared plaintiff who thinks that for the greater good, jurists will see past rigid statutes and rule in her favor even if a case is not airtight.

It is up to plaintiffs' lawyers, of course, to see that clients understand that principle alone is not enough to win a case. Evidence and timing are key.

At trial, Farber-Walter never gives the alleged harasser a chance to deny what he's been accused of during her direct examination. She will ask him such things as whether he went on a particular trip, or whether he was in the room at his hotel on a particular day, or whether he had lunch with her client at a particular time. Then she will wait for the man's lawyer to ask whether the defendant ever harassed the plaintiff. "He's going to say, 'Never. No. Of course not. I never did that. She's crazy.' I let his lawyer ask him. This is a well-rehearsed game." Once the man has denied the act or acts, Farber-Walter comes back to attempt to discredit his testimony.

The securities industry has developed other ways to keep its secrets secure. For women who quit, there were certain favored tactics. For example, after being fired, one former Shearson employee began to settle in at a new job only to learn that her new employer had been served with a subpoena seeking any records its "employee assistance program" might have in her file related to substance abuse. Her old firm,

Shearson Lehman Brothers, against whom she had filed a complaint, was planning to argue in the upcoming arbitration that her behavior on the job had deteriorated while she was with them. This might have suggested drug abuse, the firm's lawyer appeared to imply in his closing argument when the case came before the panel.

The woman's lawyer told the panel of arbitrators that there were reasons to be suspect of Shearson's motives in serving the subpoena. For one thing, Shearson had no good-faith basis to believe that she had been in a substance abuse program, he argued. And, in any event, if they had thought she had been, they might first have inquired whether her new employer even had an employee assistance program, which it did not.[89] No such effort at discretion had been made.

The second brokerage firm had hired the woman despite a regulatory record that said she had been fired from Shearson as a result of poor job performance. The December 20, 1993, subpoena requesting substance abuse information, however, was a deal breaker: she was called in by one of the firm's partners who was concerned that Shearson was inquiring about drugs and alcohol and was fired on January 14, 1994.[90] The message she took from the subpoena and subsequent firing was that Shearson had sent the subpoena in retaliation for her having filed an arbitration complaint, and that her new bosses had responded exactly as Shearson had hoped they would.

One could speculate about a brokerage firm's intentions in the battle that ensues after a complaint is filed. There was little room for speculation, however, when statistics became available about the percentages of women in particular spots at Pam Martens's firm in the mid-1990s.[91] Among 400 Smith Barney branch offices, only 10 women occupied the top spot of branch manager. Fifteen percent of the 11,000 brokers at the firm were women. By comparison, five years earlier, women made up 33 percent of insurance industry sales jobs and 51 percent of real estate sales jobs.[92] And in the four years that ended in 1995, only 2.35 percent of the women who began as sales assistants had moved on to be brokers. By comparison, 21.6 percent of the men who started in 1991 as sales assistants had become brokers by 1995. Even in traditionally female jobs where pay is lower, women did not make as much as men who performed the same job. In the 1991–1995 period, 93 percent of the secretaries in the investment banking division were women, but they were paid only 87 percent of the secretarial payroll.

The higher the stakes, the wider the gaps. Men held 95 percent of the banking jobs and 97 percent of the managing director spots. When women got in the door of the banking department, they did not move to the highest-paying jobs at the rate men did. Women occupied 2.67 percent of all the Smith Barney jobs paying between $450,000 and $549,999. Among jobs paying $550,000 and up, not one woman could be found.[93] And though they comprised 36 percent of the investment banking workforce in 1995, women earned only 11 percent of the payroll.

Despite much talk through the 1980s and 1990s that women did exceptionally well doing research, only 24 percent of Smith Barney's analysts in investment banking were women. The lopsided mid-1990s data from Smith Barney came at a time when women were pursuing higher education at a higher rate than men were: in 1994, women made up 54.8 percent of all bachelor's degree recipients, 57.2 percent of those getting a master's degree, and 44.1 percent of those receiving a doctorate.[94] There was no shortage of educated women in the job pool.

The statistics about employment at Smith Barney, had they been available, would have provided a solid starting point for the firm's frustrated women to fight back. Statistics are derived in the discovery phase of lawsuits and arbitrations, though. Wall Street employees rarely had a chance to get to court. And the industry's private arbitration system left much to be desired when it came to compelling the defendant to produce documents.

———

IN THE EARLIEST DAYS, the few women who worked on Wall Street simply didn't put their jobs at risk by talking about their complaints. As the ball got rolling and women began going public with their grievances, though, a lawyer in Chicago who had fought the case for Susan Jaskowski as well as the one for the Olde women began to see commonalities among stories of women who called telling of how they were sent to smaller branch offices after their accounts were taken away—or stories of bullying of other sorts. A pattern began to emerge.

"Someone will start on a story, and I'll say 'May I interrupt you?' and I complete their story." The lawyer, Mary Stowell, was almost always on target. "The woman will say 'How did you know that?' They're amazed. Some of them still think they're alone."

Dear Mr. Dimon: Martens Fights Back

One managing director went out onto the fire escape to urinate through the bathroom window onto another who was using the toilet.

—MICHAEL R. LISSACK, FORMER MANAGING DIRECTOR, SMITH BARNEY PUBLIC FINANCE DEPARTMENT, IN A PUBLIC SPEECH[1]

IT WAS PAM MARTENS who orchestrated the mass awakening. She had no idea of how ready her colleagues were for some leadership. Management got a clear signal that they had pushed things too far at the "volunteer or else" meetings. Immediately afterward, Nicholas Cuneo huddled in his office with Glenn Fischer, his assistant manager; Tom Ferris, the operations manager; and Cuneo's two sons, Nicholas Jr. and Leslie Cuneo. They stayed behind closed doors until 6 P.M.; the sales assistants who were still at work speculated that it had something to do with the blowup between Pam Martens and the boss.

Roberta Thomann came home that night in tears. She told her husband, Rich, about the demand for unpaid work and the threat of withdrawn benefits. "Cuneo told us he wasn't looking good in front of the hospice people," she said. His mandatory volunteer work would mean more time away from her four-month-old daughter, her firstborn.

To Rich Thomann, it was the last straw. Roberta was way too stressed. "This is unbelievable," he said, struggling with the story. "You've got to get out of there." Roberta called her mother that night and heard more of the same. The job was not worth the heartache, her mother said.

Dragging herself out of bed the following morning, Roberta dressed herself and the baby, dropped her daughter at her mother's house, and drove to 901 Franklin Avenue wondering how she'd make it through the day. When she got in, she found a memo from management in her mailbox. A meeting for all sales assistants was scheduled at 9 A.M. Attendance was again mandatory. What next? she thought. Can this get worse?

Twenty-four women filed into the conference room with emotions in upheaval. Cuneo stood in front of them. What he seemed to be offering was an apology; what they heard, though, was a series of excuses and reconstructions of reality. "I just want to clear up anything that I said at last night's meeting that may have been misconstrued," he said. He had not threatened them; he had simply asked for "a favor."

"We did not misconstrue anything," Roberta Thomann shot back. "You did threaten us." Others asserted that they knew he was taking advantage of them. He knew perfectly well that most of them could not afford to lose their jobs and needed to stay in his good graces. Morale was terrible, someone said. You treat us like dirt.

Cuneo's brief attempt at contrition turned to venom. "Well, before now, I've been an easy lay," he said, departing in a huff and letting uncertainty settle over the room. A dispiriting thought gradually suggested itself—that Cuneo's bosses had put him up to making some sort of an apology, and that they had just heard the best they were going to get.

Word moved quickly from the assistants to Pam that Nick Cuneo had backed off his demands. Recalcitrant sales assistants were starting to view Pam as the efficient repository of any antimanagement information at the branch. The assistants now knew of Pam's speech of the previous day, and it was causing some of them to reassess her. She had, up to then, been a stranger to many of them. In fact a contingent of wary sales assistants had actually steered clear of Pam until then, put off by her righteous tone and her closed office door. But now that some of them thought about it, it made sense that Pam would be the one to stick up for them. It was Pam who would jump in and quarterback a wedding shower or write a note if there was a death in a colleague's family. The wife of one broker who had died still kept Pam's letter of condolence in a drawer eight years later. And it was Pam who, while the men curried favor with the boss on the golf course, used her personal time to help the junior staff: in one instance, she learned that a sales assistant was aching to learn how to swim and began to teach her each week at a local gym.[2]

Pam has a lot of heart, Judy Mione thought as she reflected on Pam's courage at the previous day's meeting. Thomann, who was hardly accustomed to being protected, having grown up in a family of six children, thought Pam's outburst was among the most admirable acts she'd ever heard of. It was like Norma Rae taking on Wall Street. And to think she barely knew this woman.

In the wake of Cuneo's September 1 "I take it back" speech, Pam asked Roberta to stop by. Roberta said she would come around in a few minutes.

They met in Pam's office. Pam sympathized with her junior colleague over the anguish Cuneo was putting her through. "I saw your face, and I just lost it," Pam said, talking about their elevator encounter the day before.

The two went back over the previous day's debacle and—for the first time—shared with one another what they'd suffered at the branch. It was an eye-opener in particular for Roberta, who—like Pam and others—had been taking the abuse personally. What a relief not to be alone, she thought. It might actually be possible to get something to change. Then, Roberta challenged Pam: A rumor is going around that you have put your complaints in writing.

"That's true, but it happened six years ago," Pam said. She told Roberta that she had written a letter to former CEO Hardwick Simmons, but all that came of it was a visit from a human resources executive.

Roberta told Pam about the broken promises that she would have her job back when she returned from maternity leave. She told her how she had helped out through her leave whenever her boss, Eugene Trudden, had a question about the monthly money-management statements for which Roberta had been responsible. She reminded Pam of the intimidating memo telling the staff that any complaints of sexual harassment would be "dealt with" in the Boom-Boom Room.[3] And, of course, of the infamous condom-through-the-pneumatic-tube "gag."

They think it's a joke, Roberta said. They don't consider us the least bit threatening.

"Maybe it's time we make it threatening," Pam said. "We should get everyone to put in writing exactly what's happened to them—all the things they've had happen personally, and everything they've witnessed."

IT WAS WORTH A SHOT. Pam got on the telephone, calling a handful of women who had worked in Garden City but had become frustrated and moved on. She called Lorraine Parker, the brilliant former accountant who had joined Shearson in 1986 from Touche Ross. Would Lorraine put in writing what she had experienced in the Garden City branch? Parker said she would. She called Kathleen Keegan, the former school-teacher who had come to Shearson only to have Cuneo turn her into a sidekick to a male broker, losing even the privilege of having her name on the customers' statements. Keegan said she was in. She spoke to Peppy Henin, whom Cuneo had dubbed the "Jewish bitch."[4] Pam called three women she knew from when they were cold-callers in the bullpen. They were not willing to put their grievances on paper, but they suggested Pam call Lori Hurwitz, a broker who had left eight months earlier. Hurwitz promised a statement, too.

Pam told Judy Mione about the plan to compile written statements. Mione said she, too, would get one to Pam. Where does this all lead? Mione wanted to know.

We may actually sue Smith Barney, Pam told her. We've tried complaining to the manager. We've tried complaining to human resources. When an officer from human resources can stand by as Robin Leopold had on Wednesday, saying nothing while the boss threatens his employees, it's clear we have no allies there.

The two knew that they were declaring war. What they didn't know then was how much artillery the enemy had.

Pam asked Judy and Roberta to refrain from consulting with each other but rather to sit down independently and write what had happened, both at Cuneo's meeting and at their jobs in general.

The statements that came in painted a grim picture. Peppy Henin said she went to a branch dinner for brokers at a local restaurant only to be verbally harassed "about being a rich Jewish woman"[5] and having to listen to Cuneo tell "filthy jokes."[6] Cuneo's acting assistant manager, Henry Chin, "told me that a woman wasn't welcomed at these dinners," she wrote.[7]

Pam found the expected patterns in what she, Henin, and others wrote. Kathleen Keegan spoke of Cuneo's boasting that "he could say anything he wanted because no one would do anything about it."[8] She told of how Cuneo moved her clients to a male broker's book and made her give up her commissions[9]—a variation of a scheme he had tried to foist on Pam in 1988.

Keegan had been exposed to Cuneo's hostility toward women from the start. When Cuneo interviewed her in 1985, he told her that Shearson was "forcing quotas of women" on him.[10] It didn't take long before she found out what it was like to socialize à la Cuneo. She described in her memo her one and only venture into the Boom-Boom Room and told of her horror at the vulgarity in the office. During her initiation to the securities industry, Keegan had figured that as a former schoolteacher, she just didn't understand how business worked.

Keegan conceded in her statement that Cuneo's secretary, Gladys Lawson, once passed on a client to Keegan who had walked in cold to open an account. Accounts that come in that way are considered gravy in the brokerage business. But the largesse was not doled out with the blessing of the boss. According to Keegan's statement, Cuneo yelled at Lawson, "Why the hell did you give that to Keegan?"

To this was added the statement from Lori Hurwitz, who had quit in disgust on January 28, 1994. Not even the connection of a male relative—her father, who worked as a broker in a different office of the same firm—had protected her. In the statement she sent, she described a job interview with Glenn Fischer during which he told her not to apply if she thought she would be taking "significant time" off for maternity leave. Hurwitz said that management repeatedly raised the bar when she tried to qualify to enter the training program, increasing the number of new accounts she would have to sign up. She gave up on getting management to pay for the books for the broker's test and bought the material herself. Hurwitz passed the Series 7 test despite the lack of support and then was told she must continue to pass on any clients she wooed to other brokers until she passed another test, the Series 63. She passed that test, but then learned she could not keep the clients she signed up until she passed yet another test, called the Series 65. Although most of the senior men in the office would later have the Series 65 license, Hurwitz at the time stood out because her colleagues were required only to get the Series 7 before keeping their accounts.[11]

Hurwitz was told that, as a cold-caller, she would be fired if she flunked the Series 7 test on the first try (she passed the first time), yet she knew of male brokers who flunked and got another shot.[12]

During this time, Hurwitz's statement said, not a single one of the accounts she opened was passed on to a woman broker.

Pam sat back and considered the wide-ranging problems of the women past and present at 901 Franklin Avenue. She decided that before acting aggressively with a lawsuit she would detail the problems to management. On October 3, 1994, she posted an explosive dispatch to the thirty-eight-year-old workaholic president and CEO of Smith Barney, James "Jamie" Dimon:

Dear Mr. Dimon:

I am writing to request your review of a systemic problem of sexual harassment, sexual discrimination and lewd conduct on the part of the Branch Manager of the Garden City office, Nicholas Cuneo ... Mr. Cuneo's illegal conduct began on the very first day we met for my job interview. He told me that he would not be giving me the same trainee stipend that he gave the male brokers; that he knew it was illegal and I should not bother to try to sue him since many before me had tried and failed ...

The next memorable encounter with Mr. Cuneo came on a bus trip to the Waldorf Astoria to hear Peter Cohen (then CEO of Shearson) speak. Mr. Cuneo had just had some kind of run-in with a male broker in our office, Mel Colby ... During this bus trip, Mr. Cuneo stood in the aisle at the front of the bus, like a tour guide, and repeatedly pointed to the lower part of his body and said "Mel Colby, eat my d—-!" He called Mel Colby every disgusting name you could imagine ...

Shortly thereafter, Lorraine Parker was hired through the Shearson training program. Lorraine had been a CPA with Touche Ross and was very attractive. Mr. Cuneo paraded around the upstairs yelling out that he had just hired a Playboy Bunny.

At one point, there were a number of female trainees in our office ... Mr. Cuneo placed flyers in all brokers' mailboxes inviting "All Garden City Brokers" for a day of golf and dinner at his Country Club. When we rsvp'd, Mr. Cuneo told us that this was just for the male brokers. When Lorraine (Parker) said she would like to come for the dinner, he told her she was not invited.

I wrote to Human Resources about this conduct. Jody [*sic*] Beth Galos set up a luncheon meeting ... We told her about Mr. Cuneo's vulgar language at sales meetings, about the golf outing, about the fact that he gave only the male brokers books when a broker left. She responded that "we" should try to get along with him. That was the last that we heard of our complaint. Shortly thereafter, Mr. Cuneo began to harass me in the office...

His meetings were always rambling, unfocused, and punctuated with unbelievable vulgarity. A sampling: about the one and only time we had a black sales assistant: "tell that to the watermelon kid upstairs." About the time Peppy Henin made broker of the month: "I'd rather give it to that broker that has a plaque up on the back wall and shot his in-laws in the head than give it to that bitch." About too many phone calls to home from the office: "If you miss your wives that much, go home and lay between their legs." About the sales assistants' complaints: "that pack of humps." About his invalid wife: "You guys don't really think she is crippled—I just keep her in a wheelchair so that she can't cheat on me." At the 1993 Christmas Party—with the microphone in hand, from the center of the dance floor as part of his message of "good wishes for the holiday season": "We've achieved the status as the biggest whorehouse in Garden City." And, an expression I have heard him use time and again: "You guys who nailed Jesus to the cross."

The six-page missive was the making of a management nightmare. Pam detailed the treatment endured by Kathleen Keegan, saying she "had repeated bouts of upset stomachs while he was harassing her and I believe she finally decided it was this job or her health." She noted that both of Cuneo's sons worked at the office, in "direct violation of the regulations spelled out in the Shearson employee handbook." And finally, she devoted a full page to the details of the August 1994 meeting of Cuneo and the sales assistants.

Given the extremes of Cuneo's transgressions, Pam suggested to Dimon that "someone, for some reason, is covering his tracks." Pam noted that it was an open secret in the office that broker Stanley Feminella had a single big-paying client, because his huge monthly commissions frequently came from a single trade. The office knew it because of a practice of displaying daily sales runs for everyone to see, she told Dimon.

She didn't have the global perspective of the business to know how plausible her speculation about someone covering a manager's tracks was. Brokerage firms routinely protected errant big-earning managers when they were able to, negotiating settlements of both customer disputes and regulatory charges so that the firm took the rap and no individuals were named.

In closing, she noted that she recently had asked Glenn Fischer, the assistant manager, whether the staff should be concerned that Cuneo might come unglued and use the gun that he kept in his drawer.

JAMIE DIMON'S SECRETARY, Theresa, didn't let him get very far the next morning. "Read this right away," she said, handing a document to Dimon, who with his thick brown hair and baby face always looked a little young for the job he was in. He took the six-page, single-spaced letter and sat down in his office. Dimon, having just taken charge of the former Shearson branches in an acquisition that had closed months before, was about to inherit a massive headache from the previous management. It was no secret that the culture of the Shearson branch system was a notch cruder than that of the big-firm competition. Now Dimon, the executive in charge of all those brokers, was reading the gory details about a manager whose alleged behavior was off the charts even by Shearson standards. The acquisition was turning out to be no picnic for Dimon. He had engineered the deal with Sandy Weill, his boss and mentor, who worked his young protégé hard. No one could question that Dimon's career had benefited vastly from his close association with Weill, a "Mr. Outside" socialite who was chairman of Carnegie Hall, among other highly visible public roles. Weill, however, was adept at staying miles away when a crisis was on. Dimon, Weill's "Mr. Inside" known for his fastidious financial analysis and blunt management style, was in the hot seat.

He looked up from his unwelcome piece of mail and summoned John L. Donnelly, senior vice president and director of human resources, and George Saks, general counsel. When they arrived, Dimon recapped the contents of the Martens diatribe and had Theresa make copies for Donnelly and Saks to take with them. "We'll get right on it, Jamie," Donnelly told him.

Dimon separately began to ask around, to get a take on Cuneo. He's a good guy, he was told. He's had a tough life, with a wife who has multiple sclerosis. And whatever you may have heard about Cuneo, he's

been much better recently. Cuneo, in fact, had advised one of the brokers at the branch several years before that he was feeling pressure to
manage the office in a more professional manner, and that he and his
staff would have to behave more like the brokers that were depicted in
television commercials.

Donnelly, meanwhile, moving on Dimon's instructions, got in touch
with Pam Martens promptly. He told her, in a brief telephone conversation, that management would be looking into her allegations. Then he
pressed her on a question: Did Cuneo still have his gun, and did she
know whether it was on his person or in his office? He got his first taste
of Pam's fearless approach even when dealing with top management:
She told him that she didn't consider herself to be the gun-control sher-
iff of 901 Franklin Avenue. Donnelly responded that it was important to
find out whether Cuneo still had his gun and whether he had a license.[13]
Martens suggested that the pursuit of that answer lay more in his jurisdiction than in hers.

Donnelly told her to expect to hear from regional director Hugh
O'Hare, who would call her about a meeting. By brokerage industry
standards, Pam had moved a mountain.

But Cuneo had already set in motion a counteroffensive. Three days
after her October 3 letter to Dimon, a Thursday morning, Pam noticed
that a group of the men in the office had shown up outfitted for golf.
They departed for an outing with Cuneo before noon. Over the course
of the following day, Pam got unexpected visits in her office from three
of them. They each arrived with a curious assortment of defenses,
bribes, and threats. One told Pam she could get anything she wanted if
only she would retract her letter. The second implored her to consider
the failing health of Cuneo's wife; and if Pam didn't sympathize with
Cuneo and retract her accusations, well, he would be digging up dirt on
her. Pam responded that he might start with her shamefully filthy basement, which had even more dirt than the Garden City office. The third
emissary told her she simply had it all wrong. Garden City was
"Camelot," he said, with apparent sincerity. Pam, who had recently
been to a women's rights meeting to bone up on civil rights law,
remembered that she had a flyer in her briefcase that discussed the
concept of a hostile environment in the workplace. She took it out and
handed it to him, pointing to the phrase "an environment that a reasonable woman would find offensive." He crumpled it up and threw it at

her, then walked out of her office. So much for Camelot, and chivalry.

In any competitive and political branch office, the men, too, were subordinate to the boss and had to keep on his good side. Whether in Garden City or potentially any branch office, men who were not interested in the degrading sexual shenanigans were sometimes chided as wimps or told that they were not team players. Some of the men who took part in brokerage-house harassment, or in supporting the harassers, were reluctant participants.

Emboldened by Pam's actions, Roberta Thomann sent a letter to Hugh O'Hare on October 11 with a copy to Jamie Dimon. In it, she recapped the handling of her maternity leave. In order to show that she was not going behind the boss's back, she handed copies of the letter both to Fischer, the assistant manger, and to Trudden, her immediate boss. Thomann had expected that her efforts would result in a serious discussion of her career and management's missteps. She quickly learned she was wrong. A friend tipped her that she should run down the stairs to peek in Trudden's office. "They're all down there laughing," she told Thomann, bracing her for what she would see. Indeed, Thomann arrived outside Trudden's door to discover her boss, Fischer, and compliance manager Karen Sendel laughing uproariously over what Thomann believed to be a copy of her letter.[14] Thomann was devastated. She vowed at that moment that she would sue Smith Barney. Clearly, she concluded, nothing less would work.

Robin Leopold responded in writing to Thomann on October 13 to say that the letter to O'Hare had been forwarded to her and that she would be conducting "a thorough investigation."

More questions were being asked by management in New York, and fires seemed to be kindling everywhere. On October 25, Lorraine Parker, who had departed in July 1993 for PaineWebber after six years in Garden City, sent her own letter to Jamie Dimon, corroborating many of Pam's charges and adding several of her own.[15] Parker told Dimon that Cuneo behaved in an absurd manner during the Anita Hill/Clarence Thomas hearings, yelling one day, "I left a pubic hair on my Coke can" for all to hear. (Clarence Thomas was alleged to have made a similar remark to Anita Hill.) She told Dimon that she walked into the office one Saturday to see several male brokers going through microfiche records of client accounts. The information should not have been available to them, said Parker, who later discovered that some of her clients were being wooed by men who had inexplicably gotten their hands on their names and phone numbers.

Parker's letter also recited that, during a regular audit of the branch, the auditors, as was their custom, circulated around to the brokers to conduct individual interviews. When it was her turn, Parker told them that she considered it a conflict of interest that Cuneo supervised his own son, an observation that was met with an attempt to change the subject. She pressed the point, at which one of the auditors simply shrugged, according to the letter. The son got preferential treatment in the form of receiving large accounts when other brokers left for a new job, Parker wrote to Dimon.

Six days after Lorraine Parker's letter to Dimon, Roberta Thomann sent him one asserting that her charges had been investigated in a one-sided manner.[16] Thomann had received a follow-up response on October 22 from Robin Leopold, who said that after her maternity leave, Roberta had been placed in a job working for the highest-producing broker in the office, a sign of both prestige and potentially large bonuses. Thomann was outraged by Leopold's rosy description. She sent a two-page letter to Dimon on October 31, telling him, among other things, that she did not work for the biggest producer. She had been relegated to a spot where she worked both for the producer's junior partner and for the producer's assistant. She was assistant to the assistant.

Twenty-seven miles and two rivers to the west, in Paramus, New Jersey, other women—including Eileen Valentino, who had been attacked in the storeroom—had already registered complaints. Darlene Livingston, a former Shearson employee in New York City, one month before had begun a sequence of forty-five arbitration hearings that would extend over nearly a year, from September 1994 to August 1995. It was an exhausting battle that the tenacious former employee would win at a huge price: she testified to the arbitrators that when it became clear to her that no one in authority on the job was going to listen to her, she began to think about killing herself.[17] Edna Broyles, the Florida broker, had complained about her branch in Tampa. Broyles, the second-biggest producer in the office, by her performance qualified automatically for a promotion to vice president on May 25, 1994. Six days after the promotion, Broyles received a written warning saying that she must cease such behavior as asking for a transfer to a different branch or criticizing company policy.

The Women Issue was an increasingly live one internally at Smith Barney. It would be important to keep it within corporate walls.

As the in-house investigation of Garden City proceeded, management started getting the unwelcome news that more and more of the allegations were true. Yet even as Dimon was learning that, he was feeling the pressure from his lieutenants to take it easy on Cuneo. To come down hard on Cuneo would be to put Dimon's popularity at risk, some of them warned.

But even as the first round of letters was landing on Dimon's desk and complaints from Los Angeles to Paramus to Tampa were accumulating, higher-ups in the municipal bond department were behaving in classic Wall Street–meets–Animal House style. Weeks after Pam's first letter to Dimon, one group of senior managers went after work to Landmark Tavern in Manhattan's west 50s, where they started a food fight in a private upstairs dining room during a raucous evening bankrolled by the company, according to whistle-blower Michael Lissack. "At one point the office manager—a female—was barricaded behind a smoked glass door to the bathroom and ordered to dance if she wanted to be let out," he said. "Finally a food fight broke out, with the head of the public finance department an active participant. The penultimate act was the targeting of the female directors present with shaving-cream pies."[18] These were the revelers who asked how large might be the penis of Marianne Spraggins, the African American woman who had been an investment banker at Smith Barney. It didn't sound like top executives at the firm were terribly concerned about advertising their biases.

(When Spraggins gathered her settlement money and left, nine months before Pam's first letter to Dimon, Smith Barney told the *Wall Street Journal* that it denied "any allegations of racial and sexual discrimination." During private testimony in another case before the American Arbitration Association, however, James Boshart, managing director of Smith Barney's capital markets division, later said that $500,000 of the $1.35 million settlement Spraggins received was allocated to emotional distress, humiliation, and other personal injury. The Reverend Jesse Jackson spoke with Sanford I. Weill on Spraggins's behalf, Boshart testified. And the Reverend Al Sharpton, the black activist, also visited to send a message for Spraggins, although he was left in the waiting area during a meeting that concerned her. Boshart testified that Sharpton's presence was "some indication of what we might be facing if we didn't settle this in a way that everybody walked away feeling good about it."[19] Several times in his testimony, Boshart mentioned Smith Barney's concern over bad publicity.)

If Dimon was preoccupied by the nonstop flow of complaints, legal filings, and settlement negotiations, he didn't show it to the complainants. Pam had heard only from his minions. From Dimon's point of view, his staff people were on the case, taking action where none had been taken before, so there was no reason for him personally to get in touch with her. Dimon additionally had his hands full with upheaval in the investment banking department, where a pricey senior hire from Morgan Stanley & Co. was proving to have been a mistake, costing him not only money but an inordinate amount of his management time.[20]

In November and December, the correspondence to Dimon mounted; Eugene Clark and Mary Reisert of the general counsel's office traveled to the Uniondale, New York, Marriott Hotel on Long Island to hear from the Garden City women. Clark, who struck some of the women as a thin version of Clark Kent with his brown hair, glasses, and straight-arrow demeanor, reported to George Saks, the general counsel. Reisert, another lawyer from the general counsel's office, appeared to play a role secondary to Clark's, asking fewer questions than Clark did during the sessions. One by one, the sales assistants and brokers went in and responded to their queries.

Pam, meanwhile, had two private sessions at the New York head-quarters. Sensing that she should have a witness, Pam took Russ along for both conferences.

The two first met with Clark and Reisert in a private session in November. Pam and Russ stopped briefly at Clark's office at 388 Greenwich Street before settling in at a conference room; she was taken aback to see what she considered the unkempt state of his beautifully appointed office, with legal briefs stacked on his desk, his chairs, and his couch. Later, in early December, there was a second meeting to tell Hugh O'Hare and Robin Leopold about the branch's problems. It did not appear to Pam and Russ that the meetings had been set up to earnestly explore what might have gone wrong. Pam began to conclude that these sessions were nothing more than informal depositions without the benefit of having a lawyer present.

As tension rose, things got proportionally worse for Pam. Word got back to her that Cuneo was extremely agitated over her complaint to

Dimon. She heard that Cuneo told several of the men in the office that he would "fuck her where she bleeds." He had allegedly said to the men that he would snap Pam's neck if she hurt his career. Pam contacted George Saks, the chief counsel, who called her back with Eugene Clark on the other line, in mid-December. Pam reported the neck-snapping and rape threats, expecting that the executives would be concerned even if the talk had been nothing but bluster. Instead, she received a dismissive response from the chief counsel. Saks told her that she sounded like a hysterical woman and suggested that she resign. Pam struck back quickly. "How would that sound to a jury, Mr. Saks?"

"Oh, well, I say that to everybody, don't I, Gene?" came the reply.

Pam pressed the point. Yes, Saks conceded, that would sound awful to a jury. The conversation ended with Pam asking how much longer the investigation would go on.

It would take another two weeks. She asked if she would get to see a copy of the report and was told "absolutely not." The conversation was over as quickly as it had begun.

It was as a result of that phone call that Pamela K. Martens decided it was time to move ahead with plans to sue Smith Barney. She had had enough, and she was ready to take on one of the largest brokerage firms in the United States.

———

PAM CALLED LORRAINE PARKER to convey the gist of her conversation with Saks. She told Parker—who needed no convincing—that a lawsuit was now a must.

Parker already had a notion of how to get started. She faxed Pam a copy of a story she had seen in the *New York Times* profiling Judith Vladeck, the leading civil rights lawyer.[21] She had ripped the article out of the paper when it was published back on February 13, 1994, knowing even then that she wanted to sue.[22] Vladeck was known in particular for taking on Wall Street. "We should look into this person," Parker wrote on a Post-It that she stuck on the corner of the article before she fed it into the machine.

Pam wasted little time. She managed to get on the calendar of the nation's most famous employment lawyer for a meeting just a few weeks later, in December 1994.

Chapter Nine

Getting Lawyers,
Getting Fired

*Our managing director was a woman. The word "cunt" was written
in the dust on her computer screen.*

—A FEMALE BOND TRADER WHO LEFT THE BUSINESS

THE OFFICE TOWER at 1501 Broadway did not strike passersby
as the command center of a law firm that planted terror in the
hearts of corporate racists, bigots, sex discriminators, and
power-abusing sexual harassers. A greasy-spoon deli was within yards
of the front door, and in those days New York City's crudest pornography shops were within blocks of the address. The smell of grilled
sausages and Greek gyros from the sidewalk vendors was much in the
air. Bright lights from Times Square beckoned from every angle even
during the day.

Yet on the eighth floor of the nondescript building was the office of a
seventy-year-old attorney who had taken on corporate giants from
Western Electric to City University to Chase Manhattan Bank. Companies cringed to learn that Judith Vladeck was representing one of
their employees, but some escaped the embarrassment of revealing

headlines. That's because Vladeck, like many an employment lawyer, will advise a client to agree, for the right price, to go silent about her corporate ordeal in exchange for a sum she can't refuse. Her clients, who had usually suffered a lot by the time they hired her, were relatively powerless against their gigantic companies and were rarely rich. In fact, their emotional and financial situations were sometimes dire.

Vladeck herself was no less a surprise than the somewhat undignified neighborhood where she did business. At five feet three inches tall, the trim, bespectacled woman was not Hollywood's usual idea of a powerful and slick negotiator. Her gravely voice, the result of too many years of chain-smoking Merit Greens, was never mistaken in a crowd and provided her with a distinctive courtroom identifier. She exploited the attention she was able to command, too, taking every opportunity— public or private—to catalog the ignorances of oppressors of every variety, be they men, women, black, white, Jewish, Christian, old, or young. When Judith Vladeck spoke, audiences bestowed engrossed attention.

With Judy Mione and Lorraine Parker in tow, Pam traveled to Vladeck's Times Square office in December, waiting in a conference room dominated by the biggest, most well-polished mahogany table Pam had ever seen. Aware of Vladeck's stature, Pam felt as though she were awaiting an audience with royalty. The queen did not disappoint.

Vladeck arrived as if she expected a serious, important meeting. This *is* a big thing, Pam thought. This is significant. If Judy Vladeck takes our case, we are on the map as people to be reckoned with.

Pam was astonished at how tiny Vladeck was. She must be ninety pounds dripping wet, she thought. Vladeck, who had her hair done each morning on her way to the office, looked perfectly prepared.

She smiled at her visitors. "I am so excited that women are getting angry again," she said. "This will be a landmark case." Vladeck particularly liked the feisty woman who would be the lead plaintiff in the lawsuit. Martens had enormous energy and struck Vladeck as extremely smart.

The three women could barely contain themselves. Judith Vladeck was talking about filing a class-action lawsuit against one of the biggest financial firms in the United States.

The preliminary details seemed endless. Laura Schnell, one of Vladeck's associates, would get to work immediately filing forms with the United States Equal Employment Opportunity Commission. Individuals with a claim against a company file their own grievances, the lawyers explained, as distinct from a lawsuit that the EEOC might choose to bring on its own. But an employee must first notify the EEOC before he or she files a claim against the company in court. They would have to use a different plan of attack for Lorraine Parker: 300 days had passed since she had worked in the office, leaving her with legal standing only in New York State, where she was allowed three years to file. Pam heard Vladeck mention something about filing a class-action suit in order to circumvent arbitration but barely processed it in the excitement of getting started with the public battle.

Vladeck told them to get to work rounding up more plaintiffs. If they could rally enough coworkers, Vladeck might come out to Long Island and speak to them. The law firm might take out some ads to locate women to join the suit, Vladeck said, but she had some concerns that advertising could be deemed ethically inappropriate. She would first have to be sure that an ad would receive the blessing of the Bar Association of the City of New York.

THE MORE PRESSURE THEY BROUGHT to bear on the company, the tougher the treatment they received. Not even those who had quit felt immune from the retaliatory reach of Smith Barney—real or imagined. No sooner had alumna Lorraine Parker mailed her letter to Dimon on October 25, 1994, than she received at her office at PaineWebber a letter that jolted her. In a business where brokers' mail is routinely opened before they get it, receiving correspondence at work that referred to her discrimination complaints had the smell of sabotage. Yet there it was, a letter from Eugene Clark of the Smith Barney counsel's office.

Clark could well have been responding to her at the office innocently, because she had mentioned in her previous correspondence that she was in the middle of a move to a new home and had attached her new PaineWebber business card to the letter. Parker, however, was not about to give Smith Barney the benefit of the doubt. She sent a letter to Dimon on November 7 noting that Clark, Dimon, and anyone else in the industry surely would be aware that brokers' mail is opened by others as a matter of course for security reasons.

"If this is the person who was selected to investigate these claims, I suspect I may be dealing with someone who is ignorant of regulatory rules," she wrote. Or perhaps it is the intent of Smith Barney "to harass me and attempt to intimidate me."

Inside the Garden City office, Judy Mione was feeling the heat. Glenn Fischer summoned her at 3:30 on December 1. After asking her to take a seat, he told her, recording it in a memo to his file, that he had heard that she had been telling staff that management was going to cheat them on their bonuses. He also told her that the whispering and huddling that had been going on among the women "must stop immediately." It was unhelpful, unproductive, unprofessional. If it didn't stop, he said, she would "be dealt with harshly."

Two days after Fischer's threat to Mione, Pam sent another letter to Dimon. "Dear Mr. Dimon," it began. "Since filing my letter of complaint with you, Mr. Cuneo has threatened to rape me," she said, overreacting, perhaps, to what was still only a secondhand account of Cuneo's "fuck her where she bleeds" remark. She added that Cuneo's comment about snapping her neck had been reported to management but that this only resulted in "an even more hostile environment."

Pam told Dimon that there was full-scale retaliation going on against Judy Mione, too. "People are afraid to even talk to her" now that Fischer has dictated that whispering and huddling be stopped, she wrote. Mione had been spending more time than usual conferring with friends who were concerned about news that her daughter had cancer. To management, though, such consolations had the look of conspiracy. Amid the thick politics at play now that management was laboring to quiet the storm, the complaining women were working to illustrate the ways in which they were stifled. Small events were turned to big events as an increasing number of verbal exchanges were reported on paper by both management and the women in the office.

As with her first letter, Pam got no direct response from Dimon.

On December 6, Pam once more jumped the chain of command and called Eugene Clark of the general counsel's office again, this time to tell him of financial irregularities with three of her clients' accounts. Checks had been cut for the customers, Pam told him, but the checks had never arrived in the mail. Clark called her back to candidly disclose that, during the same time period, Smith Barney had had to issue fifteen stop payments on Garden City customers' checks that had never arrived.[1] Four days later in yet another letter to Dimon, she recounted the missing checks, security breaches in the branch mailroom, and other problems. Pam detailed for him her shock on the Saturday she poked her head into the office administrator's office with some homemade Christmas cookies to see a male broker poring through customer accounts on microfiche—a violation of company policy, according to Pam, who said that "numerous clients" of hers had received solicitations from the broker.[2] It was the same kind of problem that Lorraine Parker had reported in her letter to Dimon.[3]

In the December 10 letter that outlined the missing checks and the alleged clandestine Saturday microfiche viewing, Pam also mapped out for the CEO how, in a breach of the rules, two Garden City brokers had been going to the Post Office to pick up mail. In light of the mysteriously missing checks, her report should have been a screaming red flag.

Still, she did not hear from Dimon.

Dimon was a particularly busy executive by then, trying to run the company while putting out fires far and wide. By January, less than a year out of the settlement with Marianne Spraggins, he and his staff were dealing with sex discrimination and harassment charges not only at the Paramus and Garden City branches and with Darlene Livingston in New York City but also with Edna Broyles, whose clashes with management in Florida had gotten worse. Broyles, who had complained for years about slipshod operations and unequal treatment of women in the Tampa office, had earned a written warning from the company on May 31, 1994, to cease such behavior as asking for a transfer to a different branch or criticizing company policy. Frank Powers, the branch manager in Tampa, had been keeping files—not always written contemporaneously—on Broyles.[4] Now a paper trail was ready to show that Broyles had violated terms of the May 31 warning. On January 5, regional manager Doug Van Skoy, divisional manager Rudolph Hlavek, and Jack Horn and Diana Winoker, two brokers from the Tampa office, spent much of the day together. During the course of the day, Horn told Hlavek and Van Skoy, "Edna is a loose cannon waiting to go off."[5] At 7 P.M. that night, Hlavek called Powers and said that, based on Broyles's repeated violations of the May 31 warning, he wanted Powers to fire her. When Powers fired Broyles on January 6, she called Dimon seeking his support. Instead of backing her up, Dimon returned her telephone call with confirmation that she was, indeed, to pack up her belongings and get out.

On January 19, Smith Barney learned that Judith Vladeck, the employment lawyer Wall Street loves to hate, was representing Pamela

Martens. That was the date that Laura Schnell of the Vladeck office filed Pam's complaint with the EEOC, making it official that Smith Barney was on notice as a potential violator of civil rights laws.

Suddenly, a company that had put nothing in writing to Pam about any formal action on Cuneo was anxious to get a careful response on the record—and quickly. In a certified letter sent on January 19, 1995, John Donnelly, the human resources chief, told Pam that, while some people in Garden City agreed with her assessment of Cuneo, "many employees hold Mr. Cuneo in high regard." (In fact, management was concluding that Cuneo had run amok in the office but was still hearing testimonials from well-placed Cuneo advocates who came to his defense.) The divergence in views had caused "dissension and disruption" in the office, Donnelly noted, implying that Pam and her fellow complainants were troublemakers.[6] While Donnelly did concede the undeniable—that Cuneo's "conduct and manner have fallen short of the high standards which Smith Barney expects of its managers"—he also took the opportunity to instruct Pam that she'd be wise not make further trouble.

Should she have other concerns, she should discuss them with members of management (as opposed to her coworkers) and do nothing that "disrupts or impedes" management efforts to provide a good working environment.[7] The letter said that any such behavior by Pam or others "will necessitate an appropriate response."[8]

Most important, this first written correspondence to Pam concluded with the news that while Donnelly "had sought to meet with you to further discuss this matter,"[9] he had been informed that day that she "had retained legal counsel."[10] The presence of Judith Vladeck was apparently reason enough for Smith Barney to send this letter implying that there would be no further discussions with a current employee and that it was putting on its fighting gloves.[11]

Roberta Thomann quit that month, unable to justify leaving her infant at home while living with the stress at the office. Pam threw a going-away party with her customary bagels and orange juice. It differed from prior send-off parties in an important respect: Thomann would be very much remaining with her former colleagues as they continued their fight.

After quitting, Thomann took a secretarial job for the Catholic Archdiocese in Brooklyn, with a pay cut and no benefits. Pam, in the meantime, made a connection with another lawyer she'd heard about,

Cliff Palefsky, a partner at the San Francisco firm McGuinn Hillsman & Palefsky, which was known for the efforts it had made to fight companies that forced employees into arbitration. On February 8, 1995, she sent him a seven-page letter describing the work environment in the Garden City office, maintaining that women had been hired for two purposes: to gather accounts for the men, and to amuse and visually entertain them. She did it to line up another backer and get her branch's story out.

PAM WAS INCREASINGLY BUSY helping the lawyers at Vladeck's firm compile the statistics necessary to make their case. She kept up her one-way correspondence with Dimon despite the mushrooming legal battle.

Pam wrote another letter to the CEO on June 2, pointing out that he now had received written testimony from five current and former female employees from her branch. She noted that Smith Barney was perhaps missing a business opportunity: 40 percent of America's wealthiest investors were women, but of Smith Barney's 11,066 brokers, only 676 were. "These figures, under practice and pattern models recognized by the EEOC, clearly suggest that both investors and female brokers are being denied a level playing field at Smith Barney."

Still, no communication from Dimon.

She wrote him again in the fall, a year and two days after the first letter she had sent. Harassment and unprofessional conduct were continuing in Garden City, she wrote—this time including Gene Clark as an addressee. The latest troubles, she alleged, were caused by Eugene Trudden, a broker at the branch.

As always, Pam was blunt. "I have a sworn affidavit that Mr. Trudden sent condoms through the wiring tubes to the wire room. Roberta O'Brien [Thomann] has also filed this charge with the EEOC," she wrote. "This area is staffed by predominantly women."[12] And Trudden that summer and fall was continuing to verbally abuse women, her letter said.

He yelled to Judy Mione, "You should be shot! You are a trouble-maker!" on June 16, Pam wrote. In late September, "he loudly used the word 'bitch'" while referring to Pam's assistant, the letter continued. And Trudden went on a "verbal rampage" against Pam in full hearing of everyone on October 6, she said in an addendum she attached. During this tirade, according to the letter, he repeatedly called Pam a "silly little girl" and further stated that she had "no respect in the building."[13]

"I would like to hear from one of you immediately as to what the firm is going to do to prevent any further verbal attacks on me by Mr. Trudden," Pam wrote.

What she got, six days later, was a memo from the Garden City office administrator, Lisa Bardenhagen.

> To: Pam Martens
> Re: Follow-up to 10/10/95 conversation
>
> As a follow-up to our conversation yesterday, I want to once again remind you that you are not being singled-out with reference to the Compliance meeting that is being held this Friday October 13, 1995 at 9 am in Glenn's office. Again, this meeting is being held for the 19 registered employees of this branch that missed the Internal Auditor meeting of Monday October 2, 1995.
>
> Once again, this meeting is mandatory for all registered personnel and it is required that you attend.

Pam wrote back the same day.

> To: Lisa Bardenhagen
> From: Pamela Kay Martens
>
> Reference is made to your attached letter. Please understand, Lisa, that I fully appreciate that you are simply carrying out the instructions of Glenn Fischer. Unfortunately, that is precisely what Glenn Fischer did for Mr. Cuneo. At some point, we must each be accountable for our own actions.
>
> With regard to any future meetings which would be conducted by either Glenn Fischer or Karen Sendel, this is my position: I will not attend these meetings since both individuals have participated in ongoing harassment of me, including retaliation for reporting their actions to higher management. Both have, as recently as last week,

failed to show any adherence to the sexual harassment rules recently promulgated by the firm. Specifically, this new code of conduct stated that members of management could be held accountable for tolerating harassment on their watch.

With regard to the last sentence above, I observed you standing across the atrium listening to the diatribe unleashed on me by Mr. Gene Trudden on Friday October 6, 1995. I am surprised that, as a member of management, you failed to intercede. I would be further surprised to learn that you did not provide a written account of this event to higher management. If you did so, I am now asking for a copy of same ...

—◆—

FIVE DAYS AFTER THAT, Pam received a memo from Herb Dunn, divisional director for the northeast division of Smith Barney, telling her that she had better attend the next mandatory brokers' compliance meeting or her position at the firm would be "in jeopardy." He told her that he was equally unhappy with her "general refusal to cooperate" with Garden City management and gave her until October 30 to decide whether to move to one of three other Long Island offices.

She wrote back to say that it was impossible for her to attend the required meetings at the branch anymore in light of the constant abuse, ridicule, and harassment she suffered when she arrived at the all-male meetings run by Glenn Fischer. "Both the tone and content of your memo shock me. You have never met or spoken to me yet you send me a threatening memo while management of the Garden City Branch continues on as usual."[14]

She and management were at a standoff.

And Cuneo, amid congratulations and much fanfare, was on his way out. Three days after Pam got the letter from Dunn, Cuneo was toasted at a lavish Thursday-evening retirement party at the North Hempstead Country Club in Port Washington, where Smith Barney brokers from all over Long Island and their local and New York City bosses gathered to pay homage to a branch manager like no other. Pam, who was not invited, heard that Cuneo had retired on good terms, with his benefits intact and his securities record clean.[15] With a history of heart problems and the burden of a disabled spouse much in need of medical care, Cuneo had the mercy of top management, who couldn't see fit to try to yank his benefits.[16] They even made sure that Cuneo's career on Wall Street had the final mark of a job well done. "Voluntary retirement," his official securities industry records would read. By the time Cuneo departed, Sanford I. "Sandy" Weill had been his boss two times, having owned, sold, and repurchased Shearson since Cuneo had come on board as a hungry young broker.

Pam arrived at work on Monday, October 23, one workday after the Cuneo bash and just seven days before her deadline to make a decision about moving to a different branch. Minutes after she sat down at her desk with her *Wall Street Journal*, Glenn Fischer walked into her office and told her she was fired. "You have an hour to pack and leave," he said, adding that he would provide boxes for the packing job.

Pam remained calm. She remembered times that other brokers, frazzled over being let go, would frantically throw their belongings into boxes and depart the office in a tizzy. That, Pam told herself, will not be me.

She told Fischer she didn't need any boxes, prompting a look of confusion on his face. She walked outside her office, where she saw Michelle Bonadonna and Janie Paton, two sales assistants. Looking back at Fischer, she said, "Glenn, I want you to tell Michelle and Janie that you just fired me, because I know you're gonna lie." Pam sensed that Fischer was very nervous, particularly with the target of his pink slip appearing to take control of things. "I just fired her," he told them.

As soon as Fischer left, she called Russ, told him the news, and asked if he would come to the office to give moral support. She left her desk the way it was. When Russ arrived twenty minutes later, the two made the rounds to say goodbye to Pam's favorite coworkers, exchanging hugs and kisses with several. They walked out with smiles on their faces. She had her husband on one arm and her purse and Rolodex in the other when she left 901 Franklin Avenue for the last time. That was it.

She took some satisfaction in noticing that she and Russ were both in their best gray suits.

THE STAFF WAS SUMMONED to the downstairs conference room the moment Pam and Russ left the building. It was the spot where the whole controversy had begun, at the meeting of the sales assistants almost fourteen months before. This time, executives from New York headquarters were present. Pam Martens has been fired for refusing to attend a compliance meeting, they told the gathering. We will not answer further questions about this.

LETTING THE DOOR on the screened-in porch slam behind her, Pam headed straight for the telephone and called *BusinessWeek* magazine before she had taken her purse off her shoulder. She had read an article by a reporter who appeared to have a skeptical eye toward the brokerage industry, and she figured that the reporter, Leah Nathans Spiro, might be sympathetic. Spiro picked up her phone, and Pam began telling her what had been going on at the Garden City office. They arranged a meeting four days later.

Smith Barney, however, still had a formidable hold on Pam's career. Despite the absence of customer complaints, $187 million in assets, and ten years in the business, she soon got the feeling that she was being blackballed from employment in the town where she lived. She interviewed with the local PaineWebber manager but learned from him that he was trying to recruit five male brokers away from Cuneo's shop, and that her presence in the office might not be appreciated by that quintet. And by the way, said the PaineWebber manager, I have a question. How would you feel if one of my brokers screamed at his sales assistant? Pam said that if it was an isolated event on a bad day, she would ignore it. If it were routine behavior, though, she'd have a problem.

The manager told her that he had a problem with her having a problem. Word seemed to have gotten to him that she objected to the rantings and ravings that went on at some shops.

She moved on to the next interview.

At Merrill Lynch in Garden City, Pam's $187 million in assets under management looked very attractive, and the head of the branch hinted that she might even merit a $100,000 signing bonus if he wooed her in. He took her around to meet his brokers, introducing them to her in a manner that struck Pam as bizarre.

"This is a $400,000 producer," the branch manager would say. "And this is our million-dollar guy." Pam did not know that even as she was touring the office, word was getting back to her former branch that she was interviewing at Merrill.

The Merrill Lynch manager said he would get back to her with a firm offer. But no phone call came. When Pam called days later to find out what her status was, she found out she had no status. There was no spot for her.

Dean Witter also had an office in Garden City, and the manager there said he was so interested in getting his hands on her accounts that he would push for a $160,000 signing bonus. He said it would be no problem for her to bring her sales assistant from Smith Barney, but he did request that they both take drug tests.[17] So distrustful of Wall Street was Pam by this time that she went to a local doctor to have a backup test done the same day. Just like the Merrill manager, though, the initially enthusiastic Dean Witter manager switched gears. After ignoring her calls for a week, he finally told her that her hiring had been blocked "at the regional level."[18]

She drove into Manhattan on a rainy November night and met Leah Nathans Spiro at a midtown restaurant. Over a dinner that stretched to more than three hours, Pam told the *BusinessWeek* reporter details of what it had been like to work for Cuneo—and Smith Barney—if you were a woman. Pam left the dinner feeling relieved that she had the ear of someone in the media, even if there was no assurance that an article would ever run.

Along with what felt like blacklisting in Garden City, Pam had another problem to contend with. When a stockbroker leaves a firm, the firm must file a document with securities regulators called the "U-5," which explains the reason for a termination. Judith Vladeck and her lawyers were negotiating feverishly for Pam to get a clean U-5, but in practical fact the only way that would happen would be for Pam to settle confidentially with Smith Barney. She refused to do that despite the suggestion of Laura Schnell, who wanted Pam to at least consider getting on with her life and putting Smith Barney behind her.

Vladeck, fighting hard, landed a relatively innocuous explanation under the "reason for termination" box. "Incompatibility with local management unrelated to customer matters or sales practices culminating in her refusal to attend a required meeting" is how her records read to this day. It was completely out of character for the Garden City office and for the times. Firms were falling on their swords in negotiations with regulators in order to keep even a disreputable producer from having a blemish on his record if the broker was a moneymaker, but Pam Martens lost the coveted "clean U-5" status with abundant customers and without ever having suffered a customer complaint.

Late in November, she contacted management at A. G. Edwards & Sons. During her visit to their local office, she learned that a broker from Cuneo's shop had recently stopped by to give the Edwards branch a heads up that Pam was in the market for a job and to warn that she was "a bitch." Pam met with the branch manager, though, telling him about her $187 million book of business and showing him the plaque she received in 1995: "In Recognition of 10 Years of Dedicated and Loyal Service" to Smith Barney. Eleven of her 557 clients had been colleagues from Cuneo's branch and their relatives. In one case, the elderly mother-in-law of a Garden City sales assistant in Cuneo's branch turned her money over to Pam. Previously, the woman had felt safe only when she kept her stock certificates under her bed.

"Look at my record," she said to the branch manager. "I run a clean business, I've never had a complaint in ten years, and 557 clients trust me with $187 million." That was good enough. On November 9, 1995, Pam set her Rolodex down on a desk in her new office at A. G. Edwards. If she was a bitch, it sure didn't look like her customers thought so.

———

SHE WAS PLEASED with the damage control Vladeck did on what could have been a more injurious U-5 statement, but Pam was getting antsy that Vladeck was not pressing the case with the speed she wanted. Particularly now that she had been fired, Pam was fired up, and she couldn't get the lawsuit together fast enough.

Vladeck during this time was slugging it out on another sexual discrimination and harassment case against Smith Barney. Alicia DeGaetano, a former public finance analyst, had rejected the sexual advances of her boss only to be told that she'd better succumb or be hurt on her bonus, her performance evaluation, and her promotion possibilities. Vladeck was in heated negotiations over the dispute, disgusted that a young woman just out of Cornell University had been mistreated not only by her boss but by the human resources department, which had advised DeGaetano that perhaps she was suffering as a result of problems at home. Pam began to feel that Vladeck would not make the Garden City case a priority until the DeGaetano case was resolved.

Vladeck was not choosing between the two cases. She was, however, of a mind that the case should proceed more cautiously than Pam wanted. For one thing, Vladeck was concerned that not all the plaintiffs Pam had lined up had the greatest stories to tell. Some of them also had exceeded the statute of limitations for such cases. Vladeck had sought and received approval from the Bar Association of the City of New York to advertise to recruit new plaintiffs, but that process, too, took time, and Pam was getting impatient. Vladeck saw the friction developing between Pam and the associates in the law firm who were doing most of the work on the Martens case, and was regretful that she couldn't persuade Pam to slow down while the lawyers did extensive up-front research. In her client's view, though, the lawsuit simply had to go faster.

―――――

HUNGRY FOR INSPIRATION AND FEEDBACK, Pam asked Roberta Thomann to drive with her to Hempstead, a neighboring town, for a gathering of Women on the Job, a coalition of sixty women's groups. There the two told their story, complaining that they were losing patience with the process. An attendee sitting nearby looked at them and said, "It sounds like you need a new attorney."

Renowned though Vladeck was, maybe this woman was right. Roberta and Pam left the Family Services Building in Hempstead that night and got into Bluey. They agreed that it was indeed time to part ways with Vladeck. But they had completely different ideas of what that implied. Pam was elated at having a new direction in which to move. Roberta was crushed.

"It's all over, isn't it?" Roberta said.

"No, it's not," Pam replied. "We're going to find a new attorney."

Pam dropped Roberta off, drove back to the house, and began to go through her meticulous files, searching for a story she had read in the *New York Times* about allegations of sex discrimination and sexual harassment at Olde Discount. She found the story and called Roberta right away to give her the names of the two lawyers mentioned in it.

Roberta called their Chicago office the next morning, reaching Linda Friedman, one of the partners at Leng Stowell Friedman & Vernon. "Our case is just like Olde," Roberta began. She offered a few details about the oppressive Garden City atmosphere. Friedman said she and her partner could be in New York to meet her later that week. She sounded very interested in the case.

Chapter Ten

Attacking the
No-Court System

I got the kangaroo court.

—SUSAN DESIDERIO, A BROKER WHO SUED NASD WHEN IT
REFUSED TO LET HER SCRATCH OUT ITS ARBITRATION CLAUSE

ORDINARILY, LINDA D. FRIEDMAN and Mary Stowell would insist on a face-to-face meeting before signing with a client who wanted to file a lawsuit. When they looked into what Pamela Martens had, though, the two lawyers in Chicago found so much of the documentation already in order that the need for a personal meeting didn't seem so pressing.

Pam had statistics about how many women worked as stockbrokers. She had written statements from women who had worked in the Garden City office. And she was an inveterate communicator, whether it be by e-mail, by phone, or by overnight mail, furnishing her two new lawyers with names, dates, and documents that buttressed the Garden City case. In one of those documents, written back in November 1994 (and previously shared with lawyer Judith Vladeck), Pam outlined forty-one examples of alleged harassment and discrimination.

So, rather than flying to New York as they had first offered, Stowell and Friedman set about poring through the material that was streaming in. By February 2, 1996, the two lawyers and Pamela Martens were ready to sign a contract to move ahead with a lawsuit. It would be a contingency contract, one that would pay the lawyers only if the women got a monetary award. Stowell and Friedman said they would take a fee calculated at either one-third of any money awarded or their hourly rate, whichever was higher.[1] (The contract did not specify what their current rate was.) They were sufficiently hopeful about the case that they agreed to pick up "outstanding legal costs related to this matter from Vladeck, Waldman, Elias (et al.)."[2]

Signed by Mary Stowell and Pamela Kay Martens, the two-page contract memorialized their purpose in the second paragraph: "VINDICATION OF CIVIL RIGHTS: I understand that the primary purpose of this case is to establish a violation of my civil rights and to remedy that violation through declaratory injunctive or other remedial relief."[3]

Obtaining all that would be easier said than done. Stowell and Friedman sued employers all the time, in industries as diverse as computer software and health care. But when it came to clients who worked in the brokerage industry, the upholding of civil rights was a far trickier endeavor.

Given their combat experience with brokerage firms, though, Stowell and Friedman knew better than most lawyers that companies on Wall Street had a nearly airtight way of avoiding lawsuits and the publicity that comes with them: in order to get a license for a job selling stocks or commodities or managing people who sold those products, a professional had to agree never to sue his or her employer. The licensing documents signed by hundreds of thousands of such people bound them to use arbitration in the event of a dispute, rather than filing suit in the public courts. Stowell and Friedman knew that the industry had bound thousands of *un*licensed employees to arbitration, too. Firms accomplished that by compelling unlicensed employees to sign private contracts. Sometimes the firms would get those employees—who ranged from word processors to senior vice presidents in the investment banking department—to give up their right to sue as a condition of employment up front. Other times, they would get the commitment to arbitration retroactively, first publishing a copy of the mandatory arbitration agreement in an employee handbook and then asking employees to sign a separate form on which they agreed to the terms of the handbook. The chances of a busy full-time employee of any rank actually taking the time to read the entire handbook could not have been very high.

Just as Vladeck had done earlier, Stowell and Friedman explained to Pam that she and her colleagues would have to get around those barriers. The best way to do that, they explained, would be to file a class-action lawsuit. Neither the New York Stock Exchange nor the National Association of Securities Dealers will hear class-action complaints in their arbitration systems, Stowell and Friedman explained. That will enable us to sue Smith Barney in court.

The tactic, by its very ingenuity, would at a minimum get the story out to the public, regardless of whether the case actually went to trial. If all went well, a judge would actually grant class status, giving Pam, Roberta, and Judy their day in court.

———

STOWELL AND FRIEDMAN had been learning about Wall Street's peculiar judicial system since 1989, when they set up shop together in Chicago. They had worked together unofficially even before that, in a relationship that made them seem destined to be partners. Friedman, a stout young lawyer with a hint of red in her dark brown hair, had previously worked as a legal assistant for a civil rights trial attorney. She suffered from the potentially career-killing handicap of getting flustered when she had to take depositions from women who had been sexually harassed. Friedman could be self-conscious, and she appeared to want to be liked by people. She simply couldn't bring herself to repeat some of the repulsive words and phrases that the defendants allegedly had used. The flip side of her people-pleasing trait was that when she felt crossed or threatened, Friedman could attack an opponent viciously.

Stowell, a statuesque former prosecutor who at that time worked down the hall from Friedman in a small office she shared with another white-collar-criminal defense lawyer, was fazed by nothing after nine years of murders and drug busts. Often prickly and seemingly immune to what others thought of her, she coached Friedman to ask the shocking questions directly. Otherwise, Stowell told Friedman, she would never get the key information she needed to present to a jury.

At first, "I couldn't say 'nipples' or 'penis' on the record," Friedman says. "I couldn't ask the follow-up."

Stowell did not have her friend's modesty problems. She told Friedman to ask the deponent whether she had told the truth when she said, "He wanted to take off my bra and play with my nipples."

"You can do it," Stowell said. "Just say 'nipples.' Say it."

Friedman was no less undone when she had to depose a defendant who said, "I have the Lord between my legs."

"Just ask him if he means his penis," Stowell said matter-of-factly.

With their complementary personalities, the two became friends, then joined forces to found their own firm. From a personality point of view, it was a perfect union: Friedman, the people pleaser, would establish the relationship, make the promises, and stroke the difficult personalities. Later, if things got tough, she would take to heart that someone might be angry with her. Stowell, the steely prosecutor, played a quieter background role, often towering over Friedman in grim silence in the lobby outside the courtroom while her more loquacious partner chattered away with clients before the judge arrived.

Friedman had a dazzling knowledge of constitutional law and an ability to stick with a tough case when others would have given up. Stowell, no less sharp, had the courtroom cool that comes with years of government work and the tough litigation techniques that it teaches. Friedman would outfit herself for trials in standard black suits with long black skirts; Stowell, who sometimes sported blue nail polish outside of court, went the same conservative route when she was in front of a judge, favoring form-fitting knit dresses, typically in black. Of the two, Stowell was the environmentalist, retrieving used manila file folders from the office garbage bins after her partner had tossed them. Stowell could visibly relax and speak in earnest about her family and her passion for women's rights in the privacy of her office. In the courthouse, though, she showed a cooler, reserved persona.

Their firm differentiated itself from stuffy old-line operations the moment a visitor walked into the reception area. The walls were sunset-reminiscent shades of pink and blue and orange. The boardroom's lawyerly mahogany table was surrounded by mahogany chairs upholstered in dainty pastel patterns. It would be difficult to miss that this was a firm run by women.

Mary Stowell, born in Memphis, had actually been trained for what was traditionally thought of as "women's work": before getting her law degree she had graduated with a secretarial certificate from the

Katherine Gibbs School. While she went to school wearing white gloves and a hat to get equipped with a trade, her two older brothers were educated at the Massachusetts Institute of Technology.

With her year of Katie Gibbs training behind her, Stowell joined the Teamsters union in order to qualify for a typing job at Anheuser Busch outside of Elizabeth, New Jersey. Typing for the Teamsters did not turn out to be her calling, and she quit to pursue a degree at the University of Missouri at Kansas City. It was a time that suited Stowell to be in college: the late 1960s and early 1970s. She participated enthusiastically in antiwar and women's activist efforts and graduated in 1971 with the Outstanding Student in Political Science Award. She moved on to Northwestern Law School and then landed a job in the United States Attorney's office in Chicago. It was in Chicago that she met Linda Friedman in 1988.

Friedman got her law degree from Chicago's DePaul University in 1985 and worked as a law clerk for her first two years out of school. After that, she signed on with a litigator who represented plaintiffs in civil rights cases, but she had to throw in the towel in 1988 when her boss neglected to pay his rent—apparently not for the first time—and the landlord deposited the delinquent lawyer's belongings on the Chicago sidewalk five floors below. Using a spoon, Friedman stood outside the door of her old office and scratched her name off the glass.

Stowell gave her the $500 deposit she needed to get an office of her own. In less than a year after they met, they had set up shop together. Although Friedman typically was the firm's link to the outside, Stowell, with her confident, sometimes bossy manner, had an aura of being the dominant one in the partnership.

From the start, the two fought tough civil rights cases and won some big publicity coups in the Chicago press. In their second year, they got the Rodman & Renshaw cases, which initiated a chain of publicity dominoes, establishing their reputation as a team that fought brokerage firms.[4] Their first Rodman case was that of Susan Jaskowski, the human resources executive who alleged that she had been replaced by a man during her maternity leave—a man who she said was hired at 40 percent more than she had been paid.[5] Friedman and Stowell took the blame all the way to the top, implicating Rodman's CEO.[6] The suits they filed against Rodman produced legal papers loaded with the kind of quotable, juicy details that reporters relished.

The coverage did not go unnoticed by similarly distressed women. At Olde Discount Corporation, the women who were getting harassed or pushed out read about Stowell and Friedman's success and signed the two on as their attorneys,[7] winning handsome settlements. Stowell and Friedman were not the only lawyers who successfully negotiated sex discrimination cases against Olde, but their cases were the most widely noticed. The Olde cases were even splashier than the Rodman ones, with allegations against a CEO who kept homes in Canada, Florida, and the Cayman Islands and who lived the high life with a net worth estimated at the time to be over $400 million.[8]

The Olde cases made the front page of the business section of the *New York Times* in April 1995.[9] It was this article that Lorraine Parker clipped and eventually passed on to Pam Martens, who dug it out of her files and passed it on to Roberta Thomann.

In many of their winning cases, Friedman and Stowell would prevail after refusing to accept bullying and this-is-how-we-do-it assumptions. Executives at one firm told Friedman that she had no right to file a complaint with the U.S. Equal Employment Opportunity Commission because her client's grievance was a private matter between the firm and the New York Stock Exchange, where the charges would be heard in arbitration. She ignored them and carried on with her plans to file papers with the EEOC.

PAM AND THE LAWYERS let their over-the-telephone relationship develop. Stowell and Friedman officially took over from Judith Vladeck. They filed a new EEOC charge—the form that had to be filed with the EEOC before a civil rights suit could be submitted in court. It was a revision of a prior claim that realleged what Martens previously had told the EEOC but added retaliation and defamation to her grievances. The latter was a reference to the fact that her regulatory files now stated that she had been fired. Pam Martens's EEOC filing would be the lead claim on which all the other Smith Barney women could piggyback.

In the minds of both Pam and her lawyers, this was not just a complaint about catcalls and condoms. It was also importantly about the tiny clause in the women's licenses that kept them from taking their sex discrimination and harassment claims to court. Pam had not heard of this catch-22 before June 9, 1994, when the *Wall Street Journal* ran a page-one story about three nightmarish experiences that other women had had with arbitration panels.

The sweeping power to mandate arbitration instead of allowing employees a courtroom trial derived from the fine print in the regulatory document called the Form U-4 Uniform Application for Securities Industry Registration or Transfer—the U-4 for short—that has to be signed by the securities industry employee. "I agree to arbitrate any dispute, claim or controversy that may arise between me and my firm, or a customer, or any other person ..." the U-4 application read.

An early version of the ultimately explosive little clause had been launched innocently enough. In 1958, the New York Stock Exchange established a rule that any controversy between a broker and the broker's firm would be settled by arbitration.[10] Behind the ruling was the notion that brokers squabbled with their firms over issues best handled in a forum sponsored by arbitrators who understood the industry. (Cynics conjecture that the brokerage industry would also prefer that the public not learn any more than it has to about the sums of money its employees make.) Typical disputes involved such things as being denied accrued bonuses or fighting over a broker's right to take clients with him if he were to leave for another firm.

A similar rule was set up by the National Association of Securities Dealers in 1968, stating that disputes "between or among members and/or associated persons" would be subject to the same kind of arbitration.[11] Brokers would formally agree to be bound by the arbitration rule by signing a U-4, a copy of which the NASD kept on file for every stockbroker in the nation.

Both the NYSE and NASD arbitration rules came under the auspices of the Securities and Exchange Commission in the late 1970s, by way of an amendment to the Securities Exchange Act of 1934. The amendment said that "self-regulatory organizations," such as the New York Stock Exchange, had to file rules with the SEC before implementing them. Existing rules would also be swept under SEC jurisdiction—sometimes after a review—and any new rules would subsequently have to pass muster with the SEC. Officials at the SEC do not recall whether they ever formally expressed an opinion about the U-4 when the SEC was going through the process of taking on all those existing NYSE and NASD rules.

In 1983, the U-4 was amended with unambiguous language that said arbitration was mandatory for stockbrokers and others who had to sign the form in order to qualify for a licensed job. But some firms were already thinking of a way this idea could be extended to benefit the industry further.

Mandatory arbitration could be a godsend in customer disputes, too. In court, juries could be terribly sympathetic to the innocent investor fleeced by an errant broker, and that could cost millions to any firm unlucky enough to employ a rogue. Arbitration panels, by comparison, did not typically allow punitive damages and tended to rule in favor of the brokerage firm about half the time. If anything, they stuck to the notion of so-called compensatory damages, which would seek to make an investor whole but not richer than when he started. On those occasions when a customer won, he usually was awarded less than he claimed to have lost.

Because this philosophy of adjudicating employment matters within the confines of the industry had been firmly established since 1958, it was not much of a stretch to apply the idea to business dealings with the public. All the brokerage industry had to do was find a place to print a little clause that, like the one in the U-4, would preclude lawsuits. So brokerage firms added the fine print in their "customer agreements"— account-opening documents that covered everything from the client's investment objectives to his date of birth. Squeezed in amid the pages of caveats and disclaimers there began to be clauses that said that the customer agreed, in the case of a dispute, to use an arbitration forum run by the NYSE or the NASD. Customers had to sign the document or they couldn't open the account; they rarely noticed the section that said they could not sue if they were swindled by their broker.

The customer arbitration clause was a boon for securities houses, whose legal teams took pains to be sure that customers could not wiggle out of the arbitration promises they frequently did not even know they had made. It was, among other things, a wonderful way to keep complaints quiet: no lawsuit, no public filing, no public embarrassment or loss of faith by investors. Mandatory arbitration was well worth fighting for. In 1987, a brokerage client of Shearson tried to sue and then fought the firm when it said he was barred from court. It was no small matter to Shearson, which trundled out the big guns. The firm took the case, brought by investors Eugene and Julia McMahon, all the way to the United States Supreme Court in an effort to force the McMahons to accept arbitration. The Supreme Court ruled in favor of Shearson, saying that the McMahons had agreed to arbitration by signing the account-opening documents.

Arbitration was getting to be a big, important business area for the brokerage houses, considering the money it was saving them in legal costs and monetary damages. Around the time of the McMahon decision, some securities firms began to get more professional about their arbitration efforts, compiling databases that included names of all the arbitrators they'd had dealings with and keeping notes about whether they appeared to be pro-industry or pro-consumer. In the late 1990s, *Registered Representative* magazine reported that Merrill Lynch and Smith Barney were the two firms that had put together the most comprehensive information about these men and women.[12]

What worked so well to keep customers out of court thus had the potential to work equally well in keeping employees out of court when civil rights claims began to be filed and the stakes were raised in job disputes. Robert Gilmer, a stockbroker at Interstate/Johnson Lane, learned how important mandatory employment arbitration was to Wall Street when he sued his firm for age discrimination. Interstate fought hard to keep Gilmer from telling his story to a jury. Gilmer had signed a U-4 agreement that bound him to arbitration, Interstate argued before one court, then another. In 1991, just as Stowell and Friedman were getting into their first Rodman case, the Supreme Court ruled in favor of the brokerage firm.

That year was an important one in which to win court backing for the industry's arbitration rules. In 1991, Congress reinforced certain protections under Title VII of the Civil Rights Act of 1964, allowing jury trials for the first time in sex discrimination cases, and allowing jurors to grant awards for emotional distress. An employment discrimination case that found its way to court was now more threatening to the employer than ever. So Gilmer was a welcome win, making Wall Street the only industry in America to have barred the doors of the nation's courts to any employee—such as a stockbroker—who required a license to do business. And to think the abridgement of the Constitutional right to a trial was happening under the jurisdiction of a federal agency, the Securities and Exchange Commission.

"Employers could never get together in another industry and do this—it would be an antitrust violation," says attorney Cliff Palefsky. "It's only because they have the protection of the Securities Exchange Act of 1934" that they can make rules that suit them, Palefsky says. The authority given to the industry through self-regulation allows it to create rules favorable to business.

The result was that while the rest of corporate America got hit right and left with discrimination suits in the 1980s and 1990s, the casual observer could easily imagine that Wall Street must be a nearly egalitarian utopia, where women and other groups protected under the civil rights laws worked without finding any discrimination to complain about. For all anyone knew, people in the nation's financial districts were working so hard that there was no time for shenanigans.

Statistics kept by the Equal Employment Opportunity Commission, in fact, would have one believe that not only was Wall Street no worse than any business, it was a measurably better place to work for women and minorities. Only 27 complaints were filed against New York–based brokerage firms in 1992—a year when the EEOC was flooded with 21,796 gender-based complaints in all. Another 27 gender-based complaints came in against New York–based securities firms in 1996, the year Pam Martens hired Stowell and Friedman; a total of 23,813 were filed with the EEOC that year. The pattern remained the same through 1999, when only 18 complaints were lodged against New York–area brokers while 23,907 complaints were filed across all industries. The EEOC has those numbers because of the requirement that an employee who wishes to sue any employer on civil rights grounds must first file papers—such as those that Vladeck and Stowell and Friedman filed for Martens—with the EEOC and wait for it to issue a "right to sue" letter. The person who works for a brokerage firm, though, is not able to sue.[13] He or she can only ask for an arbitration. And because the National Association of Securities Dealers—which hears most of Wall Street's employment arbitration cases—doesn't require that anything be filed with the EEOC, those cases don't get into government statistics. So, while the federal government operated with extensive information about the prevalence of civil rights complaints in other industries, it was largely in the dark about problems on Wall Street.

Not every employee went along with the mandatory clause without a fight. Gilmer or no Gilmer, those with enough spunk continued to struggle for the right to go to court. Rita Reid, a fourteen-year-veteran investment banker at Goldman Sachs, sued that firm in New York

State Court in November 1991, seeking $18 million in damages. Her complaint asserted that she was paid less than men doing the same work; that she wasn't promoted to a partnership she deserved; and that she was terminated in a restructuring during which Goldman kept less qualified men.[14]

As Reid's fight went through the courts, brokerage firms got more aggressive in their methods. More firms were establishing policies in which new employees other than brokers would sign private contracts that barred them from court. Firms would wait until the prospective employee came in to sign a mountain of pre-employment documents, then include a page requiring arbitration, a form that a distracted new employee rarely would notice. Some firms even employed a "belt and suspenders" approach of having stockbrokers—who already had lost their right to sue through the U-4—sign a private contract, too. In early 1992, Olde Discount Corporation was using a "Stockbroker Employment Agreement" in which president Ernest J. Olde reserved the rights to modify anything in the agreement without cause or notice; to terminate an employee at any time without cause or notice; and, in the event of a dispute, not only to force arbitration but to choose whether it would take place at the NYSE or the NASD.[15]

In late 1992, Pam's firm, transformed to Primerica/Smith Barney as the result of further acquisitions by Sandy Weill, was using a similar pre-employment document. In its "Principles of Employment" manual, the firm said any employee with a gripe would have to go to arbitration.[16] Particularly for women, it was not a good time to be at Olde or Primerica if discrimination or harassment problems came up: at the end of 1992, 89 percent of all NASD arbitrators were men.[17]

Susan A. Desiderio learned the hard way about how arbitrary arbitration could be. She was just getting out of her car to go to work at 8:15 on an August morning in 1992 when her boss met her in the parking lot of the Lantana, Florida, Great Western Bank. He handed her a box containing her sweater, a plant, and two bottles of water, and told her she was terminated effective immediately. She'd been a successful stockbroker in the brokerage division of Great Western Bank since 1989 and had recently gone along with instructions to share commissions with a twenty-six-year-old woman whom she had trained.[18]

Desiderio filed to request a hearing based on a complaint of age discrimination. When the hearing came, she was distraught at the paucity of legal procedures. Desiderio thought the rules were being made as they went along. Indeed, one arbitrator confirmed to her how loose the rules really were when he told the group "We have a wide latitude here. This is not court."[19] At another point, when Desiderio's lawyer was putting a question to the woman who replaced her, the opposing counsel actually managed to change the young woman's testimony. Asked if she was making healthy profits because Desiderio had coached her, the young woman replied "yes." The Great Western lawyer didn't like the answer, which would have been his tough luck in a courtroom. In an arbitration hearing room, though, he had room to maneuver. "Don't say yes," he told the witness. She changed her answer to "no."[20]

Desiderio got $7,850 for "medical damages" and started to look for another job.[21]

Brokerage firms were largely winning their war to keep discrimination claims out of court. In 1993, the NASD asked the SEC to approve a rule change to make the U-4 say specifically that employment disputes—as opposed to just "business disputes"—were subject to mandatory arbitration.[22] The SEC approved the change, saying that this was "designed to protect the public interest."

The Securities Exchange Act of 1934 requires employers to properly supervise employees as part of its job of protecting investors. While it is obvious how the rogue broker churning an account would be viewed as harming the public, it is not clear how the fellow who grabs the buttocks of his sales assistant is jeopardizing the financial health of his customers. The SEC never explained why it would be appropriate that disputes over employment matters be restricted to arbitration, or, indeed, why it was in the interest of the public to do so. Yet the SEC was laying the groundwork for a system in which the self-regulatory organizations like the NASD were adjudicating discrimination violations over which they had no enforcement authority: although their arbitration panels might hear disputes over civil rights issues, the self-regulatory organizations had no fines, sanctions, or consequences to levy for discrimination or harassment.

Wall Street officials who defend the status quo say that women in particular graft discrimination claims onto employment cases that are largely about other matters. Women shouldn't be allowed to bifurcate cases like that and must be forced to keep the entire claim in arbitration, they say. People in the industry also advance the argument that whether the case is against a rogue broker or an accused coworker, the public interest is generally upheld when the industry polices and judges its own, because the public ultimately learns through enforcement proceedings and public records that a wrong has been done.

The fallacy of these arguments, though, is that in those few cases where a broker has actually lost a job as a result of committing harassment, it is anything but public. Although almost all violations against customers are subject to being written up on his regulatory records, rarely can a mention be found in the public records that a man has been fired for harassment. Thus, the broker with multiple customer complaints might have a record that exposes those complaints, provided he or she didn't get the record expunged via certain loopholes. But the broker with multiple *coworker* complaints (about discrimination or harassment) would have little reason to worry about exposure in a public record kept by the securities industry. That's because the industry, with no enforcement authority over such misbehavior, has no mechanism set up to track it.[23]

Indeed, neither the securities industry nor its regulators have the authority to enforce civil rights laws in general. Nor has either shown a particular interest in doing so.

The benefits to employers of arbitration over the courts were of such note that a well-known employment lawyer who represented brokerage firms openly praised arbitration's one-sided advantages. At the annual meeting of the American Bar Association in Chicago in August 1995, Stuart H. Bompey of the law firm Orrick, Herrington & Sutcliffe told his audience at an arbitration committee session that, based on what he called an "unofficial survey" of Wall Street discrimination claims taken to arbitration in the five-and-a-half years prior to his talk, brokerage firms had "a good measure of success" defending them.

He looked at sixty-two awards granted by New York Stock Exchange and NASD arbitrators over the period, and found that employers won 76 percent of the cases heard before NASD arbitration panels and 59 percent of the cases heard before NYSE panels. "Employers stand a greater chance of success in arbitration rather than in court before a jury," Bompey said. And where employees do beat the odds and win, "the size of damage awards in arbitrations tends to be smaller than in jury trials."[24] So tied in with the industry was Bompey that the NASD asked him to write some of its arbitrator training materials.[25]

Only five months before Bompey's speech, Rita Reid, who had claimed pay disparity and unfair termination, had become one of these favorable statistics: on March 31, 1995, a panel of arbitrators at the New York Stock Exchange dismissed her case against Goldman Sachs. (The New York Court of Appeals had said she could not use the court system and had to go to arbitration.) In an eighteen-page memo attached to its decision, the panel conceded that in 1990, a year in which Reid was passed over for partnership, Goldman had only one woman partner and that this was the only woman partner in the history of the firm.[26] Rather than consider that this might suggest discrimination at the firm, the panel posited that Goldman's partners might be trying to do their best at nominating women for partnerships "without lowering partnership election standards."[27]

Later in its memo, the panel described Goldman's destruction of many of the documents it used to determine who would become a partner that year and who would not.[28] The panel acknowledged that Goldman's document destruction policy "may well violate federal law," because of EEOC regulations that require retention of documents for ten years. The panel additionally noted that it is possible that Goldman did not violate the law, because it might have destroyed the documents before the law was changed to require companies to retain such papers.[29] The documents that were not destroyed revealed no discrimination, the panel noted.[30]

As Wall Street increasingly enjoyed the perks of arbitration, its lawyers got even more sophisticated about deterring people from coming even to the arbitration system with their discrimination and harassment claims. An example is Eileen Valentino's case against Shearson in 1993. She claimed that on December 15, 1992, a male colleague had followed her into the stockroom, pushed up against her body, and grabbed her breasts, telling her "Now you know the myth of the black man is true." She screamed at him never to touch her again and ran into the ladies' room in tears.[31]

Her sales assistant, Patti Hanlon, made a similar complaint. She said that the same man came up behind her in the office kitchen area in July 1993 and ran his hands up the inside of her leg. Although they had filed their request for a hearing and Smith Barney had answered their complaint on September 7, 1994, the two women waited until 1996 before they got a hearing date. A week before the hearing, though, the firm (which by then was called Smith Barney) forced the two women to undergo examinations by a psychiatrist of the brokerage firm's choosing.[32] The women had claimed emotional distress among their complaints. Had this charge been made in court, the defending employer would have the right to make a case that a woman already was damaged when she arrived at the firm—an outgrowth of the 1991 law that opened up the possibility of damages for emotional distress. Smith Barney wound up demanding and getting this courtlike benefit. Valentino, however, did not get the accompanying protection that a court would have provided. She was subjected to a grilling by Smith Barney's consultant that included questions about her sex life, the opening of her gynecological records, and queries about her menstrual periods, her marital counseling, and her divorce.[33] The psychiatrist even had copies of her therapy records.

Hanlon, who was placed in a chair in the middle of a room, was similarly grilled with two-and-a-half hours of questions that ranged from her sexual experience to her childhood. The consultant had had access to her counseling records, too. When, in an utterly bizarre moment, he asked her to recite the names of all the U.S. presidents in reverse order, Hanlon broke down and cried.

The night before the arbitration for which they'd waited three years, the two decided during a tearful 9 P.M. telephone conversation that they could not go through an appearance before an arbitration panel where their examinations would be unveiled, and that they could not face the possibility that the details of the examinations might get back to that man and to others in the office who had harassed them. They called their lawyer and said to settle.[34]

In courtrooms, women are similarly vulnerable to the trauma of a psychiatric evaluation, but courtrooms provide more protections than do the more informal auspices of an arbitration. In court, for example, Linda Friedman could get her client a protective order to keep invasive information private, and if the order were violated, it could lead to contempt proceedings. "It has teeth," according to Friedman, who adds that that's a far cry from "a bunch of people in a hotel room who decide it will be confidential, and then, oops, it isn't." Feisty defendants who tried to push the limits with invasive discovery or invasive questioning in court got a clear message from the U.S. Court of Appeals for the Eighth Circuit that they'd better think twice. On December 5, 1997, that court made the key decision in favor of the iron mining women of Eveleth,

Minnesota, whose personal lives had been brutally probed.

Some arbitration panels do exercise great care about psychiatric exams; it's simply that women have not been able to count on getting a panel that does. The panel of NASD arbitrators that heard Darlene Livingston's case said that Shearson would be allowed to examine Livingston only if the examination was tape recorded and if she could have a health professional of her choice in the room during Shearson's examination. Shearson initially declined the opportunity to examine Livingston after the terms were set, then later chose to examine her despite the arbitrators' terms.[35]

Claims by securities industry officials that arbitration is fair ring less than true when one considers how different its arbitration system is from those of other arbitration forums—which, incidentally, are rarely offered to Wall Street employees as options. Arnold M. Zack, former president of the National Academy of Arbitrators, said in an interview in 1996 that under a system of "due process protocol" that his group developed, a fairer system is available for plaintiff and defendant. In the case of Valentino and Hanlon, for example, the arbitrators, not the defendant, would have selected the psychiatrist—if there was to be one at all. The due process rules also would provide that the detailed results of such an exam be kept private from the defendant. No such assurances were made to Valentino.

The securities industry, though, for nearly five years made no move to incorporate the rules that Zack's group unveiled in 1995. Although lawyers in other widely used arbitration forums had embraced the rules—the American Arbitration Association and JAMS Endispute, another dispute resolution group, endorsed and used them—the securities industry was conspicuous by its absence in the use of the due process methods. "The securities industry wasn't interested in negotiating away from the position of strength they have pursuant to the Gilmer case," Zack said in 1996. Eventually, amid political and regulatory pressure emanating from the increasingly militant faction of women on Wall Street, a version of the protocol was incorporated into the NASD arbitration rules in 2000.

As discrimination and harassment cases began to filter through the arbitration system and hit all these obstacles, Friedman watched as the advantages enjoyed by Wall Street firms began to discourage lawyers from taking a woman's case. This was ironic because Congress had intended to further the civil rights cause by giving certain advantages to victims of workplace harassment or discrimination: legal fees can be shifted to losing defendants, for example, encouraging plaintiffs' lawyers to take a chance with unemployed people who had to hire a lawyer on contingency.

"So if a woman comes into the office and says 'I have a great claim,' I know if it's federal court, if I have to front costs, I will be reimbursed," says Friedman. "I know fees are awarded at a market rate. And I know that if something goes awry, I can appeal. But say a woman has a phenomenal claim against a securities firm. I sit here and say 'Uh-oh, they don't usually award fees,' and 'Uh-oh, she doesn't have a job.' I have no idea how they will value her claim, and I know for certain I can't appeal. And then I don't even know if they're going to follow the law." While both arbitration and court proceedings are often unpleasant and not always fair, it was important that the right to the courtroom not be shut off.

Incredibly, at the time Pam Martens was signing up with Stowell and Friedman, stock exchange arbitrators did not have to follow the law on such things as rules of evidence and legal precedents; they were discouraged from explaining how they came to their decisions; and unlike jurors, they were not permitted to talk about a case when it was over. Discovery—the process of demanding evidentiary documents from the other side—is limited, which puts the employee at a big disadvantage in any case in which company employment records of total hirings by sex and race are key. The average arbitrator at the time Rita Reid went to arbitration was a white, sixty-year-old male to whom the plaintiff sometimes needed to convey the trauma connected to having had a white, sixty-year-old male boss touch her where he shouldn't. And depositions are limited or not permitted at all—the ultimate example of fighting with your hands tied behind your back. Employers are the ones with the information: the statistics on women's salaries versus men's, the records on other harassment and discrimination complaints. If there is no process to force companies to share that information, the plaintiff is severely limited in getting arbitrators to believe her complaint.

The General Accounting Office released a study about securities industry arbitration on March 30, 1994, pinpointing areas for improvement in arbitration but stopping short of saying that there were abuses in the system. The GAO confirmed that nine out of ten adjudicators were white males, and that the average arbitrator was sixty. Half the arbitrators were retired.[36]

Less than three months later, the *Wall Street Journal* took a more painstaking look at the dark side of securities industry arbitration, high-lighting on page one allegations made in the case of Helen L. Walters, a trading assistant at Bateman Eichler Hill Richards Inc.[37] Walters, a Bible-college graduate who aspired to be a stockbroker one day, worked for a 300-pound boss who she claimed regularly called her a bitch, a hooker, and a streetwalker, according to the article. She said he would leave condoms on her desk from time to time and once referred to her as a "fucking idiot," the story said. She told the panel that this boss, who himself had served as a securities industry arbitrator, would sometimes get her attention by cracking a riding crop. She further told them that once, when she didn't respond quickly enough, he told her he would "tear" her "titties off," according to the story. Two former male employ-ees and a female former human resources official corroborated much of Walter's testimony, the story said.

The panel dismissed her claims.

The *Journal*'s saga, which is known among lawyers as the Riding Crop story, irritated securities industry officials who saw the story as a threat to arbitration. By August 1, the Division of Market Regulation at the SEC was writing to the self-regulatory organizations, including the NYSE and NASD, to ask whether they really wanted to handle discrimination claims. Wall Street fought back. On August 24, William Fitzpatrick, a consultant to the Securities Industry Association, wrote an alerting letter to the gen-eral counsels of all the self-regulatory organizations to ask them to "Please hold the line on this issue." If they didn't hold the line, they would "have very cranky members" after them, the letter said.[38]

The stakes were high and the stacking of the deck blatant. While presenting a paper at an NASD arbitration training session that year, one speaker urged his audience to avoid issuing written opinions on cases in order to avoid the unlikely situation in which the thinking of the arbitrators could be used by a plaintiff to show that they had delib-erately flouted the law. Don't express opinions, he told his audience, because that way "there are few (if any) ways to show that the arbitra-tors were aware of the law and intentionally ignored it."[39] While the NASD did invite a second presenter who gave the opposing view—that opinions should be given about arbitration decisions—the balance was tilted heavily in favor of arbitrators refraining from saying how they came to a decision: the NASD over the years had routinely coached arbitrators not to.

A forum that adjudicates disputes ideally would go to extremes to ensure participants that its approach was neutral, but NASD had history that said the opposite. Even the members of a subcommittee of the NASD Legal Advisory Board showed their apparent bias in the way they voted one year. NASD and the securities industry overall had for years taken the position that arbitration should be binding and that appeals should not be encouraged. Yet the Legal Advisory Board in 1994 put out recommendations that included a virtual turnaround in the no-appeals policy—but only in the event that arbitrators came out with a big judgment in favor of a plaintiff.

The beauty of arbitration, its defenders frequently say, is that it is final and nearly impossible to overturn. But here was an NASD subcommittee trying to set things up so that firms would have fodder for an appeal if they lost big.

"Arbitration panels awarding punitive damages should set forth in writing their reasons for doing so," the subcommittee wrote. "First, it will facilitate any appeal of the award of damages. Second, it is necessary to ensure that the public is clear on why the defendant is being punished,"[40] it added, a disingenuous commentary considering that the NASD had gone to such lengths to ensure that the public learned as little as possible about what transpired in its arbitrations. Although the NASD board of directors did not approve the proposal, the fact that such a pro-defense policy was seriously proposed for a judicial forum showed how far some NASD arbitration proponents will go.

Indeed, keeping arbitrations confidential was an objective in which a great deal of energy was invested by the industry. In September 1995, *Fortune* magazine and *The Bond Buyer* asked the New York Stock Exchange's permission to attend the arbitration hearings over the dispute between Michael Lissack and Smith Barney. "Such access would be routinely granted if this case were being heard in court," wrote Terence P. Paré, an associate editor at *Fortune*, who asked to attend the hearings and to examine the NYSE's case files "on behalf of *Fortune*'s readers and the general public."

Stuart Bompey's law firm, Orrick, Herrington & Sutcliffe, which represented Smith Barney in the Lissack case, told the New York Stock Exchange "that neither the Exchange nor the arbitrators have the discretion to permit members of the press to attend hearings," because arbitration is a private forum. Bompey wrote that the attendance of a reporter at the private meeting would breach public policy, which he ambidextrously referred to as "the public policy of privacy" in arbitration. "No spectators, especially those from the press, should be permitted to attend the hearings," he wrote to the NYSE, which saw things Bompey's way.

That is not to say, though, that the self-regulatory organizations were never swayed by views other than those of their own industry. Amid the flap over the riding crop story, some higher-ups at the New York Stock Exchange began to think that perhaps discrimination complaints should not be included among cases forced to arbitration after all. Such claims were not anticipated when the various arbitration forums were put in place, the director of NYSE arbitration, Robert Clemente, told Deborah Masucci, his counterpart at NASD.[41] To make that happen would take some rewriting of the form U-4 that stockbrokers signed when they got their license.

By late that year, though, a straight-up counteroffensive to the riding crop brouhaha was on. Masucci sent a letter in late September 1994 to members of the NASD's National Arbitration Committee, saying that a subcommittee had recommended that the U-4 *not* be amended to exclude discrimination claims.[42] Not surprisingly, not a single member of the subcommittee came from the ranks of lawyers who represented employees. Masucci said in her letter to the NASD's National Arbitration Committee that "We should convince Congress and others that action should not be taken based on the one *Wall Street Journal* article." The article was inflammatory, in Masucci's view. Still, the brass at NASD had better start considering where all the flap was heading, Masucci warned.[43] Should the NASD keep the U-4 as it is, then the NASD might be required to extend its regulatory duties to actually enforcing the nation's discrimination laws.

It was a comical concept at best: an organization run largely by men and controlled by the industry might, by clinging to control over adjudication of discrimination and harassment complaints, end up having to take responsibility for cracking the whip over the men who violated civil rights laws. And it would be forced to do this because its parent regulator, the SEC, was a federal agency that empowered NASD with its self-regulatory ability in the first place. Up to now, the industry had been able to exercise exclusive power over adjudication of its civil rights cases while taking no responsibility for enforcing civil rights. The trick now would be finding a way of getting around any pressure to begin enforcement without giving up the power to compel arbitration.

In fact, that work had already begun. Plenty of firms were now using pre-employment agreements in which all employees—licensed or not—had to agree to industry arbitration. So if the day were to come when the U-4 licensing process no longer ensured that civil rights cases must be arbitrated, the firms would have backup private agreements that mandated arbitration.

In August 1994, as Nick Cuneo was preparing his charity speech to his sales assistants, his firm was modifying its policy that already funneled civil rights claims.[44] Incredibly, the revised policy went on to say that arbitration hearings would be conducted by rules of the NYSE except "as modified by The Travelers Group/Smith Barney Employment Arbitration Policy"[45]—basically a case of a member firm telling the regulators how it would be regulated. So complete was Smith Barney's control over the process that it required employees to submit any complaint to the human resources department along with a $25 check payable to Smith Barney.[46] That had the effect of letting Smith Barney take early control over the process, where under normal circumstances the claim would be filed with the NYSE first. An added insult: the arbitrators "shall be bound by Smith Barney policies and procedures," it said, and "shall not have the authority to award punitive damages" or to make any award that Smith Barney deemed arbitrary or capricious.[47]

Lawyer Judith Vladeck's big case against Smith Barney came only months after these revisions were published. On March 8, 1995, Alicia DeGaetano filed her discrimination and harassment claim of emotional distress against the company and Frederick Hessler, her boss in public finance.[48] It was not a hopeful time for taking on brokerage firms: By the end of the same month, the arbitration panel on the Rita M. Reid case had ruled against her and in favor of Goldman Sachs. Reid said the process had stumped her at every juncture: she said that she was not able to compel testimony from clients of Goldman Sachs for whom she had performed extensive services and that the panel declined to hear testimony from former Goldman employees who themselves had experienced discrimination that would corroborate her experience.[49] A Goldman lawyer told the *Wall Street Journal* that "what's right is what was done" in the case.[50]

While DeGaetano waited for word on her case, some stalwarts enjoyed victories of a sort—but at great cost. Darlene Livingston, the tenacious former Shearson employee, was awarded $130,000 in compensatory damages in January 1996 for the hostile work environment she experienced.[51] In addition, Shearson had to pay $10,000 for abuse of process and $3,500 in connection with its failure to offer certain evidence. The company also had to pay $32,500 in attorney fees.[52] Despite an unsparing defense against Livingston, who was analyzed by therapists and whose personal life became the stuff of routine conversation at her forty-nine hearing sessions over a period of twenty-five days, one of Shearson's own witnesses corroborated the conditions under which women worked, testifying that people in the office would send pastries from a local vendor called the Erotic Baker—"breasts, maybe a penis or two."[53] The witness presented by Shearson also had to admit that the manager would "rub back and forth against my breasts," and that she would have complained, except that women "didn't complain at that point."[54] Shearson stopped at nothing in its defense, including among its attempts to discredit Livingston an allegation that she had body odor.

In February, a month after Livingston's award, the U.S. District Court for the Southern District of New York told Alicia DeGaetano that she would have to go to arbitration.[55] It would prove to be an active winter on the arbitration front. By mid-March, Susan Desiderio, who had gone through the 1992 arbitration in which arbitrators said they needn't follow the law, was flouting the NASD's rules and editing the U-4 that a prospective employer asked her to sign. Sun Trust Bank had hired her in mid-March, and on March 13, she signed the U-4 but crossed out three key words on the document. Where it said "I agree to arbitrate any dispute, claim or controversy that may arise between me and my firm or a customer or any other person," Desiderio struck out the words "my firm, or …," figuring she was not going to risk being burnt in arbitration a second time.[56] Sun Trust, which was willing to go along with the alteration, called the NASD to be sure it was kosher. NASD said no: Desiderio could not alter the document to delete the clause, even if her employer agreed to it. Desiderio lost her job.

In Desiderio, the industry was up against the sort of foe it hated. Like Pam Martens, Desiderio was righteous and willing to fight tirelessly. On January 15, 1997, she sued the National Association of Securities Dealers, Inc., and the Securities and Exchange Commission, saying that they had usurped her Constitutional right to a jury trial.

The U.S. District Court dismissed her case in April 1998.[57] She

appealed, but the Second Circuit Court of Appeals in Manhattan affirm-
ed the District Court's decision. The NASD is a private actor, and thus
has no obligation to confer Constitutional rights, the courts said. Despite the NASD's relationship with the SEC, in which the federal agency
granted it power to regulate brokerage firms, the court did not find a
nexus that would point to the NASD as a "state actor." So Desiderio
could not sue it for denying her rights.

Somehow, the securities industry had set up a system that gave it all
the government-conferred clout it wanted for enforcing policies on its
members without exposing it to the responsibilities that might go along
with such power. Ellen Varygas, legal counsel for the Equal Employment Opportunity Commission, said it was ironic that "an industry
which one would think of as capitalism at its purest has created a cocoon
to take itself out of the marketplace."

Like Vladeck handling the Martens case before them, though,
Friedman and Stowell had ideas about how to work this system to their
advantage. As they had explained to Pam, there was a loophole that
could get the Smith Barney women's case into court: the one thing neither the NYSE nor the NASD would recognize was any complaint that
purported to be made on behalf of a class. And the precedent had been
set for sex discrimination cases to be certified as class actions five years
earlier, when a Federal District Court in Duluth, Minnesota ruled that
the women who worked in the iron mines of Eveleth, Minnesota, constituted a class. So the *Martens* case, if given class action status, should
be relegated to a court. This was a somewhat risky strategy. It wasn't so
simple to get a judge to declare that a group of employees constituted a
class. Among other requirements, employees would have to show common problems that were systemic throughout the firm. A judge could
easily dismiss their contention that women who worked at Smith Barney
constituted a class. Considering, though, that they'd been stuck from the
start with the arbitration system and all its flaws, they had little to lose
in at least trying for class status.

So Stowell and Friedman drafted the complaint, deciding that
along with Smith Barney, Nick Cuneo, and Jamie Dimon, they also
would name the New York Stock Exchange and the National
Association of Securities Dealers as defendants. The NYSE and
NASD were the forums where most Wall Street employment cases
were heard, and to sue them would bring public attention to the

unfairness of mandatory arbitration. Pam Martens, who couldn't recall ever having signed the U-4 document, would not be included in the counts against the stock-trading organizations. (If she wasn't certain that they had forced her into arbitration via the U-4, she might not have had a legitimate claim against them, and no one knew a way to immediately get their hands on a copy.) She already was aware, though, from having worked with Vladeck, that women who worked for Smith Barney across the country had a civil rights dispute with the company much broader than the complaints about how women were treated in Garden City. And she had further educated herself by talking with Palefsky, to whom she had sent a long letter during the months when she was working with Vladeck.

Along with a trove of documents she stuffed in a box and shipped to Chicago, Pam had included her own version of a complaint against Smith Barney—a version that she previously had given to Vladeck. ("Pam, it has to be much shorter," Kathleen Keegan had scribbled across the top, hoping that Pam would edit it back before presenting it to Vladeck. Pam didn't cut a word.) The complaint was rich with anecdotes that would wind up being highlighted in their lawsuit. Friedman located a New Jersey–based law firm to be her local counsel for the case, which would be filed in the Southern District of New York in lower Manhattan. They also made sure to comply with local New York City codes that required advance notice that a civil rights complaint was about to be filed. On Friday, May 17, 1996, Stowell and Friedman served copies of the complaint to the City Commission on Human Rights and the Corporation Counsel of the New York City Land Department. Their ducks were now in a row, with the complaint ready for a Monday filing in federal court, two hotel rooms booked at the New York Helmsley, and three plaintiffs prepared to drive in to Manhattan early Monday morning to meet their lawyers face-to-face for the first time.

Smith Barney, for its part, was not entirely sure of the timing, but its attorneys did know that Martens had filed a complaint with the EEOC and that a lawsuit could come at any time. The company was ready to downplay the women's assertions, and it hoped that any lawsuit would not be taken too seriously.

Litigation was just lawyering. Its hazardous by-product, publicity, was the weapon Wall Street most feared.

Chapter Eleven

Going Public

It's hard for me to talk this way. They talked about sucking a woman's nipples until they bled.

—DONNA, A FORMER STOCKBROKER, AT A PUBLIC HEARING

FOR ALL THEIR FELLOW COMMUTERS could tell, they were another car pool of groggy Long Islanders creeping through the miserable Monday-morning traffic to New York City on May 20, 1996. The last thing anyone would tag them for was a trio of crusaders about to make history.

Pam Martens was at the wheel of her Jeep. Most families would by now have relegated Bluey to be the train station car. The strips of dark blue paint peeling from the hood were numerous and long.

Dressed in a conservative black suit with matching black shoes, Pam negotiated the bumper-to-bumper parking lot whose official name was, oxymoronically, the Long Island Expressway. Judy Mione sat in the passenger's seat. Pam had picked Judy up at her modest home in North Bellmore.

In the back, Roberta Thomann tried to get as comfortable as the

Jeep's aging rear seat allowed. It was Roberta who heard the dispatch from WBBR-AM, a New York all-news station owned by Bloomberg: Three women, the announcer said—two former employees and one current employee—had filed copies of a complaint with the New York City Commission on Human Rights that charged Smith Barney with sex discrimination and sexual harassment. The plaintiffs intended to file the complaint in federal court later in the day, he said.

Roberta shouted to get Pam's attention. "That's our story—they're talking about our lawsuit." Over the din of honking horns, they strained to hear the rest. Pam turned up the volume. The complaint alleged that the Garden City office of Smith Barney had a "Boom-Boom Room" where partying went on, the announcer said. Among defendants were not only the firm and the branch manager, Nicholas Cuneo, but James Dimon, the chief executive officer of Smith Barney.

Hearing the words on the public airwaves put Roberta in a state of panic. Somehow in the emotion and exhaustion it took to get to the point where they actually had gone public, Roberta had kept too busy to focus on where it would lead. Pam could see that she was nervous and breathing too quickly. She and Judy tried to persuade her that she needn't be so anxious. At that, they didn't have much success.

They drove into Manhattan and parked Bluey in a garage that seemed too fancy for it. A few blocks away, at 212 East 42nd Street, was the New York Helmsley, where Friedman and Stowell had taken two rooms from which they would field calls from the media. Pam mentally forgave the lawyers for booking a hotel associated with Leona Helmsley, who had been jailed for tax evasion.

When they got to the front desk, they found that their lawyers had not yet checked in. They went to the hotel coffee shop, ordered coffee, tea, and muffins, and waited. The quarter hour of enforced downtime calmed Roberta a bit. They paid an astonishingly large check and went back to the front desk. Reception told them that their lawyers had arrived and were upstairs. Pam called Mary Stowell and Linda Friedman from a house phone in the lobby, and the two came down promptly to meet their clients. Pam was too caught up in the excitement of the moment to take in much detail about her new lawyers, but she couldn't help but be struck by how tall Stowell was. Pam was pleased that her lawyers looked so professional, so confident. Apparently they were pleased by the presentation of their lead plaintiff, too. "You look great," Stowell told Pam. It occurred to Pam that her lawyers had represented more than their share of exhausted and bedraggled women who were worn out from the fight. They headed for their rooms. A publicity war was about to begin.

Until then, Smith Barney had said little about the complaint. Bloomberg News had called them the week before it was filed, and the company said it had not seen the complaint and that any specific allegations were "one person's word against another's."

Bloomberg had broken its story about the allegations at 6 A.M. that morning, a few hours before Martens and her former colleagues had headed to Manhattan. Smith Barney's public relations department was not yet aware of the filing of the complaint.

By 9:30 A.M., though, the complaint was filed in court and a copy was served to Smith Barney. The firm prepared a statement, saying, in effect, that even if some of the charges were true, the behavior described would be an exception at the firm. In an interview with the *Washington Post* that day, and published May 21, spokeswoman Mary McDermott called the complaint "much ado about very little," adding that the allegations were "totally without merit."[1] The complaint is about "one former broker and two sales assistants who are unhappy with one manager," McDermott told *BusinessWeek*. The notion of discrimination and harassment problems being widespread at the firm was "absurd," she added. (Two days later, in its May 22, 1996, edition, the *New York Daily News* would report that "A Smith Barney spokeswoman said this was an isolated incident" at one branch out of 470.)

As they awaited press calls at the hotel, Pam and Linda Friedman realized that they needed extra copies of the complaint for reporters. They dashed across the street to a tiny quick-copy center. In the short time it took to get the duplicating done, a thick stack of messages from reporters had accumulated back at the hotel. Within minutes things were more frenetic than any of them had anticipated. Press people were showing up at the suite. At one point, Friedman was being interviewed by the *New York Daily News* in the bedroom while Pam talked to a *USA Today* reporter from the phone in the bathroom. When Pam came out of seclusion to do the next phone interview from the bedroom, tension broke out between her and Friedman. Pam was talking about things she considered to be criminal acts by her former employer, contrasting this with the character of A. G. Edwards, where she worked now. Friedman was livid when she overheard Pam—on the telephone with a reporter—using the word "criminal" with regard to Smith Barney.

The makeshift press conference began to come undone when television crews started to arrive. Pam called the front desk to see about getting a meeting room on short notice. The New York Helmsley accommodated, at no extra charge, opening up a huge banquet room with an incongruous doorstop—a grand piano—parked just outside. The space filled quickly with television cameras, blinding lights, and silver photographers' umbrellas. Energized by the media, Pam took center stage. She posed for a still photographer, spoke righteously for a television crew, then recounted workplace indignities for a print reporter before starting the cycle again. A *BusinessWeek* photographer asked Pam and Roberta Thomann to walk toward him from the end of the corridor outside the meeting room. They repeated the exercise a half-dozen times until he was satisfied that he had his shot.

Amid the bustle of news crews and lawyers delivering sound bytes of measured outrage, a lonely figure with short brown hair and brown eyes sat silently in a metal chair in the corner. It was Judy Mione, looking tired and uncomfortable. She was still employed as a sales assistant at Smith Barney in Garden City and thus was prohibited by company policy from speaking to the press. She wanted to be there for the historic occasion. She did not, however want to give Smith Barney an easy reason to show her the door.

Roberta, who was falling back into near-panic, made it through the *BusinessWeek* photo but waved off the television interviews and spoke only to several print reporters who persuaded her that talking to them would help her cause.

Once most of the media had packed up and gone, Pam went back to the hotel room with Roberta, Judy, and their lawyers. There, from her seat on the queen-sized bed that was serving as an interview stage, Pam looked up to see a familiar face. It was Leah Nathans Spiro, the *BusinessWeek* reporter whom she'd called after being fired. She had not written a story after meeting Pam the previous fall but was well-prepared now, armed with her notes from their interview seven months earlier. She sat down to review with Pam what had transpired since then. Pam was impressed that Spiro remembered the salient details of their previous interview and had digested the facts of the complaint. She spent twenty minutes with the reporter, then gathered her things and headed for the garage and Bluey.

———

PAM DROPPED OFF ROBERTA, then Judy, and drove back to Garden City. None of the three got home in time for the evening news, though Pam's sister, Diana, taped the news on her VCR to give to Pam the next day. That night, the brass at Smith Barney understood for the first time how attractive the story was for reporters on and off the business beat. This was not the latest statistic on new-housing starts or an update on personnel changes at a mutual fund. Customers would see these stories. Female customers in particular. Employees would be demoralized. The lawsuit would attract readers who typically were strangers to financial news. How often did commuters see allegations of lewd language, booze, and condom pranks on pages better known for chronicling the quarterly Gross Domestic Product?

Company-paid golf outings, and they ban the women brokers? Even Archie Bunker would read that story—if only to see how the guys got away with it.

As Jamie Dimon and the other higher-ups at Smith Barney watched the evening coverage, it was obvious that they wanted top help to make the whole thing go away. Its spokespeople might have been pooh-poohing the lawsuit publicly, but Smith Barney already knew it would spare no expense in snaring the toughest litigator it could find.

———

MARK BELNICK WAS A SENIOR PARTNER at Paul, Weiss, Rifkind, Wharton & Garrison, which had represented Smith Barney for years in litigation, securities law matters, and contract negotiations. His firm had long been a powerhouse among law firms doing mergers work and litigation, soaring to thirteenth place (from twentieth the year before) in 1989 on the *American Lawyer* magazine "100" survey. Paul Weiss had remained as a top-tier player, with Belnick ensconced as a profitable senior partner, ever since.

Belnick learned about the Boom-Boom Room complaint filed that morning the same way Smith Barney executives did: at home, watching the evening news. Belnick, slightly balding at forty-nine, was a famous

New York litigator whose assignments included work for the firm he was hearing about on TV. He was a trusted adviser whom the firm sought out when tough problems came up.

Belnick's phone rang the next morning with a request from Smith Barney's George Saks, asking him to come in that day to counsel the firm on whom to hire to deal with these women. Charles O. Prince III, general counsel of The Travelers, had authorized the call. Belnick was the natural person to seek out for advice as they were mapping out a strategy. He told Saks he would be happy to help them select the right lawyer to run the case.

There was no shortage of attorneys who wanted the job, either. The phones in the general counsel's office of Smith Barney were ringing with big-name trial lawyers offering their services. As those pitch calls were coming in, though, Smith Barney's senior deputy counsel Joan Guggenheim, George Saks, and Prince, known as "Chuck" among his colleagues, were meeting with Belnick and telling him that it was Belnick himself they wanted.

Belnick said he was not interested; he would much prefer to help them find someone else.

But they pressed him. Enlisting a twenty-six-year Paul Weiss veteran would send a signal that Smith Barney wasn't fooling around. Belnick was a fellow of the American College of Trial Lawyers, a man who had done work for Merrill Lynch, the National Association of Securities Dealers, Donaldson Lufkin & Jenrette Securities, American Express, and Morgan Stanley. He led the review for a major reorganization of the NASD and the Nasdaq stock market. In 1987, he was deputy chief counsel to the United States Senate's Iran-Contra Committee. Obviously no stranger to controversy, he had represented billionaire Michael Milken, the former Drexel Burnham Lambert junk bond boss who went to jail. And he had been the principal lawyer for Pennzoil in its battle with Texaco that brought an $11 billion verdict for his client. He had graduated from Cornell University in 1968; he got his law degree from Columbia Law School in 1971.

When he saw how ardently Smith Barney wanted him personally, Belnick laid out his requirements and his strategy. If they didn't like his terms, he'd help them find someone else.

For one thing, he would not pursue a scorched-earth strategy, he said, referring to the aggressive litigation style in which the defense opposes everything. Scorched-earth fights were a particularly bad idea with civil rights suits, because you look as if you're pitted against your employees. Once you allow yourself to be labeled as antiemployee, he explained, you're stuck with the black hat, and the plaintiffs get to wear the white one. The good guy/bad guy labels fuel publicity, too. "The most important thing is from the beginning to stop it from becoming a wildfire," he told them. If that ever happens, the only possible winners are the plaintiffs' lawyers.

At all costs, settle before you take the risk of going to court, he advised them. Belnick figured it was "at least a fifty-fifty proposition" that the women might get a court to certify them as a class. So imagine if they go to court. A parade of witnesses will take the stand. Some may be telling God's honest truth. Others may be making it up. In either event, the stories would be played out in the media day after day, dragging the firm through the mud relentlessly. The public already had the impression that Smith Barney was running some kind of after-hours sex club in the basement in Garden City, if they believed the tabloid-style TV reports. Don't make it worse by fighting the plaintiffs on every point and keeping a debate alive in the press, Belnick said. Everyone in the room already had the impression that Jamie Dimon was ready and willing to talk to the press. Dimon and any other executives trying to influence coverage have to be made to understand that they simply won't win the public relations battle, Belnick said. Don't talk to the media, he said.

———

AS BELNICK COUNSELED HIS CLIENTS, Linda Friedman was on the telephone to Pam, asking her back into Manhattan for more interviews. Pam Martens and Roberta Thomann were on the cover of that morning's *New York Daily News; Good Morning America* wanted to get her on camera. Pam had some trepidation over the potential reaction of her branch manager at A. G. Edwards to all the publicity she was getting. Pam asked him for permission to be taped for the television show. "What you do outside of this office is your own business," he told her. Pam took off for the city, where the *Good Morning America* crew greeted her with a buffet spread of juice, bottled water, yogurt, fruit, and iced drinks. She felt like a runway model.

———

BY THE TIME Pam got back to her office at Edwards, calls from women at Smith Barney locations all over the country had begun to pile up. Marianne Dalton, a Los Angeles broker, called at 12:50. Pam called her back and heard a story about a branch manager who smacked Dalton with his shoes and a broker who would regularly change for the gym— stripping nude in front of her—each day at noon. Pam told Dalton where she could reach the Chicago lawyers.

Another message was from a sales assistant named Patricia Clemente, who worked in the same branch as Dalton. She'd had a broker's license since 1989, but she claimed that the branch manager would not let her go into the training program. Pam gave her the lawyers' number.

A former sales assistant in the nearby Jericho, Long Island, office had called. Her story sounded familiar: she had beseeched management to back her efforts to become a broker, but they would not support her.

Another call was from someone whose name Pam knew. Lydia Klein had been Pam's retail liaison on the municipal bond desk in New York. Klein called to tell her about harassment she'd been living with on the trading floor in one of Smith Barney's Manhattan offices. Pam referred her, too, to Stowell and Friedman.

That night there was a second wave of television coverage on the Boom-Boom Room story. And the next day, more tabloid stories. Belnick wasn't too far off course: although the *Martens* complaint alleged a number of illegal policies and practices, the public was getting the impression that women had been groped and fondled in the Boom-Boom Room. No one had alleged that.

———

THE CALL ASKING BELNICK officially to take the assignment, on his terms, came the next afternoon. Belnick accepted. Thus, the lawyer who had fought the U.S. government on behalf of Michael Milken was defending Smith Barney against three Long Island moms who worried about everyday things like gas prices and mortgage payments. Assisting Belnick would be another attorney experienced with Wall Streeters in trouble, Brad Karp. Karp, an intense thirty-six-year-old Harvard Law School graduate, was poised to step in when Belnick was not available for court calls. Karp had defended Dennis Levine, the convicted insider-trader from Drexel Burnham Lambert Inc., escorting him out of jail, helping protect him from the media, and earning Levine's praise as his "guardian angel."[2] Karp also had defended Lazard Freres in a high-profile case brought by the government against brokerage firms that were cheating their municipal government customers. It was a curiously potent legal team, given Smith Barney's public stance that the complaint was a meritless gripe of three workers who were unhappy with one branch boss.

Belnick compiled employee names and telephone lists and got to work talking to employees. In fact, in order to get an idea of exactly what the plaintiffs were talking about with this weird room in the basement of 901 Franklin Avenue, he drove out to Garden City to take a look. After a glance around, he was less than impressed. I've seen nicer finished basements, he thought. The artwork at least was fitting. Brokers had put up homemade posters listing successive names of the firm, which had changed hands so often.

As he toured the branch and talked to employees, he picked up pieces of lore about the office and about the Boom-Boom Room. The hanging bicycle, according to one account, had belonged to Gladys Lawson, Cuneo's secretary, who rode her bike to work in her younger days. (Lawson did ride a bike to work, but she says that the bike that hung from the ceiling was not hers.) The toilet seat next to the bike had come from the previous branch office down the street, according to people Belnick spoke to—from an uncooperative fixture that had never quite flushed properly. As for the allegations in the suit, his sources were telling him a different story than the plaintiffs had told. "The stories we checked out were bogus," he said.[3]

Belnick was successful in keeping his clients quiet, but he was not exactly keeping the press away. Leah Spiro's story in *BusinessWeek* the week after the lawsuit featured Pam's picture and recapped the sensational charges, alongside Mary McDermott's comment that the allegations were "absurd."

The *BusinessWeek* story set Pam's phone ringing anew. This time, women from Goldman Sachs, Bear Stearns, Merrill Lynch, and Nuveen were calling to report discrimination and harassment at their firms. Later in May, a Smith Barney stockbroker from Eugene, Oregon, contacted Pam to tell her story of unequal treatment in the Pacific Northwest. Soon after, Lorraine Parker called to tell Pam that she had spoken with Eileen Valentino, the woman who claimed she was molested in the Paramus, New Jersey, branch.

McDermott, the spokeswoman, was meanwhile telling Bloomberg News that the practice of compelling complaining women to be examined by Smith Barney's psychiatrist was commonplace at all brokerage firms and was thus nothing to pick on Smith Barney for.

While Pam was rallying these callers to make mandatory arbitration a constitutional-rights issue, the NASD was asking its arbitrators that same month to fill out a form that would supply it with demographics on its arbitrator pool. Of the pool of 2,669 arbitrators completing the form, 346 were women. As for the cases that the arbitrators were hearing, relatively few had anything to do with civil rights. By the end of 1996, only 109 of the 5,631 arbitration complaints filed with NASD concerned women alleging discrimination. But the tiny number belied the frustrations of the women who entered, then gave up on, the system. And it revealed nothing of the quantity of preemptive settlements wrapped up by brokerage firms that did not want to risk even the employer-friendly system of arbitration.

Just as the month ended, with firms up and down Wall Street growing queasy about their potential exposure to civil rights claims, a U.S. District Court judge ruled that the brokerage unit of a big bank had gone a step too far. First Union Corp. of Charlotte, North Carolina, had been taken to arbitration by broker Laura A. Park, who was fired in mid-1994 after blowing the whistle on improper sales practices by the bank's brokerage unit. A panel of NASD arbitrators turned Park into one of the rare wins in the arbitration game, telling First Union to pay her $722,045. First Union immediately went to court to overturn the award, presenting to an apparently incredulous judge the argument that the three-person arbitration panel couldn't be unbiased, because one of its members was a woman. First Union made other arguments. Among them was a protest that it was entitled to rights of due process that it was not receiving at NASD.

The judge suggested that if First Union didn't like the NASD arbitration requirement, perhaps it might choose not to participate in the securities business.[4] It was a rare, role-reversing moment for the cause of employees forced to accept arbitration, like it or not. The edifice of Wall Street's private justice was developing its first small chinks.

Chapter Twelve

Momentum:
Merrill's Women Sue

*If you talked to your immediate managers, nine times out of ten,
they were the source of the situation to begin with.*

—A MERRILL LYNCH WOMAN

Survey respondent quoted in the plaintiffs'
Expert Report on Merrill Lynch women

I T WAS THE BUZZ IN GARDEN CITY. Even Sean's sixteen-year-old
friends were excited that the lady who had once been their Cub
Scout den mother had become a local celebrity. When Pam pulled
up in front of Garden City High to collect Sean, students hanging
around after school would notice Bluey and perk up.

"Hey, Mrs. Martens, how's it going? Are you winning that lawsuit?"

The story had broken first on television, radio, the wire services, and
in the New York tabloids, but within a week it also began to get attention from the *New York Times* and the *Wall Street Journal,* and the
bad publicity appeared to be getting to Smith Barney. On May 31, John
L. Donnelly, the director of human resources who had contacted Pam
the day after her letter to Jamie Dimon arrived in October 1994,
shipped out his own "Dear Colleagues" letter to everyone in the company. "A great deal of media attention has been devoted to a recent

lawsuit against Smith Barney alleging sexual harassment and discrimination at one of our branch offices," the letter began. "Unfortunately, many of these media accounts have been inaccurate, incomplete and unfair to the firm ..."[1]

Donnelly went on to tell employees that he had responded to Pam's letter to Jamie Dimon and that an "intensive review" had taken place as a result. He took credit for the "prompt and responsive action" of relieving the branch manager of his duties and naming a replacement, though the firm would continue to waffle on whether Cuneo had retired voluntarily or had been told to leave.[2] The story seemed to change depending upon whether it was useful to exonerate Cuneo or to take credit for throwing him out.

Donnelly pointed out that there was a hotline to call in the event of work-related problems, and that the firm was proud to provide support services such as back-up child care, adoption assistance, and flexible scheduling.[3] To the horror of the plaintiffs, Donnelly also noted that "employees are always encouraged to talk with their managers or to call on our Human Resources department." Pam read the letter in disgust.

On July 2, the lawsuit was amended to add Lorraine Parker to the list of named plaintiffs.[4] Now four names appeared at the top of the complaint.

———

LATER THAT MONTH, Anne P. Kaspar, a broker at Merrill Lynch, called her lawyer to say that it looked like the Smith Barney women had found lawyers who were willing to work with a class of women to fight Wall Street. Kaspar asked her lawyer to call Stowell and Friedman.

———

EMPLOYEES RECEIVED ANOTHER "Dear Colleague" letter from Donnelly on August 27.[5] It's possible that "there will be periods of renewed media interest in the case" as the legal process plays out, he said. He urged employees to report inappropriate behavior in the office.

Belnick, meanwhile, was playing hardball with the Chicago team. Stowell and Friedman wrote to Belnick asking for depositions of top Smith Barney human resource executives in September, additionally demanding employment statistics to back their case. Belnick opposed the requests.[6] Smith Barney was holding fast to its position that a handful of women in the suburbs of New York would not a class make. The court, they said, would not certify this group as a class. Perhaps Smith Barney's legal team was feeling lucky in September.

———

SEPTEMBER 11, 1996, was the kind of day that underpaid, over-worked civil service lawyers live for. Attorneys for the Securities and Exchange Commission were in their second consecutive day of depos-ing Stanley J. Feminella, the former broker from Cuneo's branch, who already had been charged by the SEC with giving payoffs to a customer in return for exorbitant commissions. Now Feminella was implicating management in the excessive commissions. If Feminella's knowledge were to be let loose on the media panting for dirt on the Boom-Boom Room boss, it could turn Smith Barney's simmering corporate head-ache into a migraine.

Feminella told the SEC that day that Cuneo had repeatedly explained to him during his employment interview that he would pay Feminella a commission the SEC had now deemed excessive. The bro-ker described scenes in which Cuneo telephoned colleagues to verify the high percentages that he was promising. To compound matters, SEC lawyers showed Feminella copies of documents he had been given by Glenn Fischer, Cuneo's assistant manager, that would help the firm avoid disclosing details to Consumers Union about commissions it had paid.[7] Feminella's testimony included specifics on how Fischer had guided him through the process of filling out regulatory paperwork to make it look as though Consumers Union didn't need to be informed about commissions. Those documents included the signature of a regional director of the firm.

The next day, September 12, 1996, the SEC accepted a settlement offer from Lehman Brothers Inc.—corporate successor to Shearson Lehman Brothers in the SEC lawsuit—that was a gift to the former management of the Boom-Boom Room by any measure. The SEC issued a cease-and-desist order and imposed sanctions on Lehman even as it was continuing to depose Feminella about the particulars of his scheme with David Granston, his former customer at Consumers Union. Lehman settled without admitting or denying the findings in the cease-and-desist order.[8] (Although neither the sanctions nor the cease-and-desist order mentioned Smith Barney in the title, that was, in fact, the name now on the door of the operation where the alleged actions had taken place during Cuneo's reign.) Lehman would pay $55,000. At a time when the SEC had put firms on notice that it would charge individual managers with responsibility for "failure to supervise" employees who had broken securities laws, neither Cuneo nor Fischer was mentioned in the settlement. It had been only six months earlier that Arthur Levitt Jr., chairman of the Securities and Exchange Commission, had said in a speech before the Securities Industry Association that the industry wasn't policing its brokers well enough and that regulators would increasingly hold management accountable for brokers who broke securities laws.

By comparison, a month before the Lehman settlement of the Feminella case, Refco Securities Inc. had settled a failure-to-supervise case with the SEC for $3.5 million. Elaine Cacheris, Levitt's regional director in Los Angeles, was quoted on the Dow Jones wire saying, "This case today illustrates the importance of responsible supervision in the brokerage industry. If a violation occurs on your watch, then you may get tagged for it." Yet amid all this pressure and precedent, Garden City management was spared.

As Feminella's testimony continued, more information related to Cuneo came out. In October, Feminella spoke extensively about checks written to him by his sales assistant, by a stockbroker in the office, and by Cuneo himself, for thousands of dollars apiece in some cases. When asked by SEC lawyers why his coworkers had written him the checks, Feminella pleaded the Fifth Amendment. For what it saved in potential new publicity about the Garden City office, the $55,000 was money well invested by the company.[9]

———

PUSHED BY BELNICK to prove that they represented much more than a fluke feminist quartet, Friedman and Stowell figured they had nothing to lose in storming the enemy. Armed with a growing list of egregious allegations, they filed a second amended complaint against Smith Barney on October 17, 1996.[10] This set off another flurry of press reports and gave the plaintiffs a better argument with which to push for status as a class: Now the plaintiffs included twenty-three women in ten states.

The new plaintiffs' allegations broadened the appeal of the story among broadcast and print reporters. This time, there were allegations that a branch manager offered $100 to each woman who would take off her shirt at a Christmas party; that a broker told a colleague he would like to take her to Victoria's Secret, the lingerie store, to model under-wear for him; and that a branch manager told his assistant that he would fire her if she didn't help him falsify documents to build a case against a female broker.[11]

Bad publicity can be costly for a company that sells stocks, bonds, and mutual funds, because it's easy for customers who get turned off to buy and sell through the competition. A hundred shares of Microsoft is the same hundred shares of Microsoft whether a customer buys them from Smith Barney, Charles Schwab, or Brand X Securities. With women tak-ing command of their own finances like never before, a scandal about alleged mistreatment of women brokers was a problem.

Apparently responding to its growing media problems, Smith Barney made Dimon available to *BusinessWeek* in what would turn out to be the eye of the storm. "Whiz Kid," a largely flattering cover story about Dimon, appeared in the October 21, 1996, issue. The profile, which went on for some 3,000 words, made no mention of his handling of the lawsuit. It was written by Leah Nathans Spiro, who had written about the suit earlier in the year.

———

ELEVEN DAYS AFTER FRIEDMAN AND STOWELL filed the amended complaint, they launched a second, separate action against Smith Barney—this one in California.[12] Judges in the Northern District of California in San Francisco had been ruling favorably when securities industry employees demanded the right to go to court, so the Chicago lawyers decided to take a stab at circumventing arbitration there. More plaintiffs, more embarrassing allegations. The public so far had been served up a menu of official reactions to the women's various complaints that ranged from "patently absurd"[13] to "totally false"[14] to "an isolated incident" restricted to one wayward office.[15] That position was becom-ing tougher for Smith Barney to justify.

Not all the men implicated in the charges were as nervous as their employer. On October 31, the former boss of one plaintiff who had been fired from the Kansas City, Missouri, branch of Smith Barney took the opportunity to ridicule his former employee at an office Halloween party, according to court papers filed later.[16] John Kuddes, a branch manager who allegedly had denied basic office support—such as postage and clerical help—to Beverly Trice, ordered one of his brokers to dress up and mock Trice at the Halloween party.[17] He gave the broker first prize for best costume.[18]

Smith Barney took another hit on November 13, when the *Wall Street Journal* ran a story on the front page of its investing section raising the question of whether the firm had fueled its own bad publicity by playing hardball with the plaintiffs in the *Martens* suit.[19] At 1:15 the same afternoon, James Dimon took to the in-house speakerphone system that linked all the company's 360 branches, telling his 10,000 brokers—and whoever else might be listening in—that not all the allegations were legitimate, but enough of them were true that Smith Barney had taken action.[20]

He reassured the troops that after getting Pam's letter, management had responded immediately. His analysis of what that response had been sounded inconsistent: First, he gave the impression that Cuneo was pushed out. "Within two months [of Pam Martens's letter] the branch manager was on leave of absence and soon after retired," Dimon said. Then he gave the opposite impression: "The retirement had nothing to do with the lawsuit whatsoever," he immediately added. The CEO did not explain the juxtaposition of the two apparently contradictory statements.[21]

Dimon told his listeners that stock brokering was "a great career for women" and that 12 percent of Smith Barney's 10,500 brokers were female. After saying that the firm was doing "as much as we can" to raise that number, he gave as an example that 20 percent of the previous year's trainees were women, which in 1996 was presumably something to boast about. Several people in his audience tape-recorded the speech and sent copies to former colleagues who had quit or been fired. Those who were fighting the firm were entertained by the part about stock brokering holding such great promise for women.

Two days after Dimon's November 13 chat with his employees, African American employees at Texaco settled with the oil giant for a record $176.1 million, a number noted by both sides in the *Martens* matter.

While Smith Barney management worked at shoring up its image with employees, lawyers for the firm spent the autumn trying to persuade the court that the plaintiffs should not get the documents that they had requested: no spreadsheets with recent history on discrimination and harassment complaints, no confidential employment statistics. In one of the tedious pretrial conferences that invariably follow the filing of a lawsuit, Smith Barney's counsel went up against Stowell and Friedman and said that it would be overly burdensome to produce firm-wide data about such complaints, and that they could not provide employee information because it was, after all, confidential. But Smith Barney lost both battles.

On the first, Stowell and Friedman suggested to the District Court judge assigned to the case that Smith Barney simply contact its operations managers—most of whom were women, and many of whom were clients of Stowell and Friedman—to ask for complaints about discrimination and harassment that had come in over the past eighteen months. The judge found that reasonable, particularly given that Stowell and Friedman were amenable to receiving spreadsheet data that would replace the names of both the complainants and the accused with numbers. Thus, in November 1996, an e-mail to the firm's operations managers elicited word that 270 discrimination and harassment complaints had been made in the preceding eighteen months—a number that gave the two lawyers further confidence that discrimination was pervasive and provable.[22]

On the matter of firm-wide employee data about hiring, salaries, and promotions, the judge once again found the plaintiffs' request reasonable. Stowell and Friedman were going to be expected to show that there was a pattern and practice of discrimination in order to proceed with their case, and the company was the only one with the data that would prove or disprove that. Smith Barney did win on one related point that was of great concern to it: keeping the information confidential. Apart from wanting to protect employee privacy, there was a lot to be gained by keeping the data under wraps: 98 percent of branch managers were male and 2 percent were female in 1995. Among lower-paying jobs, women were predominant and still lower-paid than men with the same responsibilities and titles. Men predominated in high-paying stock broker jobs, taking up 89 percent of those spots. When the lower-paid males tried to get ahead, they had a relatively easy time. In 1994, out of a pool of 1,725 female sales assistants and 78 male sales assistants, 24.5 percent of the men moved on to become brokers but only 2.9 percent of the women did. Thus, male sales assistants were more than eight times as likely to advance to become brokers as female sales assistants were.

In individual job categories, differences existed too: the median female income in control administrator jobs in 1995 was $50,405, while the median male income was $67,614.[23] So far, the raw data behind this information had been seen only by Smith Barney officials.

Smith Barney, of course, had to protect the individual employees whose names were attached to the payroll data. The firm, however, wanted more protection than that. Even if the names were deleted and the data were collated, the firm wanted assurance that the totals and percentages would be protected from public exposure.

Friedman and Stowell were obliging when Smith Barney's counsel made a request in front of the judge for a letter agreement that would bind them and others assisting them on the case to confidentiality over these data. It was Friedman's assessment that too much back-and-forth over a topic like confidentiality might annoy the judge and lead him to dismiss their request entirely. Better to be accommodating and get the statistics, Friedman figured.

Besides, she knew that Illinois law would not have permitted her to possess the Smith Barney employee data except on a confidential basis in any event, and she knew that it was standard legal practice to exchange payroll statistics as "attorneys'-eyes-only." This letter agreement didn't strike her as a big concession. It didn't even strike her as something that must be shared with her lead plaintiff.[24]

Things were going smoothly, yet Pam began to express concern that the momentum that had been so favorable to the plaintiffs might turn. Brokerage house managements had long relied on the common reluctance of women to come forward—a dynamic Pam knew well. She figured that when challenged, the securities firms would stage a show of force to deter recalcitrant females. She e-mailed her lawyers in late December 1996 to say how important it was to Smith Barney to "convince their brokers and employees that you never go up against this powerful machine."[25] She worried now that Smith Barney would be pulling out all the stops.

On December 31, 1996, she told her lawyers that she would be starting to put together a list of proposed demands, and congratulated them for their hard work. "I think you are doing everything perfectly!" Pam e-mailed Linda Friedman. "It's when SB's attorneys stop yelling at you that we need to worry."

Forced to proceed with delivery of statistics and other documents, Belnick on January 10, 1997, sent a letter to Stowell and Friedman memorializing the terms of the confidentiality agreement. This January 10 Letter Agreement was a complicated document that obligated the viewer of Smith Barney's statistics to work with Smith Barney, within the law, to avoid subpoenas and even court orders. It was not the sort of document that Pam Martens would have liked. In Stowell and Friedman's view, though, having the data was a coup, so they signed it.

News events separate from the *Martens* case were serving to boost its importance. Susan Desiderio, the former broker who refused to sign away her trial rights, filed her complaint on January 15, 1997, against both the NASD and the SEC.[26] Wall Street was now under a blinding spotlight. The civil rights angle was becoming irresistible to politicians. Reporters were getting press releases announcing that Edward J. Markey, the Massachusetts Democrat, and Constance Morella, the Maryland Republican, had introduced a bill proposing that it be illegal to require arbitration as a condition of employment in *any* industry, and offering their critical opinions on Wall Street's practices while they were at it.[27] Markey, Jesse L. Jackson Jr., the congressman from Illinois, and Anna G. Eshoo, the congresswoman from California, sent a three-page letter to SEC Chairman Arthur Levitt saying they were "deeply disturbed" that employers were forcing employees to relinquish their rights to court as a condition of employment.[28]

With political winds blowing in their direction, Stowell and Friedman accepted an invitation to meet with representatives from Smith Barney and The Travelers and, on January 20, 1997, flew from Chicago to New York City to face a half-dozen stone-faced lawyers and executives, Belnick and George Saks among them. Saks offered himself up as an example of how anything was possible, even for minorities, at Smith Barney. You just had to put your mind to it. After all, said Saks, Smith Barney was not considered a good place for Jews to work, and yet he, a Jewish man, had been able to get ahead.[29] Friedman listened in disbelief. She thought back to Pam's story of Saks telling her that she was a "hysterical woman" when she called him to discuss continued problems in the Garden City branch.

Another company representative floated the idea that perhaps something was genetically different about women: women simply didn't have what it took, for example, to make a cold call to someone's home and interrupt a family that was gathering for dinner. Maybe women just couldn't do a job like this.

Friedman by now was boiling. "Let me get this right," she said. "A woman has to go to the office, fight off some guy grabbing her breast for five hours, and then meet production goals?" The hyperbolic question was not intended to elicit an answer, but Friedman's next question was:

"Are you trying to market to women?"

"Yes, we are," came the answer.

"Mary and I are successful professional women with money to invest," she told them. "So we would be just the type of women you would want as clients, right?"

"Yes, you are."

"Well, let me tell you something. I hate everything about you. Why would I give you my money?"[30] At this, Friedman could sense her partner, Stowell, clenching her jaw. "And I would tell my friends not to give you their money. And I would tell my family not to give you theirs, either."

The disastrous meeting broke up, and the two lawyers were escorted out to an impressive hallway with an elegant spread of food laid out for lunch. Then, as quickly as their hosts had walked them there, the contingent from Smith Barney and The Travelers vanished, leaving Stowell and Friedman to dine alone. No one from the company reappeared for another hour and a half, at which time it was mutually decided that the meeting was over. They were on a plane back to Chicago by 2 P.M.

On the flight back they derived one encouraging insight from their bristly meeting. "They can never go to court and say all that out loud," said Friedman. The argument that women were somehow genetically programmed to be incompetent at making difficult sales calls couldn't possibly be made in court. Smith Barney either had to become enlightened or was destined to be very embarrassed over its mores. In fact, the worst case for the plaintiffs might be if Smith Barney got smart about women's issues, legal issues, and image issues all at the same time. The worst case for Friedman might be if Smith Barney were to call her, or selected clients, on certain impassioned, off-the-cuff accusations. No one, of course, had their breast grabbed at for five hours. But some plaintiffs were sloppy in their recollection of events, potentially damaging their credibility.

The plaintiffs would have other obstacles should they ever get to court, and their adversary Belnick knew those obstacles well. They would have to prove a pervasive pattern of discrimination—no easy task in the cold light of judicial scrutiny. They also would have to show that any gender imbalances were caused by discrimination. Arbitrators had a reputation for bias, but judges could show partiality, too. A judge could demand that the parties first pursue mediation privately in the court-room, which would mean the absence of a jury. And cases that move for-ward beyond mediation do not necessarily go to trial, because judges can dismiss them before trial, on a motion by defendants for summary judgment. Court presented risks just as arbitration did.

Here, in the Smith Barney case, Belnick would have an economist prepared to make a case to a jury that Smith Barney was restricted not only by the pool of qualified, educated women, but by the numbers of those women who wanted the jobs.[31]

THE FIRM MIGHT HAVE BEEN maladroit on matters of gender equality, but it was masterly at the art of lobbying. While Pam was on the telephone with a client at A. G. Edwards on January 21, she got an urgent message from her secretary that Kathryn Rodgers, executive director of NOW's Legal Defense and Education Fund, was calling from an airport. Pam took the call. Rodgers said she had received a call from Travelers and that the company wanted to meet with her organization to discuss the lawsuit. "I can't tell you who to meet with or not to meet with," Pam said.[32]

ON JANUARY 29 AND 30, many of the plaintiffs finally met one another for the first time at Manhattan's Westbury Hotel. The ABC News pro-gram *20/20* was interested in doing a big story on the lawsuit, and a film crew arrived the first night to begin videotaping the women telling their stories. It was a warm gathering—the first time the prospective class representatives and other plaintiffs had come together in such numbers. Indeed, the ABC News crew had hit the television-production jackpot: sixteen current and former Smith Barney employees were there, as were Stowell, Friedman, and a lawyer from PaineWebber sent to monitor the comments of four former Smith Barney brokers who had moved on to PaineWebber: Lorraine Parker, Eileen Valentino, Edna Broyles, and Patti Hanlon. One former Smith Barney office manager had traveled to the New York meeting despite nearly debilitating late-phase breast cancer; Carolyn Metzger, a class member but not a named plaintiff, had been so angered by a news article in which Smith Barney was quoted calling the Garden City accusations an "isolated incident" that she summoned up what was left of her strength to be there. The women felt awkward at first in the stark studio, layered, as they were, in more makeup and hair spray than they would ever normally wear, even for an evening out. But by the time reporter Deborah Roberts had asked two or three questions, cosmetic issues were forgotten. Only afterward, when the camera crew was packing up and the women faced each other to chat, did they realize how different they looked in their TV makeup.

Next for ABC would be picking scenes for the show, a process that would take several weeks. Meanwhile, Belnick had approached Stowell and Friedman to talk seriously about a mediation that might circumvent a court trial and appease both sides. Stowell and Friedman liked the idea, already having brainstormed about mediation with Pam and Rene Ellis, executive director of the Duke Adjudication Center. Belnick also said that he would allow two plaintiffs of Stowell and Friedman's choice to see the confidential data for purposes of the mediation. But those plaintiffs would have to sign an amendment created to go with the January 10 Letter Agreement promising not to reveal the information to anyone else. Friedman would have to persuade Pam to sign in order to see the statistics.

Pam told Friedman that she didn't feel it was worth it to assent to confidentiality over statistics of any type, given that their team already had accumulated so much information on its own: disparities in salary, disparities in training stipends, and trades done by women who weren't paid at all. Friedman replied that the data coming from Smith Barney might not even have to remain confidential.[33] Confidentiality "was only a temporary agreement until the Court can decide the issue," she wrote in an e-mail to Pam on February 5.[34] She suggested that the statistics might even be filed publicly along with the impending request for class certification—something for which Pam was pushing hard, and which Friedman was estimating would happen by the end of the month.

Pam remained emphatic about the notion of being muzzled by Smith Barney, and she e-mailed her lawyer to that effect. "I'm not at all averse to looking at stats," she wrote back on February 6. "I'm averse to signing any type of confidentiality agreement. I should not have to give up one constitutional right to gain another constitutional right—i.e., I'm not prepared to swap freedom of speech for due process." Pam also proposed $1.2 billion as an acceptable figure should Smith Barney seek to settle the lawsuit. Though Pam's intention was to pursue a jury trial, Friedman had explained to her that the judge would be looking to see if both sides had at least attempted to reach a settlement, which is what Friedman and Belnick wanted to accomplish through a mediation. A $1.2 billion award would have been unprecedented for an employment case. Pam at the time justified that amount as "viable" from a jury "listening to tales of attempted rape, assault and battery, death threats, and sexual assault."

Friedman, though, did not want to go before the judge with a record-setting demand and appear to be acting in bad faith. She also was concerned that her lead plaintiff was not willing to look at the Smith Barney statistics on a confidential basis—the only condition under which they could be seen. Friedman wanted Pam to see the data and understand the broad picture, not just the anecdotal evidence that Pam and the other women had compiled.

Although lawyers during information-gathering negotiations frequently exchange correspondence like the Letter Agreement without discussing its provisions in detail with their clients, this particular letter planted the seed for later controversy. The January 10 document alone ran three-and-a-half single-spaced pages and included an agreement by Stowell and Friedman that they would "take all lawful acts necessary or appropriate to resist response" to any court order, subpoena, notice of deposition, request for production of documents, or similar court paper asking for access to the data on the 60,000 employees.[35] Yet Pam had not even seen that Letter Agreement with all its caveats.

———

AS THE *20/20* PRODUCERS FINISHED editing their lawsuit story, Smith Barney laid on the pressure, going so far as to suggest that the show not air out of respect for the many Smith Barney employees who considered the brokerage house a wonderful place to work.[36] Belnick's blanket prohibition on talking to the media was still in force, but the firm did craft a statement for *20/20*. It said that the lawsuit amounted to "allegations and distortions of fact asserted by individuals and their counsel who have every incentive to twist the truth."[37] Attached to the letter to *20/20* were copies of Smith Barney's policies against sexual harassment and discrimination.

Belnick's guidelines placing the media off-limits didn't stop Dimon from talking to his own troops. In a "Dear Colleague" letter sent to all employees nationally on February 10, Dimon wrote of the firm's aspirations "to be a true meritocracy" regardless of gender, race, age, sexual orientation, or religion.[38] Workers photocopied the letter and passed it on to women who had been fired or had quit, as they had done with recordings of his nationwide company teleconference five months earlier.

The CEO's letter spoke of great strides that included the sexual harassment and discrimination training already provided for 7,000 employees. Networking breakfasts for women and minorities had been set up. The number of female and minority employees in the broker training program was not given but was said to have doubled in the previous year.

Dimon wrote that employees could look forward to even greater efforts at targeting women and minorities for broker jobs and management spots. His letter outlined everything from a new mentoring program to the new 800 hotline to call with employment concerns. The pièce de résistance was the addition of the highly respected Johnetta B. Cole, president of Spelman College, as a consultant on matters of diversity. From every indication, Cole was going to bring great things to their company.

A "Special Diversity Issue" of Smith Barney's internal newsletter also was coming off the press in advance of the television show. Published on the heels of Dimon's letter, it included excerpts from anonymous responses by employees who praised the brokerage firm's efforts. These unsigned testimonials included the concern of "some employees" that efforts to advance women and minorities "would reduce focus on finding the most qualified, talented individuals." A groundless fear, responded the "spotlight mailbox": "At Smith Barney, we are committed to hiring the best, most qualified candidates for each position."

Page one of the midcrisis diversity newsletter had a photograph of Cole, the new "senior diversity officer" who would be implementing aggressive programs to create a more inclusive workforce.[39] The front page also featured a large-type reference to "The new SMITH BARNEY EMPLOYEE HOTLINE" to call between 8 A.M. and 6 P.M. with any harassment concerns. The special edition included a gallery of photographs of female and minority employees.

The plaintiffs were keeping up their side of the PR battle. On February 24, Pam Martens was walking down the concourse to US Air flight 6431 at New York's LaGuardia airport just before 10 A.M. with Russ, *20/20* producer Dean Irwin, and two cameramen from the show. Linda Friedman was in Washington awaiting them for a session with Congressman Edward J. Markey, cosponsor of the antiarbitration bill. Blasting the securities business was becoming an increasingly popular sport: just before boarding the plane, Pam spotted the new *Forbes* magazine on the newsstand with a cover story about Wall Street's illicit bucket shops.[40] She bought a copy and tucked it into her briefcase alongside her copy of *Registered Representative* magazine, whose cover story was about securities price-fixing in the over-the-counter stock market. Next to that was her copy of the December 16, 1996, *BusinessWeek,* whose cover story told a stunning tale of how the mob had infiltrated Wall Street.

When their plane landed at Washington National Airport, Pam and the news crew embarked on a round of shooting what is known as "B roll" for the *20/20* segment: pictures of Pam near the Capitol Building, a long shot of the American flag wafting inspirationally in the wind above the White House. Getting the footage took longer than expected; Pam, Russ, and the news crew got stuck in traffic on the way to Markey's office.

As soon as Pam arrived, nearly an hour late for her appointment with Markey, Linda Friedman grabbed her shoulder and steered her out into the hallway. "How dare you be late for this meeting?" she asked. Friedman (who had her mother in tow for a weekend in Washington) had spent $3,000 for the trip. The least Pam could have done was show up on time. In fact, she had asked Pam to arrive a half-hour early so that she could review the law on defamation with Pam and give her suggestions on how to proceed with the meeting.

"Linda, I had no control—I was in the back seat of a car with a TV crew," Pam replied. And wasn't the whole purpose of this trip to get the news crew the footage it needed?

"You think their B-roll is more important than our meeting?" Friedman said. She was not to be mollified. It was a bad start for their first major appearance in the political spotlight.

Now the feud was pushed aside, as Jeff Duncan, Markey's legislative director, introduced himself to Pam and Russ Martens, Linda Friedman, and the news crew, and escorted the group into a reception area just outside of Markey's private chambers. They settled into a row of chairs on the right.

In the lull before her audience with the congressman, Pam spread out the three Wall Street–berating magazine covers in front of Duncan. "If there was justice, and not a secret justice system, this wouldn't be happening," she said.

That exasperated Friedman, who again buttonholed Pam. "I told you not to go into the criminal aspect of anything," she said. Was there no direction from her lawyers that Martens would follow for forty-five minutes?

Then Markey was ready for his group, radiating sound bites and a quintessential politician's charm and concern. Wall Street "is the last plantation in America," he told them. It was a high-wattage performance for an audience consisting, for the moment, of just Pam, Russ, three TV newsmen, one lawyer, and the lawyer's mom. The *20/20* people, though, had a gem of a quote and a politician who came across as genuinely angry at the notion that the men who ran the financial world could maintain a semiprivate justice system.

Pam was pleased with Markey's performance and, in fact, with the whole day's taping, notwithstanding the run-in with her lawyer. When the TV crew began to shut down the lights and pack up their gear, the rest of the group moved from Markey's office to a nearby pub, where Linda Friedman's mother took a spot next to her daughter and Pam sat across from them.

Linda and Mary are underestimating the people they're up against, Pam told Friedman's mom. Pam had to concede, though, that Linda Friedman had managed, so far, to give Wall Street a run for its substantial money.

⸻

THREE DAYS LATER, on February 27, an independent new salvo was fired in Chicago, with the legal team of Stowell and Friedman in charge there as well. In Federal District Court for the Northern District of Illinois, eight women filed a complaint of sex discrimination, retaliation, pregnancy discrimination, and fraud against Merrill Lynch & Co., the world's biggest brokerage firm. (The head of Merrill Lynch was David Komansky, who had once been assistant manager of Merrill's branch in Garden City.) The eight plaintiffs included seven former and one current Merrill Lynch broker, all of whom had read of the success of their colleagues at Smith Barney and been led to hire Linda Friedman and Mary Stowell.

In a fifty-nine-page complaint, the Merrill plaintiffs asserted that only 15 percent of Merrill's brokers were women. Of 480 "resident vice presidents," only 25 were women. Just seven of seventy-six sales managers were.[41] They sought certification as a class representing all women who worked at Merrill, just as the Smith Barney women had.

The Smith Barney suit was noteworthy for its cases of sexual harassment—an embarrassing edge that likely made Smith Barney a softer negotiator than Merrill Lynch would be. The Merrill suit went to the heart of the other critically important but less headline-grabbing issue: job discrimination.[42] It painstakingly mapped out the sometimes subtle ways in which women were left behind. In particular, the Merrill complaint described the slow demise of lead plaintiff Marybeth Cremin, who began at the Northbrook, Illinois, office in 1982 and by 1994 was producing $400,000 in annual commissions. The complaint alleged that Cremin's boss frequently commented negatively about the fact that she had children and told her that he would not consider a transfer to California that she requested unless he could assure the branch manager at the West Coast office that she had no intention of having another child. She did move to California and continued to work for Merrill.[43] Her suit described other problems that she said were gender related. For example, when other brokers were sent to financial planning seminars, Cremin alleged that she was left out.

Before the birth of Cremin's daughter Mary Claire in May 1995, her boss in Illinois said she could come back to work after the baby was born "if she could ignore that she had children and a husband," according to the court papers,[44] presumably meaning that she should perform in all ways as if she had neither. In June 1995, the Illinois manager offered Cremin a lump sum of half of her 1994 taxable income if she would transfer her $60 million–plus in assets to other brokers. When she hesitated, he offered her a permanent part-time position in exchange for giving away her accounts. Cremin accepted, turned over the business, called clients to assure them that she would still be at the office even though a new broker had their accounts, and then, the complaint said, awaited the promised first of two payments, due at the end of August 1995. On August 25, after Cremin had contacted most of her clients and transferred them to other brokers, she was terminated. The payment she was promised in August didn't arrive until November, and the amount was less than what Cremin and her manager had agreed upon.[45] Merrill countered that she was a valued member of the Chicago-area district, and that she and her managers worked over the years to structure arrangements to accommodate her changing situations.

One particularly large account, which Cremin had attempted to transfer to a female colleague whom she admired, was instead given to a male broker. Cremin claims that the colleague was bypassed because she was pregnant.[46]

Over and over in the fifty-nine-page filing, the Merrill plaintiffs cited ways in which they were kept back. The women said that they would not be assigned mentors, would not be given walk-in business, and would be denied basic support, from business cards to answering machines to secretaries. If they failed to meet production goals and cried foul at not having received equal support to the men, deadlines for production goals might be extended but greater dollar requirements would be tagged on, making it even harder to catch up. Women charged that they tended to be given accounts considered "problems," such as the elderly clients who call several times a day about their tiny holdings.

It added up, they said, to a toxic combination that undermined them at every juncture: without the support, they spent more time on clerical duties while their male peers had time for prospecting. Seeds of doubt would be sown in the minds of the customers the women did drum up: why was there no secretary, no business card, no club membership for this broker? Were the men who had those trappings perhaps more competent? Customers draw conclusions when their broker answers her own phone and the men around her appear to have full-time assistance.

Some of the Merrill women claimed in the complaint that they, like the Boom-Boom Room women, were not invited to branch golf outings where bonding and mentoring went on. Merrill paid for the club memberships of male brokers, according to the complaint, but told a Harvard graduate that they would not pay for her membership at the Harvard Club in New York, where she could have recruited and entertained clients.[47] Merrill countered that only brokers at a very high and objective standard qualify to have club membership reimbursed.[48]

Like their Smith Barney counterparts, the Merrill women faced three possibilities: settle, fight for certification as a class and win, or fight for certification as a class and lose, which would mean falling back on industry-run arbitration. Merrill, for its part, was planning to argue in court that the plaintiffs did not constitute a class that was representative of all women at the firm. The women were pushing the argument in their complaint that the problems they suffered were endemic to women at Merrill offices all over.

By this point, the stories being told by the Merrill plaintiffs were so similar to those of the plaintiffs who had come before them that one could almost imagine some global court hearing their claims. It was not only at Merrill that women said jobs were given away after pregnancy leaves. It was not only at Olde that women gathered clients only to see the accounts later redistributed to men. It was not only at Smith Barney that it was suggested that men were more entitled to jobs than women were. Had a court system existed for cases against entire industries that were violating civil rights, a lawyer would have joined the women of Merrill, Smith Barney, Olde, Rodman, and Lew Lieberbaum and called them a universal class.

The claim against Merrill documented a climate of constant reminders to the women brokers—as there had been for plaintiffs at Olde and Smith Barney—that they were subservient to their male colleagues and professionally out of their league. After an office lunch, a male broker in a San Antonio, Texas, branch said, "Let the women do their jobs and clean this up instead of being brokers," according to the suit. When one of the plaintiffs complained about that and similar statements, she was called a "man hater." Later, when she asked why she was left out of seminars that male brokers had attended, she learned that it was because she had a "rotten attitude." The women were in a trap, continually baited, sprung, and reset: Denied equal privileges, they would get frustrated and angry. If they complained, they'd be chastised for having bad attitudes.

History already suggested that this process could operate all the way up to senior levels. The New York Stock Exchange arbitration panel that ruled against Rita Reid of Goldman Sachs said that Reid's performance had declined by 1990, resulting in a pay cut. But Reid worked under a co-head of the firm who thought it acceptable to keep women off a "pitch team" if the potential new clients didn't want women pitching them.[49]

Reid admitted in her testimony that she may have told a colleague that she intended to work less in response to the cut in pay—an example, the women would say, of the kind of "bad attitude" that is bred in the cycle.[50] Apparently oblivious to any irony, the arbitrators said that Reid "admitted" that people may have found her abrasive, a quality frequently found and tolerated in successful investment bankers. On the eve of the October 1990 partnership election, Goldman had only one woman partner, the only one in the history of the firm. The arbitrators ventured no conclusion about whether that statistical aberration might be the result of discrimination, but Reid, like other women there, had only to look up at the partner ranks to see bleak possibilities and adjust her expectations accordingly.

Strain in the workplace could take a heavy toll. Nancy Thomas, who in 1983 qualified for Merrill's Executive's Club based on her high production during her first year of work, rose to become mutual funds coordinator in her New York City branch and ranked in the top ten brokers selling funds in the large Manhattan office.[51] She continued to be successful, developing an insurance class to teach Merrill brokers and increasing her production in her fourth and fifth years, enough to qualify for Merrill's President's Club. By her sixth year, Thomas was one of eighteen brokers named to Merrill's Financial Planning Advisory Board, according to the 1997 complaint. Merrill at that point had 12,000 brokers nationwide, according to the complaint.

She transferred to a branch in Atlanta, Georgia, where she was greeted with no stationery, no business cards, no sales assistant, and a computer that wasn't programmed with the standard data services that a Merrill broker needs. She returned to New York, where she was welcomed back, she heard later, largely because of a discrimination claim against her manager there, who needed to appear supportive of women.[52] Her top fifteen clients from Atlanta were doled out to male brokers in the Atlanta office, notwithstanding the desire of most of them to stay with Thomas despite the geographic distance. The Atlanta manager told customers who called looking for her that she no longer worked for Merrill Lynch, the complaint said.[53]

Back in New York, she was assigned a series of sales assistants who had been bounced by brokers who complained that they couldn't do the job. With no one competent to answer her phones on a regular basis, not even a request for a telephone answering machine would be honored: Thomas said she was told to pay the $200 cost of the machine on her own. She also learned that she would not be reimbursed for industry publications, a cost her male colleagues were permitted to submit as business expenses.

Although the crux of her grievance revolved around discrimination, Thomas said she also put up with harassment on the job. She received a package one day that included a dildo, lubricating cream, and an obscene poem. She brought it to her branch manager's attention. He suggested they wait and see whether anything happened in the future.[54] The broker who sent the package to her was later promoted to sales manager, according to the suit. (Merrill says it was unable to determine who sent the package, the contents of which it considered outrageous and inappropriate.)[55]

By the time the complaint against Merrill was filed, Thomas was suffering from stress-induced chronic fatigue syndrome that restricted her ability to work. She had visited a collection of doctors and had even attempted to recover by seeing an unconventional healer. On the day the complaint was served, she still worked at Merrill in an open bullpen typically reserved for rookie brokers with far less than her fifteen years' experience.

When news of the lawsuit became public, Merrill Lynch handled the media much the way Smith Barney had: a statement went out saying that any problems that existed were isolated in nature. A Merrill spokeswoman told Bloomberg that the firm took discrimination claims seriously and had investigated the women's complaints. "The facts do not support the claims," she said, later dispatching copies of articles in *BusinessWeek* and *Working Mother* magazines that profiled Merrill as a great place to work if you were a woman. Lead plaintiff Cremin shuddered on hearing about the media praise. Merrill's exemplary *written* policies about family leave and flextime, Cremin said, likely helped the brokerage firm score with those magazines. The policies "could be held out to the public as wonderful," she said, "but the realities inside Merrill Lynch are different."

Despite all these pressures, the Securities Industry Association, a trade group for the brokerage industry, was engaged in a last-ditch effort to explain the virtues of arbitration. In a ten-page letter to the NASD on March 11, the SIA said that arbitration provided "broad leeway" to employees to receive documents in the discovery process and was "proper, effective and useful" as a way to settle disputes. The NASD should not cave to the pressure to ban industry-run arbitration that "has served, and continues to serve, so many so well," it said. Bear Stearns, Dean Witter Reynolds, Goldman Sachs, Lehman Brothers, Merrill Lynch, Oppenheimer & Co., PaineWebber, Smith Barney, and Morgan Stanley (which had a month before said it was merging with Dean Witter) all signed the SIA's endorsement of the status quo.[56]

Two days after Smith Barney joined in signing the SIA letter, the National Organization for Women threw a punch in the other direction, naming Smith Barney its first Merchant of Shame and threatening to boycott Smith Barney retail offices. Jamie Dimon responded in part by stating publicly that his mother was a member of NOW. He wrote to Patricia Ireland, president of the National Organization for Women, on March 12, 1997, saying that she was simply parroting the views of the plaintiffs' lawyers rather than seeking out Smith Barney's side of the story. Dimon outlined changes Smith Barney had made.

In the midst of this debate, there was a hint that the system's beat cops, the arbitrators themselves, might be feeling the heat. In mid-March, a panel of American Arbitration Association arbitrators hit Smith Barney's general counsel George Saks and a company attorney junior to Saks with a $12,000 fine. The case involved a former branch manager at Smith Barney who was fired after he—by his account—took the advice of the legal department not to follow up on sexual harassment complaints. The executive, who argued that he was a scapegoat for Smith Barney's lawyers, won his case and was awarded $300,000 in all. The arbitrators noted that Smith Barney had failed on at least six occasions to produce the documents they had ordered, including the notes of a meeting with Smith Barney's former president Joseph Plumeri that resulted in the firing.[57]

In the course of hearing testimony, the arbitrators learned that an analyst who worked for investment banker John Reagan received a settlement of more than $700,000 after the analyst claimed that Reagan had asked her to sleep with him and had tied his requests to her continued employment.[58] She had made the complaint in the early 1990s, according to a transcript of the hearing.[59] (Two years after that 1996 testimony, Reagan was named a managing director at Smith Barney.) James Boshart, managing director of the capital markets division, testified at the same hearing that he was in charge of the eight-person diversity committee at Smith Barney from 1993 to 1995. Boshart reported directly to Robert Greenhill, CEO of Smith Barney. Although the firm during that time conducted training programs on how to avoid sexual harassment, the committee collected no information about complaints of sexual harassment, nor did it keep track of disciplinary actions taken against employees for harassment.[60]

Throughout the late winter of 1997, brokerage executives, politicians, and regulators declared their concerns on the issues of women's rights and mandatory arbitration. Richard R. Lindsey, director of the Division of Market Regulation at the SEC, produced a ten-page memo on March 17 in response to the letter that representatives Edward Markey, Jesse Jackson Jr., and Anna Eshoo had sent. Yet despite press reports that by then had raised serious questions about the competence and fairness of arbitrators who handled civil rights cases, Lindsey wrote, "We are aware of no systemic problem in the handling of these claims in arbitration.".

That let SEC chairman Levitt off the hook. In his official response to the politicians, he said that while they had raised an "important and difficult issue," there was "no clear answer" on the question of whether self-regulatory organizations such as NASD or the New York Stock Exchange even had jurisdiction over civil rights claims. Rather than take a stand, he left his options open, suggesting the SEC wait for a proposal to come from NASD on ways to approach the issue.

———

BY LATE WINTER, Pam had become a fixture in the Wall Street women's rights crusade. She was turning into a clearinghouse, fielding calls from women at securities firms all over the country who wanted to know how to go about filing a claim against their company. Pam in particular was viewed as a mentor to younger complainants, whom she found time to help regardless of her workload or the demands of her own lawsuit.

Linette Cinelli, one of the sales assistants who had left Lew Lieberbaum, was working as a wire operator at A. G. Edwards & Sons in Garden City—Pam's branch—by the time her lawyers had prepared a lawsuit against Lieberbaum. Just days before the suit was to be filed and a press conference held, the twenty-five-year-old Cinelli learned that her colleague Pam Martens was the Pam Martens of the famous lawsuit. She followed Pam into the ladies' room one late-winter morning. "Pam, I've got to talk to you," she whispered. Cinelli was nervous about how her new boss, their branch manager, would react to the upcoming publicity. Pam invited Cinelli and her mother to come to her house after work that night.

Over cookies and tea with her visitors, Pam told Cinelli that she was alarmed to hear that one of the lawyers on the Lieberbaum case was Thomas P. Puccio, the same trial lawyer who had represented Alex Kelly, the Darien, Connecticut, silver-spoon teenager who was convicted of raping a sixteen-year-old. Pam showed Cinelli a news clipping in which Puccio was characterized as saying that a girl fabricated a story of rape because she was Catholic, and thus "ashamed of having sex with a boy she had just met."[61] After her meeting with Pam, Cinelli approached her branch manager in a professional and direct manner about the coming press conference, preempting any unsettling surprises for her boss.

When she wasn't engaged in a one-on-one with a fellow industry employee, Pam could frequently be found with a member of the media. *Newsday* sent a photographer to her house in the weeks just before the *20/20* show aired, an opportunity Pam exploited. With the camera focused on her, she picked up a prop she had prepared for the occasion. It was a copy of the Civil Rights Procedures Protection Act—a bill now sponsored by twenty-eight members of Congress that proposed an end to mandatory arbitration of employment disputes. She held it up next to her face and got it into her newspaper photograph.

THE SECURITIES INDUSTRY was working hard to counter the onslaught of publicity that Pam and others had set off. But the action wasn't just on the corporate side. With its role in the arbitration issue under fire, NASD was hustling, too. Mary L. Schapiro, president of NASDR, the regulatory arm of NASD, on April 2 issued an invitation to nine gurus of arbitration and workplace rights to meet with her later in the month to discuss ways to address the issue of civil rights claims.[62] At the meeting, which took place on April 14, 1997, Jeffrey Liddle, a well-known plaintiffs' lawyer, blasted NASDR for allowing Stuart Bompey, the renowned defense lawyer who frequently worked for brokerage firms, to speak at training programs for arbitrators. Judith Vladeck, the lawyer who had initially represented Pam against Smith

Barney, proposed amid the back-and-forth of the meeting that there was a simple solution to address the abuses of the arbitration system: Allow hearings to be open to the press, and the shenanigans would stop under the threat of public exposure. Schapiro would later say she did not remember Vladeck's idea.

What Vladeck was suggesting could most politely be seen as rabble-rousing to anyone in the securities industry. Keeping the media out of arbitration hearings was a hard-fought goal won long ago by NASD member firms, who treated the privacy of these proceedings like a constitutional right.

———

ON APRIL 4, 1997, *20/20* aired its eighteen-minute segment on the lawsuit against Smith Barney. It was a frontal assault on Smith Barney's image. The familiar face of Hugh Downs appeared on the screen, and the avuncular newscaster asked the viewer a question: "Does this go on where you work?" he began. "Lewd comments, unwanted sexual advances, and—it's hard to believe—the boss stripping naked in plain sight?" He went on to introduce the "largest sexual harassment lawsuit ever filed against a big Wall Street firm."

The camera cut to Barbara Walters, who said a few words about aggressiveness on Wall Street and sexual harassment. She introduced reporter Deborah Roberts, and the camera panned across three rows of women sitting in bleacher seats on a television set. They were well-dressed, attractive, articulate. These were not the hysterical kooks that companies frequently describe in sex harassment cases—the would-be scammers out to shake down a deep-pocketed corporation. They were intelligent and well-spoken, hailing from Smith Barney branches all over the United States, yet telling stories that were remarkably similar. Most had never met one another before they had assembled for the taping.

What they said was chilling.

"It went to the point that he would follow me outside, rub my shoulders, rub up against me at the copy machine," said one. "He would just—I couldn't work. I would sit there at my desk and cry because I had no recourse."

"He said that he wanted to pull my stockings down and sit me on his lap," said another. "And that was the—that would be the greatest thing. He got an erection, showed me."

"Somehow, he got behind me, and I was up, like, against this wall, I was trying to get free from him," said a third woman. "He was actually lifting up the back of my skirt. It was like a Spandexy-type skirt, and so he was lifting up the back of it, and somebody came in the front door. I heard the front door move. And I was just kinda like, Oh, thank God." She reported the incident to a female manager, who patted her on the leg and said, "It's OK, you're doing a good job here."

Smith Barney had sent 20/20 a letter objecting that "from everything we have seen and heard," it was apparent that the program would present only the women's side. "ABC is intending to broadcast a portrait of Smith Barney that is based on allegations and distortions of fact asserted by individuals and their counsel who have every incentive to twist the truth—because they are seeking millions of dollars from Smith Barney in litigation and they evidently believe there is value to them in waging a misinformation campaign," the letter read.

Yet Smith Barney declined to correct that ostensible distortion and misinformation by participating in the interview process. The show aired with little defense by the defense.

It was a new low for the company and the industry. The floodgates seemed to have opened. On April 28, Linette Cinelli and the three other women from Lew Lieberbaum & Co. filed their lawsuit. Lieberbaum already had four censures by the NASD, charges by regulators in Florida, Colorado, and Connecticut, and a quarter-million-dollar ruling against it by a panel of NASD arbitrators—and the firm was only seven years old.[63] Yet the sexual harassment charges, including in-office strip acts and ambiguous rape threats, were proving far more explosive than the existing regulatory problems.

A week after the Lieberbaum women sued, Gruntal & Co., a medium-sized New York–based broker-dealer and investment bank, without admitting liability signed a consent decree with the EEOC concerning six women who had reported similar abuse.[64] The women said that the two branch managers in the firm's Madison Avenue office touched them on the breasts and buttocks and between the legs and repeatedly asked them for sex.

On July 10, the EEOC put out a policy statement opposing mandatory arbitration. Something significant had changed. A taboo was lifting.

Chapter Thirteen

Martens without Martens

A broker told me he would masturbate in the bathroom at home and think of me, and that his wife came in and caught him once.

—MICHELLE, A SALES ASSISTANT WHO STARTED AT A SMALL FIRM
IN 1994

AFTER THE 20/20 AIRING, there began a gradual metamorphosis, from Smith Barney as defensive target to Smith Barney as confident adversary. The TV exposé, with its bruises to the company's brand name, had been a bottoming out as far as its reputation was concerned.

After so many years of keeping most sex suits quiet, none of the financial firms had much experience with the sort of grass-roots public relations battle they were now facing. Ugly news coverage of inside traders or rotten-to-the-core stockbrokers was embarrassing but rarely had the staying power of sex complaints. This was a story that literally had legs. Moreover, none of the firms anticipated the domino effect that took over as women heard about the plights of others similarly situated and grew bolder. To anyone who appreciated how threatening a giant brokerage firm could look to an employee, the confidence that had built among women with stories to tell was remarkable. Those who had suffered in silence, or striven to be one of the boys, were talking—first among themselves and now to the media.

Smith Barney would have to get ahead of the story. Crazy as it might sound, if they got really lucky, they could even wind up looking like heroes.

The first order of business was to learn from its public relations mistakes. Management saw that its resistance to produce documents the previous fall had worked against them: The compromise that was reached—the fresh e-mail survey of operations managers—had brought to light 270 harassment and discrimination claims. Calling a complaint by three women an "isolated" incident had similarly worked against them, because Friedman and Stowell simply countered by filing their juicier amended complaint that added twenty new plaintiffs. Frat-house behavior at an esteemed white-shoe firm was right back in the news, and this time, the news was that such things happened at branches all over.

As Smith Barney began the shift from defense to offense, there was a sense that someone had taken command of its swelling platoon of public relations people. Michael Schlein was put in charge of getting Jamie Dimon's word out to the press. Schlein, the former right-hand assistant to Arthur Levitt, the SEC chairman, was a natural in understanding the ways of the media, assisting reporters on a background basis that kept his name out of the paper while still giving him a shot at influencing coverage of the scandal. Robert Connor, the longtime Smith Barney spokesman who had called the initial charges "lurid," had retired. Arda Nazerian, a well-thought-of spokeswoman hired from the American Stock Exchange, began to play more of a role. Belnick, meanwhile, was talking to reporters himself.

It was, perhaps, not "an isolated incident" after all. But in a war over public perceptions, the facts can be a sideshow to strategy. Smith Barney wanted to look like a good guy, and it was going to make every legitimate effort to do so. Johnetta Cole's name was dropped by management frequently, even though company telephone operators routinely told callers that they did not have her in the directory and did not know who she was.[1] In March 1997, she had been described in the in-house magazine as a new officer of the company.

During its shift out of defensive posture, the new Smith Barney also became a Friend of Women. Print advertisements painted a Smith

Barney that loved women and cherished families. One magazine ad showed a Norman Rockwell–style assemblage in which mom, dad, son, and two puppies were smiling and embracing. For a free copy of "Empowering the Young Investor," the family-friendly Smith Barney provided an 800 number beneath the photograph. No kids in the family? Smith Barney had an ad for that, too. A beaming man and wife nestled together, with the caption "She manages a career, a family and the household assets. Super woman? No, the average woman." There were television ads of kindred spirit.

After spending between $198,900 and $2.7 million a month on advertising in 1995, Smith Barney Inc. stepped up its ad efforts in print and on television during 1996, the year the lawsuit was filed. In May 1996, the month of the suit, it spent $3.6 million on advertising, more than it had spent in any month the year before, according to Competitive Media Reporting, a New York firm that tracks print, television, and other ad spending. In autumn of that year, when the amended complaint with its new allegations came out, Smith Barney upped advertising to as much as $4 million in one month. (That fall, visions of big awards were in everyone's mind because Texaco had agreed to put $176 million in a pot to settle its race discrimination claims. Mitsubishi Motor Corporation's American subsidiary was facing a lawsuit brought by the EEOC seven months earlier on behalf of more than 300 women at its Normal, Illinois, automobile assembly plant, as well as a separate suit by 10 women at the plant, who would settle for $9.5 million the following summer.)

Between March 1997 and the end of the year, monthly ad spending never dipped below seven figures and reached as much as $6 million in some months.

In tandem with the advertising, there was a blitz of seminars for women: a free program to give investment guidance to single women; symposia for mothers and daughters on the importance of establishing financial independence; and, later in the year, after The Travelers Group purchased Salomon Brothers, luncheons to raise awareness of breast cancer in the Salomon Smith Barney Women's Health Issues program.

Smith Barney couldn't sponsor events for women and minorities fast enough: there were five women-only "Career Opportunity" seminars, the 22nd annual Catalyst Awards dinner to honor businesswomen of achievement, the Black Entrepreneurship in America Conference, and "Charter Day" at Howard University, the historically African American institution. The breast cancer efforts seemed to include not just PR but real dollars: One manager sent a memo to the New York City suburban branches asking that their brokers call the women on the breast cancer guest list "to ensure their guests respond and actually come." The manager, Steve Fields, noted that women's events yielded better results than advertising.[2]

The company that once had the Reverend Jesse Jackson pounding on its door on behalf of Marianne Spraggins launched a joint venture with *Black Enterprise* magazine in which companies owned or managed by African Americans or women would be bought out by a fund sponsored in part by The Travelers Group, the brokerage firm's parent. It was formed on May 8, 1997, less than two weeks before a scheduled picketing of Smith Barney to mark the one-year anniversary of the women's lawsuit.

Pam, as always, stayed in communication with Stowell and Friedman, constantly suspicious of possible trickery by Smith Barney. She received information at one point that a sales assistant in the Garden City office had seen on a computer at work a reference that she was listed as a licensed sales associate—yet she had no license.[3] Pam suggested to Friedman that Smith Barney might be doctoring the numbers. Friedman was confident that the numbers had not been doctored, having consulted with Smith Barney on the matter.[4] Increasingly, when Pam put questions to her lawyers, they conferred with the opposition and came out considering the opposition's version more credible than hers. She was losing ground with her lawyers.

———

IN THE DAYS JUST AFTER the April 4 *20/20* show aired, Pam's phone at A. G. Edwards rang incessantly with clients telling her they had seen the blistering television piece. She had told only four of her clients in advance that *20/20* would be featuring Smith Barney in an imminent show. Two weeks after the program had aired, ninety clients had mentioned seeing it.

Mediation was increasingly a topic of discussion now. Pam was distressed, though, when Linda Friedman began to offer details about one of the players in the coming negotiations. The word was that the mediator they and Smith Barney had chosen together could be hard-nosed about presenting the realities of settlement offers. In sessions that stretched into the wee hours, plaintiffs could be reduced to tears. Pam wanted to learn more about this man, whose name was David Rotman.[5]

She somehow preserved energy for mothering and mentoring. Cinelli, her wire-operator colleague, now found herself with her name in headlines and her face on television, and Pam was giving her daily pep talks. On May 1, the manager of the A. G. Edwards & Sons Garden City branch called a meeting to remind the staff to practice the golden rule. He now had two female employees in the news as the result of their roles as litigants against Wall Street firms, and he told the staff to stick to business and to be kind to their colleagues, who were under stress. The A. G. Edwards branch manager "should be NOW's Man of the Year," Pam wrote to Friedman that night.

She also wanted to light a fire under her lawyers. They should make big demands now, Pam thought, while Smith Barney's reputation was well-tarnished. She sent an e-mail to Friedman on May 1 to persuade her that they—not Smith Barney—had the upper hand. "Linda," she wrote, "we are finally meeting critical mass and I believe, as many of our women believe, that we should take our chances and go ahead and file our petition in Federal Court." She suggested they file the petition to request certification as a class on the May 20 anniversary of the suit, capitalizing on the upcoming rally. *Ms.* magazine founder Gloria Steinem already had written a press release for it. "Apparently, Smith Barney thinks women should make money the old-fashioned way— sexually or by putting up with sexual innuendo," it said. To Pam, it looked as if everyone—Steinem, the media, her counterparts in the Merrill Lynch lawsuit, and the National Organization for Women—was in her camp. We are dealing from strength, she thought. This is the time to push for everything on our wish list. But the petition was not filed.

The focus instead was on the push to settle the lawsuit in mediation—a commitment made by both sides. Several dates in July had been penciled in for a round of mediation, and Friedman had no intention of filing a petition for certification unless the mediation failed.[6] This was a shift from fall 1996, when Friedman's partner, Mary Stowell, had written that it was the plaintiff's obligation to file the petition for certification "early in the litigation" in order to get the court's approval, and that they were working toward that end.[7]

The lawyers had embarked on, and were sticking to, a strategy of negotiation rather than Pam's preference for a fight to the bitter end in court. Although Stowell and Friedman had long expressed a philosophical desire to secure brokerage industry employees the right to fight their employers in court, they appeared to back off from that goal—by their critics' estimation—during negotiations with the Smith Barney legal team.

Had things gone Pam's way at this point and the class petition been filed, the judge would have looked at the facts in the plaintiffs' brief that supported the request for certification. The judge might then have granted them preliminary certification, which could have been withdrawn later if the judge became persuaded that the group did not represent a class of all women who worked at Smith Barney.

If the judge did certify the group as a class, he would have to define exactly who was in the class—did it include brokers, sales assistants, investment bankers?—and for what period of time—that is, when they had to have been working there. In this hypothetical pursuit of a trial, the two sides would continue their battles over discovery, demanding documents and deposing witnesses. It would have been typical in such a case for Smith Barney to make a motion for summary judgment, asking the court to dismiss the case. Only if all those hurdles were surmounted would the matter have gone to trial—an event that carries risks for plaintiffs as well as defendants, regardless of whether the defendant is a Wall Street firm or not.

To Stowell and Friedman, the obstacles in May 1997 were too numerous compared to the possibilities of mediation. They would not make the combative move of filing to certify in the middle of preparations for that mediation.

Pam, meanwhile, was elated to learn on May 19 that the Smith Barney plaintiffs had been chosen by NOW to receive its "Women of Courage" award on July 4.

ON THE MAY 20 ANNIVERSARY DATE, Pam awoke at 6 A.M. and jogged in the rain at 6:30. It was pouring by 8, by which time she, Russ, and Sean were in "Greeney," the family's latest Jeep Cherokee, en route to Manhattan with visions of the ink on her fastidiously produced posters dissolving into unintelligibility. Instead, they arrived at the rally site and saw the sun break through. Sean, who had taken the day off from school to be there, carried a poster that said "Secret Systems of Justice Have No Place in a Democracy." Now over six feet tall, with his father's sandy brown hair cropped short except for his bangs, he towered over Gloria Steinem, his mother, and the other two original plaintiffs from Garden City. His poster, which depicted a beaten-up kangaroo, was captioned "No more kangaroo courts."

Women from NOW carried signs that read "Merchant of Shame" and unfurled black umbrellas—a red umbrella was the logo of Smith Barney's parent, The Travelers—bearing the same words. Television cameras caught the rally, and print reporters came over with their notebooks out. For the cameras, the women broke into a chant. "Smith Barney, you can't hide. We know what goes on inside." The demonstration had two purposes: to commemorate the anniversary of the filing of the complaint, and to capitalize on NOW's Merchant of Shame designation two months before.

Weighing on Pam's mind was her correspondence with her own lawyers. The confidentiality issue was heating up again in her perpetual e-mail traffic with Friedman. Pam was firm: she must see a copy of what she and the other women were now being asked to sign before any mediation talks with Smith Barney.

Stowell and Friedman had scheduled a meeting to discuss settlement possibilities with nine of the plaintiffs in New York City on June 19. "Can you bring a copy of what it is we have to sign with you or e-mail me a copy," Pam wrote on June 15, four days before the New York meeting. "Linda, I am quite firm on wanting to see this agreement before I travel to Chicago [for a mediation] .... It will only make all of us look bad if SB wants an agreement that no one is willing to sign and we had not done our due diligence on this issue beforehand."

There were several things Pam didn't know. Along with a pledge to sign for anyone viewing the statistics, there now might be a second document, David Rotman's standard nondisclosure agreement for protecting mediation discussions. And the January 10 Letter Agreement that she still hadn't seen had meanwhile been shared with the outside counsel for Merrill Lynch, with whom Stowell and Friedman also were negotiating in that firm's discrimination suit. On June 9, at Friedman's request, one of Belnick's colleagues mailed a copy of the Agreement to a lawyer at Morgan, Lewis & Bockius, LLP, which was representing Merrill. The idea was to assist Merrill in coming up with a similar document in its settlement negotiations.

———

THE TWO LAWYERS, Pam, and eight other plaintiffs (Judy Mione, Roberta Thomann, Lydia Klein, Patricia Hanlon, Eileen Valentino, Beverly Trice, Lorraine Parker, and Lori Hurwitz) assembled at New York's Westbury Hotel on June 19, 1997, as planned. But Friedman did not have a copy of the confidentiality agreement. Pam asked if she had brought it, but as Pam remembers the evening, Friedman dug through her briefcase looking for it and said that she forgot.[8]

It was a tense evening for Friedman, who complained to the assistant manager of the hotel about the women's suite. She had requested a nonsmoking suite yet had been given smoking accommodations down the hall from a convention whose members, on their cigarette breaks, sent their secondhand smoke directly into the women's meeting place. Friedman already had an excruciating migraine set off by her allergies, and the hallway smokers were pushing her over the edge. It didn't help that the normally fastidious hotel also was doing renovations.

Pam—one of the smokers among the plaintiffs—grimaced as her lawyer barked into the telephone that the hotel's treatment was "outrageous" and that she had "never been treated like this."[9] Friedman complained that even an elegant replacement suite was unacceptable. Pam was befuddled. It was a perfectly charming suite, she thought. What on earth is wrong with Linda? Salad plates were served for dinner, and the nine women and their lawyers settled in for a 5:30 to 10:00 P.M. session to map out their strategy.

Linda and Pam were professional toward each other, though not as warm as before. Pam told the lawyers that they must have unanimous approval of all the "named plaintiffs"—the ones whom the judge had preliminarily approved as "class representatives"—before any settlement was reached. Friedman assured everyone that would be the case.

Mary Stowell told the group about David Rotman, the $10,000-a-day mediator whose work was so well regarded both by Stowell and Friedman and by the Smith Barney lawyers. Rotman would be an excellent choice to oversee the mediation, she said. Pam brought up the reports she had heard from Friedman herself, citing an account by

Mary, that Rotman was known to make people cry during all-night mediations. Rotman is wonderful, Pam, Stowell replied, describing the lawyer's tranquil San Francisco office with a meditation room that had water gently flowing over an assemblage of rocks. That said, they also did their best to get the message across that mediations could be wearing and that everyone should be prepared to roll up their sleeves and work hard to see if they could reach some kind of an accord.

We will not let the mediations go past 9 P.M., Friedman assured Pam. That requirement having been established, Pam mapped out three other conditions of settlement: abandoning the $1.2 billion number she had floated months earlier, she asked for a $200 million lump sum to compensate the class; abolishment of the practice of requiring employees to arbitrate civil rights cases; and a separate fund of money to launch a foundation for women in finance.

It became clear as the meeting progressed that some of the women were willing to volunteer to sign a confidentiality pledge in order to review the employee statistics. Several were weary after thirteen months of litigation; they were anxious to settle the dispute and get on with their lives. Pam and Lorraine Parker, though, hung tough on their position. It was a contest between practicality and principle. "I'm not swapping my First Amendment rights to hear a settlement offer," Pam said again. She told the assembled group that neither she nor Lorraine would attend the first mediation session, which was scheduled for July 9.

———

PAM ATTEMPTED INITIALLY to lace her immovable position on "gag orders" with amiable reminders of her admiration for her lawyers' courageous work. The job of a lead plaintiff was not an easy one; it was no coincidence that women in civil rights suits frequently hired and fired lawyers. A copy of the Rotman nondisclosure agreement had arrived—finally—on her fax machine the day after the contentious meeting.[10] Lorraine Parker, meanwhile, had received a copy of the Belnick Letter Agreement via U.S. mail the same day. Pam read Friedman's fax cover letter, which explained that the attached agreement had been sent "specifically for the upcoming *Martens et al. v. Smith Barney et al.* mediation," then read the document. Pam settled in at her home computer to compose an uncharacteristically long e-mail to Friedman.

Dear Linda,

It has become clear from our meeting in New York that you and Mary have decided that you will handle the Smith Barney case in the format that has become status quo for what is laughably considered justice in America of the 1990s. Please clearly understand that this will not be the case. Please finally come to terms with the fact that I will never let this happen. I have worked three years to build trust among the women of our group, and what occurred in New York must never happen again. I repeat, it must never happen again.

You have indicated to us that you are willing to serve as our personal attorneys in addition to representing class claims. Ethical personal representation requires that each and every woman has a right to fully read and understand any contracts that she is being asked to sign. Ethical personal representation requires that each and every woman has a right to understand what she is giving up when she signs a contract. Ethical personal representation requires that women are rested and cognizant when they agree to a settlement of their claims.

Mary's story, of a woman "lying on the floor at 4 a.m." when the mediator tells her what her claim is worth, did serious damage to your credibility. I repeat, it did serious damage to your credibility. I believe that you and Mary need to step back and look at what you are doing and why you are doing it. Up to now, you have brilliantly handled this case. Up to now, we were clearly on the road to hold the two of you up as role models for the legal profession in general and the female legal profession in particular.

Only a few months ago you promised that we would have filed our class petition for certification before a year had lapsed from our original filing. What brought on the idea of round-the-clock mediation and confidentiality orders?

I have great compassion and understanding for what you and Mary are going through. I think by now you both understand that I can be your greatest ally to achieve an honorable settlement of this case if you will only be candid with me. I am willing to use my individual claims as leverage for an honorable settlement for all. But you must come out of denial about what is going on right now. You have worked a year and a half without pay. You have listened to a pattern of stories that collectively show a growing tide of degradation of American women. You are women, this has to emotionally impact you personally. Despite working your butts off without pay, you have some women complaining about everything from the petty to the absurd. You have women laying the burden of an imminent need to find money for living expenses at your doorstep. You have women pestering your staff and tying up your ability to earn a living from other cases.

In short, you have every reason to want to see an end to this case. Every reason except the one you embarked upon when you undertook the practice of law—justice.

I think you should carefully consider the issues I have raised and evaluate if you need to bring in a big, rich law firm to assist you. Just the prospect of that might change the posture of Smith Barney. You may also want to consider seeking funds from women's foundations or legal groups. There is no disgrace in asking for help. We would all back you completely.

By pursuing the course that you are presently on, you run the risk of having 25 women hire personal attorneys to represent their personal claims to be sure that they are not negotiating from the floor in a stupor at 4:00 a.m. in the morning. Please understand that I have a tremendous stake in seeing the two of you succeed.

I understand that women cannot gain confidence in themselves without role models. If our role models sell out, one by one, the other side wins … Can you imagine the humiliation that we would bring to Patricia Ireland and NOW if we accepted their award and five days later [at the mediation] sold out to Smith Barney. Please get some rest and think carefully about what I am saying. With love and gratitude for all that you have done and every confidence that you will continue to do the right thing, Pam.

What happened after that was like a whirlwind. Lorraine Parker sent a memo to Stowell and Friedman on June 27 saying again that she would not attend the mediation sessions scheduled for July 9 and 10 in Chicago because she had not been advised on a timely basis "that our attendance at this mediation meeting was contingent upon our signing a confidentiality agreement."

Like Lorraine, Pam canceled her airline and hotel reservations and advised the other plaintiffs that they should hold out for a minimum of $200 million in any settlement in order to send "a loud and clear message to Wall Street, don't do it again."

Pam was able to shelve the discord in order to bask in the glory of the National Organization for Women's award on Independence Day. Pam and Judy Mione flew to Memphis, Tennessee, for the event at the Peabody Hotel, receiving the award from Patricia Ireland on behalf of all the named plaintiffs in the Smith Barney suit. Linda Friedman was not there for the occasion.[11] The event was by Friedman's estimation, though, a watershed that would mark the onset of rigid activism by Pam Martens. Friedman became convinced that Pam's refusal to compromise on settlement talks was linked to a sense of obligation to NOW—a feeling that if she accepted mediation she would be selling out.[12]

<hr />

FIVE DAYS LATER, on July 9, fourteen of the plaintiffs showed up for the first collective mediation in the Chicago offices of Stowell & Friedman, Ltd. Belnick; his Paul, Weiss associate, Joyce Huang; and Smith Barney's Chuck Prince were there on behalf of the firm.[13] Rotman, the high-priced go-between, was present to keep peace and streamline communications. He had not enforced his requirement for a nondisclosure document. Conspicuously absent were Pam, Judy Mione, Roberta Thomann, and Lorraine Parker.

Smith Barney was firm from the outset that the company would not settle for a large amount of money the way Texaco and Mitsubishi had. "We're not gonna wear a sign," they told Friedman.[14] In the face of that resolve, the women took a course that would surprise the outside world, considering their initial fight against closed-door hearings: they began creating the outlines of a mini-court that would hear cases only of women with claims against Smith Barney. The "court" would advance from simple mediations to more complex arbitrations in the event no settlement could be reached at mediation. No arbitration award could be lower than the last mediation offer—something the plaintiffs felt strongly about.

Stowell and Friedman ducked out for coffee at Starbucks, leaving their clients with a computer to compile a list of provisions they would insist on should they agree to end the lawsuit with neither a trial nor a lump-sum settlement. The lawyers returned less than a half-hour later to see the beginnings of a thoughtful itemization of settlement demands.

If the plaintiffs were to give up on the idea of a specific settlement amount, then there must be no cap on how much money an individual could be awarded through the private adjudication system they were starting to envision. No matter what state a woman came from, she could use the longest statute of limitations available in the country for seeking damages. All women in the retail division, including sales assistants, would qualify for the settlement.

The latter provision was no accident. Sales assistants, who were heavily represented among the named plaintiffs but who would likely have been sacrificed in a court determination of class status, held big sway in the settlement talks. There had always been a risk that the sales assistants would be tossed aside if the lawsuit came to trial because judges grant class status based, in part, on a professional group's having been precisely defined. The largely administrative functions of the sales assistants were defined, compensated, and evaluated quite differently than were the jobs of stockbrokers. While some labor lawyers speculated that a judge might have considered splitting the class into subgroups that included a group for sales assistants and a group for brokers, the complaint was not presented that way. Here at the bargaining table, the plaintiffs were telling Smith Barney that the class would include everyone.

The women's wish list included even more. There was the notion of a $30 million fund for diversity programs; the setting of goals and timetables for women in particular jobs; the abolishment of a gender-biased psychological entry exam; and the establishment of unlimited emotional-distress and punitive damages. Smith Barney was more likely to agree to such unlimited damages because of legwork the plaintiffs' lawyers had done over the previous year. Stowell and Friedman had painstakingly filed individual EEOC claims for women who came to them from what the lawyers considered good states for civil rights claims: New York, California, Michigan, and New Jersey. Those women already had the right to enter the federal lawsuit by piggybacking on the *Martens* EEOC claim. In their individual states, however, they had unique legal opportunities that Stowell and Friedman did not want to forgo. The idea was both to reserve these women's rights to go to court for their Title 7 federal claims *and* to preserve their statutes of limitations in their states, thus holding back-up claims over Smith Barney's corporate head. Smith Barney would not risk imposing a settlement likely to encourage hundreds of women to opt out and pursue separate court actions.

Stowell and Friedman had a similar ax over Smith Barney when it came to the separate lawsuit that had been filed in the Northern District of California. In that suit, too, one hundred or more women stood to benefit by opting out to exploit California law, which was uniquely favorable to Wall Street workers who had signed arbitration agreements. Thus, it behooved Smith Barney to throw the women a bone on issues like punitive damages and emotional distress in order to entice the California contingent into the settlement.[15]

As soon as Friedman and Stowell finished reading their clients' negotiation proposals, they went back to Belnick and his colleagues.

"You will be pleasantly surprised that our clients have not told you to go to hell," Friedman said.

Friedman went to sleep that night with an envelope to write on next to her bed, popping up to turn on the light all through what was left of the night. "No mental exams" she wrote at one point, concerned that the brokerage firm not be permitted to put her clients through humiliating psychological tests again. "No tests" to screen, pre-employment, for the classic male broker's personality, she wrote in another bleary-eyed scribbling in the wee hours.

———

WORD QUICKLY GOT BACK TO PAM, the self-exiled lead plaintiff, that there was serious talk about a private-mediation-then-arbitration setup. She was enraged. She thought back to the original complaint the lawyers had advised her on. Not just Smith Barney, Nicholas Cuneo, and James Dimon had been named as defendants in the *Martens* suit; it also took on the New York Stock Exchange and NASD, for their brokerage-industry arbitration systems. Count VI of the complaint discussed the U-4 form that brokers had to sign in order to get a license. The U-4 said that the employee agreed to arbitrate employment discrimination claims before the NYSE or NASD, yet the document's language made no effort to disclose to women that they were waiving any rights. Count VII said that mandatory arbitration was a violation of the Fifth Amendment to the United States Constitution, in that it denied women access to their rights to a jury trial and violated the Civil Rights Act of 1991.[16] Even the letter her lawyers had sent her two months before the initial complaint

was filed attested to their fervor about the issue. "Finally, I am enclos-
ing a recent report on arbitration results," Friedman had written. "I am
sure you will agree that our fight to stay out of arbitration is important."[17] Had no one remembered one of the core reasons they'd begun
this whole thing?

SMITH BARNEY WAS LIKING its own idea of finding some neutral third
party to resolve each woman's claims. That would take the old-boy curse
of NYSE or NASD arbitration off the proceedings. But it would still
protect Smith Barney from the courts, where juries could get carried
away with spending the defendant's money.

Day Two of the Chicago mediations got more specific about what
these individual adjudications would look like. The hearings would go in
stages, with first a written offer, then, if no agreement resulted, a one-
day mediation that would be private, and then, if there still were no
agreement, an arbitration that would be open to the media.[18] Any
woman who was savvy to the firm's public relations priorities would
know that Smith Barney would make its most munificent offer just
before the third-stage, public airing of allegations.

There would also be a presumption against depositions in the arbitrations. That meant that each side began with the proposition that there
would be no depositions. But then, if you could present a good reason
why you absolutely needed one for your case, it would be considered.

They moved on to psychological testing. The women had had it with
the tests that sought to determine how aggressive they were by probing
their interest levels in such things as motorcycle racing and football
viewing. The Smith Barney side initially argued that the test had no
problems. The women persisted. "If you're going to ask if we want to
ride a motorcycle, then we want a question that asks if you prefer natural childbirth or an epidural," one of them said. Smith Barney agreed
to end the tests.

Talk began about having Smith Barney pay some of the attorneys'
fees for the women pursuing their claims. And they made progress on
the notion of curtailing the firm's ability to probe sexual histories and
other highly personal aspects of a woman's life when she filed a claim of
emotional distress—one of the items that Friedman had written down
during her largely sleepless night.

When Pam learned what had gone on during the two-day session, she sent an angry letter on July 12 to Cliff Palefsky, Patricia Ireland, and Gloria Steinem. Each of the addressees was carefully selected for what Pam considered a white paper on a landmark case: Palefsky for his activist role as a civil rights plaintiff's lawyer; Ireland for her support of the *Martens* lawsuit and efforts to quash mandatory arbitration; and Steinem for her recent help with Pam's picketing efforts. It was signed not only by Pam but also by Lorraine Parker, Judy Mione, and Roberta Thomann, all of whom had boycotted the first mediation sessions. The letter complained that their lawyers had been pushing a confidentiality agreement in a lawsuit that had much to do with ending such agreements. It also pointed out that in Rotman's current round of mediation sessions, the sides were leaning toward a setup in which just one person would mediate each woman's claim. Even the abhorred Wall Street–run arbitrations the women were fighting allowed for three-person panels, the letter said.

Palefsky spoke with Pam Martens on the phone, and he tried to reassure her that Rotman, the mediator, was a respected and impartial person to handle the job. He also tried to get her to understand that no company would allow confidential employee statistics to be viewed by plaintiffs in a lawsuit without first obtaining confidentiality promises. This was not a conspiracy, he told her. The request is standard operating procedure. Pam, though, wouldn't buy it.[19]

Patricia Ireland came to New York to meet with Pam, Lorraine, Roberta, and Judy before the second set of collective mediation sessions began on July 26. Ireland encouraged the women to attend the mediation. "No way in hell," said Pam, who showed Ireland what she referred to as the "gag orders" that the women had been asked to sign. Ireland was not able to persuade Pam or Judy, but Lorraine and Roberta came around to seeing virtue in participating in the mediations.

In a letter Pam sent to Linda Friedman on July 20, no traces of cordiality remained. "The fact that the plaintiffs in the Smith Barney suit were not properly counseled in advance regarding the contract of adhesion imposed by the mediator" was to the women's detriment, she began. Pam was referring to the faxed copy of Rotman's preprinted nondisclosure agreement which she had received in June. Her letter ended with a curt demand for copies of all correspondence between the Chicago lawyers and Smith Barney. It was an affrontive step, signaling plainly that she thought her attorneys had gotten too cozy with the New York defense team.

She was inadvertently promoting just such an alliance between the opposing legal teams—an alliance to defend the developing settlement against her vehement protests. So much work had been done by both the plaintiffs and defendants by midsummer that neither side appreciated Pam Martens's seemingly mutinous objections to their proposals. They'd all worked very hard to create the skeleton of a settlement. They were not about to let even the lead plaintiff destroy it.

The second round of the Rotman mediations, on July 26 and 27, was attended by fifteen women—one more than the previous session. Lorraine Parker had decided to give the settlement talks a chance. Women were getting revved up over the dangling prospect of big-money awards, but in reality there would not be the big media splash that a nine-figure sum would attract, so the story would have to be carefully spun in order for this to look like a win for the plaintiffs. Still, maybe settling would be a victory. Court, after all, was no sure shot. If they had tried and failed to be certified as a class, they would have been bounced back to Wall Street–operated arbitration. Thus, to be feisty and insist on trying the case in court would be a big risk. Four of the fifteen named plaintiffs at the mediation came from sales assistant and operations jobs, giving voice to the administrative contingent. In court, that group was at risk of being sliced out, but in mediation the group could define itself as it wished.

So the negotiations kept going. The women agreed to drop the separate—and key—lawsuit against Smith Barney that had been brought in California. In agreeing to merge the California case with the *Martens* case, they gave Smith Barney a plum. In exchange, the plaintiffs got the prospect of unlimited emotional distress and punitive damages in the upcoming individual mediations and arbitrations. They held onto the provision that said an arbitration decision could be no lower than the last offer in a failed mediation.

Most were elated over the diversity programs to be set up under the agreement, including quotas that Smith Barney would have to meet in hiring women for broker jobs and management spots. They agreed to $15 million for the program, after having initially asked for $30 million. Even Belnick and others on the Smith Barney team were genuinely happy about this aspect of the proposed deal. When a defense lawyer is able to back an idea that costs relatively little but works toward a commendable goal, it can be a rare moment of personal reward in a sometimes ruthless job. In that light, the opposition truly did have a commonality of interest with Stowell and Friedman.

There was another practical plus for the plaintiffs. While there was a clear downside to replacing one arbitration system with another, the very act of settling a high-profile suit and setting up a process for dispute resolution was likely to embolden more women to come forward. Had there been a big but finite fund, the way there was in the Texaco case, it arguably could have worked as a disincentive for current plaintiffs to encourage others to come forward. This way, there was no reason not to rally more complaints, because a larger group of claimants would not mean smaller pieces of the pie.

The euphoria of this honeymoon, though, did not touch Pam Martens. Lorraine Parker tracked Pam down on vacation with Russ and Sean at the Pridwin Hotel on Shelter Island in New York and told her the terms of the rough settlement that had been worked out as of July 28. No end to mandatory arbitration? asked Pam. No, said Lorraine. No lump-sum settlement? No, no lump sum, Lorraine conceded. No fund for women? No, but we have $15 million toward a diversity program at Smith Barney. "It's a wonderful settlement," Lorraine said, wishing her former colleague would give it a chance.

"I'm going to the press," said Pam.

Lorraine stayed calm. "But it's a wonderful settlement—"

"I will expose this as a fraud," Pam told her bluntly.

"Can I make you change your mind?"

"This is fraud," Pam said again, and their conversation was over.

She sounds like a cult follower, Pam thought as she hung up. Wonderful settlement. Wonderful, wonderful. They've forgotten why we went through all this hell in the first place.

━━━━

PAM WROTE TO EDWARD MARKEY five days later, telling the congressman that a tiny Chicago law firm had caved to Smith Barney's demands.[20] She attached the letter complaining about confidentiality agreements and arbitration, dated July 12, that also had been signed by Parker, Mione, and Thomann. On learning August 7 that Pam had included a copy of the three-week-old letter in her package to Markey,

Parker wrote to Pam that she considered it a breach of confidentiality for Pam to circulate the outdated correspondence.

"You have my blessing to continue on your personal crusade to have vindictive victory against Smith Barney and your aggressors," Parker wrote. But although in the past she had allowed Pam to speak and write on her behalf regarding the lawsuit, "this no longer prevails," she added. "I would like to add that I am extremely saddened by the fact that you have acted in this manner." Parker also sent a letter to Markey telling him that Pam was not authorized to send copies of her correspondence and that Parker had been "guilty of pure ignorance" in previously questioning her lawyers. "I feel terribly embarrassed that I acted in such an arrogant manner," she told the congressman.

As Lorraine was writing her letters to Pam and to Markey, plaintiff Bette Laswell of Tucson, Arizona, was trying to bring Pam around to seeing the mediations the way the majority did. By bringing Smith Barney to the negotiating table at all, Laswell wrote, Pam had already won. "I look forward to welcoming you back to the team," her letter said.

But Pam had no intention of rejoining a team whose judgment she so questioned. Instead, she complained more vociferously to politicians and to the press.

BY MID-AUGUST, Stowell and Friedman had had enough. They wrote to the U.S. District Court in New York to say that they no longer wished to represent Pamela Martens in the lawsuit against Smith Barney. Their brief court filing simply cited irreconcilable differences. It did not detail what Linda Friedman felt: that she could not represent Pam because Pam had crossed the line between privately challenging the settlement (such as it was, in its formative state) and lodging public barbs. Friedman said that once Pam began her public criticisms, it put Stowell and Friedman in the position of representing diverse parties in the litigation—a violation of legal ethics.

On September 10, 1997, the judge gave the Chicago lawyers permission to drop Pam as a client. In a letter September 11, they informed Pam of the judge's decision.

The lawsuit of *Martens et al. v. Smith Barney et al.* would proceed with the lawyers representing all the named plaintiffs except Pam Martens.

Chapter Fourteen

Settling the Settlement

> *The men in the office got away with* Playboys, *strippers, comments, jokes, touching, wearing glasses with penises hanging from the center. One of the girls in the office got slapped by a broker. She was fired and the witnesses forced out.*

> —A WOMAN WHO LOST A CIVIL RIGHTS ARBITRATION AGAINST E. F. HUTTON, A FIRM THAT WAS ACQUIRED BY SHEARSON

IN THE FINAL WEEKS of polishing the settlement document for presentation to a judge, what had been a case against a brokerage firm seemed to evolve into a case of the brokerage firm and the plaintiffs' lawyers versus the lead plaintiff.

Stowell and Friedman went out of their way not to allow duplicates of the work-in-progress out of their hands. To release even one would inevitably lead to a copy in Pam's possession, they figured,[1] and that could only mean more criticism. Thus the women bringing the action received no document that they could take home and mull over as the settlement language—and indeed its substance—began to move through several versions.

Pam sought out reporters, saying that the group was going along with a settlement they weren't being allowed to examine in its entirety: Stowell and Friedman had abandoned their battle to stamp out mandatory arbitration, she said when she got the ear of the media.[2] The lawyers indeed had sounded more militant in the past. As recently as July 1997, *Registered Representative* had quoted Linda Friedman saying, "I can't imagine that the Smith Barney or Merrill Lynch plaintiffs would resolve their claims" without insisting on some provision to address the way the arbitration issue was handled in the future. Friedman had been quoted in a *Wall Street Journal* story on May 14, 1997, speculating that a jury award or settlement could be worth more than $100,000 per class member, and that the amount paid by Smith Barney could top the $176 million paid by Texaco. Such comments had the tone of a lawyer set for a court fight, or at least for some combative negotiations.

Yet she and her partner were now putting the finishing touches on a deal that had no promise of removing mandatory arbitration for *any* employees—past, present or future. Not even a morsel of a future commitment for a potential change at Smith Barney bore fruit: At the Chicago mediations in July, the firm's general counsel, Chuck Prince, had left Friedman with the impression that he intended to honor any philosophical shift by NASD's regulatory arm on the issue, but he and his team refused to commit to that in writing.[3]

Friedman and Stowell pooh-poohed Pam's contention that they were selling out, saying that they had long been fighting the arbitration battle and that Pam was a newcomer to the subject. They defended their stance as an exercise in fiduciary responsibility: the arbitration issue was a deal breaker for Smith Barney, and they didn't want their clients to wind up with no settlement, then have a court decline to certify them as a class. Neither lawyer saw herself obligated above all else to quash mandatory arbitration; their focus was on the aspects of the settlement that addressed discrimination—a more direct attack on the problem, they thought. Besides, separate claims in the *Martens* suit challenging arbitration were still outstanding against the New York Stock Exchange and National Association of Securities Dealers Inc. Stowell and Friedman were working with other clients who would be filing separate charges against Smith Barney. So the lawyers knew that they would be facing off with the firm again on the arbitration debate.

Discourse reached ever-lower lows. Friedman referred to Pam as a "footnote" in the story at one point:[4] At another, she said that a book about Wall Street women's rights would best be written without mention of Martens.[5] Pam, in the meantime, continued to be openly critical of the settlement. They brought others to the dispute: Patricia Ireland, the president of NOW, came out in favor of the settlement, but the New York State and New York City NOW branches supported Pam.

As an increasing number of lawyers, plaintiffs, and defendants got involved in passing information about who might be doing whom in, gossip could carom around the country in a single morning, resulting in anger, hurt feelings, and ultimately a long telephone call from Friedman, who sometimes spent hours defending the settlement to a skeptical plaintiff.

With these same two lawyers also suing Merrill Lynch, and women from both actions confiding in one another, a corresponding atmosphere began to pervade the Merrill Lynch group. One plaintiff mockingly accused two women involved with her lawsuit of "a lesbian relationship" and said that they were jealous of her beauty. When plaintiffs disagreed, conversation quickly degenerated to the petty.

Players in both contingents claimed special knowledge of various reporters' motives, opinions, and future stories. The barbs traded between the camps made it tough for the press covering the story, says Patrick McGeehan, who wrote about both lawsuits for the *Wall Street Journal*. "It was difficult for me all along," he said. "It seemed that all the players in this wood were capable of personal attacks. It often felt like I was refereeing a schoolyard battle."

Friedman declared on October 27, 1997, that she was no longer talking to McGeehan.[6] Several Merrill plaintiffs were angry that those on the Smith Barney side were getting more media attention. Telephone calls to the two lawyers from clients now ranged beyond questions about harassment, discrimination, and legal rights. There were inquiries about press conferences, television appearances, and reporters' points of view about the case. Stowell and Friedman themselves were no strangers to media games: they would be posing for dozens of photos for *People* magazine in the months ahead and were letting reporters know when they didn't like the tone of their questions.

Dan Jamieson, editor in chief of *Registered Representative* magazine, said that he received a letter from Stowell and Friedman asserting that one of his reporters, Rosalyn Retkwa, had meddled in the Merrill Lynch lawsuit. "They alleged that my reporter had provided a phone number of Pam Martens to a Merrill Lynch class representative," said Jamieson. He said the lawyers made the claim, without offering any evidence, "that her techniques crossed the line from investigative techniques to 'tortious interference.'" (A person committing "tortious interference," in legalspeak, is one who wrongfully interferes in another's business affairs.) The reporter was sufficiently rattled that she asked to be taken off the story. "I've never had that sort of experience" as an editor, said Jamieson, a journalist for sixteen years. His reporter was "really spooked" by Stowell and Friedman.[7]

McGeehan of the *Wall Street Journal* says that while he never received a direct threat of a lawsuit from Stowell or Friedman, "they raised the specter of 'tortious interference' in conversation with me"—an implicit threat to sue, in McGeehan's estimation. They were quick on the trigger when criticized, says McGeehan. "We're talking about lawyers who took offense quite easily."

By the five-week mark after Stowell and Friedman's September 11 letter dropping Pam, visions of big settlements were in many women's minds.[8] Amid this celebratory environment Friedman wrote on October 16 to all the plaintiffs to applaud one of their number, Edna Broyles, who had just been designated Woman of the Year by the 70,000-member Business and Professional Women's Association. The image set forth by the laudatory communiqué was that of one big happy family among the cooperating plaintiffs.

No one who had labored at the long mediation sessions and subsequent grunt work to finalize the text of the agreement was interested in having potshots thrown at what they'd achieved, compromised though it might have been. Friedman began to depict Pam as uninformed on the facts of the current mediations and on the settlement-in-progress and thus unqualified to issue an opinion on either.

Friedman and her partner by now had made it to the inner ring of regulars on the Wall Street employment lawyers' circuit. When a panel of civil rights attorneys was put together in late October to discuss the developing controversy over arbitration, Friedman was among the dignitaries invited to speak at the downtown headquarters of Merrill Lynch & Co. (Merrill provided the space; the gathering itself was sponsored by the American Bar Association.) She awoke on the morning of the event in her room at New York's Plaza Hotel and dressed in a black-and-taupe silk outfit that was notches above the humbler attire she had worn in the days when she fought for the Olde women. As she took a taxi south from 59th Street toward Merrill's headquarters in the financial district, she considered how difficult Pam was. She recalled that Roberta Thomann, not Pam, had been the first to call her firm. In earlier days she had credited Pam with making the introduction, perhaps because it was Pam who directed Roberta to call. Back then, they'd worked together and supported one another. Those days were gone now.

———

BY MIDNIGHT NOVEMBER 17, the pieces were in place. The U.S. District Court would be hearing the settlement proposal in the morning. It would not be a hearing for the judge to approve or disapprove the deal that the two sides had worked out. Rather, the proposal simply would be publicly presented to the judge, who would have an opportunity to ask questions of the architects of the plan. A few journalists had been leaked its terms. Press releases had been prepared, framing Smith Barney and the plaintiffs as being in pursuit of the same philosophical goals. In a carefully worked out deal, both sides had agreed on how they would handle the money issue: Smith Barney would not crow over the fact that it had not been required to cough up a specific pot of cash (instead, there would be the one-by-one mediations or arbitrations), and the women would not float estimates of what the firm might wind up spending under the special dispute resolution system that had been created.[9]

The first piece of the plan soon went awry.

Fax machines were whirring at news organizations around the United States just after midnight as publicists for Stowell and Friedman began selectively distributing a press release. In the early hours of November 18, though, Friedman got wind that a representative of Smith Barney was already boasting to reporters that they "didn't have to pay a penny." All bets were off, Friedman told herself. The next reporter who reached her was John Schmeltzer of the *Chicago Tribune*. Livid with Smith Barney for breaking the pact, she abandoned it, too, speculating to Schmeltzer that the settlement would cost Smith Barney more than $115 million. He reported that number and quoted Friedman as saying that victims in the Texaco settlement received $40,000 to $60,000 on average, and that that was not enough for her clients, who would have unlimited punitive damages and emotional distress damages available to them.

The press release from the brokerage firm later that morning was remarkable for what it did not include. The headline read "Landmark Settlement of Class Action Suit Against Smith Barney Reached." Reality was that not only would there be no pool of money and no relief from compulsory arbitration for employees left behind at the brokerage firm, but the settlement's dispute resolution system was in some ways more advantageous to Smith Barney than Wall Street's standard process.

In the existing system of resolving disputes with NASD or NYSE, it's likely that a much higher percentage of cases would actually have made it to be heard by an arbitration panel. That would have meant more cases whose final terms would have been made public. Although that outcome would not have been as negative for Smith Barney as having all the cases go to trial, it would have involved some of the same downsides of trials. At the very least, the plaintiffs could have collected the results of arbitration proceedings to show how various branches, branch managers, or brokers had fared when charges were brought against them. With that data, they could have begun to suggest the sorts of patterns that litigants need to persuade a jury that discrimination or harassment is pervasive.

In the settlement, though, Smith Barney wound up avoiding the worst of what happens at trial while still enjoying a courtlike benefit: it would receive the claims of nearly 2,000 women at once and get the chance to determine patterns and weaknesses for itself before making initial offers to claimants. Thus, it would know exactly where it would be most advantageous to settle most generously at an early stage, while still avoiding the exposure of a quasi-public arbitration. In the existing arbitration system, Smith Barney would never have had the opportunity to pre-examine so many cases at once—a key benefit considering that, in many cases, several women in a branch had complained about the same harasser. Not only that, but because the two sides ultimately agreed that Stowell and Friedman would deliver all the claims to Smith Barney at once, the firm in one fell swoop got a good idea of who the central witnesses might be, since women in the same office filing against the same man would be likely to help one another.

Smith Barney would be motivated to settle credible cases either in the first stage, via written exchanges, or in the second stage, a one-day mediation, both of which carried confidentiality clauses. The firm would be able to dispose of the most embarrassing cases before negotiations reached the third stage, an arbitration proceeding that could lead to negative publicity. The signing of confidentiality clauses in stages one and two would also benefit Smith Barney by minimizing available witnesses.

At settlement time, Smith Barney in its official statement said that this system was better than a fixed settlement fund because it placed no limits on the amount of money a woman might be awarded. If they were worried about how much money they might have to pay out, though, Smith Barney and its various parent companies never let on. Publicly held companies have obligations to warn shareholders about extraordinary events that might drain earnings or large expenditures that would require putting money in reserve. From the point of view of what accountants and securities lawyers call material information—in this case, the possibility of unexpected costs of mediations—nothing had occurred. The cost of the dispute resolution process wouldn't even merit a footnote in the next Smith Barney annual report.

Pam's dream of a foundation for women found no place in the press release, either. Smith Barney did list as its top item that Johnetta Cole "will have an enhanced role," further raising expectations that Cole would be high-profile. And Smith Barney would spend $15 million on its own in-house diversity programs to encourage employment of women and other minorities. Among the directors of the program was Robin Leopold, one of the human resources officials who had disappointed the Garden City employees when they turned to management for help. When Pam learned that Leopold was among the new inclusivity czars, she hit the phones to express her disgust to reporters.

————

WINTER WAS IN THE AIR on the morning of the settlement announcement. The temperature dipped below freezing in New York City, and the plaintiffs who came to watch their lawyers present the conciliation plans to the judge were dressed for the cold. The doors to the courtroom opened at 9:50 A.M.

Presiding would be Constance Baker Motley. She was one of eleven female federal judges among the forty-four in the Southern District of New York, and one of only three African Americans. At seventy-six, she had spent thirty-one years on the bench. Motley got her law degree from Columbia University in 1946 and passed the bar in 1948. She spent twenty years as a lawyer for the NAACP Legal Defense and Educational Fund before running for and winning a race for New York state senator in 1964.

In the first rows of seats, clustered on the right, the gathering plaintiffs looked more like habitués of a fur salon than spectators at a federal court. Stowell and Friedman could be thankful that no one would be occupying the jury seats at this hearing. With the exception of Roberta Thomann, who had given up on Wall Street and was working at her local Catholic archdiocese, the plaintiffs wore designer suits under their fur coats. Beverly Trice, with coiffed red hair and exquisite jewelry, could have stepped off a page of *Town and Country* magazine in her St. John ensemble. She had laryngitis from two nights of making telephone calls to rally support for a foundation for women that she was trying to start. One of the other plaintiffs showed an associate a new purse she had picked up on a recent trip to Spain. In fact, she had bought two, a beige and a gray.

The scene was reminiscent of a divorce hearing, with Pam, Russ, and Judy Mione seated by themselves across the aisle, on the left. Plaintiffs blessing the settlement were all on the right. Friedman, in the minutes before the judge arrived, made several circuits between her chair at the front in the lawyers' section and her clients sitting in the audience behind her.

At 10:26, the clerk called out "All rise." Judge Motley, bespectacled with short black hair, stepped from her chambers to the left of the courtroom. With the judge in her seat, the room was hushed. Pam presented herself without being called on, but Motley stopped her immediately. "We didn't sever you at the last pretrial?" the judge asked, referring to an October 9 conference with lawyers for both sides in which she had reviewed an array of issues, including an agreement in principle to settle and the desire of Stowell and Friedman to dismiss Pam as a client.

"I am still the lead plaintiff in the suit," Pam told the judge, explaining that Stowell and Friedman had merely dumped her as a client. Linda Friedman, however, was already at the podium.

"Your honor," she began, "it is with great pleasure—" But the judge interrupted her, too. She wanted to dispose of Pam's request for five minutes to speak about the legality of the settlement. The class members can challenge the fairness of the settlement later, the judge said. This is not a hearing on fairness.

Thus by 10:31, Judge Motley had sidelined Pam and given the floor to Friedman to describe the accord with Smith Barney. Friedman spoke of the settlement as an "impetus for change" on Wall Street and alluded to the significant presence of Johnetta Cole as a player at Smith Barney. Amid the excitement of having a settlement—and perhaps stemming from her fatigue at finally having gotten there—Friedman spoke so rapidly that the judge had to ask her to slow down a bit. The settlement heralded real change, Friedman continued, ticking off target dates by which Smith Barney would have to have certain percentages of women in its professional workforce and boost the numbers of women in management spots. If the settlement was implemented, Smith Barney would be a model for Wall Street.

Friedman told the judge that the twenty-three named plaintiffs expected to divide $2.05 million to compensate them for their service as class representatives. This was not settlement money but what is known in class-action litigation as incentive, or "bonus," money. Courts award such payments for everything from the outlays these plaintiffs make for their trips to lawyers to their time off work to make their case to the media, politicians, and the public. Friedman was proposing that the twenty-three be paid from $20,000 to $150,000 apiece depending on the work they had done. This would be separate from any money they might get in a mediation.

Lawyers' fees were not part of her presentation to the judge. Friedman's firm, when all was said and done, would be paid $12 million by Smith Barney—a figure that loomed large in a case where the size of the settlement was a blank slate to be filled in later. Fees had not been discussed with Smith Barney until the night before the hearing.[10]

Friedman finished her introduction to the settlement and gave the podium to Mark Belnick, representing Smith Barney. Belnick had a commanding voice, and in his pinstriped suit he looked and acted the part of the confident corporate lawyer.

"This is not rhetoric," he said. Smith Barney was to be a leader in the industry. It would set a "new standard" for women professionals. Belnick, the rough-and-tumble litigator who had been on call for Michael Milken, was projecting a statesmanlike tone in the courtroom, noting even that Smith Barney's nemesis, Pamela Martens—he motioned in her direction—would have the opportunity to object at the fairness hearing.[11]

Lawyers for the New York Stock Exchange and the NASD stood to discuss their respective motions to dismiss the remaining counts against them in *Martens et al.*

Pam stood and addressed the court yet again.

"We have been denied a copy of the final settlement document," she said.

"We have no problem," Friedman told the judge, surprising those in the room who knew how contentious things had gotten when Pam had tried to obtain a written version of the settlement. Friedman meant that she would be willing to give Martens a copy of the settlement later.

Court was dismissed. Now that Motley had been presented with the terms of the proposed deal, the combative groups would not meet again until they debated the pros and cons of the settlement on April 9, 1998, the date of the fairness hearing.

The crowd filed back out into the frigid fall air to reconvene as a court of public opinion. Belnick held an audience with reporters, making a case that there was no systemwide problem at Smith Barney. He calmly deflected hostile questions. Although it is often part of the game that defendants who settle get to state officially that they did not admit to the accusations, even though they're making huge concessions, Smith Barney went a step further: the firm actually denied the allegations. Parity, though, was ultimately in the eye of the beholder. The industry at large employed 16 percent women. Smith Barney so far had only 10 percent to 12 percent women on its payroll.

As Belnick held his impromptu press conference outside the courthouse, Stowell, Friedman, and fourteen of their clients were traveling to the financial district. They were using the services of The Dilenschneider Group, a New York-based public relations company. Dilenschneider's Chicago office had coordinated a press conference to be held in the third-floor Hudson Room of the Marriott World Trade Center, and the women who filed in encountered a setup of press kits, microphones, and well-prepared public relations people. It was the big-time for brokers and sales assistants who got no respect at the company picnic. Several hundred reporters, photographers, and sound technicians packed the room, many of them elbowing to get a choicer spot or a better angle. Stowell and Friedman opened the session to questions, and reporters continued to file in even after that. Cameras flashed and video was rolling. The plaintiffs were lined up behind a lectern that bristled with monogrammed television microphones. CNN. CNBC. Bloomberg. NBC. Almost immediately they were answering questions with words like "landmark" and "fantastic" as publicists moved through the crush taking down names of reporters and passing out the press kits. Smith Barney has turned itself around, they were saying. It will be a leader in the industry. It is sincere.

Honest, it's changed.

They eyed each other nervously on being told by reporters that Belnick had just said, outside the courthouse, that there was no systemic discrimination at the firm. Mary Stowell declared that "women in the securities industry should not be satisfied that they can't go to court," leaving a long distance between her stated goal and the outcome of this particular settlement. Then NOW president Patricia Ireland took the podium. "We're very pleased Smith Barney will no longer be doing business the old-fashioned way," she said. In fact, Smith Barney already had made progress toward some of the settlement's gender targets.

Stowell spoke a second time, keeping the fourteen women lined up in back of her. This *was* a landmark case, she said. Some plaintiffs bowed their heads as if in prayer and closed their eyes. They had worked hard and won some important coups through the settlement. The dispute resolution system would be up and running within two years, Stowell told the media. It was her hope that by then, mandatory arbitration "will be a thing of the past."

THE NEXT FIVE MONTHS were marked by posturing and politicking in various camps. Proponents labored furiously to protect the deal they had created. Wall Street policy makers meanwhile fretted over the potential loss of their ability to force arbitration on employees. And at Merrill Lynch, the pending final settlement of the Smith Barney suit meant additional pressure to settle. Merrill was in serious negotiations with Stowell and Friedman in hopes that its suit could be ended as well.

Amid all the action on Wall Street and on Capitol Hill, Pam was planning to expose as many warts as she could find in the settlement proposal that had been unveiled on November 18.

Countering her, there were grass-roots efforts to ensure that the deal wouldn't come unglued at the upcoming fairness hearing. On December 7, Lorraine Parker and Lydia Klein stopped in for a drink at a piano bar owned by Judy Mione's son in Rockville Centre, a town on Long Island. The two women tried to persuade Mione's son that his mother was ill served by opposing the settlement and that he should try to get her to change her mind.[12]

WALL STREET LOBBYISTS were in a letter-writing war with civil rights advocates. On December 17, 1997, the NASD published a letter in *The Federal Register* inviting public comment on changes in its rules that it had proposed to the Securities and Exchange Commission: Should the language of the U-4 be changed in such a way that employees would not have to take civil rights disputes to industry-run arbitration? If such a change were made, should brokerage firms be given one year to adjust to it? Should a due-process protocol adopted in 1995 by most other arbitration forums be used at NASD?

The answers to those and other questions depended, of course, on which ax the respondent had to grind. New York state attorney general Dennis C. Vacco wrote in December that the industry should be given only two months to adapt to changes.[13] The National Employment Lawyers Association said the NASD's suggestion of a one-year wait to implement changes was nothing more than an opportunity for the industry to set up in-house policies to compel Wall Street employees to arbitrate even if the U-4 language no longer required it. NELA called the suggestion to wait so long "transparently disingenuous."

Jeff Liddle, the civil rights lawyer, told NASD that the current system's problems included lack of judicial review, the fact that arbitrators could make decisions irrespective of the law, and the absence of any process through which to correct errors by the arbitrators. Liddle also made the point that arbitration was loaded with secrecy for secrecy's sake.[14]

Securities-industry advocates, of course, defended the status quo. An official of Charles Schwab & Co. suggested that the files kept by the Equal Employment Opportunity Commission should not be shown to arbitrators because they would be "likely to misunderstand the information in these files and its relevance to the case before them." This ran counter to prevailing depictions by the industry of arbitrators as fair, intelligent judges. If Schwab was right that panelists really would misunderstand data, why were persons too dense or inexperienced to read a government report of that sort selected for arbitration panels?

The Securities Industry Association insisted in its correspondence with the SEC that one year was necessary to notify the "556,000 registered persons of the change." To critics, the suggestion that disseminating a change in the Internet age would be burdensome strained credulity.

When the comment period closed, NASD's regulatory officials retired to consider the information and the opinions it had gleaned. After a period of bureaucratic silence, NASDR would be making a recommendation to the SEC, which would affirm or deny the proposal.

As THE LAST FEW LETTERS were straggling in to the SEC, Mary Stowell was drafting an unrelated correspondence of her own. On January 14, she sent a letter to her Smith Barney clients warning them that they might be invited to appear at a hearing about sex discrimination and harassment later that month, and to decline any such solicitation. New York state attorney general Vacco had scheduled a Vacco Public Hearing on Gender Discrimination in the Securities Industry for January 22, 1998, and he wanted the Smith Barney plaintiffs to attend. Mark Belnick would not approve if you attended, Stowell said in her letter. Should anyone wish to have some input, it would be acceptable to write a letter, Stowell wrote—but she or Friedman must approve it first. And if you do draft a letter, you might like to "say something positive" about Smith Barney, she wrote.[15] The lines between adversaries and allies were becoming increasingly blurred.

THE ONLY REPRESENTATIVE from the landmark case that would forever change Wall Street who attended Vacco's hearing on January 22 was Pam Martens, who did not endorse the landmark case's landmark settlement.

Women from several firms told of unwelcome touching, vulgar talk, and personnel departments that kept harassment problems low on their priority lists. One witness said women in her office were routinely called "dumb fucking cunts." Another described a scene where a colleague told her that "in case of fire," she should slide down his penis. In one case, when a firm showed a sexual-harassment training video, the men laughed uproariously at the reenactments of illegal workplace behavior. "That's just like what we do to Michelle," one of them called out.

Toward the end of the all-morning hearing, a woman related that men at her office would talk about what they would do with various parts of a woman's body. "It was becoming an effort in the morning just to take a shower and get to work," she said. She ultimately was fired for insubordination and low production. One of Vacco's witnesses said she had requested that a woman sit on her arbitration panel. The brokerage firm objected. To require that there be a woman on the panel would be discriminatory on its face, they said.

After a late-morning break, Pamela Martens went to the witness table; but by then, most of the media people had left to meet their midday deadlines. The only voice from inside the Boom-Boom Room suit went largely unremarked.

———

THAT SAME MORNING the *Wall Street Journal* ran a story of high interest to the litigating women. Merrill Lynch "is drafting a new policy that could let employees sue in court," said a headline on the front page of the paper's third section, where brokerage-industry news is featured. The story, written by Patrick McGeehan, reported that people familiar with the situation had said that Merrill intended to adopt a new policy in which employees would no longer be restricted to industry-run arbitration in the event of a dispute with the firm.

Four days later, in a separate fight in Boston, U. S. District Court Judge Nancy Gertner said that Susan Rosenberg, a former Merrill Lynch consultant, would be allowed to take her discrimination case to court. Gertner said that Merrill could not force Rosenberg to go to New York Stock Exchange arbitration because the NYSE arbitration system was dominated by the industry. The judge said she was "deeply troubled" by the "structural bias" in the system.

These developments made Stowell and Friedman look weaker for not having pushed Smith Barney harder. Friedman in particular was boiling over the *Wall Street Journal* story, which she assumed to have been leaked by someone at Merrill. To her, this story looked like the second time a major brokerage firm was breaking a behind-the-scenes deal that was to have shaped the way the public viewed a settlement. She and her partner had expected her clients to get credit for having Merrill drop mandatory arbitration for its employees. In exchange, Merrill was to get the continuing cooperation of the plaintiffs in playing down the harassment aspect of their experiences at the firm. Women at Merrill Lynch had, in fact, experienced pervasive sexual harassment.[16]

The two sides had been in intense negotiations toward a settlement and were close enough that another *Wall Street Journal* story, this one on January 27, 1998, said that an agreement would be announced the following day. The deal, however, never happened. Both the Journal and the *New York Times* ran subsequent stories saying that talks had broken down in the early morning of January 28.

The judge on the Merrill Lynch case, Ruben Castillo, could see how hopelessly apart the two sides had become. Come back on February 25, he said. Stowell and Friedman could use the time. There was work to be done before the April 9 *Martens v. Smith Barney* fairness hearing in New York.

The last thing they needed was any more bad press.

ON FEBRUARY 10, with less than two months to go before the fairness hearing—the official airing of the settlement's pros and cons—the *New York Post* hit Smith Barney with a pie in the face.

Smith Barney had taken bows over its improved employee hotline. *Post* reporters, though, tried for four consecutive days to get through and for the most part got no answer.[17] A lone answered call was forwarded to a receptionist, who put a reporter on hold for six minutes, their story said. When someone finally took the call, the reporter was told "We'll get you someone to talk to, honey." Instead, the call was disconnected, according to the story.

Unamused by the horrific publicity, Jamie Dimon picked up his telephone and told his minions that the hotline had better get fixed fast. It was. In the next day's paper, the *Post* reported that the firm had restored its ailing hotline after discovering that it was down. "Smith Barney: Sex Hotline Was on Fritz," the headline read.

On March 7, Pam filed papers in opposition to the Smith Barney settlement for the fairness hearing. The settlement was a violation of EEOC policy, she said. It didn't allow the claimants to prove a pattern of discrimination, because there would not be depositions or multiple-branch testimony. (Multiple-branch testimony, the interviewing of witnesses in diverse offices, would have given the plaintiffs the opportunity to prove that certain practices—such as firing women who complained, or relocating men who were caught harassing—were omnipresent.) It was flawed in that it did not contemplate depositions of defendants or employees of the human resources or legal departments.[18] And it exempted all individuals from liability. She said that a recent issue of the *New York Post* had pointed out that Paul, Weiss, Rifkind, Wharton &

Garrison, the law firm that represented Smith Barney, had just been ranked the worst firm in the nation for women lawyers. It ranked seventy-seventh out of seventy-seven firms in a study, "Presumed Equal: What America's Top Women Lawyers Really Think about Their Firms," conducted by two Harvard Law School students in 1997.

(Sixteen of the eighteen Paul Weiss women who responded to the survey that provided the basis of the critique of Paul Weiss criticized the firm's advancement opportunities; seventeen of eighteen said they had low job satisfaction.[19] The survey, sent to 7,000 women attorneys at 105 firms, included questions on a range of matters from job satisfaction to the likelihood of getting a senior male mentor. After learning of the bad results, Paul Weiss hired a management consultant to help it find ways to solve the problems.)[20]

On March 16 the New York State chapter of NOW filed a friend-of-the-court brief to register its objections to the use of an alternate dispute resolution system in the Smith Barney settlement. NOW's national office continued to support the settlement. Two days after that, Mary Stowell wrote a letter to Judge Motley asking permission to drop Businesswoman of the Year Edna Broyles, the Tampa, Florida, stockbroker, as a client. The judge approved Stowell's request to jettison Broyles. Like Pam, Broyles had been criticizing the proposed settlement.

On March 21, Pam and Judy Mione officially opted out of the settlement, saying that they would pursue a lawsuit against Smith Barney on their own. Unlike Martens and Mione, Broyles remained in the class of women who intended to settle, but no longer having legal representation, she joined with Pam and Judy in pursuit of a new lawyer.

Martens, Mione, and Broyles began talking to Gary Phelan, an employment-law expert at Garrison, Phelan, Levin-Epstein, Chimes & Richardson who was willing to work on a contingency basis. Tall and soft-spoken, with a thick shock of prematurely white hair at age thirty-seven, Phelan had come to Pam's attention because one of his partners, Joseph Garrison, had written an article in *ADR Journal,* a scholarly publication that focuses on alternate dispute options to court. Pam was impressed by Garrison's knowledge about mandatory arbitration and called to arrange for a meeting in New Haven, Connecticut, with Garrison and his colleague Gary Phelan. Pam drove up to Connecticut from Long Island on Saturday, March 28, with Mione and Rene Steinhagen, a public interest lawyer who had been helping Pam on her case without pay. Edna Broyles called in from Florida. Martens, Mione, and Broyles now planned to have Phelan represent them. It was important to have representation before the fairness hearing, a little over a week away.

———

JUST BEFORE THE HEARING, Smith Barney got an opportunity to show that it meant what it said in its postlawsuit statements about fighting discrimination. On March 31, the *Wall Street Journal Interactive Edition* Web page published word that two men in the Smith Barney research department had been fired for their use of pornography on the Internet.

———

MARY STOWELL, FOCUSED ON THE GOAL of a favorable settlement hearing, on April 7 filed an objection to a filing that Edna Broyles had made, arguing that Broyles could speak only on certain issues. Stowell additionally said that the New York State chapter of NOW should not be allowed to speak at the hearing because it had no standing in the suit. Stowell nonetheless noted that national NOW supported the settlement and called it "groundbreaking" and "fair."

She had criticism, too, of the New York City chapter of NOW, which Stowell said should not have given the court a copy of the February 10 *Post* story about the nonworking Smith Barney employee hotline. Stowell described the story as having been subsequently retracted. The story, however, was not retracted or corrected.[21]

The Stowell objections were far-reaching. Not only did she seek to spike briefs from the two NOW chapters, but she also told the court that Pam and Judy Mione did not have standing to express an opinion on the settlement because they had opted out of it. Stowell apparently did not want questions to be raised about the deal with Smith Barney in a public courtroom.

———

WHAT PAM HAD SOUGHT when she started her letter-writing campaign to Dimon in 1994—management's ear—was given to eight plaintiffs who now disdained her. On April 8, 1998, a day before the hearing on the merits of the settlement, chief executive Jamie Dimon met for three hours with the women who had sued him and his firm. With Dimon at the meeting was Chuck Prince, The Travelers' general counsel.

Dimon came prepared to listen, and they told him first-hand what had happened to them and how bad the strain of work had been. For a stretch, the session resembled a group therapy exercise. Dimon looked out at his audience. An executive can be so high up that he simply doesn't know some of the problems going on on his watch, he told them. Tracy Gibbs, the plaintiff who had learned two days before her maternity leave ended in 1995 that her job had been eliminated, was moved at the CEO's words. The detailed letters he had received from Pam four years earlier did not come up.

Several women broke down and cried. Lorraine Parker, who wanted a more businesslike conversation, eventually pounded the table after hearing one too many anecdotes. "I would like to talk to Jamie," she said. That, however, was also a disappointment to Parker. She listened intently as Dimon told a story that they assumed he was summoning up in order to show his humanity. A Smith Barney broker who was suspected of having turned the corner to senility was writing double tickets for his clients' orders and making other mistakes on the job. Out of compassion, though, Dimon decided to keep him for some months. Parker was incredulous at what she considered a stupid management decision. This was not the sort of noblesse oblige we're asking for, she thought.

His ace in the hole was the fortuitously timed dismissal of the two research analysts for their use of pornography on the company's computer system. Most of the women were heartened, knowing how unusual it was for a high-level securities analyst to be dismissed for such behavior.[22] Even Parker was impressed at that point.

When the encounter wound down, several of the plaintiffs refused to shake Dimon's hand on leaving the meeting. For the most part, though, he had won over his audience. These guys seem genuinely sorry for what happened to us, they said afterward.

———

ACT TWO OF THE *MARTENS V. SMITH BARNEY* court show, the fairness hearing, opened amid a circus atmosphere and continued clashing among the divided class representatives. This was the day that the judge would hear the opinions of parties deemed by the court to have standing in the case.

Judge Motley would not be coming out with a ruling today. After the hearing she would retire to her chambers and consider the evidence she had been shown. She would not be reviewing all the objections that had been submitted: There had been intense jockeying by class counsel to limit the challengers from having their voices heard.

Outside the courthouse, representatives from the New York City and New York State chapters of NOW protested the settlement. Galen Sherwin, president of New York City NOW, was dressed in a kangaroo costume and carried a placard reading "No More Kangaroo Courts." Inside, Pam and Judy entered the twenty-sixth floor ladies' room just around the corner from Judge Motley's court, only to bump into Beverly Trice and encounter further discord. "Give me something so I can get the stench out of here," said Trice to another woman in the powder room.

Pam took the remark to be a comment about her presence.[23] "Don't make an ass of yourself here today," she snapped at Trice from inside her stall.

Another dissenter, Cara Beth Walker, a named plaintiff who had grown critical of the settlement, noticed that morning that many of her coplaintiffs were no longer speaking to her. She later heard rumors that Friedman had told the women to stay away from her.[24]

The court was called to order at 10:30 A.M. This time, the rival factions did not have the luxury of avoiding one another as they had on November 18, when they sat on opposite sides. It was standing-room-only, and opponents were forced to squeeze in together. Tempers were high. The judge had granted Stowell's motion to keep New York City NOW from speaking, while allowing the brief itself to be accepted. Pam, too, was struck from speaking.

Motley called attorney Gary Phelan to the podium to speak on behalf of Edna Broyles. Phelan had been curbed by Stowell and Friedman via court filings before the hearing and would be permitted to speak on three narrow issues, including the settlement's violation of EEOC policies. Other objections by Broyles had not been filed by a March 16 deadline.

Phelan told the court that something important was being lost by abandoning a trial. "The guidance issued by the EEOC on July 10, 1997, states that arbitration systems are not suitable for resolving class or 'pattern or practice' claims of discrimination," he said. "They may in fact protect systemic discriminators by forcing claims to be adjudicated one at a time in isolation without reference to the broader and more accurate view of the employer's conduct." He cited work done in 1996 by a task force of the Department of Labor, which deemed that arbitration should not ordinarily be used for such cases.

"Under this agreement, Smith Barney has succeeded in the very effective and very typical defense strategy in sexual harassment and sex discrimination class actions of divide and conquer." Phelan told the judge that a higher principle had been forgone by separating the women's grievances into individual hearings.

"By forcing these claims to be fought in individual, isolated arbitrations, Smith Barney has won the war," he said, because the settlement agreement provided no opportunity to prove liability or to show a pattern and practice of discrimination. He finished speaking, staying within the scope of permitted argument. Phelan, a lawyer more suited to the brainier environment of an appellate court or perhaps even academia, was not the type to resort to the litigation trick of sneaking in an argument that the court had ruled out. In a courtroom where his adversaries were willing to push the envelope, Phelan's professional and courteous ways didn't always seem to serve him well as a litigator.

"That's all I'm allowed to say," he said at 10:44, having spoken for less than fifteen minutes.

Friedman took the podium. "Good morning, your honor," she began, getting quickly in command of her audience. Friedman was speaking as much to the clients to her left as she did to the court. "We have today in the courtroom many of the class representatives, who traveled from around the country to show their support for this agreement." Each woman will have the opportunity to go into a hearing with classwide statistics to show how women have fared at Smith Barney, Friedman said, responding to Phelan's allegations that there would be no information about pattern and practice. She was apparently referring to statistical studies being done by experts, some of which were made available in 2000 after the mediation process had begun. Ultimately, however, Smith Barney successfully fought many plaintiffs' use of those statistics.

Judge Motley asked Friedman whether the availability of easy legal fees would attract lawyers who were not competent to handle discrimination claims. Smith Barney had offered to pay fees up to $5,000 for each woman who came forward with a claim.

"They will be moving in on this gravy train and looking to represent people, and they can't represent them, they are not competent," the judge said. "This is a highly specialized field now in the law, but now everybody and his brother is an expert on Title VII, and that's a serious problem, in my view."

"Your honor, we absolutely share that view," said Friedman.

"I think that's one of the problems with this plan that's going to have to be worked out, that is, that it should be a panel of lawyers in advance, such as we have in this court, say, when we have panels of criminal lawyers."

"That's a wonderful suggestion, and we would be happy to amend the agreement," said Friedman, glancing back to Belnick, who was nodding his head in approval. The two would work out a clause that provided for experienced lawyers only.

The hearing ended with Belnick and Friedman reiterating to the judge that $2.05 million in "bonus" payments would be going to named plaintiffs. By morning's end, Belnick, Friedman, and Phelan—on behalf of Broyles—had been heard from. Pam Martens had been only a spectator.

With the hearing over, Judge Motley would begin her review of all that she had heard, considering everything from the practical aspects of a class that included 22,000 women to the legal concepts that governed, practical or not. It could be months before the *Martens* players knew what the judge's opinion was on the proposed settlement.

Pam held her own session just outside Motley's court with a knot of reporters. "Mark Belnick is sadly mistaken if he thinks we'll all go back to our knitting," she said. But most of her audience was already melting away, headed for the elevators, anxious not to miss the 12:30 press conference.

⎯ ⎯•⎯ ⎯

THE PLAINTIFFS LINED UP in front of the cameras just as they had on settlement day. The cast was the same, but this time the script included no horror stories. Stepping to the microphone in a red turtleneck sweater, Lisa Mays told the assembled group, "I'm one of the California plaintiffs, and I'm just thinking how exciting it will be" to help women. Mays made no mention of what she had gone through in her job.

Lorraine Parker, chic as always in an electric blue suit and three tiers of pearls, remarked on Smith Barney's firing of the two analysts who had been exchanging pornography. "Two years ago they would have made copies and disseminated it." Change was really in the works, she said.

Beverly Trice stepped to the microphone and thanked the press corps for getting word out about their plight. "And before I get into tears," she said, her voice cracking, "I want to thank Linda and Mary." Trice made an immediate recovery from her emotional moment, keeping command of the microphone while she had the chance.

Friedman deflected questions about the arbitration issue. This was no time to diminish a moment in history.

———

WHILE THE *MARTENS* LAWYERS and plaintiffs awaited word from Judge Motley, the Merrill Lynch case came back to life. On May 4, the two sides said they had come to a settlement agreement. The proposed dispute resolution system, with a three-stage process that moved from a written complaint to a one-day confidential mediation to a public arbitration, was strikingly similar to the model that Smith Barney had agreed to.

Very different, though, was Merrill Lynch's concession that starting July 1, its employees would be allowed to go to court in the event of an employment dispute, just as the *Wall Street Journal* story that so riled Friedman had foretold. Merrill also agreed to certain diversity initiatives. A month later, Judge Ruben Castillo gave preliminary approval of the Merrill accord.

The *Martens* settlement, though, hit a snag. On June 24, Judge Motley sent the lawyers back to work with her ruling that the proposed settlement was "not fair, reasonable, and adequate." Then, on July 2, Edna Broyles wrote to the court to object to aspects of the settlement, including the fact that age and race claims had been bundled into the sex suit. Broyles pointed out that persons with those claims might not be well served by a sex discrimination settlement.

In the meantime, publicity from the Wall Street cases had finally had an impact on the SEC, which had been the quiet sponsor allowing Wall Street's licensing process to include provisions for mandatory arbitration. On June 23, the SEC said that starting January 1, 1999, the securities industry licensing process would no longer shut off the courts in civil rights cases. Previously, SEC chairman Levitt had said there was "no clear answer" on the matter. Without the government abetting arbitration, firms would have to establish policies of their own to keep employees out of court.

Another court conference was called for July 23 to see how the settling parties had addressed Motley's concerns and to hear Broyles's objections. Friedman was irritated over the opposition filed by Broyles, muttering that morning in the cafeteria of the U.S. Courthouse that it was her opponents' "most desperate move yet" to foil the settlement. Although only Broyles's name was on the official document, the fact that she had become friends with Pam over recent months was no secret, and Stowell and Friedman always suspected Pam's influence in filings by her supporters.

Friedman by this point in her career was fully cured of the old symptoms of shyness that used to require pep talks from her partner. Friedman could, in fact, be ferocious if necessary, using badgering, dramatics, put-downs, or threats to get what she wanted or needed in litigation. As she entered the courtroom that morning, she stopped at the back to talk to Gary Phelan, who had filed the motion on Broyles's behalf. With his retiring, intellectual demeanor, Phelan had never seemed to fit in with the rest of the *Martens* case legal crowd. Despite the volume of in-person and written interactions Friedman had had with him over the preceding three months, she persisted in calling him "Jerry" for the first few minutes.

At one minute before eleven, the judge arrived, and Friedman broke off the discussion. While the other lawyers seated themselves at the front of the court, Phelan took a seat in the back of the room. Counsel began the exercise of introducing themselves, and Judge Motley looked quizzically at Phelan when he stood from the peanut gallery and said who he was.

"Why don't you sit up here?" Judge Motley suggested, motioning to the lawyers' section at the front of the court. Phelan walked forward and took a seat in the same row as Stowell and Friedman, leaving a seat between himself and Mary Stowell.

Friedman and Belnick were by now sufficiently comfortable with their close working relationship that Belnick would openly assist her in court. As the judge began to raise questions related to Broyles's motion, Belnick held up a sign that read "ADEA" for Friedman as she stood speaking at the podium. (The reference was to the Age and Disability Employment Act.) When Friedman pondered an amendment to the settlement, he gestured to her and mouthed "sure." Belnick passed notes to Friedman as she addressed Motley. To the outside observer, the two would have appeared to be colleagues from the same firm.

From the start, the settlement had aspects that read like brain-teasers on a final exam. There would be statistical evidence to assist the plaintiffs at their hearings, but the statistics were under a confidentiality order under most circumstances. Depositions were not prohibited, but there was a "presumption against depositions." There would be "no burden of proof" imposed on a claimant when she submitted her claim, but nothing in the settlement would "relieve any Claimant from the burden of proving" that she suffered injury and damages.[25]

Motley already had read the briefs before she came to court. Fully prepared to hear Phelan argue his case for Broyles, the judge was suddenly confounded to hear Friedman announce that she had been authorized by her adversary—Phelan—to tell the court that all but one of his objections had been worked out. "There has been so much change that I haven't been able to keep up with," said Motley. "I've spent the last two days going over Mr. Phelan's objections, and that's been abandoned?"

Phelan approached the podium. "No, your honor. If I may address the court."

Phelan, though, did not get to speak to Motley for long. Friedman took over, telling Motley that she and Smith Barney could prepare amendments that would repair any problems that were brought up that morning. As Friedman spoke, Phelan moved back several steps and leaned against the railing that separated the lawyers' section from where the public was sitting. Trying to get a handle on things, Motley asked why Smith Barney and the plaintiffs were proposing that the settlement include employees other than women. How would that work, she wondered? How, for example, would the dispute resolution system handle a case brought by a black man?

There seemed to be more confusion than answers, with two lawyers on the floor and now a third injecting himself: Mark Belnick attempted to assist Friedman in explaining a point, and Motley called a halt. "I don't know if I can hear three lawyers at once," she said. Although it was arguably he who initially had had the floor, Phelan voluntarily took his seat.

Motley tried to get straight the status quo on the rapidly changing events in the nation's courts regarding mandatory arbitration, and the complicated relationship of those events to the changes in the SEC and NASD rules that governed broker licenses. No sooner would she tease apart one tangled aspect of the settlement than another knot would present itself.

Then Judge Motley saw a reference to a sealed document that she had not been aware of. What was in that sealed envelope, and why was it sealed?

The clerk found the envelope, and the judge began to open it. Belnick, clearly agitated, rose to ask that if the judge insisted on opening the envelope, she do so outside of public court. Motley ignored the request, reading from the document and revealing for the record that if 100 or more of the 22,000 Smith Barney women in the class objected to the settlement, the firm would be able to walk away from the deal.

Belnick defended the move. It was done "to avoid someone who wants to run in effect what becomes a proxy fight," he told Motley. "It's in every class-action fight I've been involved with, filed with the court under seal."

"Well, I've never seen it, and I've been here for thirty-two years, for your information," the judge replied.

Phelan, sounding more confident after the showdown between Motley and the settlement's proponents, said that, on behalf of Broyles, he was withdrawing the approvals he had given Friedman earlier that day on certain changes in the settlement. "We didn't know about this," he said of the sealed agreement. He restated his objection to the notion that claims outside of gender discrimination be included in the settlement, pointing out to Motley that no discovery had been done in those areas.

The judge looked at Friedman.

"Let me ask Ms. Stowell, Ms. Friedman, has there been any discovery with respect to race discrimination at Smith Barney?"

Friedman glanced back at Belnick, who shook his head no.

"No, your honor," she said.

"Hispanics?" the judge asked.

Another glance at Belnick.

"No, your honor."

"Asians?"

"No," Friedman answered.

Motley went back to the issue of Smith Barney's ability to bail out of the settlement. "The one hundred figure can readily be reached. You already have thirty-eight," she said, referring to the number of women who had opted out. After a short back-and-forth between Motley and Friedman, the judge said she was utterly confused by the settlement, which, after all the effort going into it, could be undone by Smith Barney if only sixty-two more people objected to it.

"I feel like Alice in Wonderland," she told Friedman. "The more you talk, the more confused I get."

As Friedman tried to get herself back in the good graces of the judge, she made an assumption that she was speaking on behalf of Phelan. Phelan, exasperated, had an uncharacteristic moment of lost temper. "I would object to Ms. Friedman saying what I believe—repeatedly," he snapped. Minutes later, when the judge began to read a passage from Phelan's objection to the settlement, Friedman got into a private conversation with Belnick. If the incidents were accidental—preempting Phelan's testimony, calling him Jerry, or having a side conference when the judge's attention was on his work—they were fortuitously dismissive and affrontive.

Friedman and Belnick emerged from their talk soon enough to promise the court, along with Stowell, that they would work on more amendments that would address the concerns brought up that day. Given Judge Motley's displeasure over the surprise envelope and her questions about everything from the lack of discovery on minority groups to the potential incompetence of lawyers who would flock to represent individual class members, the room emptied amid a feeling of defeat for the settlement.

The next morning, July 24, newspapers reported that the judge was unhappy with a convoluted proposal.

No matter. News of the settlement's demise was premature.

By the afternoon of July 24, with the hastily produced amendments from Friedman, Stowell, and Belnick in hand and with assurance from Smith Barney that it was willing to scrap the bailout provisions that had been under seal, Judge Constance Baker Motley gave her approval. A final order was signed, and the women now officially constituted a class.

On August 6, the court issued an order of settlement on *Martens et al. v. Smith Barney et al.* Claims were dismissed against James Dimon, Nicholas Cuneo, and every other male and female employee of Smith Barney who had been mentioned by name in the suit. It meant that, no matter what a woman settling with the class accused a Smith Barney man of, he was financially and legally free of her claim, with nothing on his securities industry record to show for it. Not a single deposition had been taken of the people named as defendants.

Chapter Fifteen

Pariah or Visionary?

"Everyone is afraid of arbitration. They mark you in the industry for the rest of your life."

—A WOMAN WHO TOOK A LARGE MONEY PAYMENT
IN EXCHANGE FOR HER SILENCE. SHE LEFT THE INDUSTRY.

P AM'S FORMER LAWYERS, her former employer, and her estranged coplaintiffs were on a roll. The judge in *Martens* had OKed the settlement against Martens's wishes, and in Chicago a month before, another judge had given provisional approval to a very similar accord with Merrill Lynch.

Pam's supporters were fewer and fewer, yet she persevered even as sympathy dwindled, filing a motion to request that the judge reconsider her approval of the settlement. Submitted on August 13, 1998, it criticized a range of the settlement's features and history. Pam argued that the plaintiffs had given up their right to trial, yet had not seen the settlement document until after it was presented to Judge Motley.[1] She contended that Stowell and Friedman developed "an untoward coziness" with opposing counsel, an accusation she based in part on copies of two letters written by Stowell. And she pointed out that Paul, Weiss, the law firm representing Smith Barney, had offered jobs to two of the judge's clerks. Pam filed this contentious motion cosigned by Edna Broyles and Judy Mione. Her salvo quickly drew a rejoinder on August 26 from the settlement's supporters. At this point, they had little good to say about her.

A year before, Lorraine Parker had written her letter demanding that Pam cease speaking on her behalf; similarly, coplaintiff Lydia Klein had posted a letter telling Pam "do NOT speak for us." Another, Bette Laswell, wrote Pam saying she had a "significant problem" with Pam's view on the mediation. By now, there was a chorus of critics, calling Pam everything from unstable to an out-of-control publicity hound to a megalomaniac. One coplaintiff called Pam "The Puppet Master."[2]

To Pam's partisans, she was a purist who would not compromise on the big issues. As time went on, though, her loyalists tended to be a rung down in the feminist power structure—people like Galen Sherwin, president of the New York City chapter of NOW, rather than Patricia Ireland, president of national NOW, who was in Stowell and Friedman's camp. Pam had support at the grass-roots level, where she had helped frightened young women who called for advice. Those allies, though, had no political muscle.

When Pam's name came up, there were plenty of examples of how her unyielding, extreme position had been harmful. Because she had filed the motion to reconsider the settlement, the judge could not release any of the $2.05 million in bonus payments to the named plaintiffs. And there was criticism of Pam for engaging Judy Mione as an ally: Mione was said to be particularly needy of the bonus payments; ergo, Pam had been self-ish in wooing Mione to side with her, the argument went.[3]

She did, though, have supporters whose clear-sightedness made up for what they lacked in clout. "Pam takes what's right and goes with it so severely that it upsets people," says Claudia Galvin, the former Garden City sales assistant. She also, however, could be overly confident of her ability to analyze legal situations—perhaps the result of her vast layperson's exposure to the courts and the law. She knew far more than the average educated person but misspoke at times about the legal implications of events—particularly meetings she had not attended.

Her opponents Stowell and Friedman got a new boost on September 2, 1998, when, in federal court in Chicago, Judge Ruben Castillo gave his enthusiastic final blessing to the pact that had been reached on May 4 between Merrill Lynch and the eight named plaintiffs there. Like the Smith Barney deal, it had no large money fund; it offered a dispute resolution process; a diversity adviser would oversee problems at Merrill in the future; and targets were set for achieving numbers and percentages of women in particular programs and jobs by particular dates. (It also had a provision to end Merrill's in-house policy of requiring arbitration in the case of a civil rights dispute, but that would not apply to the class, which was agreeing to mediate its claims in lieu of court.) The settlement even included the sealed-envelope provision of a secret number known only to Merrill Lynch and Stowell and Friedman: the head count of objectors, if ever reached, that could void the agreement. The envelope had never come unsealed in the Merrill case, and Marybeth Cremin, the lead plaintiff, was never made privy to the number of objectors that could nix the settlement, even long after it had been approved.[4]

On September 2, 1998, Judge Castillo said, "Certainly there have been no more competent counsel that I've ever had in a case than have appeared here on behalf of the plaintiff and have appeared on behalf of the various defendants we've had." Stowell and Friedman deleted the portion of Castillo's compliment about the defense teams and used only the first half of his sentence—ending with the word "plaintiff"—to validate the "high regard in which Stowell & Friedman are held" in a later filing to Judge Motley in New York.[5]

The public face of the Merrill settlement was much like that of the Smith Barney accord: good news for the brokerage firm, good news in many respects for its women, and very good business for the lawyers who crafted the deals. Behind the scenes, however, there was scrapping. One class representative snarled that Stowell and Friedman had promised "a big press conference like the Smith Barney women had." But no such media bash was forthcoming. The Boom-Boom Room group had had the glory of big headlines and television cameras, whereas the Merrill plaintiffs were getting treated like yesterday's news. Some class representatives wondered whether their lawyers had struck a deal with Merrill to quiet their clients down once the agreement was approved.

On the day after Castillo approved the Merrill Lynch deal, New York state attorney general Dennis Vacco staged a follow-up to his Public Hearing on Gender Discrimination in the Securities Industry of eight months before. His September 3 press conference was a noticeable backpedaling. Last time, he had featured witnesses from Donaldson Lufkin & Jenrette Securities, the Bank of New York, and Shearson Lehman Brothers, whetting the appetite of the press and the public for a serious investigation. Now, however, he was naming a single curious target: Garban Intercapital GLP, a largely unknown British firm whose New York satellite office employed 300 people in the 120 Broadway building in which Vacco himself worked. On hearing the company's name, even veteran Wall Street reporters exchanged puzzled glances and asked "Who?"

There was no question that the allegations against the Garban men were serious. Vacco told the group that one broker had allegedly passed around a photograph "of himself engaged in an act of bestiality of himself and a dog." But it was an eyebrow-raiser that Vacco did not target a U.S. firm when he unveiled the fruits of his probe.

Asked why his office hadn't pursued the allegations brought up in the *Martens* suit, Vacco said, "That impact wasn't observed by us."

Eight months earlier, Vacco had invited Pam Martens to be a witness at his explosive hearing. Somewhere along the line, his interest in civil rights violations at Smith Barney appeared to have waned.

At Stowell & Friedman, interest in civil rights, of course, was considerable as word got out about the suit to women who qualified to be in the class. In October, Max Fischer, a junior lawyer at Stowell & Friedman, conducted a disturbing telephone interview with a former cold caller at Smith Barney who told Fischer that her life had been reduced to steel-plated doors, recurrent nightmares, and keeping a gun by the side of her bed as the result of having been raped by her boss. The woman said she had a recurring nightmare: she would race up a long flight of stairs trying to get inside her door in time to avert danger. She would always awaken from the frightening dreams the same way: her heart would be pounding so loudly that it would wake her up.

ON NOVEMBER 19, Judge Motley rejected Pam's request to withdraw approval. The settlement that Pam had painstakingly critiqued would move forward without obstructions.

THE YEAR CLOSED with a major announcement from the New York Stock Exchange for which Friedman and Stowell claimed much credit. On December 29, the NYSE said that starting January 11, it would only hear civil rights cases in those instances where the brokerage and the employee agreed to arbitration *after* the alleged violation had occurred. The new policy kept firms from entrapping employees with mandatory arbitration contracts signed at hiring time, or at some point after they had been hired but before they encountered a problem. Given the SEC's announcement in June that civil rights cases could no longer be bound to arbitration via the securities industry licensing system, the NYSE's decision was critical if firms were to be kept from compelling to arbitration employees who preferred court.

The NASD, however, made no parallel change in policy, which meant that firms still had a viable dispute forum available to hear their civil rights cases. In the view of Cliff Palefsky and other plaintiffs' lawyers, this was an example of the NASD's weaknesses as a regulator. "The board of directors and the executives at NASD are too afraid of the industry," says Palefsky. "It's a trade organization dominated by the industry in a way that NYSE isn't quite."[6] As a result of the closed justice system that the NASD club has cultivated, "Wall Street is thirty years behind every other industry or profession," says Jamie Franklin, a civil rights lawyer in Minneapolis.

Wall Street was behind the times, and yet its backwardness had bred a cutting-edge private adjudication system that other industries had by now envied and imitated. When the Smith Barney and Merrill Lynch lawsuits were in the settlement stage—and the brokerage industry was beginning some reform of its private court system—copycat industries were just starting to feel the heat. Court cases that challenged mandatory arbitration in other industries were coming into the news just as Wall Street was surrendering some of its prerogatives.

———

DILUTED THOUGH IT WAS by the weaker stance of NASD, the NYSE's new rule became effective on January 11, 1999, and the settlement that Pam Martens hated continued to chug along. On February 1, the settlement's effective date, the claimants began officially to file their individual grievances, although the Stowell and Friedman staff had begun to take information over the telephone from the alleged rape victim and others as early as the previous fall.[7]

That the telephones of Stowell and Friedman's Chicago office were ringing with eager class members was notable, given how grueling it could be to go public with an allegation. Women are known to be greeted with hardball intimidation and other retaliation from the men they report and those men's supporters. Creative companies can draw on all sorts of ploys: Strategically granted promotions can engender loyalty—and lapses of memory—in witnesses who might otherwise have been hostile.

It might seem reasonable to expect that supportive witnesses could be found among women of higher position. Smith Barney's plaintiffs already knew, though, that a few high-ranking women had worked against them and that women at the top were not likely to help. There is a dearth of senior women on Wall Street. To talk with some of them is to discover how often they speak in conflicted ways, denigrating female peers for lacking critical attributes such as aggressiveness—even in cases where the colleague clearly has it. The same senior women have been known to furnish management with a veneer of feminism when it is time to sack a female, yet complain privately of how frequently they feel uncomfortable on the job. Even senior women who are mentors in their departments have their limits. When a woman junior to them is being wronged, to support the cause can mean career suicide.

Similarly, sympathetic women in human resources face a limit in what they can do. Susan Jaskowski, the Rodman & Renshaw human resources executive who wound up suing and settling with the firm, said that it was her job as an officer of the company to smooth things over. "I could never advocate that somebody go see a lawyer," she says.

Corporations, of course, instinctively discredit employees who challenge them. A Smith Barney representative whispered in a reporter's ear that Pam Martens never earned her accounts but had them handed to her by a senior broker who had retired.[8] The story was repeated by one of Pam's former friends, once Pam and the other plaintiffs had parted ways. Yet a sales assistant who worked for the broker whose office was next door to Pam's and observed her habits said that Pam was one of the hardest workers in Garden City and that she got none of the breaks the men got. "They hated Pam for her success," says Claudia Galvin. "The guys got that all the time," she says, referring to the practice of accounts being passed on from departing brokers to their protégés.

A complaint nationwide had been that men got an unfair share of these accounts. Galvin said that Pam earned hers but that she saw many instances in which male brokers took over such accounts without even knowing the customers. No one carped in those cases about any inequities, Galvin said.

Smear campaigns can take other forms when the complaining woman has moved on. Lorraine Parker arrived at a new job at PaineWebber in Boca Raton, Florida, to learn that a male broker with whom she had worked in Garden City had told her new colleagues that she was "bad news."

Those who complain can be marked long before they get into their new jobs. Marybeth Cremin was shunned when she sought to get back to work after a maternity leave.[9] She called PaineWebber and Dean Witter, among others, but they would not return her calls despite her good record and loyal clientele. She ultimately got a job at A. G. Edwards. "By the time I came in for an interview at A. G. Edwards, no one else on the North Shore of Chicago would even talk to me," she said. "One guy at a brokerage house who was a friend said he didn't want to touch me. It was very difficult." Jaskowski said the publicity that accompanied her case backfired on her. "It's a small world, and word gets around when you sue your employer. It took me three or four years to come out of that. It's still hard, and I have a completely different life now."

BACK IN GARDEN CITY, things were harder and harder for Judy Mione. Although her sister Joan Chasin still worked in the office with her, it was lonely being a class representative under branch manager Glenn Fischer, former right-hand man to Nicholas Cuneo, while also remaining a combatant in *Martens v. Smith Barney*. Her sister Joan, while supportive of the lawsuit, was not viewed as being as militant as Judy, who had taken a lead role. For months now, Judy had opposed the same women she initially had sought to battle *for*. The branch was now split into two factions.

Gossip went through the branch about sales assistants being coached by management to remember or forget certain events if they were called as witnesses in arbitrations. Employees anticipated being pitted against coworkers or former coworkers. Mione was not considered safe to talk to. She approached her office friends one morning for their contribution to a regular lottery pool that five or six of them took part in but was told that they wouldn't be playing the pool with Judy and Joan anymore. After having chest pains for several weeks, she decided that the stress of sticking it out at Smith Barney was too much. On March 8, 1999, she quit.

Darlene Livingston had sunk into a major depression that had rendered her suicidal. Her hair began to fall out. Lorraine Parker stopped working nights because she ultimately deemed it useless. (Ironically, a male colleague would later denigrate her for putting in short workdays.) Susan Jaskowski's husband told Linda Friedman, her lawyer, that his wife had been transformed by being demoted and replaced as head of human resources after her maternity leave. Friedman said she will never forget the despairing phone call she got from him. "He said, 'I don't know this woman—she wants to become a hairdresser.'" Jaskowski became clinically depressed after she was fired.

When Pam got the call from Judy Mione saying that she had quit, Pam considered it remarkable that Judy had lasted so long. Few who went public stayed at their jobs. Many left the industry altogether. The backlash left them too beaten down or too distracted to stay where they were. Many eventually dropped their complaints.

Only days after Judy Mione walked out of 901 Franklin Avenue for the last time, at corporate headquarters in New York, Jennifer Solomon was signing an agreement that would raise her compensation as a securities analyst from $450,000 a year to a minimum of $850,000. Solomon, a respected beverage analyst, had been offered $1.25 million in March to join PaineWebber Group Inc. Salomon Smith Barney persuaded her that, by sticking with them, she would have greater global career opportunities. Jennifer Solomon, who previously was operating without a contract, did not pay attention to the language in the new document she was signing. It said that in the event of a dispute with her employer, she would have to pass up court, and use securities industry arbitration. Smith Barney, however, would have the option of going to a court of competent jurisdiction should it wish to seek injunctive relief against Jennifer Solomon.

WOMEN WHO SUPPORTED the Smith Barney settlement were developing their claims, frequently hiring attorneys for advice separate from whatever Stowell and Friedman were giving them. Friedman exchanged e-mails with one, Cara Beth Walker, on April 19 to say that her lawyer, John Davis, "Seems very nice." She told Walker (known as "Beth") ten days later that her second lawyer, Kent Spriggs, was "very well respected." The previous fall, Friedman had invited Spriggs onto the official panel of lawyers approved to handle arbitrations for individual class representatives. This panel was created to allay Judge Motley's fear that the settlement might attract lawyers who were inexperienced in and unqualified to handle sex discrimination cases.

Spriggs and Davis had one of the settlement's better cases: Walker, a named plaintiff in the *Martens* matter, put up with one boss who would publicly rub his crotch with a lint brush and another who once told her to zip up his fly, according to the complaint. The two bosses insulted her customers and reassigned them to male brokers without telling her, it said.

Stowell and Friedman continued to support Smith Barney and laud the changes at the firm, which had come a long way since the days of Nick Cuneo's Bloody Marys in the basement. It had fired some offenders. It had advanced women to new positions. Diversity programs had been started even before the settlement compelled the firm to do something.

Thus it came as something of a surprise when, on May 21, 1999, a memo was circulated to branch managers instructing them that employees must get permission before filing a securities-related lawsuit. Branch employees also must get an OK before appearing as a witness in such a suit, the memo said. Given that a pool of 22,000 class members was considering whether to participate in a class-action settlement that surely would involve the use of witnesses, the memo's timing had the potential to be used in an intimidating way. It might deter a woman thinking of filing a claim, and might unnerve any person considering stepping up to be her witness.

The memo gave a broad definition of a "securities-related" lawsuit. "Securities-related" would include a "class-action lawsuit against a corporate or municipal entity." The discrimination class action brought in 1996 would seem to qualify; there was nothing in the memo that stated otherwise. The memo was distributed to managers, leaving it anyone's guess in what form its contents might have been communicated to employees.

IN THE SETTLEMENT with Merrill Lynch & Co., where 939 claims had been filed, Stowell and Friedman were bristling over that firm's behavior. On June 3, 1999, 370 of those women from seventeen states—nearly all of the claimants who still worked at Merrill—filed interim complaints citing continuing discrimination and retaliation. The following day, a clearly unfazed Merrill said that 50 of the 939 initial claims had merit and that they were reviewing several hundred others.

It was a hot summer by any measure for players in both big class actions, and the judgment of Stowell, Friedman, and Pam Martens was about to come into question for their selection of associates or business connections.

Although Gary Phelan was representing Pam in her legal matters, Pam was a backstage booster of Kent Spriggs, the Florida lawyer who was working for Beth Walker and Teresa Tedesco. Friedman liked Spriggs, too, and in the spring had referred to Spriggs and his partner, John Davis, as "vg lawyers" in an e-mail to Walker.

By June, though, Friedman's fondness was waning. On June 14, 1999, she wrote to Spriggs to express her concern over statements that had been repeated to class representatives and attributed to him by his client Walker. Among the alleged statements were that Smith Barney had loopholes to get out of the settlement; that class counsel had engaged in improper conduct in seeking extensions to file claim forms; and that class representatives could be sued for their bonus money if the settlement fell apart.[10]

By now, Friedman had begun to look into Spriggs's professional background. Pam, Walker, and Tedesco, though, continued to support him.

———

PAM'S DREAM OF A SEPARATE TRIAL that would allow her to tell her story in court was not materializing. Three days after Friedman's letter to Spriggs, one of the Paul, Weiss lawyers working for Smith Barney sent a letter to Judge Motley about Martens's and Mione's push for a court trial. "Should Ms. Martens and Ms. Mione now attempt to assert such claims, Smith Barney will—at a minimum—be forced promptly to move to compel Ms. Martens and Ms. Mione to arbitrate any claims they wish to assert against the firm." Brad Karp, the Paul, Weiss lawyer who wrote the letter, said that he had the right to compel them to arbitration: both had entered into mandatory arbitration agreements as a condition of employment at the firm, he wrote.

Pam didn't need Karp to explain the terms of Smith Barney's various employment contracts over the years. She had copies of all of them filed away in her basement, in file drawers stuffed with information about the company.

What she did not have these days, though, was entrée to fresh knowledge about the lawsuit she had launched. She was out of the communication loop when big claims came in, and thus had eroding clout. It was Stowell and Friedman who had a grip on the information about big cases, and it was Stowell and Friedman who could get the word out to the media or keep a case quiet. On June 17, the same day Karp sent his letter, Linda Atkins Smoot's explosive complaint against her stockbroker boss in Charlotte, North Carolina, was shipped out of the office of a lawyer in Matthews, North Carolina. It was among many hundreds of stories on which Pam would have no influence.

Smoot was the former sales assistant who said that her supervisor, Roger Shuster, had demanded that she have sex with him, calling her names and grabbing her in the office.[11]

It had been Pam's vision that such allegations would be aired in a public trial. But by the terms of the Smith Barney class-action settlement, neither Shuster nor any of the other individual men accused of harassment were held liable for any alleged actions, and most were never publicly accused, with the exception of the handful of men named in the initial lawsuit. These men were, depending on one's point of view, either deprived of the opportunity or spared the necessity of rebutting in open court the accusations being made against them.

Smoot rejected several settlement offers from Smith Barney before accepting one in 2001. Roger Shuster, who works at Prudential Securities in Charlotte, said in an interview with the author in August 2001 that he swore on his five children's lives that Smoot's allegations were "a total fabrication." Sondra C. Collins Maddy, a sales assistant at Smith Barney, also filed a claim that focused on Shuster's behavior and echoed many of Smoot's allegations.[12] Smoot and Maddy sat in the same area of the Charlotte, North Carolina, branch. Others in the office also filed claims in the class action.

Shuster's regulatory records show no violation of internal policies at Smith Barney and state that his termination was "voluntary."[13] He says that Smoot's complaint was "99.9 percent garbage" and that she and the others who filed complaints in the Smith Barney settlement were mercenaries. "It's what screws up this country," he says. "People wanting free money because of bloodsucking lawyers."

The nature of Wall Street sexual harassment cases is such that almost no trials with discovery and testimony exist; irrefutable conclusions about whom to believe are thus hard to come by. What is clear, however, is that men who have been the focus of problems that cost their firms dearly have been able to move on without any trail of evidence one way or the other.

Like Shuster, John B. Reagan has a clean regulatory file. Under the heading of "reportable disclosures," Reagan's file in 2001 said "none submitted in CRD as of this date." Smith Barney paid more than $700,000 to settle the claim that Reagan had demanded that an analyst he supervised sleep with him as a condition of keeping her job.[14]

The man who allegedly molested Eileen Valentino and Patti Hanlon had no mention of any violation of firm policy on his regulatory records when the author retrieved them in 2000. By 2002, his records could not be retrieved at all: NASD had established a new policy of deleting records of brokers if they were out of the business for two years. He subsequently became a practicing attorney on whose behalf Smith Barney apologized to Valentino and Hanlon during their mediations. Initially, the firm had defended him and six other men.[15] Smith Barney said that Valentino and Hanlon "themselves engaged in sexual banter." Nicholas Cuneo, whose CRD says he left Smith Barney in a "voluntary retirement," is likewise a beneficiary of this system.[16] A member of the public would never know by obtaining Cuneo's official CRD records that he was the key named defendant in a historic sex-discrimination lawsuit.

In contrast, when it comes to investor-broker disputes, the NASD requires that brokers report customer complaints, pending arbitration hearings, decisions by arbitrators, and settlements. Although there are exceptions—small settlements go unreported, as do customer complaints that are abandoned—at least the starting expectation is that brokers will report publicly when there is a complaint or a lawsuit. No parallel requirement exists, however, when a civil rights complaint is filed in the same arbitration forums. When brokers or other licensed industry professionals become defendants in discrimination or harassment cases, they suddenly enjoy a special privacy within the public reporting system.

Pam had the fury of knowing that although Cuneo's record was clean, hers was not: her CRD says she was fired for her inability to get along with management. Beverly Trice, a coplaintiff with whom Pam had worked harmoniously in happier days, had told her she was fired for "keeping a messy desk" after complaining of discrimination in her Kansas City branch. Others Pam had spoken to in the years since the lawsuit was filed said they had lived with trumped-up customer complaints that were contrived as revenge when they refused to drop their threats of a civil rights suit.[17]

At this point, not even Pam's rare victories were satisfying. After badgering by Phelan and consequent inquiries from the media, Smith Barney issued a corrective memo on June 18 to address the May 21 internal memo about lawsuits. The new memo clarified that the rules would not apply to civil rights cases like *Martens*. The incident played out in such a way that Pam's objections, which helped quash the memo's potential harm, looked foolish once Smith Barney responded to them: How silly to think that the harassment and discrimination scenarios alleged in the *Martens* case could be deemed securities-related, said Pam's critics in the matter, who included Linda Friedman. And how irresponsible it was to ask for a corrective memo that might intimidate women who never saw the May 21 memo in the first place. Besides, no one had proved that the memo was deliberately drafted to have that effect.[18]

Less equivocal, though, was a public relations gaffe reported to have occurred later that summer, during a meeting of top-producing Chairman's Club brokers at Merrill Lynch.[19] Vice chairman and executive vice president John L. "Launny" Steffens reportedly told his audience that the women who had filed claims in the class action were low producers, in the fourth and fifth quintiles, and that only 50 of the 900 claims filed had merit. Among the listeners were female Chairman's Club brokers who had filed claims and were by no means low producers.

DESPITE THEIR STRING OF DEFEATS, Pam and her compatriots at the New York City chapter of NOW banded together to picket Citigroup, parent of what was now called Salomon Smith Barney, on July 15. Having quit four months before, Judy Mione was a transformed woman from her unhappy days at the firm—a time when she would have been prohibited from taking part in a demonstration against it. Rested and happy, she looked serene in her role as a militant.

It took only fifteen minutes for police to be called to the unthreatening gathering. A police officer on the scene told a reporter that a call had been made to 911. Minutes later, Michael Schlein, senior vice president, arrived.[20] Schlein made the rounds to reporters but was not willing to speak for attribution. In the background, Pam and a half-dozen demonstrators chanted "Smith Barney, you can't hide, we know what goes on inside," protesting the continued use of private contracts that kept employees out of court. They picketed and chanted in the summer heat, competing with calypso music playing in the Citigroup band shell below, until their permit to demonstrate expired at 1 P.M. Two professional men in their twenties on their lunch break offered sympathetic interviews to a reporter after hearing a summary of what the protest was about. A half-hour later, after having returned to their offices in the Citicorp building, they rushed back down to the sidewalk and appealed to the reporter not to use their quotes. "Smith Barney is a big client," one of them explained. The protest received some attention from the media, and Pam took her NOW group off to lunch when the demonstration ended.

A month later, a glowing article about Stowell and Friedman appeared in *People.* Over a four-page spread with five photos, the two lawyers were described as having "forced these companies to take notice." Beneath a photograph that included Pam and Sean Martens, the caption read. "Gloria Steinem (center) and plaintiffs Roberta Thomann (right) and Lorraine Parker (in hat) protest against Salomon Smith Barney in Manhattan in '97." Neither Pam nor Sean was identified.

Days later, Merrill fired three women from its Providence, Rhode Island, office. All had filed claims against the company. It was not an encouraging sign to think that a major brokerage firm would take such a step despite the attention focused on sex discrimination in the industry. What would firms do when the heat was off? several of the more militant Merrill women wondered.

On September 8, 1999, citing retaliation and failure to implement the Merrill settlement, Stowell and Friedman filed a corrected status report with Judge Castillo. As that report and its charges were pending in federal court, the NOW Legal Defense and Education Fund was preparing festivities to honor Merrill at its annual Equal Opportunity Awards and Dinner—the kind of event at which honorees are expected to sponsor expensive tables. Anne Kaspar, a class representative in the Merrill lawsuit, wrote an angry letter to Kathryn Rodgers, executive director of the NOW Legal Defense and Education Fund, on September 17 to protest retaliation against women who had filed complaints; bad-faith settlement negotiations; and failure by Merrill to get going with settlement promises such as fairly distributing sales leads to women. She was disgusted that the diversity initiatives were not introduced until contempt charges were filed.

Kaspar took some comfort when she heard, only one week later, that Judge Denise Cote in U.S. District Court in New York ordered Morgan Stanley Dean Witter to hand over files to the Equal Employment Opportunity Commission related to its investigation of a discrimination case brought by Alison Schieffelin, a securities saleswoman. At least someone was being held accountable.

The news from Judge Cote's chambers, however, had a dark side. Kaspar had for some time now been questioning the wisdom of both the Merrill and the Smith Barney settlements, increasingly viewing both as the products of compromise run amok. A crown jewel of the Merrill accord had been the firm's agreement that in the future, employees could go to court against the firm. Yet in Kaspar's view, here was Morgan Stanley Dean Witter, a company that also allowed employees to go to court, finding new ways to thwart the process, so hindering the EEOC that a federal judge had to order the firm to supply the necessary documents. What will it take to make this industry accountable? Kaspar wondered. How much worse will things be when the Boom-Boom Room is out of the headlines?

Schieffelin was not the only high-level woman running into problems. Kaspar didn't know it, but Schieffelin's peers at other firms were facing frustration but still trying to find a way to work things out. Virginia Gambale, the chief information officer at Deutsche Bank, had just come back from a stressful but mandatory business meeting in Cannes, France. She would later say in a complaint that a Marilyn Monroe look-alike entertained her 100 male colleagues at the meeting, publicly fondling several. To enter the meeting, she and her four female colleagues had to walk past a welcoming committee of "sex goddesses" who wore revealing clothing. By year's end, she was passed over for a job promotion. Women at Gambale's level, though, rarely spoke out. The noise at this point was largely in the ranks of retail brokers.

There were now so many legal actions against brokerage firms and their employees that sub-battles were taking place within the battles. On October 5, lawyer Spriggs sent an e-mail to his client Beth Walker saying that he was waiting for a particular court motion that would clear the way for him to "move to dethrone" Friedman and Stowell. Talk of insurrection was in the air.

Kathryn Rodgers posted an unsatisfying response to Anne Kaspar on October 12, crediting her for her courageous role as a litigant but skirting Kaspar's specific disappointments with Merrill's behavior. Rodgers told Kaspar that it was important "to work with corporations once we have their attention, to make sure that the progress continues and grows." Thus, the awards dinner would go on.

As far as Kaspar was concerned, the lure of corporate sponsorship at the NOW Legal Defense and Education Fund's Equal Opportunity Awards and Dinner was too much for NOW to pass up.

―――――

LINDA FRIEDMAN HAD KNOWN of the campaign to replace her and her partner as attorneys for some of the Smith Barney class representatives only from secondary sources up to now, but on October 25, it came out in the open. Paul C. Sprenger, a partner at the Washington, D.C., law firm of Sprenger & Lang, wrote to Friedman to say that he was representing four women in their capacity as class representatives. He also noted that he was working with Kent Spriggs and John Davis, who represented Beth Walker, Marianne Dalton, Lisa Mays, and Teresa Tedesco. His assignment, he wrote, was to investigate whether the terms and conditions of the settlement with Smith Barney had been breached. Thus began a string of contentious letters between Sprenger and the Chicago firm.

Four days later, Pam sent a fax to Spriggs to say that she had heard thirdhand that Friedman and/or Stowell had threatened to sue him.[21] She offered him information about other such threats made by Friedman, noting that he had joined a "distinguished roster" of targets. On November 19, Spriggs filed a motion to replace Stowell and Friedman as counsel for certain of the named plaintiffs.

That opened a legal can of worms. On December 8, Stowell and Friedman filed their response. Their Memorandum in Opposition to Kent Spriggs's Motion to Substitute included a profile of Spriggs that was unattractive at best, citing cases in which he had been sanctioned by the Florida bar, questioned regarding his fees, and even sued by his own law partner.

ON DECEMBER 15, Smith Barney released its list of new managing directors. Of the 152 names on the roster, fourteen, or 10.8 percent, were women. Elsewhere, the numbers occasionally looked more encouraging. Warburg Pincus at the start of 2000 put out a list of sixty-seven new officers, of whom twenty, or 29 percent, were women.

Women in the Smith Barney class were showing up for the earliest mediations in spring 2000. Patricia Clemente, one of the class representatives and a big ally of Stowell and Friedman, was eager to have a mediator hear her case. She had started as a sales assistant in 1981 at the firm then known as Shearson/American Express and had been repeatedly denied the opportunity to become a broker. She was confident that she could line up witnesses to back up important points she wanted to make to her mediator.

Two weeks before her hearing, though, Clemente began to get disenchanted with the process. She didn't get the statements she wanted from her witnesses, although Linda Friedman's law firm did tell Clemente's story, debating the issues and presenting statistical evidence to boost her position. Clemente was distressed when, at 11 P.M., Friedman and Brad Karp, the Smith Barney lawyer, left the room for a private discussion. On returning, Friedman told her that if the offer on the table were to be increased, Karp would lose his job. From Friedman's point of view, the statement was one that could be made with regard to any lawyer who came to a negotiation with limited spending authorization,[22] but from Clemente's standpoint, it had the tone of Friedman protecting the defense. Dejected, Clemente accepted the offer, which was 10 percent of her lost wages and exactly the amount that a junior lawyer at Friedman's firm had told Clemente she would get two weeks before.[23]

Pam knew nothing of the disappointing mediation; Clemente signed a confidentiality agreement.[24] Pam was aware, though, of a complaint filed on May 8, 2000. Three women submitted a claim in U.S. District Court in San Francisco[25] that day seeking class status against Piper Jaffray & Hopwood Inc.

Four years after all the negative publicity of the *Martens* and *Cremin* suits, brokers were still describing conditions much like those in the *Martens* case. According to the Piper complaint, women made up only 14 percent of the firm's brokerage force but 93 percent of its sales assistants. Only 13 percent of the firm's managing directors were women, it claimed. On a percentage basis, the latter statistic actually put Piper ahead of Smith Barney. In the gory details summarizing life at Piper Jaffray, one plaintiff described how a new assistant branch manager called her on the phone the week after he got his new position. Not knowing where he was calling from, she asked, "Where are you?" He said, "Under your desk, looking up your skirt."

Pam still felt there was hope for her case. A hearing was coming up in seven days. Lawyers Spriggs and Davis would tell Judge Motley the ways in which they believed Stowell and Friedman had been deficient in representing the class. Pam, who had not thoroughly read Stowell and Friedman's court filings criticizing Spriggs, was expecting a day of vindication.

<hr>

KENT SPRIGGS ROSE at the clerk's command at 10:25 A.M. on May 15, 2000. His client, Beth Walker, looked striking standing beside her stocky attorney. Taller than Spriggs and thin, she had her golden blond hair tied in a braid down her back. To her right was Teresa Tedesco, a class representative who had suffered a stroke in recent years and carried herself with less energy than her friend. The three stood in a row and watched as Judge Constance Baker Motley emerged from her chambers on the left and took her seat.

Looking down at the papers on her desk, the judge seemed momentarily confused about something.

"Mr. King? Mr. King Brent?" the judge said. Then a pause. "Mr. *Spriggs*, I'm sorry."

Judge Motley got down to business. She was not pleased with the history of this lawyer from Florida who had asked permission to be heard in her courtroom that day. The judge cited from Stowell and Friedman's court papers the damaging information that had been unearthed about

Spriggs. "Your conduct as a lawyer was noted and disapproved" in the cases that class counsel had found, Motley told him. The judge noted that she had previously permitted him to appear *pro hac vice* in her court, meaning that, although he was not a member of the bar of the Southern District of New York, she would allow him to represent his clients in this particular proceeding.

Many of those who were watching had come expecting to hear Spriggs take the floor and assail the entire settlement. But here was Motley challenging the challenger. She zeroed in on Spriggs's past conduct as a lawyer and addressed his record harshly. "We can't permit a lawyer with a history like yours to appear in the Southern District," she told him. "You may be allowed to appear in other courts, but you're not allowed to appear here."[26]

There were gasps from the back of the courtroom where Pam and Judy sat. The tables were being turned, or rather, upended. Now Friedman, who was to have been the one being disparaged in this proceeding, was preparing to address the court. She began to speak of a "wonderful settlement" and credited defendant Smith Barney for having set about a complete reversal of bad behavior. Spriggs had taken potshots at her and Stowell and slung mud at them, Friedman told Judge Motley. "We ask that the court consider our motion to sanction."

John Davis, Spriggs's rail-thin partner, asked to approach the bench. He tried to focus the judge's attention on the affidavit of his clients Teresa Tedesco and Beth Walker, but Motley cut him off to ask who else had filed affidavits to support his allegations against class counsel. Motley was short-tempered with Davis, raising her voice at one point. He brought forth "tsks" and head-shakings from Friedman when he suggested that she and Stowell had repaired the settlement in response to his own clients' having flagged its deficiencies. He seemed overmatched in the majesty of the federal courtroom, at one point looking too casual for the setting with his left hand on his hip, too much the out-of-towner with a practical buzz cut in a courtroom of more stylishly coiffed big-city lawyers, at another waving his hands expansively to make his points and addressing the judge as "Ma'am."

As Davis stood before Motley, the now-banished Spriggs attempted from his seat to supply his partner with names of women who had had problems finding lawyers when Motley asked for examples of such plaintiffs. But the judge chastised Spriggs for butting in.

Friedman and Stowell burst into theatrical laughter when Davis named a particular woman as an example of someone who had settled her case without the assistance of a study that would have helped her. Both were dressed in black plaid that morning, and their outburst had the look of best-friend schoolgirls on a mission to be cunning.

Friedman presently stood and solved the mystery of why Davis's example was so amusing. The woman, who had brought a race discrimination claim, would not have been able to do so in an ordinary court proceeding, because she would have been time-barred by statutes of limitations. The more liberal statute of the Smith Barney settlement, however, allowed her to be included. Friedman's statement did not even address Davis's objection about the absence of the study; instead, she had created an opportunity to highlight a benefit of the settlement to a particular class member. Pam sat in the back of the room seething. How was it that every misstep of the opposition could be turned into a victory?

Brad Karp approached the bench to speak on behalf of Smith Barney. He was the ultimate corporate lawyer, fit, stylishly suited, with cropped curly black hair. Confident, even cocky, Karp advised the court that it had three legal bases on which it could impose sanctions on the Florida lawyers in order to "prevent shenanigans of this type." Karp rarely appeared to be caught off guard in the courtroom; he sometimes seemed so prepared, in fact, that he gave the impression of guiding jurists to a conclusion. He read Rule 11 from the Federal Rules of Civil Procedure.

The judge followed Karp's suggestions precisely.

"Pursuant to Rule 11 and 28 U.S.C. 1927, sanctions are imposed," she began. Looking down at her desk for a long pause, she again appeared puzzled for a moment and called her clerk. Then she looked out at Spriggs's partner.

"What is your first name, Mr. Davis?"

She imposed sanctions on both lawyers in the amount of $5,000 each.[27] Davis then asked if she would hear their motion on behalf of their clients.

She denied it. Pam and Judy gasped again. Court was dismissed at 11:34 A.M.

Tempers were high as the room emptied. Pam stood and glared at Karp. "Brad Karp, you're lucky I didn't get up and ask for sanctions against *you*," she said loudly. She had her finger pointed at him. "We're going to see the chief judge now. Corruption of this sort is a total disgrace against America."

Pam shouted at Karp as he walked away that he had said on the record that she had resigned from Smith Barney, not been fired, but he was through the courtroom doors by the time she got into detail. In fact, Karp had filed a memo of law on August 2, 1999, that said Pam had resigned. Even the regulatory document filed by the firm itself said that she had been terminated. Assuming the worst of Smith Barney's counsel, Pam figured that they were now switching to a stance that she'd resigned because courts were looking harshly on companies that fired employees after they made civil rights complaints.[28]

Accompanied by Judy Mione, Beth Walker, and Teresa Tedesco, Pam marched around the corner from the courtroom and into the reception area of the chief judge, who declined to meet with the group. They went from there to the 26 Federal Plaza office of the Federal Bureau of Investigation, where an investigator came to the lobby armed with his laptop computer and took down their information to open a file for the Department of Public Integrity.

Later that day, Motley issued an opinion in which she said that Pam Martens and Judy Mione were no longer part of the lawsuit and that they had lost their opportunity to pursue their individual claims. Her six-page opinion was harsh, charging them with "pettifoggery" and "interloping in the affairs of the class."

MOST OTHERS WOULD HAVE GIVEN UP. Pam Martens, apparently afraid of no one, filed a complaint against the judge.

Replete with news clippings about the job offers that Paul, Weiss had made to Judge Motley's clerks, and making multiple references to the business that Motley's banker son got from Salomon Smith Barney (a firm so big that it is hard *not* to get their business),[29] the complaint ran 257 pages and four sections.

It was filed in late June by Pam, Beth Walker, Edna Broyles, Teresa Tedesco, and Judy Mione. According to the complaint, Judge Motley was in a conflicted position because her son, Joel Wilson Motley III, "was a principal of a member firm of the National Association of Securities Dealers," which was a defendant in the suit, they wrote. Her son "Engaged in multimillion-dollar bond dealings" with Smith Barney, they added. The document pointed out that Motley would not let Broyles's attorney talk about the potential for conflict of interest between Smith Barney and the entity slated to administrate the dispute resolution process established under the settlement. The proposed administrator was a legal unit of Duke University, which had a long-standing investment banking relationship with Smith Barney.

If the latest noise from Pam was bothering Friedman, it was not showing. She was feeling confident throughout the months after the hearing in which Spriggs and Davis were sanctioned, and she predicted in early July that the Smith Barney mediations were going so well that only 4 or 5 of the 1,900-odd cases would fail to be settled at the mediation stage and thus need to advance to arbitration.[30] Friedman said that her firm had a body of 3,000 Wall Street women in its database at that point, giving her and Stowell potent negotiating leverage when they represented women who had discrimination claims. "We can say 'Change, or we open the phone lines,'" she said. "At any given point in time, we can probably muster up ten complaints against any firm on Wall Street, and they all know it."

Her firm's profile had risen to such an extent that deeply troubled women would call to say that they had become suicidal as the result of their experiences. "Over the past six months, we've made a dozen suicide referrals. Five of them were in the past two weeks," she said on July 11. The work had taken on a humanitarian and counseling aspect.

Friedman, Stowell, and the defendants at Smith Barney had been in the good graces of the court and most of the plaintiffs in part because of their substantial plans for change. Policies would be revamped, the workplace would be diversified, attitudes would be reformed, and targets for numbers of women in professional jobs would be set. It was hard to argue with such a solid blueprint.

Those goals, though, looked excessively ambitious with the publication of a survey of Smith Barney women on July 17, 2000, that Stowell and Friedman had commissioned. Louise Fitzgerald, a respected psychologist in the fields of sex discrimination and sexual harassment, contacted 1,853 women who had worked at Smith Barney four years earlier and received information from 1,210—65 percent of those she surveyed. One-third had the symptoms of post-traumatic stress disorder. One-quarter of them had been stroked or fondled in a sexual way while on the job. Seven out of ten said they had been stared at, leered at, or ogled in a way that made them feel uncomfortable on the job.

"I've been studying sexual harassment for almost twenty years, and I have never seen anything like this," she says. "It was amazing to me how damaged some of these women were." Because Stowell and Friedman had commissioned Fitzgerald, and because Fitzgerald got her information directly from women who agreed to participate in the study, the results were not subject to confidentiality agreements, as other studies of class-related issues were. The Fitzgerald study, however, was not widely disseminated, either, and was not part of the court file.

One-third of the women surveyed claimed they had been sexually coerced during the period Fitzgerald studied. Workplace studies done prior to this one typically showed no more than 5 percent complaining of sexual coercion, defined as the extortion of sex either through the promises of job-related rewards or threats of punishment, Fitzgerald says. She saw the same kinds of problems at company offices all over the country, she adds. Fitzgerald found it remarkable that an industry culture could breed such similar conditions in disparate locations.

Thirty-three percent had been called a bitch, a dyke, or a cunt during their tenure; 41 percent had seen coworkers or supervisors display or distribute pornography or other sexist or suggestive pictures in the office. Eighty—6.7 percent—reported unwanted attempts at sexual intercourse that required them to plead with or physically struggle with the Smith Barney male involved.

In addition to the harassment, they reported that they were demeaned and held back. Asked if they ever were in situations where their statements or opinions were ignored, 95 percent said yes. Eighty-three percent said that they had been in situations where their coworkers and supervisors had withheld information about career opportunities. It was powerful information to be added to the firmwide data that Stowell, Friedman, and many of the class representatives had been privy to once they signed the confidentiality agreements and looked at the confidential employee statistics: among other disparities, only 2 percent of the women who initially were hired as cold-callers, compared to 60 percent of the men, moved on to become stockbrokers.[31]

The harassers and discriminators were seen as powerful figures. Eighty-one percent of the women in Fitzgerald's study said the men involved could affect their professional reputation; 86 percent said the men could affect their pay and their chances of advancement. But it was too late to hold the men responsible for their actions. In both the Smith Barney and Merrill settlements, the individual men accused were off the hook from both a legal and a financial point of view. In any event, not every woman could survive that kind of workplace intact to credibly pursue a complaint. Day-to-day office life left some in a state where they came off as paranoid, untrustworthy, nervous, and prone to over-stating or understating their stories. They could become, in short, the epitome of the terrible witness.

MORGAN STANLEY DEAN WITTER fired Allison K. Schieffelin on October 25 and escorted her to the lobby to be sure that she left the building without her identification card. Schieffelin was the securities saleswoman who had filed a complaint with the EEOC in late 1998.

Earlier that month, according to Morgan Stanley, Schieffelin had had a confrontation in which she swore at her female boss and raised her middle finger. From Schieffelin's point of view, however, the firm had been on a crusade to push her out ever since she filed her EEOC complaint. Since then, traders had given her less competitive quotes on the bonds she sold, colleagues had cut her off from important market information, and coworkers generally had treated her as a pariah to be socially avoided.[32] Previously, she had been the highest-paid convertible bond salesperson at the firm; she had tried to parlay her good record into a promotion starting in 1996, but had had no success. On November 28, U.S. District Court Judge Gerard Lynch denied an appeal by Morgan Stanley Dean Witter in which it had tried to limit the information it would give to the EEOC about its investigation of Schieffelin and others. The judge said "the subpoenas will be enforced."

Plaintiffs in the Smith Barney suit were not sharing Schieffelin's winning streak. Laura Sweezey, hired as a broker but used as a sales assistant in her years at Smith Barney, went to mediation in November feeling unprepared. Exhausted at 11:30 P.M. and facing a long drive home, she gave up and left. The lawyers thought they had represented their client well, but Sweezey went away with the feeling that Stowell and Friedman were no longer being aggressive enough on her claim.[33]

Before the year was out, Stowell and Friedman shut down the web-site they had been maintaining for the women in the Smith Barney class, classactionsb.com. Friedman learned that someone was trying to buy the domain names classactionsb.net and classactionsb.org, perhaps to set up confusing or critical copycat pages. Rather than give anyone the opportunity to communicate with the class, she bought the other Web addresses herself, investing $1,500 to be sure that classactionsb.org and .net were not available. Although no outsider could tamper with Stowell and Friedman's existing page and copycat pages were now foiled, Friedman shut down her page anyway. Her clients would have to find other ways to keep informed.

Pam stayed fired up. In January 2001 she chaired a seminar for the Women in the Workplace subcommittee of the New York City chapter of NOW. It was by now her modus operandi to make lemonade out of lemons. She had an audience of only two: a NOW intern who was a student at New York University, and Amy Segal, an investment banker who had sued J. P. Morgan & Co. for discrimination after the company had fired her in November 1998. Pam made an ally of Segal. The two swapped stories about their experiences with the brokerage industry, with lawsuits, and with attorneys whose representation was a disappointment. Pam told Segal that a panel of appeals judges would be hearing her challenges to Judge Motley's elimination of her and Judy Mione from the *Martens* suit on February 9. Segal said she would be there.

IT WAS 11:04 A.M. "Good morning, your honors. May it please the court. Brad Karp on behalf of, happily, Smith Barney."

By now, courtroom groupies following the *Martens* case knew the key lawyers by sight. There was Friedman, with her deliberate, scholarly style. And Phelan, with his intelligent but too-retiring ways. Belnick, the shrewd statesman who could recast an image for an ailing client, had left Paul, Weiss for a corporate job at Tyco International in September 1998. So now Karp, Belnick's intense understudy, had stepped up to the plate.

The Second Circuit Court of Appeals had gathered that day to address three issues: Had Judge Motley improperly dismissed Pam and Judy's claim against Smith Barney? Had Kent Spriggs and John Davis been improperly sanctioned and dismissed from Motley's court on May 15, 2000? And should Judge Motley's denial of a motion that challenged the way in which the settlement was being carried out be vacated? The Honorable Ellsworth A. Van Graafeiland, seemingly inattentive through much of the hearing, sat at the left end of the judges' bench. Guido Calabresi, the goateed judge in the middle, often infused his questions and comments with charm and humor. Judge Sonia Sotomayor, a straight talker who could comfortably preface a question with an impatient "Come on, counsel," sat on the right.

Brad Karp was not the first to give oral arguments that day. As often happened, though, he was the most memorable speaker so far that morning, standing out with a self-assurance that could go over the top. "This Circuit has made crystal clear—" he began.

"I have a huge problem," interrupted Judge Sotomayor, looking down at him through her glasses.

"Yes, your honor?"

What, Sotomayor wondered, was his problem with Martens's problem? Karp was demanding that she arbitrate her claim against Smith Barney because she no longer had standing to sue the firm. But why hadn't he done this much earlier? Why was he complaining that Martens was stalling on her lawsuit when Karp's client, Smith Barney, had itself taken so long to demand arbitration?

Karp tried to explain to Sotomayor and the other two judges why he was on strong legal ground in asserting that Pamela Martens should not have delayed so long in taking steps to seek a jury trial.

"If I could just finish the sentence," said Karp. "In the *Shannon* case, the situation was identical to the situation here," he said, attempting to give the judge a legal precedent for his position.

"That's always a dangerous statement," Sotomayor interrupted. "Since I wrote the opinion, I know. There were vast differences. Why don't you move to the bottom line. But don't try arguing my own case."

No sooner had Karp gone through that browbeating than Judge Calabresi, in the center chair, took him to task for having sided with Motley in dismissing Martens and Mione.

"These people were trying to say something about their suit in the class," Calabresi said. "And the court is annoyed that they pulled out of the class. But they have a right to their individual suit. They have a right to that individual suit. And the whole tone of Smith Barney in this period of time is that somehow by pulling out of the class, they did something which is gross immorality." The courtroom burst into spontaneous laughter. The judge finished his thought. "These people were in no way abandoning their class."

It was an auspicious moment for Pam Martens. After three years of frustration in Judge Motley's court, there was—for the first time—an audience for some of her arguments. The entire tone of the *Martens* case seemed to have changed. Pam was energized.

Next up, at 11:28, Linda Friedman approached the podium from her seat in the lawyers' section on the left side of the courtroom. Her opponent Phelan sat across from her, on the right. Mary Stowell, always in the background at these Smith Barney court events, was at a table toward the rear of the lawyers' section with Joyce Huang, one of the defense lawyers representing Smith Barney. Spriggs sat to the far left along the row of lawyers.

After taking a swipe at Spriggs for not having attended the fairness hearing, Friedman spoke to the judges about the success of the settlement, citing an increase in female branch managers to twenty-five, up from only six before the lawsuit was filed. There was even a woman running a branch in a major city, said Friedman; Boston was under female management. She further told the judges that fifty-one female branch managers were "on the bench," meaning that they were qualified to become branch managers should openings arise. Friedman was proud of her role in it all, and the results were indisputable.

Judge Sotomayor told Friedman that no one was accusing her or her firm of any wrongdoing. As counsel for so many women in the class, though, "Someone has to be monitoring you," she said. "And if it's not the class reps, who is it?" She gave the example of some subpoenas from Spriggs's law firm that Friedman had gotten quashed rather than simply cooperating with Spriggs and heading off further controversy.

Friedman took part of her allotted time to read to the judges the e-mail that Spriggs had sent to Walker suggesting that he and his followers "dethrone class counsel." Spriggs only minutes earlier had told the judges that he had not intended to attempt any such thing. If Friedman's credibility had been dented by the allegations of subpoena-quashing, Spriggs's standing had been hammered by having denied what had just been revealed in writing.

As the all-morning session wound down, Judge Calabresi came out bluntly with a strong view on one of the most important dynamics of the case. Looking at Friedman, he said, "You had a judge who, for a variety of reasons, came out on your side," he said. "You had something going your way."

Pam relished the words. It *had* been going their way, she thought. It's just that no one until now had said it publicly—except for Pam and her ever-shorter list of supporters.

After one more round of embarrassing questions for Spriggs, the dramatic session was over. Pam felt that the right questions had at last been raised. These judges are going off to deliberate with a proper understanding of the issues, she thought. Now, patience. It could be months before they came to their decisions.

As the crush of onlookers filed out, Pam spotted her new ally Amy Segal and caught up with her at the back of the courtroom. "It's like I've been in a coma for three years," Pam told her. "And now the coma has lifted."

Chapter Sixteen

Arbitration After All

"My most serious charge is attempted murder because I felt suffocated and I could not breathe when my boss forced himself upon me and raped me."

— A FORMER COLD CALLER FOR A MAJOR BROKERAGE FIRM, IN A COURT FILING

IN THE YEAR THAT FOLLOWED, more women settled and ceased to discuss their cases anymore. Several at Merrill signed off on individual deals with onerous conditions. Among the provisos were destruction or delivery of any notes taken during discovery in the *Cremin* lawsuit, and agreements never to communicate with the media about the lawsuit or their individual claims or to write any books or articles about Merrill.[1] A lawyer for a former sales assistant in Smith Barney's Cleveland office approached one of his client's coworkers about being a witness; she said she couldn't, because she had settled and signed a confidentiality order.[2]

But new cases kept coming. Karen Nelson Hackett, forty-seven, a floor governor at the New York Stock Exchange, filed a grievance with the EEOC against the securities firm ING Barings. Her complaint, alleging an environment in which men verbally harassed her and other women, forcibly kissing her and others, was filed in December and came into the open on January 11, 2001, in a *Wall Street Journal* article.[3] Hackett was the highest-profile woman yet to go public with harassment and discrimination complaints, having been the first woman to be appointed to the NYSE board of governors. Along with her description of graphic sexual remarks on the job, she claimed that she had received a smaller bonus than a male peer and that the firm frequently held meetings in her absence.

On March 6, 2001, Louise Fitzgerald published a second survey for Stowell and Friedman, this one of the claimants who had participated in the Merrill Lynch class action. Like her Smith Barney survey, it was neither subject to confidentiality restrictions nor filed in court. Friedman had commissioned Fitzgerald saying that the Merrill case was one of discrimination, not harassment. Fitzgerald had quipped back, "You wanna make a bet?"

The distressing results proved Fitzgerald's hunch correct. She contacted 915 women who filed claims against Merrill and got 643 usable responses. Sixty-two percent said men had made unwelcome attempts to draw them into a discussion of sexual matters; 80 percent said men had repeatedly told sexual stories or jokes that were offensive to them; and 37 percent had been touched in a way that made them feel uncomfortable.

By some measures, in fact, harassment at Merrill was as bad as or worse than that reported by class members at Smith Barney. The Merrill women had even less faith that "the system" would work for them. At Merrill, 83 percent of the survey participants said that their reaction to an experience with harassment was to stay away from the man or men involved (as opposed to a less passive response, such as reporting the man). That answer was given by 77 percent of the Smith Barney group. At Merrill, only 7 percent bothered to call the Hot Line for assistance, compared to 10 percent at Smith Barney. At Merrill, 12 percent went to human resources with a problem, compared to 24 percent at Smith Barney. Sixteen percent in the Merrill group filed formal complaints at work, compared to 25 percent at Smith Barney.

At both companies, victims shunned avenues for reporting harassment, saying it was ineffective and dangerous to do so. Seven out of ten at both Merrill and Smith Barney feared retaliation and said that filing a complaint would hurt their chances of advancement. Among the minority who did complain through company channels, only 1.7 percent at Merrill and 2 percent at Smith Barney said that the person about whom they complained was punished. Victims may perceive human resources and company hotlines to be ineffective or even dangerous to their careers, but the courts expect them to first pursue whatever options are offered by their companies to solve a problem. It was an airtight catch-22.

"I've gone into factories and I've gone into power companies," said Fitzgerald, but neither came close to the harassment she found in the brokerage industry. "The rate was higher than it was in the military, for God's sake, and that's kind of amazing." Both Merrill and Smith Barney established organizational climates that worked against the claimants, says Fitzgerald, with retaliation "that was incredible if they complained or fussed."

A Merrill veteran who has some perspective beyond that of Fitzgerald is Marybeth Cremin, the lead plaintiff in the 1997 class action. Cremin gives Merrill little credit for changes that came in the settlement. "We'd all be foolish if we thought they were doing this for the right reason," she says. "They're not doing something about discrimination because discrimination is bad, but because it cost them money."

One day after Fitzgerald released the Merrill Lynch survey, the EEOC said it had found reasonable cause to believe that Morgan Stanley Dean Witter had discriminated against Allison Schieffelin.

—————

As spring dawned in New York five weeks later, Pam Martens, Amy Segal, and members of New York City NOW picketed outside New York City's Carnegie Hall. It was April 17, and Sandy Weill was presiding over the annual meeting of Citigroup Inc. inside. Weill, chairman of Carnegie Hall, had the clout to arrange space there for his company meetings. With Segal looking on in horror, police arrested and handcuffed Pam for disorderly conduct at 8:30 A.M., escorting her to the local precinct, where she was jailed until 4:30 P.M. The police said she had blocked a crosswalk and disobeyed an order to disperse. No other protesters were arrested.

—————

BY NOW, WHEN A NEW CASE against a brokerage firm came to light, no connection to the Boom-Boom Room was necessary in order to attract regulatory or media attention. Jennifer Solomon, the securities analyst, filed a complaint against Citigroup Inc.'s Salomon Smith Barney unit and two of its research department executives on September 5, 2001.[4] After getting a promotion and a raise in early 1999, Solomon stayed at Salomon rather than take a competing offer. By March 2001, in an e-mail to consumer analysts worldwide, it was announced that Solomon was the new Global Consumer Supersector Coordinator.

Five other analysts—all male—also would be named supersector coordinators, the complaint said. The men were relieved of their duties as securities analysts so that they could attend to their new jobs full-time. On August 2, Solomon was told that she must give up her promotion and return to her securities analyst job because the firm could not immediately fill her old job.

She sued for fraud and sex discrimination. Four days after Solomon filed her complaint, in its first federal suit ever against a major Wall Street firm, the EEOC joined Alison Schieffelin against Morgan Stanley Dean Witter. Things like that didn't happen back in the days when EEOC statistics painted Wall Street as the place where there was no discrimination.[5]

BY THE TIME THE EEOC had joined Schieffelin, most of the claims in *Martens v. Smith Barney* had been settled through negotiation or mediation. Just as Edna Broyles's lawyer Gary Phelan had warned at the fairness hearing on April 9, 1998, those plaintiffs paid a price for the decision to adjudicate each action individually. Phelan had told the court that the settlement's dispute resolution system would protect "systemic discriminators" by judging one claim at a time in isolation. He predicted that only the weakest cases would advance through the levels of the program, because Smith Barney would likely be "picking off" the strongest cases and settling them quickly. As for the mediations themselves, several women said that, from what they could see, not much went on in their settlement hearings to increase Smith Barney's offer from what was on the table when they walked in.

One obstinate plaintiff was determined to be heard before arbitrators, although, by her account, Smith Barney worked hard to avoid an arbitration with her. In fact, it was Phelan's own client Broyles who was first in line for an arbitration hearing, and thus Broyles, now using a trial lawyer, was the guinea pig who would test Phelan's hypothesis. The crux of Broyles's complaint was against her branch manager, Frank Powers, whom twenty women in the branch cited in the individual claims they filed under the class action. Yet the arbitrators would not be able to consider the nineteen others when they judged Broyles's case. Broyles had sought a hearing date in accordance with the schedule promised in the settlement, but she had been delayed by Salomon Smith Barney because the firm wanted first to assess all the claims against Powers, according to Linda Friedman. Friedman said it was her belief that Salomon Smith Barney had a pool of money allocated for Tampa and was not willing to take on the Broyles case until it had studied the firm's exposure throughout the office.

On a broader canvas, the settlement was resolving itself in another way Phelan had forewarned: in some of the cases most embarrassing for the firm, claimants stopped talking once they got their money. For whatever reason, several whose cases against Smith Barney were particularly unsavory either would no longer answer a reporter's telephone calls or said through their lawyers that they were pleased with their settlements and had nothing more to add.

Their silence buttressed a well-financed and steadily improving image on other fronts. These days, the public was exposed to a Smith Barney and a Merrill Lynch that supported women. Advertisements by both featured more female faces. The good press that Merrill Lynch received for ending mandatory arbitration helped, too.

———

BY FALL 2001, Pam Martens had received no settlement. She had no court date. She faced the possibility of never receiving a penny from Smith Barney and claimed not to care whether monetary compensation came her way. Her stamina and ability to remain outspoken derived from her obstinacy. To a fault, she would not risk selling out. She had opened a window into what happened to women on Wall Street, letting in a little light, and had passed the idea to others to do the same.

Just as that light was exposing how Wall Street treated its female employees, the destruction of the World Trade Center Twin Towers on September 11, 2001, put a country in mourning and shifted everyone's focus. That day's copies of the *Wall Street Journal* and the *New York Times* had featured stories that detailed the historic cooperation of the EEOC with Allison K. Schieffelin in suing Morgan Stanley Dean Witter—a firm suddenly grieving the deaths of employees in the tragedy. The day before, Cari M. Dominguez, chairwoman of the EEOC, had stood before reporters in New York and said that the federal government would not tolerate the discrimination and retaliation Schieffelin had put up with in the workplace. Considering the enormity of the loss at Schieffelin's former employer, the import of that government backing had receded to a trifle in twenty-four hours. Setting the Schieffelin case back further was the destruction of the EEOC's New York office, in 7 World Trade Center. It was not until late October 2001 that the New York staff even settled into temporary quarters.

The World Trade Center attack piled economic devastation on top of a recession that already had begun. After that, many worthy ideals were rendered less urgent by comparison, including the issue of gender equality on Wall Street, which had only just begun to get attention in Washington and in the corporate suite. Bad times can serve as a foil for the promotion that never seems to come to the candidate who reaches her targets. Don't like the way you are treated? You are lucky to have a job. What do you mean, you want a bonus as big as whatshisname's down the hall? Times in which patriotism becomes an exigent priority can leave a great many things on the back burner.

The acid test of the settlement in this new environment would come when the first of the complaints wound its way up to the arbitration stage. Everyone was waiting for the first public hearing for one of the claimants, with the potential for depositions and exhibits.

And that is exactly what was about to happen, starting on Halloween.

———

FLANKED BY HER HUSBAND, Philip Broyles, and her New York lawyer, David Ratner, Edna Broyles walked into the second-floor conference room of the First Union Bank building in Tampa, Florida, on the morning of October 31, 2001. Three years, three months, and seven days after Judge Motley's approval of the Smith Barney settlement, the first arbitration was about to begin. It was more than five years since the *Martens* lawsuit had been filed.

There was plenty at stake. The defendant, Salomon Smith Barney, had done meticulous research and was prepared to use its arsenal of negative information to discredit Broyles and her witnesses. Those documents sat in big black binders that the lawyers had lugged in early that morning. Some of the memos and interviews dated back fifteen years, to Broyles's first months at the firm. They even had a fifteen-year-old memo that criticized Broyles, written by a woman who had herself filed a claim in the class action against Smith Barney and settled. That woman now worked contentedly for Edna Broyles at PaineWebber.

Three arbitrators—all lawyers—were there to hear the case. Mary Lau, quietly commanding and soft-spoken, with the hint of a Southern accent, was the lead arbitrator. Lau set a tone that was genial but reserved, taking pains to show no biases in a case that she knew was under scrutiny. Martha Cook was the heaviest note taker of the three, chronicling much of the testimony despite the presence of a court stenographer. And there was Roger C. Benson, who could surprise everyone by launching a series of probing questions on occasions when he appeared to have been paying no attention. The three kept to themselves during breaks and when they arrived and departed each day. The whole setup presented a stark contrast to the clubby, make-the-rules-as-you-go atmosphere seen at some securities arbitrations in the past.

Everyone in the room knew the outlines of Broyles's grievances by now: Branch manager Frank Powers had hired Broyles from Dean Witter in 1985, telling her that the transfer of her customers' accounts would not present a problem. In fact, he told her, the move would be "seamless." Yet Broyles's problems were many. In August 1989, Broyles and three other women in the branch met with Powers to discuss a variety of issues about the office; she was developing a history of advocating for female colleagues, including sales assistants who couldn't get into the training program to become brokers. In 1991, Broyles wrote to her manager to complain about operational glitches that she said were harming her customers. Others in the office were unhappy with operations and clashed with the branch manager, too, but Broyles ultimately was sanctioned for the commotion she made. Fifty years old by the time of the arbitration hearing, she had, over the years, moved her complaints steadily up the chain of command in human resources and management. On May 25, 1994, Broyles was promoted to vice president. Yet six days later she received a written performance warning that, among other things, she must stop raising her voice, stop asking for a transfer, and stop criticizing management. On January 6, 1995, she was fired.

Although Frank Powers, who fired her, had been named in the complaints of twenty women, he still worked as a broker at the firm. Both sides knew that Powers was expected to testify the following day.

Broyles's single lawyer, David Ratner, was up against Salomon Smith Barney's six: Brad Karp, Daniel Toal, Joyce Huang, who back in 1997 had been at the first collective mediation in Chicago with fourteen of the original plaintiffs, Joanna R. Weiner, and Becky Sacher, all of Paul, Weiss; and Eugene Clark of Citigroup. Two members of the press had been permitted to observe the proceedings under terms of the settlement. Broyles had an expert witness in the wings, prepared to present a case for $3.1 million in damages as a result of her having been fired; Salomon had an expert who had been familiar with proprietary company payroll statistics ever since Broyles's mediation talks of July 1997. Salomon's expert, who had all the numbers, was prepared to say that no discrimination had taken place. The firm had so far kept the lid on studies performed in connection with the settlement that used its proprietary data: none had entered the public domain. They were undertaken with the idea that women entering arbitrations could use them to show that discrimination had taken place at the firm; the settlement stated that they could do so. Smith Barney, however, had already reached an agreement with Broyles's lawyer to keep that data out of this hearing—an agreement Broyles said she knew nothing about, although her lawyer said he had told her.

BRAD KARP WAS WRAPPING UP his opening statement. He had characterized Edna Broyles's departure from the Tampa branch as a blessing, given the trouble she'd caused. "It was as if a malignant tumor had been excised from the office," he said.[6] It was now time to tell about Broyles's *other* rabble-rousing—the lawyers she had fired, the lawyers who had fired her, and the complaints that she had lodged against Tampa management. "Just as Ms. Broyles launched complaints against the operations personnel at Smith Barney, she also launched complaints against class counsel."

David Ratner, Broyles's lawyer, objected that Karp was getting into issues that were beyond the scope of the arbitration, and Mary Lau, the lead arbitrator, directed Karp to wrap it up and move on. But Karp laid it on thicker.

"There have been accusations made by Ms. Broyles against a whole host of individuals—class counsel, the federal district judge in this case, the law clerks who patrol the Southern District of New York clerks' office—that they've engaged in various secret frauds in an effort to try to get her," he said. He said that Broyles showed "a lack of balance."

The opening had the ring of a familiar litigation style used in discrimination and harassment cases: the nuts-or-sluts defense. When harassment is alleged, paint the plaintiff as promiscuous. When discrimination is alleged, paint the plaintiff as crazy or unstable. Karp appeared to be setting Broyles up as the latter.

There would be many rounds to go through before the Paul, Weiss team would question Broyles herself, though, later that afternoon. Among the witnesses ahead of her was her friend Connie Bladon, a former broker in the Tampa office of Smith Barney.

Bladon, who currently was branch manager of a small office of Robert W. Baird & Co. in Tampa, said that she had not experienced harassment in the office but did have problems on business trips with Smith Barney colleagues. Ratner was doing the questioning; Karp, back at his seat, listened intensely, biting his lower lip as he frequently did when he was absorbing testimony taken by other lawyers.

"There were two times in particular where I would get phone calls, you know, all through the night from two brokers, and they would knock on the door, pound on the door. Then they'd want to, after a meeting, escort me up to my room, which I learned very quickly was not because they were concerned about my safety. I had numerous things like that happen." It also was common knowledge in the office, according to Bladon, that a staff business trip to Fort Lauderdale meant that the men could go to the local strip clubs on the company. "It was entertainment, and the firm paid for it," she said. Asked by Ratner how she knew that, she said, "All the guys told us about it, and they talked about it at the business meetings the next morning."

Bladon testified that Frank Powers was "on the warpath" for certain women, and that women were out of favor with Powers because of the way they did business. "He wanted higher production, and the guys would do that." Bladon said she was fired by Powers, who accused her of doing unauthorized trades.

Paul, Weiss lawyer Joyce Huang moved quickly to discredit Bladon on cross-examination. Always tense, and expressionless with the exception of her furrowed brow, Huang presented exhibits to the arbitrators that dated as far back as 1985, when the settlement of a customer complaint against Bladon was reported to the New York Stock Exchange. Ratner objected to use of the exhibits, none of which had been shared with him during discovery before the hearing. The arbitrators allowed Huang to proceed with what turned out to be a prickly cross-examination nonetheless. Huang, a highly focused lawyer with straight black hair that came halfway down her back, navigated a somewhat risky legal course: in attempting to discredit Bladon, she exposed every available document on the broker's problems with the investing public. That process, however, equally exposed Smith Barney: if Bladon was as bad as Huang wanted the arbitrators to believe, then why hadn't they fired her after the problem in 1985, rather than keep her for another eleven years? She was in the Tampa branch from 1982 to 1996.[7]

Huang challenged Bladon directly on the question of why women remained at the branch if it was such an oppressive and discriminatory place to work. And weren't there more women in the Smith Barney Tampa branch than there were in the industry at large? Huang asked.

"We had a lot more in our branch than some others did, and—but I really think a great part of that was that we became good friends, and we just stuck it out together, commiserated together," Bladon said. "It wasn't because it was such a great working condition that we all decided to stay around." The description was reminiscent of the female camaraderie in the bullpen of the Boom-Boom Room branch.

With that, Huang gave Bladon a list of brokers at the branch. Huang had Bladon count the number of men and women on the page. She then handed the witness a calculator and told her to determine the percentage of the brokers who were women. The exercise was done to illustrate that, at that unspecified point in time, Powers employed a higher percentage of women than did most branches at the time: 21.21 percent. That was considered a commendable ratio. The arbitrators were not permitted to consider that the list included women who had claimed discrimination in the settlement and collected money from Smith Barney.

Smith Barney moved to the question of whether branch management treated the women any differently than it did the men.

Witnesses testified that Powers could be abusive and abrasive to men and women alike. "He reduced a couple of male brokers to tears," said

Tom Greene, a twenty-five-year employee of the firm, who was operations manager under Powers.

Karp buttressed this notion of Powers as an equal-opportunity bully, at one point referring to notes that Broyles had taken in which she said that one of the men in the office described working for Powers as similar to working in a prison. One male broker who had worked there agreed under cross-examination that the environment under Powers could be hostile and abusive.

But Cathy Eanes, Powers's former sales assistant, who now worked for Broyles, said, "I never ever saw him yell and scream at a male broker the way he yelled and screamed at me." She said that he demeaned her so badly that she didn't think she could ever work at a brokerage firm again. After leaving Smith Barney, she took a job as a cashier at a Publix supermarket.

Smith Barney's defense relied not just on attempting to show that the branch was no more unpleasant for women than for men but also on showing that Broyles complained in an unconstructive manner, and that the operational inefficiencies that she complained about were suffered by everyone in the branch. It put Smith Barney in the sometimes uncomfortable position of fashioning poor management, sloppy operations, and mistreatment of customers—all things Broyles complained about—as typical or acceptable. The characterization was important, though, if the firm was to successfully show that Broyles stood out among her peers for her behavior.

On November 1, the second day of what would be three days of hearings, Karp reminded Broyles that there was a campaign against her. "Have you ever heard that operations at Smith Barney became so sick of your complaining and became so accustomed to your accusations that they began to create what became known in the branch as an 'Edna File'?" Karp asked. She said that she had heard of it. Ten and one-half hours into the day's testimony, at 7:25 P.M., the arbitrators decided that they would not have time to hear from the last two witnesses that night. They would reconvene on November 27 to hear the star witness, Frank Powers, work to discredit his former broker. Before the day ended, at headquarters in New York, Jennifer Solomon quit. She was unable to continue working with the stress related to the demotion to her old job.

POWERS, TALL, SUNTANNED, and speaking with a baritone that could belong to a radio announcer, did not disappoint his lawyers at the third and last session. He testified about an incident that occurred the day before Thanksgiving 1994, when one of Broyles's customers called wanting to liquidate two accounts but not enough people were on staff to finish the job before the market closed.[8] Powers said that Broyles had yet another explosion in the office, slamming the telephone down on him after telling him in the minutes before the 4 P.M. close that the job had not been completed by operations. In telling the story, he exposed the fact that his thinly staffed branch that day was illegally executing trades that they were not licensed to do. "It's illegal for them to be entering orders in the first place," he said. "They were doing a favor to Edna by taking that risk and entering those orders." He appeared to be shifting the blame back to Broyles.

Ratner argued that Broyles had used the corporate chain of command appropriately, first attempting to settle problems with her branch manager, then moving to ever-higher levels that included human resources, the regional manager, the retail sales president, and beyond. Smith Barney painted her as a person who inappropriately went over heads.

Karp showed the arbitrators dozens of documents that illustrated the lengths that Broyles went to to validate her complaints in writing. Her memos went as high as Jon Linen, the president of Shearson Lehman Brothers. Karp, apparently not expecting the answer he would get, asked one of Broyles's witnesses, Steve Murray, if he had ever gone over Powers's head and complained about his boss.[9] Murray, a former broker in the branch, said that he had complained to Doug Van Skoy, the regional manager, about Powers. In fact, he said, he had also written to Joseph Plumeri, the head of retail sales; to Frank Zarb, chairman and CEO at Smith Barney; and to the head of the mutual fund department, to say that he did not feel the firm was dealing honestly with a matter that concerned its mutual fund fees. He said that Plumeri called him personally and said that the policy was going to be changed. Ratner followed up to establish that Murray had never been issued a performance warning.

In a separate cross-examination of Broyles, though, Karp mocked her for having written to Linen and Plumeri in December 1991.[10]

"So you thought it was appropriate at this point because your operational concerns hadn't been addressed and you were frustrated, to send a letter to the *president* of Shearson Lehman Brothers?" he asked. Broyles said that in her heart, she thought that because she was a productive employee with a spotless regulatory record, her thoughts would be welcome. She thought that she was actually helping Shearson, she testified.

"So the answer to my question is yes, you thought it was appropriate to send this letter to the president of Shearson Lehman Brothers?"

At that point, she gave him the short answer he was looking for. "Yes," she said.

Helen Fisher, the Rutgers anthropology professor, commented later that she was not surprised that Broyles fumbled in her career and in her hearing, forging ahead with what she perceived as the right thing while bungling the political and legal goals. Women in litigation "are assuming people are gonna do the right thing," she says. But while Broyles was banking on justice and righting years of what she considered wrongs, the defense was fastidiously pursuing a methodical case. Broyles's whistle-blowing was a hindrance to her case, just as her perfectionism was.

A good part of the three days of testimony was spent untangling details of Broyles's altercations with Powers. For example, Broyles and three other women at the branch had met with Powers at one point to discuss issues of concern in the branch. Powers testified that "the lady group," as he called them, did not talk about gender discrimination, although Powers could not explain why the letters "EEOC" appeared in a box in the bottom left corner of the notes he took during that meeting.[11] "I have racked my brain," he said. "I don't know how that got there or why."

Karp explored Broyles's emotional state, including an incident in Powers's office in April 1989, when Powers had said that Broyles was upset and emotional because the pastor of her church had had an affair with a congregant. Karp asked whether Broyles knew that one of her female coworkers had approached Powers in the same time period to say she was "very concerned about you and that she thought the stresses of being a mother, a wife, and a broker had really gotten to you."

Held back from this portion of the cross-examination was material that Huang would use later in her direct examination of Powers: that the coworker, Diana Winoker, had told Powers "that Edna was about to blow, quote unquote," and that Winoker thought Broyles was going to start proceedings against Powers with the EEOC. The later inquiries would make Karp's claims that Winoker had been concerned about

Broyles appear disingenuous. Powers asked Winoker at the time on what grounds Broyles was going to do this, and Winoker, according to Powers, said, "Absolutely no grounds. She's sick."[12]

Soon after that incident, Powers contacted a human resources executive, Jodie-Beth Galos, seeking guidance.[13] Galos—the same HR person who had advised the Garden City women to try to get along with Nicholas Cuneo—visited the Tampa branch in April 1990. To this branch manager, however, she issued a warning: "You're either doing something illegal, in which case you have to deal with me, or you're doing something wrong," she told Powers.[14] Powers was shaken by what Galos said to him, particularly given that Galos had planned a lunch with several women in the branch for later that day. He called his manager and friend Rudy Hlavek shortly after the visit. Hlavek said, in essence, not to worry about what happened with Galos.[15] Powers and Galos never spoke again, and she is not employed at the firm today.

Karp did not let pass the opportunity to remind the arbitrators that September 11, 2001, had brought on hard times, suggesting, perhaps, either that brokerage firms were hard-pressed to come up with money, or conversely, that the industry's workers had less earning potential. "We've all read in recent weeks of tens of thousands of people in the brokerage industry losing their jobs," Karp said, apparently to minimize Broyles's economic worth in the arbitrators' eyes, in the event they should decide that she deserved a monetary award.

———

JUST BEFORE 9 P.M. ON NOVEMBER 27, Edna Broyles readied herself to present to the panel the documentation that would, in her view, prove once and for all that the crazy things that brokerage firms said could never happen, could happen. She was going to hand over the experts' report that showed how female brokers received significantly fewer equity accounts than male brokers when colleagues departed. And she had a sociologist's study[16] that showed how female brokers increased production from the inherited accounts they received at Smith Barney by 29 percent over the previous years, while male brokers' production on inherited accounts decreased by 35 percent. The defense had frequently suggested that women in the branch did better than men because of the support of Frank Powers, the branch manager. These aggregated national statistics might indicate other possibilities.

In all, class counsel had compiled four written expert reports, only one of which had been in the public record up to now—the Louise Fitzgerald report that drew on Fitzgerald's own data. The reports had been used in some mediations, but mediations were closed to the media and to the public. Stowell and Friedman had both written reports and a video presentation that combined Fitzgerald's work with the previously proprietary work of Jerry Goldman, a mathematician who analyzed workforce patterns; Janice F. Madden, who analyzed account distribution to see if it was done on a gender-neutral basis; and William Bielby, who examined sociological implications.

Ratner had told the arbitrators and the defense team that Broyles would like to briefly address the panel before closing arguments. As the group settled in after its final break of the evening, though, Karp vehemently objected to the inclusion of the experts' reports. After a recess to discuss the controversy, the arbitrators said that they would allow Broyles to address them, but that the expert reports would not be permitted.

Broyles began to speak. She tried to discuss the statistics from the reports and was immediately cut off by the lead arbitrator. "We don't want you to talk about the statistics that we're not going to consider in this proceeding," Lau said. "We welcome your comments on any of the testimony, any of the evidence that has been presented to us on any of the issues that we have determined are before us, but we don't want to hear about the matters that we have just ruled should not be admitted into evidence. We're not going to consider those in this proceeding."

Broyles tried to come back. "OK. That's just completely contrary to what class counsel has led us to believe in this particular case," she said.

"That's not to be taken up here. We're not the tribunal to make that decision," Lau said.

Broyles turned to Ratner. "I just want it on the record that all these things have been given to them and that I have my—done my fiduciary responsibility to give it to them. And as the appellate court has ruled, I did do my job ..."

Ratner and arbitrator Martha Cook had a brief exchange in which he explained that the Second Circuit Court of Appeals had ruled seven days earlier that several issues concerning the *Martens* case had been remanded to the district court, including motions to enforce the settlement. Ratner asked his client if there was anything else she wanted to say. Suddenly, the brash pioneer who stood up to the abrasive branch manager and shouted, who counseled young women to fight, who put her name on a famous class-action suit, sounded as if she was holding back tears. A small, almost unrecognizable voice came out. "No," she said. "That's OK."

RATNER AND KARP gave their closing arguments. It was 9 P.M.

Where is the proof? asked Karp, coming from this angle and that. He gave a dispassionate, highly legal summation, exhorting the arbitrators that they must make their decision based on the law and that Broyles had no case.

The defense had been argued from the standpoint of following the rules. Now Broyles's lawyer would ask the panel to look at the big picture and do the right thing.

Why, after all this, was Edna Broyles fired, but Powers is still working there? asked Ratner. "There was one other person in that Tampa branch who yelled as much or more than Ms. Broyles, who slammed doors as much or more than Ms. Broyles, who intimidated people as much or more than Ms. Broyles, that everyone agreed on, and that was Frank Powers," he said. "And he's there with apparently lifetime tenure, and Ms. Broyles was fired."

The lawyers packed their briefcases and headed out to the temperate Florida air. Karp, Huang, Toal, and Clark walked the half-block to the Tampa Hyatt, and Ratner walked to the parking garage with his weary client.

Broyles was in her PaineWebber office before the stock market opening as usual the following morning. Enron Corp. came a step closer to bankruptcy that day, as Dynegy Inc. abandoned its plans to purchase the still viable energy trading company. It was a losing session, with the Dow Jones industrial average down 160.74 points. Edna and Phil's two children were going to stay with Grandma for the weekend. Months ago, they had decided to spend this weekend in New York without the kids. The September 11 attacks had put a damper on those plans, so they settled instead for the Florida State/Georgia Tech game in Tallahassee.

Nothing had gone the way it was supposed to. Not the settlement, which Broyles, a class representative, was not even able to read in full until after it had been announced. Not the discussions in summer of 1997 that led up to it, during which the rifts began over confidentiality.

Not the relationship with the lawyers in Chicago, who had fired her. Not her individual mediation, which happened a year later than promised. Five and a half years after the lawsuit had been filed, Broyles had just watched the lengthy testimony of a young woman on whose behalf she had fought, and yet the woman had testified against her. Janet Nichols was one of the sales assistants who kept getting turned down for the broker training program. Broyles used to go to bat for Nichols and others when management wouldn't back them. "I fought and stood up for women in that office," she said. "And I was crucified for it."[17]

Business was bad for Broyles in 2001. A stock market badly shaken by September 11 didn't help any. Neither did all the time she put into her crusade. She was a veteran in the business, accustomed, prior to her class-action work, to lavish trips that came with her high production, but nowadays she attended the same staff meetings at PaineWebber that trainees went to. Her thirteen-year-old complained about how little time he had with his mom. "I've spent half their lives with this nonsense," she says, referring to the years since she was fired in 1995.

Was it worth it?

"To change lives, yes." With pride, she speaks of how her husband fired a rainmaker at his firm in 2001 for harassing a secretary. And although many things went wrong in *Martens v. Smith Barney*, Edna Broyles says that enough change occurred, and enough people became enlightened about what they mustn't do and what must be done, that she is not bitter. "Would I do it over? Yes, I'd do it over," she says. "It's something the good Lord gave me to do. Me and Pam and Judy and all of us."

On Saturday, December 1, Edna Broyles's alma mater, Florida State, beat Georgia Tech, 28 to 17. The weekend break with Phil in Tallahassee was just enough for Broyles to get the second wind she needed to pull together a detailed letter to Judge Motley by December 13. "Dear Judge Motley," it began. "I am a Class Representative in the above referenced class action before your court." Broyles told the judge that Smith Barney had barred the experts' reports from her arbitration hearing and that the firm was similarly fighting to bar the reports in other cases.

The judge had asked Friedman, back on July 23, 1998—the day before she OKed the settlement—to explain the purpose of $500,000 that would be set aside for a statistical and other work. "For what task?" the judge had wanted to know. Friedman had said, "Preparing the statistical evidence on the class testimony so that each woman will come to the hearing not only with statistical evidence prepared by class counsel and their expert, but also with affidavits and stories and anecdotal evidence supplied by class members ... " The majority of the class members had settled by the time the expert reports were all completed in 2000. Even after they were ready, extreme efforts were made to keep them from being entered as evidence should a plaintiff begin to prepare for arbitration.

Smith Barney to the bitter end was saying that there had been no systemic discrimination, yet as Broyles's letter reached Motley's desk, it was fighting to keep Lorraine Parker from using reports that drew from the same company data in her own upcoming arbitration. Smith Barney did not win that skirmish because, in a pre-hearing phone conference, the arbitrators ruled that Parker could use the statistics. But it would not wind up mattering in the end. Before summer, Parker would settle and agree not to disclose the terms of her arrangements.

AFTER ALMOST SIX YEARS of work and dreams, the first arbitration hearing had come and gone with the much-anticipated and revealing reports unheard. The settlement's dispute resolution system, despite several clear advantages over traditional industry arbitration, still couldn't redress the vast imbalance in legal resources and sophistication between plaintiff and defendant: Broyles was out-lawyered and out-rehearsed at the hearing. Even a secondary witness for the defense had gone over her testimony four times with the Paul, Weiss lawyers. Broyles said she never rehearsed at all, although Ratner said he went over testimony with his client.

Friedman's firm was being assailed on the Web page created by Amy Segal, the former J. P. Morgan banker who by then had settled in exchange for her silence about that firm. A Web page that she had set up, womenonwall.com, was the latest recipient of a letter from Friedman suggesting that Segal might be exposing herself to a defamation claim. Segal's page was a meeting place for critics and supporters of both big settlements—Smith Barney's and Merrill's. The latest round was over the Merrill settlement: the opposing sides were gearing up for their first arbitration—the counterpart of Broyles's hearing—and word had gotten out that two of the three arbitrators who would judge the case were veteran male NASD arbitrators.

On a broader front, the outlook for women on and off Wall Street was not much more cheerful. On December 19, the *New York Times* chronicled examples of federal offices "charged with protecting women's interest" that were threatened with cutbacks or elimination.[18] Ten regional offices of the Labor Department's Women's Bureau were among those with shaky futures, according to the story.

For the players still embroiled in this battle, it was perhaps too tempting to label heroes and goats, whereas in reality all were bruised and all were champions. Twenty years before, Susan Jaskowski had joined Rodman & Renshaw as a mail clerk, become a broker, soared to the head of human resources, left on maternity leave, and gotten fired when she returned. Linda Friedman took that case just as Jaskowski was sinking into a clinical depression that would last three years—a period that might have been shorter had Jaskowski not ruled out the use of antidepressants, terrified that Rodman lawyers might find a way to use her mental condition against her. Jaskowski's was the case that the Olde women noticed, which made the Smith Barney women notice, which made the Merrill women notice. In 2002, Jaskowski, by then a volunteer for a Milwaukee breast cancer center and mother of two, hadn't kept up with all the details of the lawsuits but knew that the Rodman cases had started something big.

"That was my identity, that job. It was my whole foundation—it struck me on that deep a level. Being an HR director is what I did. I felt like I'd been betrayed by my best friend or my husband." She has no regrets. "I think I was very important. I think I helped more than one person. We were treated like a different class of people in that firm [back then]. I don't think it's like that anymore. At least now they're scared of the consequences. I never want this to happen to my daughter."

ON FRIDAY, JANUARY 11, 2002, the three arbitrators in Tampa, Florida, handed down their decision in *Broyles vs. Salomon Smith Barney*. After twenty-five pages of citations of Salomon's witnesses and the careful paper trail against Broyles, the award was cited: zero dollars would go to Broyles.

Epilogue

In the end, combatants divided in surprising ways, sometimes teaming up with those whom they previously had disdained. The long string of lawsuits that kicked off in 1992 with complaints against Rodman and Renshaw left many of its crusaders shortchanged. Their successors are reaping the fruits of the crusaders' labors.

Pam Martens won her appeal to be reconsidered for a jury trial, but Judge Motley denied her request again. Her lawyer was preparing another appeal in August 2002, with possible plans to go all the way to the Supreme Court to get his client a jury trial.

Pam still brokered stocks at the same office of A. G. Edwards where she'd gone in 1994. At the New York City chapter of NOW she ran a monthly speakers' program: "Take Back America: why is America devolving on women's rights, civil rights and human rights; how do we fight back as feminists and activists." Pam helped the NOW chapter craft a letter urging institutional investors to sell their Citigroup shares and calling for the replacement of Sandy Weill as CEO. If she should get a court hearing and win, she planned to give half to Judy Mione.

The Securities and Exchange Commission had stopped the practice of endorsing mandatory arbitration of civil rights cases back in 1998, in the heat of publicity over the Smith Barney and Merrill suits. But some firms—Salomon Smith Barney among them—had then fortified internal policies that compelled arbitration. Others garnered good public relations by giving employees the choice of taking civil rights claims to court. Apart from Merrill Lynch & Co., however, which is bound by settlement terms to its policy of allowing court, firms could reverse themselves at any time and require arbitration again.

Wall Street's men found their working environment changed. They were attending more sexual harassment awareness seminars and seeing female colleagues stepping into jobs where no woman had been before.

They also came upon the names of their own firms in newspaper stories about sexual harassment and discrimination. Some took the view that women who accused brokerage firms were holdup artists. Others groused that life at the office had become politically correct to a fault.

At Merrill Lynch, management had survived everything from picketing outside the annual meeting to embarrassing banners—"Merrill Lynch Discriminates Against Women"—flown by small airplanes over company-sponsored sports events. By its own measure the firm raised its percentage of women branch managers from 7 percent when the lawsuit was filed in 1997 to 13 percent in August 2002. The percentage of female brokers, however, barely budged, up one percentage point to 15 percent. When the two top brokers—"Directors of the Year"—were announced for 2001, one was a woman. Merrill even got through the emotions and business disruption of September 11, only to be pummeled by New York Attorney General Elliot Spitzer, who said that Merrill was riddled with conflicts of interest between its research and investment banking departments. On May 21, 2002, it agreed to pay $100 million to settle.

Salomon Smith Barney by summer 2002 had settled 1,725 of the 1,950 claims filed against it in the Martens case. The firm was recruiting more women than ever, increasing the percentage of females in its broker training classes from 12 percent at the time of the lawsuit in 1996 to more than 33 percent. Even Patricia Clemente, who was disillusioned about the firm and about the handling of her settlement, was saying that it was a good place to work. However, Salomon Smith Barney was a ferocious fighter when a woman took it to task. On the day after the Tampa arbitration panel released its decision in favor of Salomon Smith Barney on the Broyles case, one class member was given a take-it-or-leave-it deadline of twenty-four hours to accept a lowball offer from the firm's attorneys. Linda Friedman said "hundreds of millions" were paid in the combined Merrill and Smith Barney cases but would not release a specific total awarded by either firm.

Scores of lawyers pocketed fees that stretched from $5,000 to represent a Smith Barney woman in mediation to $12 million for Stowell and Friedman's firm to take on the Smith Barney class action. Fee fights had broken out. A plaintiff might grow disenchanted with one contingency law firm and move to another only to find out later that she owed money to both. One lawyer was taking on new *Martens* clients at the same time that other women were saying they had fired him. Tens and probably scores of millions had gone to lawyers involved in Merrill, Lew Lieberbaum,

Olde, Gruntal, Goldman, Garban, and other cases nationwide.

As the last 225 Smith Barney claims queued up for hearings, it seemed as if the confusion and blaming would never be over. Several who had mediations came away annoyed that they hadn't had the proper statistics to back their claims. Some said they were forced to sign confidentiality agreements before they could use reports that the Stipulation of Settlement had defined as non-confidential. Stowell and Friedman defended their work and said that several of their detractors had filed false statements. They concede that a number of women had hearings before the statistics were ready. Yet Stowell and Friedman said no one was denied the expert reports that told the story of discrimination at Smith Barney.

Kent Spriggs, alive again after the Second Circuit Court of Appeals reversed Judge Motley's rulings against him, launched a new effort to overturn the settlement. In July 2002, he filed a fresh trove of papers to Judge John G. Koeltl, who had been newly assigned to the case on May 28, 2002.

Pushing up like spring flowers through the frost came a new wave of individual lawsuits by women with big titles at big brokerages houses. J. Kimberly Mounts of Goldman Sachs Group, Jennifer Solomon of Salomon Smith Barney, and Virginia Gambale of Deutsche Bank were among them. Gambale's lawyer, Judith Vladeck, amended her lawsuit on June 21 to add a retaliation claim: the firm cut Gambale's salary in half, to $250,000, less than two weeks after she filed her suit. Vladeck, who continues to win cases, is still smoking Merit Greens.

On February 2, 2002, Jennifer Solomon's daughter was born. Solomon found out, when Salomon Smith Barney filed its answer in March 2002, that part of its defense was the fact that Solomon had not been named to the *Institutional Investor* magazine list of favorite Wall Street analysts. The firm conceded that she had been recognized by the *Wall Street Journal* for her performance in July 2001 but said it "did not carry nearly the weight" of the magazine poll, which had the ability to generate business with institutional investors. The new mother has been looking for a job on Wall Street.

Mark Belnick was sued by Tyco International Ltd. on June 17, 2002. The company alleged that Belnick, while its general counsel, had received $35 million that its board did not approve. The complaint cited an agreement guaranteeing Belnick a termination payment of as much as $10.6 million even if he were convicted of a felony. On September 12, the Manhattan District Attorney indicted Belnick for allegedly falsifying records to hide more than $14 million in company loans to himself.

Belnick's lawyer said his client had "done nothing wrong."

Nick Cuneo is no longer at the Garden City office. Number 901 Franklin Avenue is now occupied by an electronic components company, and the Boom-Boom Room is gone. The branch has moved across the street, but the new office has a Cuneo—being Leslie, Nick's thirty-eight-year-old son. Nick is in retirement with all his benefits. Investors interested in his history can no longer find his records on the CRD system that tracks the regulatory status of licensed people in the brokerage business. The NASD now purges its database of anyone who is out of the business for more than two years.

Womenonwall.com degenerated into a cacophony of disputes over lawyers, strategies, and who should take responsibility for settlements gone wrong. Women posting messages called one another "moron," "cry baby," "toilet-bowl mouth," and "felon." One woman accused another of posting "psycho-babble." Another told an enemy "You need therapy." The subject of one attack responded that she and her allies were "shaking in our Guccis."

Kept in safe hiding by a former Smith Barney broker was an audiotape, never used in court, containing these words. "I'd like to fuck her with a watered elephant's dick." People who listened to the tape said it was the voice of Nicholas Cuneo, talking to one of his brokers. A copy of the tape had been sent to Brad Karp two weeks before the scheduled arbitration of Lorraine Parker—a hearing to which the media was to be invited. On the tape, Cuneo was saying that arbitrations used to be easier to win, but with new arbitrators that included women and law professors, firms could lose now. One female arbitrator was particularly irritating, Cuneo told his charge, reaching for the elephant metaphor. Given that the panel set for Parker's April hearing included two women, the prospect of playing the tape at arbitration promised the kind of sensation Smith Barney hardly needed. They made an attractive offer of settlement, and the hearing was canceled.

At Salomon Smith Barney, a more gender-balanced group of brokers of the class of 2003 will take a training class at Manhattan headquarters, just as their predecessor Pam Martens did. Whether or not they've heard of the Boom-Boom Room case or know anything about the 225 women still waiting to settle with the firm, the lawsuits of the past six years have left the novice brokers equal in one respect: Like other rookies at certain firms on Wall Street, to earn their ticket to play as brokers, they still will have to sign a form relinquishing their right to sue their employer.

Afterword

Since Tales from the Boom-Boom Room was first published in November 2002, the question I've most often heard has been "Are things better now?" For women on Wall Street, certainly some aspects of work life have improved. For the most part, though, the answer is no.

By the time the April 2003 annual meeting of Merrill Lynch & Co. rolled around, chairman David H. Komansky was a master of the art of attending to tough questions from an audience. On the occasion of his sixth and last time overseeing the shareholder confab, though, Komansky found himself sparring with former female employees in the crowd, and, for whatever reason, leaving his practiced politesse behind.

Not that the questions he fielded were anything new or jarring. He had heard all the queries about progress for women before. What hovered as detrimental for the chairman was not that the questions hadn't changed, but that the answers hadn't, either.

Only 15 percent of Merrill's 14,000 brokers were women, the audience learned—about the same as three years before, and not much different from the state of affairs when female brokers had sued back in 1997. Despite the lack of growth in women's ranks, Komansky nevertheless made the statement that there was no "so-called glass ceiling" at his firm.

"There is nothing that holds back women or any other minority group" at Merrill Lynch, he said. As the *New York Times* described the discourse in the next day's paper—an exchange that is not disputed by Merrill spokesman William Halldin—Komansky added, "It's time to get on with life and either compete or not."

Although the noisy lawsuits against his firm and Salomon Smith Barney put the topic in the headlines for a time, the unorthodox methods of settlement of both proceedings served to quiet talk about The

Woman Issue. Since both firms cut deals in which the women had to pursue their claims individually, the power of legal discovery on a national basis was never unleashed. Class representatives agreed to the terms initially, but disenchantment over the outcome led to infighting that ultimately served the purpose of brokerage firms who benefited from a bitterly divided enemy.

When all was said and done, employee hotlines were in place, politically correct language was duly noted, and human resource departments were better versed in employment law than some law school grads.

But when it came to acknowledging that there was still a problem to work on—violators to stop and biases to correct—Wall Street had become a little like the dysfunctional family hiding the crazy uncle in the attic. Everyone knew sexual harassment was there and indeed had put much energy into urgently and quietly negotiating the crises that resulted from it. But hardly anyone spoke openly about the problem—called the doctor, if you will—and started the real work of making things better.

The reluctance to take up the topic publicly was showing itself in a variety of ways. Sanford I. Weill, chairman of Citigroup, hired Sallie L. Krawcheck to be CEO of Smith Barney's research operations in October 2002, making her the highest-ranking woman at any large brokerage firm in the United States. Weill was under enormous regulatory pressure at the time to clean up the image of Smith Barney's research department, and Krawcheck's credentials were considered among the cleanest on Wall Street.

Although one might envision that a woman of Krawcheck's newly elevated stature would use her position as a bully pulpit to advocate parity on the job and punishment for harassers, she, like other women at major firms, stayed quiet on the issue. The silence was particularly striking in front of one female audience: the Financial Women's Association honored her with its Woman of the Year award on May 14, 2003 and asked her to speak on the issue of leadership. Although her short talk was heartwarming with its gratitude for the considerable sacrifices that her parents had made toward the private educations of Krawcheck and her siblings, it had the feel of a lost opportunity for the head of a major brokerage unit (and class-action-lawsuit target) to speak to an 1,100-member women's group and skirt The Issue entirely.

"Everyone gets excited and says, 'There's Sallie,'" says Judith Vladeck, the civil rights lawyer. But Vladeck says that women in top positions need to be vocal to effect change. "Some women think that if they're silent on the subject and show themselves as great silent leaders and just hunker down and don't talk about their gender, it will work," she says. "Well, it's not working."

Within weeks of Krawcheck's address, Elaine L. Chao, U.S. secretary of labor, also addressed professional women. She greeted her audience at the Forbes Annual Executive Women's Forum in New York City on May 29 as "women pioneers and leaders." Chao gave a speech that touched on topics that included accountability and transparency in the corporate boardroom, executive pay, stock options, public disclosure, campaign finance, whistleblowers, accountability in school systems, unions, stock analysts and failed pensions. She spoke of her "special interest in the integrity and leadership of our financial and corporate institutions." Yet her prepared speech included not a single word on women's issues.

Her own agency's statistics, however, were telling a stunning story about what had been happening to the co-workers of some of her audience. Members of any New York City business audience like the one Chao addressed could tell you about the severe downturn in the brokerage industry: Wall Street had begun to enter a recession even before September 11, 2001, but the downturn accelerated once the tragedy occurred.

What people were not so aware of, however, was the degree to which women had been caught in the Wall Street downdraft. During the healthy second half of 2000, 557,000 people were employed in financial services and banking in the New York metropolitan area—284,000 of them men and 273,000 of them women, according to the Bureau of Labor Statistics. Look at those numbers two years later, after the recession had taken hold, and it was no surprise to see that total jobs were down to only 499,000. What was a surprise, though, was this: men had actually gained 14,000 jobs while women had taken the entire loss and then some, losing 72,000 jobs in the period.

A downward slope in job participation for women on Wall Street had already been in place during good times. In September 2002, the Equal Employment Opportunity Commission released a report that compared the lot of women and minorities at large investment banks as measured in the 1990 census report to that of the 2000 census.

Women had pushed ahead in percentage terms in only one category—technicians—in the ten-year period. In other categories, where women would be employing more power on the job, there were significant declines. The proportion of women in the "officials and managers" category dropped from 39.3 percent to 32.6 percent between 1990 and 2000, the EEOC said. And the proportion of women professionals dropped 5 percentage points to 44.1 percent. (In the same period, the proportion of minorities soared nine percentage points to 25.2 percent.)

"I think everything's worse" for women on Wall Street, says Vladeck. She said in summer 2003 that women managing directors were coming to her office on a regular basis with stories of having been fired. "There's no appreciable improvement that I can see over the last ten years," she said. And while she initially had been hopeful that the Merrill and Smith Barney lawsuits would stimulate change, her view had turned as she watched the litigants still at battle so many years after bringing suit. "The last two major lawsuits left such a sour taste," she said. "I don't think Smith Barney or Merrill Lynch helped because it left women angry."

Surely it left many of them confused. They had agreed to a settlement in which they would not be sharing from a pot of money provided by Smith Barney or Merrill. Rather, they would argue their cases one by one in strikingly similar three-step programs. Merrill Lynch rejected all the claims filed in the first stage, which shifted all its litigating women to Stage Two—a one-day, private mediation.

It was at this stage that some litigants began to feel betrayed by the process. Smith Barney plaintiffs had, for example, heard from class counsel about class-wide statistics that would assist them in arguing their case. As it happened, though, some women claimed that the statistics were not ready when hearings began; that the firms raised objections to the use of the statistics at hearings; and that even when the statistics were prepared, the womens' lawyers had difficulties obtaining them from Stowell and Friedman. Stowell and Friedman said that they freely shared the statistics with plaintiffs during informational meetings around the country in 1999. In August 2003, U.S. District County Judge John G. Koeltl said there was no evidence that plaintiffs who had complained to him about lack of statistics had been harmed.

By summer 2003, 58 Merrill Lynch and 70 Smith Barney plaintiffs still had cases pending. Although in the euphoria of signing off on the two settlements, much had been made of the availability of "public" arbitrations in which two members of the media could be present for cases that failed to settle, only three arbitrations had taken place out of nearly 3,000 women. In the first, Smith Barney plaintiff Edna Broyles lost and got nothing. In the second, Smith Barney plaintiff Tameron

Keyes won a $3.2 million judgment in December 2002. In the third, Deborah McCrann, a high-ranking Smith Barney sales trader, received only partial reimbursement of her legal fees. (The McCrann hearing was remarkable in several respects. One of her former bosses testified under oath that, in evaluating McCrann's qualifications for a promotion, "we factored it in" that the upcoming birth of her child might take time away from the job—something the arbitrators noted as "symbolic of illegal gender bias." Another detail of the hearing was an expert report submitted by Smith Barney in which it was argued that women seek out lower paying, less powerful jobs in anticipation of settling into a life at home with children.) A single Merrill plaintiff had had a hearing and was awaiting her panel's ruling in late summer.

While plaintiffs continued to fight the two giants of U.S. brokerage, new cases continued to be filed against firms up and down Wall Street, and firms continued to force women to arbitrate. Although most cases settled before they were reflected in the statistics, what statistics do exist suggest that brokerage firms are forcing women to arbitrate even when they don't want to.

In 1999, when the Securities and Exchange Commission voted to end the practice of tying mandatory arbitration of discrimination claims to industry licensing requirements, the stock exchanges that run arbitration forums made critical decisions: some would adjudicate a civil rights case only if both sides agreed to arbitration after the problem arose, and others would accept a case even if the brokerage firm had required an arbitration agreement as a condition of employment, but the plaintiff now wished to have access to the courts.

Since then, at the New York Stock Exchange, which insists that both parties desire arbitration, the number of cases filed has trickled to almost nothing. No gender or sex harassment cases were filed in 1999; two came in 2000; and one in 2001. Ray Pellechia, an exchange spokesman, explained that the one or two cases that do come to the NYSE arrive only when a court remands a case to arbitration because a woman has lost her fight for a trial.

The NYSE's progress was foiled, though, by NASD, which continued to accept cases even if the employee didn't want arbitration. Thus, 51 sexual harassment and discrimination cases were filed in 2000, 37 in 2001, and 45 in 2002.

The General Accounting Office released a report to Congress in late August that looked at ten years of arbitration data from the NYSE and

NASD. The GAO said that Wall Street employees who filed claims against their employers during that period were less likely to win if they included discrimination among their allegations. Forty-eight percent of the 1,546 employment cases that included a discrimination claim between 1993 and 2002 received some compensation from arbitrators. But the GAO found that 61 percent of employment cases were winners when discrimination was not among allegations.

Women can fight to the end and win large dollar amounts. Arbitrators, though, appear to be reluctant to attach the "discrimination" label to a big case. Jennifer Solomon, who sued Smith Barney after she was demoted from "supersector" analyst back to her old job as beverage analyst in August 2001, won a $1.4 million arbitration award on July 25, 2003. Although Solomon and five other analysts—all male—were named "supersector" analyst at the same time, Solomon failed to get the staff and other support of her colleagues at promotion time. Only she was demoted.

Yet the arbitrators attributed the entire $1.4 million to breach of contract, denying the discrimination claim.

Courtroom battles continue over the question of whether companies have the right to require employers to give up their right to a court trial as a condition of employment. In a three-judge ruling on May 3, 2003, the Ninth U.S. Circuit Court of Appeals called the arbitration policy of Circuit City Stores "oppressive." In a separate decision, the Third U.S. Circuit Court of Appeals said that the arbitration agreement of Anthony Crane International, L.P. was unenforceable because it was "unconscionable." While those were individual victories for the employee side, the matter was anything but clear on a national level. It would still take an act of Congress or a vote of the Supreme Court to clarify the issue.

Equally celebrated by plaintiffs' lawyers was a May 13, 2003 ruling by U.S. District Judge Shira Scheindlin against UBS Warburg. Judge Scheindlin said the brokerage firm would have to front the $165,000 to provide emails requested by Laura Zubulake, a former director and senior salesperson who said she was illegally fired from the firm. "This ruling is very important for women who are victims of discrimination," said her lawyer, James Batson. Evidence is very difficult to provide in discrimination cases, but if judges demand that companies provide email—and pay to dig it up—it will help discrimination cases enormously, Batson said. In late July, Judge Scheindlin said there was "some evidence" that a UBS banker may have hidden "especially relevant emails" after Zubulake filed her complaint with the EEOC. Judge Scheindlin noted that, although UBS had instructed its employees to save any documents that concerned Zubulake's claim, some important emails were not saved, and had to be retrieved from the firms backup tapes.

The hope of many who push for trials is the inevitable attention that will come when the curtain is lifted on men who once hid behind the mandatory arbitration shield. Yet no media blitz came on what appears to have been the first such case to go to trial.

Stacy Passeri, a former assistant vice president at the Pacific Select Distributors Inc. division of Pacific Life Insurance Co., would have had her employment grievance relegated to industry-run arbitration under the pre-1999 rules of the SEC. (Passeri sold annuities and thus required a securities license.) But, never having established an in-house arbitration policy—as many brokerage houses did after 1999—Pacific Life had to meet Passeri in court in March 2003. Passeri's testimony included an account of a two-day trip to visit clients during which her boss rubbed her feet, knees, and thighs and grabbed her buttocks.

On March 17, 2003, after two weeks of testimony and a week of jury deliberation, a San Francisco Superior Court jury awarded her $434,000 in compensatory damages and $2.1 million in punitive damages. Rather than begin the typical process of ever-higher court challenges, the two sides signed a confidential settlement in August 2003. Neither Passeri's trial nor her victory received media attention. A spokesman for Pacific Life said, "The case is confidential so we have nothing to say regarding that."

Better known disputes in the securities industry may have the lure the business media prefers. Allison Schieffelin, the former Morgan Stanley convertible bond sales representative whose case was assumed in 2001 by the U.S. Equal Employment Opportunity Commission, was back in the spotlight in summer 2003. U.S. District Court Judge Richard Berman piqued interest in the proceedings when he ordered EEOC chairwoman Cari Dominguez and Morgan Stanley CEO Philip Purcell to appear in his courtroom on April 15 to try to figure out a way to restart negotiations. While Dominguez might have been accustomed to such directives in her role as a public servant, Purcell was not. The CEO cooled his heels for three hours between *in camera* sessions on an unseasonably hot day in Berman's steamy courtroom. Several weeks later, an EEOC lawyer wrote to the judge to complain that Morgan Stanley had been negotiating in bad faith.

In the meantime, some firms that have been the subject of shocking allegations win with publicity. Racquel Whilby, a former analyst at Bank of America Securities, sued that firm in January 2003 for sex discrimination and sexual harassment. She described a vulgar work environment at the investment division of Bank of America that made the Boom-Boom Room sound like Romper Room. Whilby, a *cum laude* graduate of Harvard, was describing an office she had left only in September 2002. By May 2003, Bank of America was looking like a great friend of women with its title sponsorship of Annika Sorenstam, the first woman to compete in a U.S. PGA Tour event in 58 years. While Sorenstam smiled and chatted on network television in May 2003, a Bank of America banner was draped behind her.

If ever there was a time when Wall Street managements were vulnerable to being examined and exposed on these issues, it was now. Even Sandy Weill, who gave up his CEO title in July 2003, came down a peg or two from his management mountain and said in a July 21, 2003 television interview on CNBC that he was "sorry" about the Wall Street scandals in brokerage firms' research departments. Just two months before, the *New York Times* had reported that an autobiography proposal Weill was peddling with cowriter Leah Nathans Spiro—who had authored the *Business Week* stories about the *Martens* lawsuit and the flattering cover story about Jamie Dimon—had to be withdrawn from auction in the publishing industry. The *Times* said that Weill and Spiro had worked for two years on their project, which previously had been offered "for as much as $3 million." "It's what he's been through and what he represents and the way he'd be jumped on by the media if he tried to take a victory lap right now," said Michael Cader, the writer of the publishing newsletter *Publisher's Lunch*.

On Wall Street, managers were more contrite these less-heady days. Yet neither Weill nor any other top executive in the industry had made a similar *mea culpa* about the continuing problems of women who work in their industry.

They did, however, show a rare willingness to put women in top spots when the woman had the scarce combination of talents needed to help through a crisis, as Krawcheck did. For her $15 million in compensation over the next two years, though, Krawcheck did what all the others did: she signed a contract that said she would go to arbitration if something went wrong.

Notes

CHAPTER 1
GARDEN CITY'S PARTY SPOT

The narrative in this chapter relies in part on court filings in the class-action lawsuit filed by Pamela K. Martens and others against Smith Barney, Nicholas Cuneo, and others. (Smith Barney merged with the brokerage Shearson/American Express, including the Garden City branch run by Cuneo, in May 1994.) That lawsuit resulted in a settlement: No depositions were taken of the alleged wrongdoers for inclusion in public court files; the defendants did not file with the court answers to the allegations made against them in the complaint; and the defendants were released of liability for the claims against them. Nicholas Cuneo declined to be interviewed for this book, so the narrative relies in part on multiple interviews with his colleagues, both male and female, as well as his superiors, and on his regulatory records. The author began trying to reach Cuneo in mid-May 1996, just before the filing of the Martens complaint. The author called Cuneo at his home; approached one of his lawyers in court; telephoned and wrote to another of his lawyers; and spoke to several of his managers, brokers, and support staff. This chapter also draws from the regulatory records of stockbrokers in Cuneo's office. The author sent registered letters to the brokers seeking their responses to questions about those records; none gave responses about their records.

1. *Helen B. O'Bannon v. Merrill Lynch, Pierce, Fenner & Smith Inc.*, Case No. YPI3-017, Charge No. TPI2-0502 (Decision of the U.S. Equal Opportunity Employment Commission, Pittsburgh, Pennsylvania, January 11, 1974).
2. Ibid.
3. Ibid.
4. Edgar Fitzsimons, telephone interview by author, September 30, 1999.
5. Ibid.
6. Lorraine Parker, letter to James Dimon, October 25, 1994; Lori Hurwitz, statement supplied to Pamela Martens, fall 1994; Kathleen Keegan, statement supplied to Pamela Martens, fall 1994; *Martens et al. v. Smith Barney et al.*, 96 Civ 3779

(U.S. District Court for the Southern District of New York, October 17, 1996), second amended complaint, page 11.

7. Faces of the Nation (public database), National Comprehensive Report on Nicholas F. Cuneo.

8. Former Smith Barney broker who spoke on the condition of anonymity, interview by author, September 9, 1999.

9. National Association of Securities Dealers Inc., Central Registration Depository records of Nicholas F. Cuneo.

10. Executive to whom Nicholas Cuneo reported, who spoke on the condition that he not be identified, interview by author, New York, August 30, 1999.

11. Former Garden City employee who spoke on the condition that he not be identified, interview by author, December 5, 2000.

12. *Martens et al. v. Smith Barney et al.,* 96 Civ 3779 (U.S. District Court for the Southern District of New York, August 7, 1999), exhibits A–K to plaintiffs' consolidated memorandum in opposition to defendants' motions to dismiss, page 24.

13. Ibid.; Former Smith Barney Garden City brokers who spoke on the condition that they not be identified, interviews by author, 1999–2000.

14. Years later, when the world was watching the development of Operation Desert Storm, Cuneo learned that two of his brokers had children there—one a soldier, the other a nurse—and told both employees that they should use the company phone lines to call overseas. (One of the two employees, Lorraine Parker, disputed in a telephone interview on December 1, 2000, that the telephone lines were offered.) Ann Gordon, whose husband, Bill, worked for Cuneo, said her husband brought home the news that Nick had invited them to call their daughter in Saudi Arabia. It was just like Nick to do that, Ann Gordon said. Parker's son and the men on his ship received twenty boxes of goodies, including candy and magazines, from the Garden City branch. Parker adamantly insists that Nicholas Cuneo, Jr. and not his father, oversaw the project. Nick Jr. and his brother, Leslie, both worked at the branch. But a Cuneo supporter who worked there at the time credits the elder Cuneo for the goodwill.

15. Peppy Henin, affidavit to Patricia Hefty, Palm Beach, Florida, April 6, 1996.

16. Roberta Thomann, telephone interview by author, December 6, 2000; *Martens et al. v. Smith Barney et al.,* 96 Civ 3779 AGS (U.S. District Court for the Southern District of New York, May 20, 1996), complaint, page 9.

17. Former broker in the Garden City office who spoke on the condition that he not be identified, telephone interview by author, October 21, 1999.

18. Former Garden City brokers and sales assistants who spoke on the condition that they not be identified, interviews by author, 1997–2001.

19. Roberta Thomann, telephone interview by author, December 6, 2000.

20. Peppy Henin, telephone interview by Tracy Tait, July 9, 2001.

21. Peppy Henin, interview by author, Claremont Hotel, Roslyn, New York, September 13, 1999.

22. Former Garden City broker who spoke on the condition that he not be identified, telephone interview by author, October 21, 1999.

23. Among all the former brokers at the branch who were interviewed, one was adamant that the opposite was true: that Cuneo was outspoken about and intolerant of customer abuses. In addition, a sales assistant who was at odds with Cuneo said that it was her impression that he once reversed a decision to hire a broker from a competitor after she informed him that the man was a regular cocaine user— evidence that Cuneo was concerned that his brokers be good citizens.

24. The disciplinary records of licensed stockbrokers referred to are based on data jointly kept by the National Association of Securities Dealers Inc. (NASD) and the North American Securities Administrators Association (NASAA), an organization of state securities regulators. These records sometimes refer to awards to aggrieved investors granted by securities industry arbitrators. The hearings that lead to those awards are not public, so details are limited to the brief synopses available in the Central Registration Depository (CRD). Additionally, the CRDs frequently refer to settlements between brokers and their clients. Typically, a dollar amount of the settlement is available in a CRD, but few other details are listed.

25. Edgar M. Fitzsimons, interview by author, September 30, 1999.

26. National Association of Securities Dealers Inc., Central Registration Depository records of Edgar M. Fitzsimons.

27. Ibid.

28. After initially having granted a telephone interview to the author in September 1999, Fitzsimons did not respond to subsequent registered mail on July 21, 2000, seeking comment on his regulatory records.

29. National Association of Securities Dealers Inc., Central Registration Depository records of Taihwa "Terry" Ho.

30. Ibid.

31. Ibid.

32. Ibid.

33. Ibid.

34. National Association of Securities Dealers Inc., Central Registration Depository records of Glenn Fischer. Fischer did not respond to registered mail seeking his response.

35. National Association of Securities Dealers Inc., Central Registration Depository records of Jerry J. Alampi. Alampi did not respond to a query about his regulatory record sent to his lawyer, although he had responded to queries about other questions.

36. National Association of Securities Dealers Inc., Central Registration Depository records of Gary W. Owens. Owens did not respond to registered mail seeking his response.

37. Ibid.

38. Ibid.

39. Ibid.

40. Ibid.

41. Kathleen Keegan, telephone interview by author, December 13, 2000.

42. National Association of Securities Dealers Inc., Central Registration Depository records of John C. Gatto.

43. Ibid.

44. Ibid.

45. National Association of Securities Dealers Inc., Central Registration Depository records of Kenneth A. Gatto.

46. Ibid.

47. National Association of Securities Dealers Inc., Central Registration Depository records of Charles Slicklen.

48. Ibid.

49. The 1988 *Shearson Lehman Hutton Handbook* said it was the firm's policy that employees "may not work under the direct or indirect supervision of their relatives, or work in conjunction with a relative in the same section or unit." The 1994 handbook said that relatives could work in the same facility provided that there was "no direct reporting or supervisory/management relationship ... that is, no employee is permitted to work within the 'chain of command' of a relative such that one relative's work responsibilities, salary, or career progress could be influenced by the other relative."

50. National Association of Securities Dealers Inc., Central Registration Depository records of Nicholas Cuneo Jr.; National Association of Securities Dealers Inc., Central Registration Depository records of Leslie Cuneo.

51. National Association of Securities Dealers Inc., Central Registration Depository records of Nicholas Cuneo Jr.

CHAPTER 2
FROM APPALACHIA TO WALL STREET

1. "Taking a Shot at Another Male Bastion: Investment Banking," *BusinessWeek*, August 27, 1984, page 28.

2. Ibid.

3. The United States Army Air Corps was renamed the United States Army Air Force in 1941 and the United States Air Force in 1947.

CHAPTER 3
WILD TIMES FOR WALL STREET

1. *Wall Street Journal* News Round Up, "Illegal Insider Trading Seems to Be on Rise," *Wall Street Journal,* March 2, 1984, page 1.

2. James Stewart, *Den of Thieves* (New York: Simon & Schuster, 1991), page 223.

3. Dennis B. Levine with William Hoffer, *Inside Out: An Insider's Account of Wall Street* (New York: G. P. Putnam's Sons, 1991), page 268.

4. Ibid., page 207.

5. Dean Rotbart, editorial in *TJFR,* June 1987.

6. Stewart, page 140.

7. Ibid., pages 96–97.

8. Ibid., page 96.

9. Stephen J. Sansweet and Michael Cieply, "Disney Buys Back Steinberg's Stake for $70.83 a Share," *Wall Street Journal,* June 12, 1984, page A1.

10. "Merrill Lynch's Big Dilemma," *BusinessWeek,* January 16, 1984, page 60.

11. Ibid.

12. Richard Stern, "Come Grow With Us," *Forbes,* March 1, 1982, page 44.

13. Ibid.

14. Bob Drummond with Neil Roland and Greg Stohr, "First Jersey's Brennan Must Pay $75 Million Court Penalty," Bloomberg News, October 6, 1997.

15. Neil Roland, "First Jersey's Brennan Barred from Securities Industry," Bloomberg News, May 29, 1998.

16. David Glovin, "Stock Promoter Robert Brennan Indicted in Bankruptcy Fraud Case," Bloomberg News, August 1, 2000; David Voreacos, "Brennan Guilty of Bankruptcy Fraud, Money Laundering," Bloomberg News, April 16, 2001.

17. David Voreacos, "Brennan Gets Nine Years for Money Laundering," Bloomberg News, July 26, 2001.

18. Merida Welles, "Wall Street by Night," *New York Times,* January 1, 1984, section 3, page 4.

CHAPTER 4
NICK'S WAY WITH WOMEN

The narrative in this chapter relies in part on court filings in a lawsuit and counter-suit between Gertrude K. Berman and Pamela K. Martens. Martens's countersuit was dismissed; the initial lawsuit, according to Berman, was dropped, and Berman declined to speak in any detail about it. Thus, many details that are not addressed in Berman's court filings come from interviews with Martens and others able to recall the events of late 1976.

1. *Pamela K. Martens, Judith P. Mione, and Roberta Thomann O'Brien v. Smith Barney et al.,* 96 Civ 3779 (U.S. District Court for the Southern District of New York, May 20, 1996), complaint, page 9.

2. *Martens et al. v. Smith Barney et al.,* 96 Civ 3779 (U.S. District Court for the Southern District of New York, October 17, 1996), second amended complaint, page 11.

3. Pamela Martens, telephone interview by author, February 25, 2001.

4. Women at Pam's firm would prove in later years to have been an extreme example of pay disparity: by 1995, women would make up 36 percent of the investment banking division of Smith Barney, which merged with Shearson in 1994, but earn only 11 percent of that division's payroll, according to the Class-Wide Allegations filed with the U.S. District Court for the Southern District of New York in *Martens et al. v. Smith Barney et al.,* 96 Civ 3779 (CBM).

5. United States Commission on Civil Rights, "To Regulate in the Public Interest," *The Federal Civil Rights Enforcement Effort—1974* (Washington, D.C.: GPO, November 1974), Vol. I, page 191.

6. Ibid.

7. *Martens et al. v. Smith Barney et al.,* 96 Civ 3779 CBM (U.S. District Court for the Southern District of New York, December 8, 1999), corrected memorandum in opposition to motion to enforce settlement stipulation, Tab D, statement of claim of Patricia Clemente, page 3.

8. Ibid.

9. National Association of Securities Dealers, "EEO Survey Results" (for the period November 1, 1994–July 20, 1995, including partial results for October 1994), released July 21, 1995.

10. United States Commission on Civil Rights, *Racial and Ethnic Tensions,* page 91.

11. *Martens et al. v. Smith Barney et al.,* 96 Civ 3779 CBM (U.S. District Court for the Southern District of New York, December 8, 1999), corrected memorandum in opposition to motion to enforce settlement stipulation, Tab D.

12. *Martens et al. v. Smith Barney et al.,* 96 Civ 3779 AGS (U.S. District Court for the Southern District of New York, August 7, 1999), exhibits A–K to plaintiffs' consolidated memorandum in opposition to defendants' motions to dismiss, pages 32–35.

13. Frank Dworsky, telephone interview by author, December 18, 2000. Dworsky, the former branch manager, said that Smith Barney's lawyers defended him in the case, and that he would not comment on Clemente's claims. Dworsky subsequently took a job at Prudential Securities in Baltimore, Maryland.

14. *Martens et al. v. Smith Barney et al.,* 96 Civ 3779 CBM (U.S. District Court for the Southern District of New York, December 8, 1999), corrected memorandum in opposition to motion to enforce settlement stipulation, Tab D.

15. Ibid.

16. Ibid.

17. Ibid.

18. Ibid.

19. Ibid.

20. *Martens et al. v. Smith Barney et al.,* 96 Civ 3779 (U.S. District Court for the Southern District of New York, December 8, 1999), declarations in support of plaintiffs' memorandum in opposition to motion to enforce settlement stipulation, Tab D. Exhibits: Class-wide allegations attached to all statements of claim of women in mediations or arbitration with Smith Barney in the Martens case.

21. Ibid.

22. Ibid.

23. Ibid.

24. Ibid.

25. *Gertrude K. Berman v. Pamela Kay Martens,* 22843-76 (Supreme Court of the State of New York, County of Nassau, October 18, 1976), verified complaint, 1–10.

26. Carolyn Berman, "Focus on Woodward Mental Health Center," *Woodward News,* April 13, 1978, page 4.

27. *Gertrude K. Berman v. Pamela Kay Martens,* 22843-76 (Supreme Court of the State of New York, County of Nassau, March 4, 1977), affidavit of Gertrude K. Berman, pages 1–11; Pamela Martens, letter to the members of the Board of Directors of Woodward Mental Health Center, September 7, 1976 (presented as attachment to *Berman v. Martens,* 1976).

28. *Gertrude K. Berman v. Pamela Kay Martens,* 22843-76 (Supreme Court of the State of New York, County of Nassau, March 4, 1977), affidavit of Gertrude K. Berman, page 3. Berman contests this date in the affidavit and says that Martens gave one month's notice on August 23, 1976.

29. Michele Ingrassia, "School Accused of Illegal Billing," *Newsday,* September 3, 1976.

30. Ibid.

31. Pamela Martens, telephone interview by author, November 3, 2000.

32. Ingrassia, "School Accused of Illegal Billing"; Pamela Martens, telephone interview by author, November 3, 2000.

33. *Gertrude K. Berman v. Pamela Kay Martens,* 22843-76 (Supreme Court of the State of New York, County of Nassau, April 20, 1977), affidavit in opposition to motion to dismiss complaint, pages 1–9.

34. *Gertrude K. Berman v. Martens v. Woodward Mental Health Center et al.,* 22843-78 (Supreme Court of the State of New York, County of Nassau, June 27, 1977), order by Justice Douglas F. Young, pages 1–2.

35. *Gertrude K. Berman v. Pamela Kay Martens,* 22843-76 (Supreme Court of the State of New York, County of Nassau, July 18, 1977), verified bill of particulars of Gertrude K. Berman, pages 1–5.

36. Ibid.

37. Ibid.

38. Ibid.

39. Ingrassia, "School Accused of Illegal Billing"; *Gertrude K. Berman v. Pamela Kay Martens,* 22843-76 (Supreme Court of the State of New York, County of Nassau, July 18, 1977), verified bill of particulars of Gertrude K. Berman, pages 1–5.

40. Ingrassia, "School Accused of Illegal Billing."

41. *Gertrude K. Berman v. Pamela Kay Martens,* 22843-76 (Supreme Court of the State of New York, County of Nassau, July 13, 1977), cross motion for an order of preclusion. Motion attaches June 28, 1977, letter of Pamela Martens to *Newsday.*

42. Gertrude K. Berman, telephone interview by author, January 9, 2000.

43. Berman said she dropped her complaint against Martens after getting "satisfaction" that the former PR director's allegations were not true. It was a statement consistent with what she had said in her original court papers: that Martens's criticisms were either false or "deliberately deceptive." Martens has no recollection of signing any form of retraction and says she stands by her statements of 1976 to this day.

The current director of the Nassau County Department of Mental Health had no records of the conclusion of that agency's investigation when contacted about the flap in 2000; indeed, in his official correspondence, he referred to the investigation that was acknowledged in *Newsday* by one of his predecessors as an "alleged" investigation. During a telephone interview, he said that a fire had destroyed many records in the late 1970s. Robert Ambrose, Woodward's executive director in 2000, said the center's skimpy records indicated only that Pamela Martens had resigned in 1976 and that Gertrude Berman had retired three years after that, in May 1979.

CHAPTER 5
MARTENS'S DISORIENTING ORIENTATION

1. *Edna Broyles v. Smith Barney*, arbitration (Tampa, Florida, November 27, 2001), pages 1040, 1041, 1052, 1053, 1063; *Martens et al. v. Smith Barney et al.*, 96 Civ 3779 CBM (U.S. District Court for the Southern District of New York, May 20, 1996). The Broyles arbitration transcript is not part of the *Martens* court file.

2. Mark Belnick, interview by author, Tyco International Limited offices, New York City, September 8, 1999.

3. The golf argument would change depending upon circumstances. Some men said that inexperienced women players were not welcome because their presence was a discourtesy to other players. Others would argue that there was no reason a novice couldn't join a group and hit a few balls. The latter argument was made in the arbitration hearing of Edna Broyles in November 2001.

4. Jerry Alampi denied that this incident took place, in a letter sent to the author through his lawyer, David L. Weissman, July 17, 2000.

5. Pamela Martens, telephone interview by author, February 16, 2000; Kathleen Keegan, telephone interview by author, December 13, 2000; telephone interviews with two other former Garden City brokers who witnessed the incident and spoke with author on the condition that they not be identified, September 29, 1999, and July 2001.

6. Former Smith Barney broker who spoke on the condition that he not be named, telephone interview by author, September 1998.

7. *Martens et al. v. Smith Barney et al.*, 96 Civ 3779 AGS (U.S. District Court for the Southern District of New York, October 17, 1996), second amended complaint, page 11; Pamela Martens, letter to Jamie Dimon, October 3, 1994; former senior manager at Smith Barney, interview by author, New York, October 5, 1999; Lorraine Parker, telephone interview by author, May 1996.

8. Kathleen Keegan, telephone interview by author, March 7, 2000.

9. Ibid.

10. A former Garden City broker who spoke on the condition that she not be identified, interview by author, May 1996.

11. *Martens et al. v. Smith Barney et al.*, 96 Civ 3779 AGS (U.S. District Court for the Southern District of New York, July 22, 1997), plaintiffs' consolidated memorandum in opposition to defendants' motions to dismiss.

12. Kathleen Keegan, statement supplied to Pamela Martens, 1994.

13. Kathleen Keegan, telephone interview by author, March 22, 2002.

14. Pamela Martens, telephone interview by author, March 22, 2002.

15. *Martens et al. v. Smith Barney et al.*, 96 Civ 3779 AGS (U.S. District Court for the Southern District of New York, October 17, 1996), second amended complaint, page 14.

16. Peppy Henin, affidavit prepared at the request of Pamela Martens, notarized by Patricia Hefty, Palm Beach, Florida, April 6, 1994; Pamela Martens, telephone interview by author, March 6, 2000; *Martens et al. v. Smith Barney et al.*, 96 Civ

3779 AGS (U.S. District Court for the Southern District of New York, October 17, 1996), second amended complaint, page 12 Item i.

17. Peppy Henin, affidavit prepared at the request of Pamela Martens, notarized by Patricia Hefty, Palm Beach, Florida, April 6, 1994; Pamela Martens, telephone interview by author, March 6, 2000.

18. Peppy Henin, affidavit prepared at the request of Pamela Martens, notarized by Patricia Hefty, Palm Beach, Florida, April 6, 1994, page 4.

19. Lorraine Parker, memo to attorney Linda Friedman, April 10, 1996.

20. *Martens et al. v. Smith Barney et al.,* 96 Civ 3779 CBM (U.S. District Court for the Southern District of New York, December 8, 1999), corrected memorandum in opposition to enforce settlement stipulation, statement of claim by Lorraine Parker, page 3.

21. Pamela Martens, letter to Hardwick Simmons, July 2, 1988.

22. A spokeswoman for Prudential Securities Inc., where Hardwick Simmons was CEO from April 1991 until October 2000, said that Simmons had no memory of the letter from Martens and thus had nothing to say about it. Telephone interview by author, December 6, 2000.

23. Jodie-Beth Galos did not respond to telephone calls from author, or to a registered letter sent to her home by author on July 31, 2000.

24. Pamela Martens, letter to Herbert Dunn of Smith Barney, October 19, 1995, page 2.

25. Ibid.

26. National Association of Securities Dealers Inc., Central Registration Depository records of Peppy Saffron (Henin).

27. Kathleen Keegan, statement supplied to Pamela Martens in advance of seeking legal advice for lawsuit against Smith Barney, 1994.

28. *Securities and Exchange Commission v. Stanley J. Feminella et al.,* 96 Civ 336 AGS (U.S. District Court for the Southern District of New York, July 10, 1996), deposition of Stanley J. Feminella, pages 121 and 128.

29. *Securities and Exchange Commission v. Stanley J. Feminella et al.,* 96 Civ 336 AGS (U.S. District Court for the Southern District of New York, July 10, 1996), deposition of Stanley J. Feminella, page 97.

30. *Securities and Exchange Commission v. Stanley J. Feminella et al.,* 96 Civ 336 AGS (U.S. District Court for the Southern District of New York, July 11, 1996), deposition of Stanley J. Feminella, pages 328–329.

31. Ibid., pages 270–271.

32. Ibid., page 276.

33. *Securities and Exchange Commission v. Stanley J. Feminella et al.,* 96 Civ 336 AGS (U.S. District Court for the Southern District of New York, September 16, 1996), deposition of Stanley J. Feminella, page 864.

34. Ibid., page 864; *Securities and Exchange Commission v. Stanley J. Feminella et al.,* 96 Civ 336 AGS (U.S. District Court for the Southern District of New York, July 11, 1996), deposition of Stanley J. Feminella, pages 292–293; *Securities and Exchange Commission v. Stanley J. Feminella et al.,* 96 Civ 336 AGS (U.S. District Court for the Southern District of New York, October 29, 1996), deposition of

Stanley J. Feminella, deposition exhibit 37, includes copies of canceled checks on the account of Stanley J. and Jo Ann M. Feminella and copies of deposit slips of David W. and Priscilla Granston.

35. *Securities and Exchange Commission v. Stanley J. Feminella et al.*, 96 Civ 336 AGS (U.S. District Court for the Southern District of New York, September 16, 1996), deposition of Stanley J. Feminella, page 262.

36. *Securities and Exchange Commission v. Stanley J. Feminella et al.*, 96 Civ 336 AGS (U.S. District Court for the Southern District of New York, September 10, 1996), deposition of Stanley J. Feminella, pages 370–378.

37. Ibid., page 375.

38. Ibid., pages 377–378.

39. Ibid., pages 385, 387, 391, 399; *Securities and Exchange Commission v. Stanley J. Feminella et al.*, 96 Civ 336 AGS (U.S. District Court for the Southern District of New York, September 11, 1996), deposition of Stanley J. Feminella, pages 586–588.

40. *Securities and Exchange Commission v. Stanley J. Feminella et al.*, 96 Civ 336 AGS (U.S. District Court for the Southern District of New York, September 10, 1996), deposition of Stanley J. Feminella, pages 636–640.

41. Ibid., page 392.

42. *Securities and Exchange Commission v. Stanley J. Feminella et al.*, 96 Civ 336 AGS (U.S. District Court for the Southern District of New York, September 11, 1996), deposition of Stanley J. Feminella, pages 648–651.

43. SEC Release 37673 (File 3-9079). Order instituting a proceeding pursuant to Sections 15 (b) and 21 (c) of the Securities Exchange Act of 1934, making findings, instituting a cease-and-desist order, and imposing remedial sanctions in the matter of Lehman Brothers Inc., as successor to Shearson Lehman Brothers Inc., September 12, 1996, pages 1–14.

44. Jerry Alampi, letter to author, sent through his lawyer David L. Weissman, July 17, 2000. Alampi said through his lawyer that the checks written to Feminella "were completely proper and had nothing whatsoever to do with the operation of the office."

45. *Securities and Exchange Commission v. Stanley J. Feminella et al.*, 96 Civ 336 AGS (U.S. District Court for the Southern District of New York, October 29, 1996), deposition of Stanley J. Feminella, exhibit 81.

46. *Securities and Exchange Commission v. Stanley J. Feminella et al.*, 96 Civ 336 AGS (U.S. District Court for the Southern District of New York, September 16, 1996), deposition of Stanley J. Feminella, pages 890–892.

47. Ibid., page 918.

48. Ibid., pages 920–921.

49. Ibid., page 921.

50. *Securities and Exchange Commission v. Stanley J. Feminella et al.*, 96 Civ 336 AGS (U.S. District Court for the Southern District of New York, January 17, 1996), complaint, page 4.

51. National Association of Securities Dealers Inc., Central Registration Depository records of Stanley J. Feminella.

52. *Securities and Exchange Commission v. Stanley J. Feminella et al.*, 96 Civ 336

AGS (U.S. District Court for the Southern District of New York, January 17, 1996), complaint, page 4.

53. *Securities and Exchange Commission v. Stanley J. Feminella et al.*, 96 Civ 336 AGS (U.S. District Court for the Southern District of New York, September 11, 1996), deposition of Stanley J. Feminella, pages 550–558.

54. Ibid., pages 555–557.

55. Ibid., page 554.

56. *Securities and Exchange Commission v. Stanley J. Feminella et al.*, 96 Civ 336 AGS (U.S. District Court for the Southern District of New York, October 29, 1996), deposition of Stanley J. Feminella, exhibit 79.

57. Stanley J. Feminella, telephone interview by author, September 19, 1999.

58. Stanley J. Feminella, letter to attorney Robert Costello, August 8, 1994.

59. Exhibits attached to testimony by Stanley J. Feminella to the Securities and Exchange Commission, October 29, 1996.

60. *Securities and Exchange Commission v. Stanley J. Feminella et al.*, 96 Civ 336 AGS (U.S. District Court for the Southern District of New York, October 19, 1996), deposition of Stanley J. Feminella, exhibit 65; Stanley J. Feminella, handwritten letter to Robert Costello, August 8, 1994.

61. Pamela Martens, telephone interview by author, December 21, 2001.

CHAPTER 6
MARTENS SNAPS

1. *Martens et al. v. Smith Barney et al.*, 96 Civ 3779 CBM (U.S. District Court for the Southern District of New York), hearing complaint of Lorraine Parker, statement of claim of Claudia Galvin, page 1 (this document is not part of the court file); Judy Mione, telephone interview by author, March 19, 2002.

2. Nicholas Marinello, letter to author, July 25, 2000. Marinello said, "I categorically deny the allegations now and ten years ago" in the complaint and said that the allegations are "without merit." He said, "This unfounded claim was already reviewed ten years ago and found to be without merit. I have no idea what has motivated this woman to continue these false allegations."

3. *Martens et al. v. Smith Barney et al.*, 96 Civ 3779 AGS (U.S. District Court for the Southern District of New York, October 17, 1996), second amended complaint, page 19.

4. Ibid., page 20.

5. *Martens et al. v. Smith Barney et al.*, 96 Civ 3779 CBM (U.S. District Court for the Southern District of New York, hearing complaint of Lorraine Parker, statement of claim of Claudia Galvin, page 1. This document is not part of the court file.

6. *Martens et al. v. Smith Barney et al.*, 96 Civ 3779 CBM Tab D (U.S. District Court for the Southern District of New York, December 8, 1999), corrected memorandum in opposition to motion to enforce settlement stipulation, Tab D, statement of claim of Roberta O'Brien Thomann, pages 3–4.

7. Paula Doll Bandini, telephone interview by author, March 15, 2001. Bandini gave a different version of the conversation. She said that she was "fairly sure" that she first told Thomann the news that her job was gone, and that Thomann was likely to have spoken to the assistant manager after that "because she was annoyed." Although Bandini said that she was in charge of all the support staff and "took care of" Thomann financially, Thomann said that Bandini had no such authority over her and that Thomann received no such increase to compensate for lost bonus income.

8. *Martens et al. v. Smith Barney et al.,* 96 Civ 3779 CBM (U.S. District Court for the Southern District of New York, December 8, 1999), corrected memorandum in opposition to motion to enforce settlement stipulation, Tab D, statement of claim of Roberta O'Brien Thomann, pages 3–4.

9. Ibid.

10. Ibid.

11. Ibid.

12. Ibid.

13. Ibid.; *Martens et al. v. Smith Barney et al.,* 96 Civ 3779 AGS (U.S. District Court for the Southern District of New York, October 17, 1996), corrected second amended complaint, page 22.

14. Paula Doll Bandini, telephone interview by author, March 15, 2001. Bandini, who had been a sales assistant to Trudden, said, "I just know" that Trudden would not do such a prank.

15. Judy Mione, statement supplied to Pamela Martens, fall 1994; Pamela Martens, letter to James Dimon, October 3, 1994.

16. Pamela Martens, letter to James Dimon, October 4, 1994; *Martens et al. v. Smith Barney et al.,* 96 Civ 3779 AGS (U.S. District Court for the Southern District of New York, October 17, 1996), corrected second amended complaint, pages 13–15.

17. Roberta Thomann, statement supplied to Pamela Martens, fall 1994; Judith Mione, statement supplied to Pamela Martens, fall 1994; *Martens et al. v. Smith Barney et al.,* 96 Civ 3779 CMB Tab D (U.S. District Court for the Southern District of New York, December 8, 1999), corrected memorandum in opposition to motion to enforce settlement stipulation, statement of claim of Roberta O'Brien Thomann, page 2.

18. Roberta Thomann, statement supplied to Pamela Martens, fall 1994.

19. Ibid.

20. Paula Doll Bandini, telephone interview by author, March 15, 2001. Bandini, who was a sales assistant in the Garden City office, said that Cuneo's threats were "ridiculous" but were not of consequence because she was "in charge" of support staff and would not have enforced them. Other sales assistants including Thomann, however, say that Bandini was not their boss. Bandini, who said that Robin Leopold was her mentor, nonetheless said that she never spoke with Leopold about the explosion among sales assistants that day. Bandini said, "I don't know why I didn't" speak with Leopold about it.

21. Lorraine Parker, telephone interview by author, December 1, 2000.

CHAPTER 7
THAT WAS HAPPENING TO YOU, TOO?

The narrative here uses information from court filings and arbitration complaints against Olde Discount Corp. and Ernest J. Olde. Those lawsuits and arbitrations resulted in settlements rather than adjudication, which might have brought Olde's full defense into the public record. Correspondence to Ernest Olde via H&R Block, which bought his firm, was answered only by an H&R Block spokeswoman, who had no comment. At the time the 1995 complaints were filed, the firm strongly denied through its outside counsel that it discriminated against women but declined to provide specific information. Ernest Olde and other senior managers at the time declined to be interviewed. Certified mail sent to a Florida address that was listed as Ernest Olde's home was returned to the author.

1. By 1992, enrollment in business schools was reflecting younger women's frustrations with workplace disparities. Female enrollment in the MBA program at the Anderson School at the University of California in Los Angeles was down to 30 percent from 40 percent in 1985. In an August 1994 article, *Working Woman* magazine said that in 1990, men with MBAs from the top twenty business schools were outearning their female classmates by 12 percent in their first year out of school. The magazine said that, by 1992, men made 34 percent more than women five years after graduation.

2. *Susan Jaskowski v. Rodman & Renshaw, Inc., Norman Mains, Gregory P. Quinlivan, and Kurt Karmin,* 92 Civ 4161 (U.S. District Court for the Northern District of Illinois Eastern Division, 1993), amended complaint, page 2.

3. *Caroline L. Bouvier v. Rodman & Renshaw, Inc., and Mark Grant,* 94L09636 (Circuit Court of Cook County, Illinois County Department Law Division, August 3, 1994), complaint, page 2.

4. Ibid.

5. Ibid; *Jeannine Finley v. Rodman & Renshaw, Inc., and Mark Grant* (U.S. District Court for the Northern District of Illinois Eastern Division, September 8, 1993), complaint, page 3. Finley filed a complaint with the federal Equal Employment Opportunity Commission naming Rodman & Renshaw and Grant in April 1993.

6. Laurie Cohen and William Gruber, "Second Sexual Harassment Suit Filed against Rodman," *Chicago Tribune,* September 9, 1993, page B-1.

7. *Jeannine Finley v. Rodman & Renshaw, Inc., and Mark Grant* (U.S. District Court for the Northern District of Illinois Eastern Division, September 8, 1993), complaint, page 2.

8. Ibid., page 3.

9. Susan Jaskowski, telephone interview by author, January 6, 2002. Jerold I. Budney, a lawyer for Mark Grant, said Grant vehemently denied the allegations. He said the interpretations of Grant's demeanor or actions "are inaccurate, baseless, and unreasonable," and that it was not clear how a source could have presumed to know what Grant was or was not interested in hearing or whether or not he was annoyed about a conversation.

10. *Susan Jaskowski v. Rodman & Renshaw, Inc., Norman Mains, Gregory P. Quinlivan, and Kurt Karmin,* 92 Civ 4161 (U.S. District Court for the Northern District of Illinois Eastern Division, 1993), amended complaint, page 5.

11. Ibid., page 4.

12. Ibid., page 2.

13. Ibid., page 4.

14. Ibid., page 3.

15. Ibid., pages 3-4.

16. Linda Friedman, interview by author, Plaza Hotel, New York City, October 28, 1997.

17. Laurie Cohen, "Bias Charges Undermine Rodman Deal," *Chicago Tribune,* September 1, 1993, page 1.

18. "Thursday Ticker," *Chicago Tribune,* September 2, 1993, Business section, page 1.

19. Patricia Manson, "Disbarred Lawyer Gets Year in Fee Fraud," *Chicago Daily Law Bulletin,* June 30, 2000, page 3.

20. "Wednesday Ticker," *Chicago Tribune,* February 2, 1994, Business section, page 1.

21. National Association of Securities Dealers Inc., Central Registration Depository records of Mark Jeffrey Grant.

22. NASD Regulation Inc. Award, Office of Dispute Resolution, New York, New York, *In the Matter of the Arbitration Between Josephthal Lyon & Ross Inc. and Mark J. Grant* (94-05515), October 30, 1997.

23. Ibid.; Josephthal Lyon & Ross Inc. changed its name to Josephthal & Co. Inc. in December 1997.

24. William Gruber, "Former Rodman Exec Back After Harassment Charge," *Chicago Tribune,* November 1, 1995, Business section, page 3. James Van DeGraaf, general counsel of Rodman at the time, was attributed by the newspaper as having said that the brokerage firm had reached settlements with the women for undisclosed terms after Grant left the firm.

25. Kimberly A. Casper, affidavit to the U.S. Equal Employment Opportunity Commission (case number 160-95-2407), Baldwin, New York, June 9, 1995.

26. Ibid.

27. Ibid.

28. Mark I. Lev, letter to author, August 14, 2000. Mark I. Lev (also known as Mark Lew), chairman and CEO of Lew Lieberbaum & Co., said that Casper's allegation was "a false and misleading distortion." Given the small firm's history of reparations to both civil rights and securities regulators, however, the statements of Casper and the other women have been included despite the chairman's denials.

29. Ibid. Mark I. Lev said that he had no recollection of this having been said. Lev said that the alleged incident was not brought to his attention prior to the lawsuit.

30. Ibid; Kimberly A. Casper, affidavit to the U.S. Equal Employment Opportunity Commission (case number 160-95-2407), Baldwin, New York, June 9, 1996.

31. Linette Cinelli, affidavit to the U.S. Equal Employment Opportunity Commission, November 13, 1996.

32. Mark I. Lev, letter to author, August 14, 2000. Lev said that he did not consider Cinelli's allegations to be credible. It was his opinion that she was discredited at her deposition.

33. Linette Cinelli, affidavit to the U.S. Equal Employment Opportunity Commission, November 13, 1996; Mark I. Lev, letter to author, August 14, 2000.

34. Deanna Caliendo, affidavit to the U.S. Equal Employment Opportunity Commission (case number 160-97-0303), New York, New York, November 16, 1996.

35. Mark I. Lev, letter to author, August 14, 2000. Mark I. Lev said that the manager described by Caliendo had "strenuously denied" the allegations, but that Lev had no independent knowledge of the alleged incident.

36. Ibid.

37. Ibid.

38. Ibid.

39. Lori-Ann Pugliese, affidavit to the U.S. Equal Employment Opportunity Commission (case number 160-96-2529), New York, New York, August 8, 1996.

40. Ibid.; Mark I. Lev, letter to author, August 14, 2000. Lev said that this was not his recollection of the incident. Lev additionally said that he considered the case brought to the EEOC by the three plaintiffs to have been "horrendously misrepresentative, egregiously exaggerated, and filled with numerous untruths." He did not provide examples.

41. Lori-Ann Pugliese, affidavit to the U.S. Equal Employment Opportunity Commission (case number 160-96-2529), New York, New York, August 8, 1996.

42. Linette Cinelli, affidavit to the U.S. Equal Employment Opportunity Commission, November 13, 1996; Mark I. Lev, letter to author, August 14, 2000.

43. Linette Cinelli, affidavit to the U.S. Equal Employment Opportunity Commission, November 13, 1996.

44. Ibid.

45. *Martens et al. v. Smith Barney et al.,* 96 Civ 3779 CBM Tab D (U.S. District Court for the Southern District of New York, December 8, 1999), corrected memorandum in opposition to motion to enforce settlement stipulation, statement of claim of Lydia Klein, page 1.

46. Ibid.

47. *Darlene Livingston against Shearson Lehman Brothers,* National Association of Securities Dealers hearing before the arbitrators, case number 93-00770, August 15, 1995, page 5140.

48. Eileen Valentino, telephone interview by author, June 13, 1996.

49. Beatrice Escarpenter, telephone interview by author, November 22, 1999.

50. James Boshart, managing director, capital markets division, Salomon Smith Barney, testimony before the State of Michigan American Arbitration Association, December 12, 1996; *William S. Gray v. Smith Barney Inc., Therese Obringer, and A. George Saks,* case number 95-01185 (Southfield, Michigan, December 12, 1996), page 1357.

51. Order making findings and imposing sanctions and a cease-and-desist order,

Securities Exchange Act of 1934 Release No. 396871, February 20, 1998, *In the Matter of Michael Lissack*.

52. The author used information gleaned from Lissack's interviews because she has a history of having received credible information from him.

53. *Martens et al. v. Smith Barney Inc., et al.*, 96 Civ 3779 CBM (U.S. District Court for the Southern District of New York, October 17, 1996), initial submission of claimant Linda Atkins Smoot.

54. Initial submission of claimant Linda Atkins Smoot, pursuant to Paragraph 7.12 (1) of the Class Action Settlement; *Martens et al. v. Smith Barney et al.*, 96 Civ 3779 CBM (U.S. District Court for the Southern District of New York, May 20, 1996).

55. Roger Shuster, telephone interview by author, August 2, 2001.

56. Susan Antilla, "Three Women vs. a Broker: Olde Is Accused of Blatant Job Discrimination," *New York Times*, April 26, 1995, Business/Financial Desk, page 1.

57. *Mary Graff, Julie Quintero, and Gina Caposieno v. Olde Discount Corporation, Ernie Olde, and Dan Katzman* (before the National Association of Securities Dealers, April 21, 1995), complaint, page 2.

58. Ibid.

59. Olde Discount monthly newsletter, "Top Fixed Income Producers for April 1994," May 7, 1994, page 1.

60. *Mary Graff, Julie Quintero, and Gina Caposieno v. Olde Discount Corporation, Ernie Olde, and Dan Katzman* (before the National Association of Securities Dealers, April 21, 1995), complaint, page 2.

61. In a brief telephone interview with the author on January 16, 2002, Daniel Katzman said that he would discuss with one of his lawyers whether to grant a further interview and get back to the author. He did not call back. He also failed to respond to a July 31, 2000, registered letter from the author.

62. *Mary Graff, Julie Quintero, and Gina Caposieno v. Olde Discount Corporation, Ernie Olde, and Dan Katzman* (before the National Association of Securities Dealers, April 21, 1995), complaint, page 9.

63. Ibid.

64. Ibid., page 8.

65. Ibid.

66. Ibid., page 10.

67. Ibid., pages 10–11.

68. *Graff et al. v. Olde Discount Corp. et al.*, 95 C2494 (U.S. District Court for the Northern District of Illinois Eastern Division, April 1995), affidavit of Maura M. Cook and plaintiffs' exhibit B, page 1.

69. Ibid.

70. Dan Katzman, memo to all registered reps at Olde Discount Corporation, November 5, 1993.

71. Julie Quintero, interview by author, Chicago, April 1995.

72. In a brief telephone interview with the author on January 16, 2002, Daniel Katzman said that he would discuss with one of his lawyers whether to grant a further interview and get back to the author. He did not call back. He also failed to respond to a July 31, 2000, registered letter from the author.

73. *Mary Graff, Julie Quintero, and Gina Caposieno v. Olde Discount Corporation, Ernie Olde, and Dan Katzman* (before the National Association of Securities Dealers, April 21, 1995), complaint, page 12.

74. Julie Quintero, interview by author, Chicago, April 1995.

75. *Mary Graff, Julie Quintero, and Gina Caposieno v. Olde Discount Corporation, Ernie Olde, and Dan Katzman* (before the National Association of Securities Dealers, April 21, 1995), complaint, page 13.

76. Ibid., page 14.

77. Ibid., pages 14–15.

78. *United States Securities and Exchange Commission Administrative Proceeding File No. 3-9699 In the Matter of Olde Discount Corp., Ernest J. Olde, Stanley A. Snider, and Daniel D. Katzman,* filed September 10, 1998.

79. *Susan Bell v. Olde Discount Corporation and Ernest Olde* (before the National Association of Securities Dealers Inc., February 21, 1995), page 4.

80. Ibid., pages 14–15.

81. Ibid., page 5.

82. Ibid., page 5.

83. Ibid., page 6.

84. Ibid., page 6.

85. Ibid., page 7.

86. Ibid., page 7–8.

87. Ibid., page 21.

88. Ibid., page 16.

89. Darlene Livingston against Shearson Lehman Brothers, Inc., National Association of Securities Dealers hearing before the arbitrators, case number 93-00770, August 15, 1995, pages 5162–5165.

90. Darlene Livingston against Shearson Lehman Brothers, Inc., National Association of Securities Dealers hearing before the arbitrators, case number 93-00770, August 15, 1995, pages 5162–5163.

91. *Martens et al. v. Smith Barney et al.,* 96 Civ 3779 CBM (U.S. District Court for the Southern District of New York), "class-wide allegations" attached to individual mediation complaints of plaintiffs filed April–July 1999, pages 4–6. This document is not part of the court file.

92. Bureau of the Census, *Detailed Occupation of the Civilian Labor Force by Sex, Race, and Hispanic Origin,* prepared by Customer Services, Data User Services Division (Washington, D.C., 1990).

93. Ibid.

94. United States Commission on Civil Rights, *Racial and Ethnic Tensions in American Communities: Poverty, Inequality, and Discrimination* (Washington, D.C.: GPO, December 1999), Vol. VI: The New York Report, page 143 Table 3.24.

CHAPTER 8
DEAR MR. DIMON: MARTENS FIGHTS BACK

1. Lissack was once arrested for harassing Smith Barney executives.

2. Ultimately, the sales assistant, Shu-Fei Chan—Sophie to her friends—was fired, effective June 17, 1995. In exchange for two weeks' pay of $972.81, Smith Barney asked her to sign a release giving up her rights to all civil-rights and related claims, promising never to sue Smith Barney or speak badly about Smith Barney. She didn't sign. A copy of the unsigned letter agreement between Smith Barney and Shu-Fei Chan, dated June 21, 1995, was provided to the author.

3. *Martens et al. v. Smith Barney et al.,* 96 Civ 3779 CBM (U.S. District Court for the Southern District of New York, December 8, 1999), corrected memorandum in opposition to motion to enforce settlement stipulation, Tab D, statement of claim of Roberta O'Brien Thomann, page 22.

4. *Martens et al. v. Smith Barney et al.,* 96 Civ 3779 AGS (U.S. District Court for the Southern District of New York, October 17, 1996), second amended complaint, page 12.

5. Peppy Henin, statement supplied to Pamela Martens, October 1994. In a telephone interview by Tracy Tait on July 9, 2001, eight years after Henin submitted her written statement to Martens, Henin said she only remembered having been harassed about being a woman at the dinner, and that no one had said anything about her being rich or Jewish that evening.

6. Peppy Henin, statement supplied to Pamela Martens, October 1994.

7. Ibid.

8. Kathleen Keegan, statement supplied to Pamela Martens, October 1994.

9. Ibid.

10. Kathleen Keegan, telephone interview by author, March 7, 2000.

11. Linda Friedman, telephone interview by author, December 28, 2000.

12. Lori Hurwitz, statement supplied to Pamela Martens, October 1994.

13. Pamela Martens, telephone interview by author, November 30, 2000.

14. Roberta Thomann, telephone interview by author, 1999.

15. Lorraine Parker, memo to Jamie Dimon, October 25, 1994.

16. Roberta O'Brien Thomann, letter to Jamie Dimon, October 31, 1994.

17. *Darlene Livingston against Shearson Lehman Brothers,* National Association of Securities Dealers hearing before the arbitrators, case number 93-00770 (August 15, 1995), page 5214.

18. Michael R. Lissack, statement to the Workers' Rights Board Meeting, Trinity Church, 74 Trinity Place, New York, New York, April 15, 1998. The depiction of the party at Landmark Tavern derives solely from Lissack's statement. Lissack is a corporate whistle-blower with a confrontational history with Smith Barney, but he also carries credibility for his role in exposing a municipal bond fraud in which Smith Barney was a key player.

19. *William S. Gray v. Smith Barney Inc., Therese Obringer, and A. George Saks,* case number 95-01185 (State of Michigan American Arbitration Association,

Southfield, Michigan, December 12, 1996), testimony of James Stewart Boshart.

20. Leah Nathans Spiro, "Whiz Kid: Can Jamie Dimon Turn Smith Barney into a Wall Street Dynamo?" *BusinessWeek,* October 21, 1996, page 96.

21. Susan Antilla, "Workplace Discrimination? Don't Try It Around Her," *New York Times,* Sunday, February 13, 1994, Financial Desk, page 7.

22. Lorraine Parker, telephone interview by author, January 3, 2002.

CHAPTER 9
GETTING LAWYERS, GETTING FIRED

1. Pamela Martens, letter to James Dimon, December 10, 1994.

2. Ibid.

3. Lorraine Parker, letter to James Dimon, October 25, 1994. Women at Olde Discount suffered the same frustration of having men solicit their contented customers, but it was easier to steal a colleague's customers at Olde: the firm openly permitted brokers access to accounts in order to solicit "inactive" customers. Because the women tended to handle accounts with caution, typically trading conservatively on behalf of their clients, their accounts would frequently pop up as inactive by Olde standards, setting them up to be wooed away by more aggressively trading male brokers.

4. Powers even met with a senior vice president from the Atlanta human resources department, Karen Rollo, on May 12, 1994, for coaching on how to speak to Broyles. "She needs to know she's loved—she's a middle child," Rollo told him. Arbitration of *Edna Broyles v. Smith Barney,* Tampa, Florida, November 27, 2001, testimony of Frank Powers; *Martens et al. v. Smith Barney et al.,* 96 Civ 3779 CBM (U.S. District Court for the Southern District of New York, May 20, 1996). The Broyles arbitration is not part of the court docket.

5. Arbitration of *Edna Broyles v. Smith Barney,* Tampa, Florida, November 27, 2001, testimony of Frank Powers; *Martens et al v. Smith Barney et al,* 96 Civ 3779 CBM (U.S. District Court for the Southern District of New York, May 20, 1996). The Broyles arbitration is not part of the court docket.

6. John L. Donnelly, letter to Pamela Martens, January 19, 1995.

7. Ibid.

8. Ibid.

9. Ibid.

10. Ibid.

11. The hiring of a lawyer had led to tough tactics by a predecessor company to Smith Barney, too. Shearson Lehman Brothers assigned an innocuous "miscellaneous" termination code 384 to Darlene Livingston on January 15, 1992, when it fired her. On February 24, 1992, though, the firm heard from her lawyer and learned that Livingston would not sign papers saying that she would not sue. By February 26, 1992, her separation code had been changed to 351: "not able to perform job requirements." On March 9, 1992, Shearson issued a U-5 regulatory document, required when a stockbroker leaves a firm, citing "poor job performance" as the reason for her termination. *Darlene Livingston against Shearson Lehman Brothers, Inc.*, National Association of Securities Dealers, Inc., case number 93-00770, August 15, 1995, pages 5122–5123.

12. Pamela Martens, letter to James Dimon, October 5, 1995.

13. Ibid.

14. Pamela Martens, memo to Herb Dunn, October 19, 1995.

15. National Association of Securities Dealers Inc., Central Registration Depository record of Nicholas Cuneo.

16. Former senior supervisor of Nicholas Cuneo who spoke on the condition that he not be named, interview by author, October 5, 1999.

17. It was Pam's belief that they were the first drug tests the manager had ever requested.

18. Twelve days after the author queried Morgan Stanley Dean Witter about the incident on July 12, 2001, Martens received a recruitment letter from branch manager Mark Kelly of the Morgan Stanley Dean Witter office on Franklin Avenue in Garden City, dated July 24, 2001.

CHAPTER 10
ATTACKING THE NO-COURT SYSTEM

The narrative in this chapter concerning Patti Hanlon and Eileen Valentino is as seen through their eyes.

1. Contingent fee agreement and contract of employment signed by Mary Stowell and Pamela Martens, February 29, 1996.

2. Ibid.

3. Ibid.

4. Rodman & Renshaw subsequently went into receivership. A small group of former executives who were not involved with the women's lawsuits bought the name Rodman and Renshaw and began doing business in New York City. The new firm is not affiliated with the old one.

5. Linda Friedman, interview by author, October 28, 1997.

6. *Susan Jaskowski v. Rodman & Renshaw Inc., Norman Mains, Gregory P. Quinlivan, and Kurt Karmin,* 92 Civ 4161 (U.S. District Court for the Northern District of Illinois Eastern District, June 25, 1992), page 5.

7. Linda Friedman, interview by author, New York, New York, October 28, 1997.

8. "The Forbes 400," *Forbes*, October 16, 1995, page 248; *Susan Bell v. Olde Discount Corporation and Ernest Olde* (before the National Association of Securities Dealers Inc., February 21, 1995), complaint, pages 2, 4. Bell and her lawyer moved on to settle the case; Olde subsequently gave legal business to that lawyer.

9. Susan Antilla, "Three Women vs. a Broker; Olde Is Accused of Blatant Job Discrimination," *New York Times,* April 26, 1995, Business/Financial Desk, page 1.

10. Richard R. Lindsey, memorandum to Arthur Levitt, March 12, 1997, page 2.

11. Ibid.

12. Jim Vere, "The 'Blackballing' of Arbitrators," *Registered Representative Magazine,* January 1997, pages 83–86.

13. In the period just after Shearson won the Gilmer case in 1991, some firms appeared to be unaware of the clout they had to limit litigants: Jaskowski and her colleagues were able to press lawsuits against Rodman.

14. *Rita M. Reid v. Goldman, Sachs & Co. and the Goldman, Sachs Group L.P.,* Part 17, 31002-91 (Supreme Court of the State of New York, New York County, November 1991), complaint.

15. Olde Discount Corporation, Stockbroker Employment Agreement, February 1992, pages 1–11.

16. Primerica/Smith Barney company manual, Principles of Employment (HRD0002 10-92).

17. United States General Accounting Office, *Employment Discrimination: How Registered Representatives Fare in Discrimination Disputes,* Report to the Chairman of the Subcommittee on Telecommunications and Finance, Committee on Energy and Commerce, House of Representatives, March 30, 1994, GAO/HEHS-94–17, page 2.

18. *Susan Desiderio v. Great Western Financial Services* (before the National Association of Securities Dealers Inc., August 25, 1993), amended statement of claim of Susan Desiderio during arbitration.

19. *Susan Desiderio v. Great Western Financial Services* (before the National Association of Securities Dealers Inc., February 14, 1995), page 393. Transcript of NASD arbitration available through Brickell, Gomberg & Associates, Inc. (305-522-0067).

20. Ibid., pages 524–525.

21. *Susan Desiderio v. Great Western Financial Services,* 93-01568 (NASD award in the matter, April 27, 1995).

22. Richard R. Lindsey, memorandum to Arthur Levitt, March 12, 1997, page 2.

23. Those who endorse arbitration might legitimately complain that some women could frivolously throw in a gender discrimination claim on top of a business dispute that could or should have stood on its own. Whether that is a significant enough problem to require all women's civil rights claims to go to arbitration, however, is far from evident.

24. Stuart H. Bompey, "Arbitration of Sexual Harassment and Securities Disputes," ABA Annual Meeting, Arbitration Committee Dispute Resolution Section, August 7, 1995.

25. *Tonja Duffield v. Robertson Stephens & Co.,* C95-0109 CAL (U.S. District Court for the Northern District of California, July 25, 1995), deposition of Deborah Masucci, page 200.

26. *Rita M. Reid v. Goldman, Sachs & Co. and Goldman, Sachs Group, L.P.,* New York Stock Exchange award data in the matter of arbitration, March 31, 1995, page 4.

27. Ibid., page 4.

28. Ibid., page 8.

29. Ibid., page 9.

30. Ibid., pages 8–9.

31. Eileen Valentino, telephone interview by author, June 13, 1996.

32. Ibid.; *Eileen Valentino Charge of Discrimination v. NASD, NYSE, and Smith Barney* filed with the EEOC on October 16, 1996, page 6.

33. Eileen Valentino, telephone interview by author, June 13, 1996.

34. Ibid.

35. "Award Report in *Darlene Livingston v. Shearson Lehman Brothers Inc.*," *Securities Arbitration Commentator,* January 15, 1996, page 4.

36. United States General Accounting Office, *Employment Discrimination: How Registered Representatives Fare in Discrimination Disputes,* Report to the Chairman of the Subcommittee on Telecommunications and Finance, Committee on Energy and Commerce, House of Representatives, March 30, 1994, GAO/HEHS-94-17, page 2.

37. Margaret A. Jacobs, "Riding Crop and Slurs: How Wall Street Dealt With a Sex-Bias Case," *Wall Street Journal,* June 9, 1994, page 1.

38. *Tonja Duffield v. Robertson Stephens & Company,* Case No. C95-0109 CAL (U.S. District Court for the Northern District of California, July 25,1995), deposition of Deborah Masucci, taken in New York, New York, page 95.

39. Terry R. Weiss, "If We Wanted Your Opinion, We Would Have Asked for It: Why Arbitrators Need Not State the Reasons for Their Award," presented at NASD Arbitration Training, Washington, D.C., May 18, 1994.

40. Report of the Subcommittee on Punitive Damages of the NASD Legal Advisory Board (NASD Publication, 1994).

41. *Tonja Duffield v. Robertson Stephens & Company,* Case No. C95-0109 CAL (U.S. District Court for the Northern District of California, July 25, 1995), deposition of Deborah Masucci, taken in New York, New York, page 248.

42. Ibid., page 252.

43. Ibid., page 254.

44. Travelers Group/Smith Barney, employment arbitration policy (as modified August 1994), September 1, 1994.

45. Ibid.

46. Ibid.

47. Ibid.

48. *Alicia DeGaetano v. Smith Barney Inc. and Frederick Hessler,* 95 Civ 1613 DLC (U.S. District Court for the Southern District of New York, March 8, 1995).

49. *Rita M. Reid v. Goldman, Sachs & Co and Goldman, Sachs Group L.P.* (April 7, 1995), statement of Rita M. Reid concerning decision of NASD arbitration panel.

50. Anita Raghavan, "A Big Board Panel Decides in Favor of Goldman Sachs in Sex-bias Case," *Wall Street Journal,* April 10, 1995, page B-8.

51. "Award Report in *Darlene Livingston v. Shearson Lehman Hutton,*" *Securities Arbitration Commentator,* January 15, 1996.

52. Ibid.

53. *In the matter of Darlene Livingston against Shearson Lehman Brothers,* National Association of Securities Dealers Inc. (case number 93-00770), closing arguments, reference to the testimony of Lydia Klein, page 5187.

54. Ibid.

55. *Alicia DeGaetano v. Smith Barney Inc. and Frederick Hessler,* 95 Civ 1613 DLC (U.S. District Court for the Southern District of New York, March 8, 1995).
56. Form U-4 Uniform Application for Securities Industry Registration or Transfer, signed by Susan A. Desiderio, March 13, 1996.
57. *Susan Desiderio v. the National Association of Securities Dealers, Inc.,* 97 Civ 0312 (U.S. District Court for the Southern District of New York, April 1998).

CHAPTER 11
GOING PUBLIC

Smith Barney was largely uncooperative with the author. Before the Martens lawsuit was filed, in mid-May 1996, officials at the firm would return the author's telephone calls. In the early stages of the lawsuit, company representatives largely described the complaint as being without merit. Subsequently, requests to two members of the public relations staff, Michael Schlein and Sally Cates, were ignored or turned down. When the author approached Schlein on his way out of court, he said that he would not make CEO Jamie Dimon available for an interview. The first time Schlein said this, he said it was because Dimon was too busy; later, he said it was because the author's coverage of the lawsuit had not been fair. Cates did not get back to the author with information as innocuous as the hiring dates and work locations of Nicholas Cuneo. The manager of the Paramus, New Jersey, office told the author that the public relations staff had told him not to return phone calls about this book.

1. Saundra Torry and Jay Mathews, "Three Women Sue Smith Barney; Former, Current Employees Accuse Brokerage of Discrimination," *Washington Post,* May 21, 1996, Financial sec., page D3.
2. Dennis Levine, *Inside Out: An Insider's Account of Wall Street* (New York: Putnam, 1991), pages 42–44, 336, 384.
3. Mark Belnick, interview by author, Tyco International Limited offices, New York City, September 8, 1999.
4. Nikhil Deogun, "Bank Claims Panel Was Biased Because it Included Woman," *Wall Street Journal,* May 31, 1996, page B-11.

CHAPTER 12
MOMENTUM: MERRILL'S WOMEN SUE

The narrative in this chapter relies in part on information filed in court in the class-action lawsuits against Smith Barney and Merrill Lynch. Both lawsuits ultimately were settled without a trial. As of August 2002, the only deposition taken of an alleged wrongdoer that the author was aware of was that of Frank Powers, former branch manager of the Smith Barney Tampa branch, and that deposition was part of the private arbitration file of plaintiff Edna Broyles; it was not filed in federal court.

Depositions of accused harassers or discriminators were not filed in federal court. Defendants did not file with the court answers to the allegations made against them in the complaints. In the settlements of both lawsuits, the defendants were released from liability for the claims against them.

1. John L. Donnelly, letter to Smith Barney colleagues, May 31, 1996.

2. National Association of Securities Dealers Inc., Central Registration Depository record of Nicholas Cuneo, September 6, 1995; Susan Antilla, "Smith Barney Served Amended Sex Discrimination Suit," Bloomberg News, October 18, 1996.

3. John L. Donnelly, letter to Smith Barney colleagues, May 31, 1996.

4. *Martens et al. v. Smith Barney et al.*, 96 Civ 3779 AGS (U.S. District Court for the Southern District of New York, July 2, 1996), amended complaint.

5. John L. Donnelly, letter to Smith Barney colleagues, August 27, 1996.

6. Linda Friedman, interview by author, February 13, 2001.

7. *Securities and Exchange Commission v. Stanley J. Feminella et al.*, 96 Civ 336 AGS (U.S. District Court for the Southern District of New York, September 11, 1996), deposition of Stanley J. Feminella, pages 702, 705, 711.

8. Order instituting a proceeding pursuant to sections 15(b) and 21(c) of the Securities Exchange Act of 1934, Administrative Proceeding File No. 3-9079, In the Matter of Lehman Brothers Inc. as successor to Shearson Lehman Brothers Inc.

9. By this time, Judge Allen G. Schwartz, the judge in charge of the Feminella case, had contracted pneumonia and would not be back at the courthouse for another year. In the months ahead, the district court would begin to divvy up his cases to other judges. The Feminella case had been settled, but it meant that *Martens et al. v. Smith Barney et al.* would be going from Schwartz to another courtroom.

10. *Pamela K. Martens et al. v. Smith Barney et al.*, 96 Civ 3779 AGS (U.S. District Court for the Southern District of New York, October 17, 1996), second amended complaint, page 1.

11. Ibid.

12. *Jennifer Alvarez et al. v. Smith Barney Inc.*, 96 Civ 3919 (U.S. District Court for the Northern District of California, October 28, 1996), complaint, page 1.

13. Saundra Torry and Jay Mathews, "Three Women Sue Smith Barney: Former, Current Employees Accuse Brokerage of Discrimination," *Washington Post*, May 21, 1996, page D3.

14. Kirstin Downey Grimsley, "26 Women Sue Smith Barney, Allege Bias," *Washington Post*, November 6, 1996, page C11.

15. Douglas Feiden, "New Raps in Boom-Boom Suit: Women Told to Wear Miniskirts," *New York Daily News*, May 22, 1996, page 8.

16. *Pamela K. Martens et al. v. Smith Barney et al.*, 96 Civ 3779 CBM (U.S. District Court for the Southern District of New York, December 8, 1999), corrected memorandum in opposition to motion to enforce settlement stipulation, Tab D, statement of claim of Beverly Trice, page 5.

17. Ibid., page 3.

18. In a letter to the author dated August 2, 2000, Kuddes wrote that he "did not mock Ms. Trice, did not ask anyone to dress any way, and did not select persons to

whom prizes were given."

19. Patrick McGeehan and Anita Raghavan, "Smith Barney Defense in Suit Is Questioned," *Wall Street Journal,* November 13, 1996, page C1.

20. James Dimon, address over Smith Barney internal speaker system, November 13, 1996 (audiotape supplied to the author by a former Smith Barney employee).

21. Smith Barney was consistently inconsistent in its portrayal of the reasoning behind the leave of absence and retirement of Nicholas Cuneo. It told the *New York Daily News* on May 21, 1996, that Cuneo had been "allowed to resign." In a story by Bloomberg News on October 18, 1996, a spokeswoman stopped short of saying that his departure was linked to women's complaints. After having interviewed officials of the firm, the *Wall Street Journal* wrote on November 13, 1996, that Cuneo had been forced to retire. Ultimately, Smith Barney officials signed documents for Cuneo's permanent file with federal regulators that said the branch manager had left the firm and had a "normal" retirement.

22. Linda Friedman, telephone interview by author, May 21, 2001.

23. Jerry Goldman, *Statistical Analysis of Salomon Smith Barney Inc. Retail Workforce Patterns and Practices,* July 11, 2000, Professor of Mathematical Sciences, De Paul University, Chicago, Illinois.

24. Linda Friedman, telephone interview by author, September 7, 2001.

25. Pamela Martens, e-mail to Linda Friedman, December 21, 1996.

26. *Susan Desiderio v. the National Association of Securities Dealers Inc. and the Securities and Exchange Commission,* 97 Civ 0312 (U.S. District Court for the Southern District of New York, January 15, 1997).

27. The Civil Rights Procedures Protection Act, HR 983, March 6, 1996, 105th Congress of the United States.

28. Edward J. Markey, Jesse L. Jackson Jr., and Anna G. Eshoo, letter to The Honorable Arthur Levitt, February 3, 1997.

29. Linda Friedman, telephone interview by author, May 16, 2001.

30. Ibid.

31. Mark Belnick, interview by author, Tyco International Limited offices, New York City, September 8, 1999.

32. Pamela Martens, e-mail to Linda Friedman, January 21, 1997.

33. Linda Friedman, e-mail to Pamela Martens, February 5, 1997.

34. In fact, lawyers for Salomon Smith Barney were still fighting on November 27, 2001, to keep scholarly studies that drew from the confidential data under wraps. At closing arguments for the arbitration of Edna Broyles, Brad Karp, lawyer for Salomon Smith Barney, strongly objected when Broyles's lawyer said that his client would like to submit two studies that had been prepared for use in arbitration hearings for the Smith Barney class action. The arbitrators upheld Karp's objection.

35. Mark A. Belnick, letter to Mary Stowell and Linda Friedman, January 10, 1997.

36. "Smith Barney Chief Justifies Firm's Silence on *20/20,*" *Wall Street Letter,* April 14, 1997, page 4.

37. *Secrets of the Trade: Wall Street's Smith Barney in Big Mess,* ABC News *20/20* with Deborah Roberts, Hugh Downs, and Barbara Walters, April 4, 1997.

38. James Dimon, letter to Smith Barney employees, February 10, 1997.

39. Cole e-mailed the author on January 24, 2002, to say that she would "discuss the feasibility of an interview" when she returned from a trip on January 31, 2002. She did not respond to subsequent follow-up queries by the author.

40. "Wall Street Sleaze," *Forbes,* cover story, February 24, 1997.

41. *Marybeth Cremin, Nancy Thomas, Anne Kaspar, Sonia Ingram, Alice Moss, Linda Conti, Anne Marie Kearney, and Angela Covo v. Merrill Lynch, Pierce, Fenner & Smith, Inc., Joseph Gannotti, the New York Stock Exchange, and the National Association of Securities Dealers,* 96 Civ 3773 (U.S. District Court for the Northern District of Illinois Eastern Division, February 27, 1997), complaint, page 1.

42. While the complaint itself stressed gender discrimination, a study of the Merrill women three years later revealed a group that volunteered complaints about sexual harassment as freely as it did about gender discrimination.

43. The firm said it had been accommodating to her request for a relocation because of a change in her husband's employment, and that it had even set up a toll-free telephone number so that her Illinois clients could call her. Cremin said that Merrill Lynch had a self-interest in keeping her when she moved because she would continue to bring profits to the firm.

44. *Cremin et al. v. Merrill Lynch et al.,* 96 Civ 3773 (U.S. District Court for the Northern District of Illinois Eastern Division, February 27, 1997), complaint, page 1.

45. Ibid.

46. Marybeth Cremin, telephone interview by author, February 26, 1997.

47. *Cremin et al. v. Merrill Lynch et al.,* 96 Civ 3773 (U.S. District Court for the Northern District of Illinois Eastern Division, February 27, 1997), complaint, page 1.

48. Paul W. Critchlow, senior vice president, communications and public affairs, Merrill Lynch, letter to author, August 28, 2000.

49. *In the Matter of Arbitration between Rita M. Reid v. Goldman, Sachs & Co. and Goldman Sachs Group, L.P.,* New York Stock Exchange, award data, March 31, 1995.

50. Ibid.

51. *Cremin et al. v. Merrill Lynch et al.,* 96 Civ 3773 (U.S. District Court for the Northern District of Illinois Eastern Division, February 27, 1997).

52. Ibid., page 13.

53. Ibid., page 13.

54. Ibid., page 15.

55. Paul W. Critchlow, letter to author, August 28, 2000.

56. Stuart J. Kaswell, senior vice president and general counsel, Securities Industry Association, letter to Mary Schapiro, president, NASD Regulation, Inc., March 11, 1997. The letter is cosigned by Bear, Stearns & Co. Inc.; Dean Witter Reynolds, Inc.; Goldman, Sachs & Co.; Lehman Brothers Inc.; Merrill Lynch, Pierce, Fenner & Smith, Inc.; Morgan Stanley & Co. Inc.; Oppenheimer & Co. Inc.; PaineWebber Inc.; and Smith Barney Inc.

57. In a letter to the author from its defamation counsel at Paul, Weiss, Rifkind, Wharton & Garrison dated August 31, 2000, Smith Barney stressed that the case had been an example of the firm pursuing "the right thing" with regard to sexual misconduct of one of its brokers. It additionally said that Saks had not had any personal involvement in the case, and "was sanctioned jointly and severally with the other Respondents in connection with a discovery spat between the trial lawyers." The decision by the NASD arbitrators to levy fines upon Saks and a second Smith Barney lawyer, Therese Obringer, however, was an atypical ruling from an arbitration panel. The panel told Smith Barney, Saks, and one other lawyer to pay the plaintiff $10,000 for failing to comply with the panel's discovery orders; Saks and Obringer alone were responsible for a second payment of $2,292.51 related to the arbitrators' having had to wait—without explanation—for two days to hear testimony from Joseph Plumeri, former president of Smith Barney. Although Smith Barney's outside counsel cites the case as one that shows the firm's diligence regarding the policing of sexual misconduct, transcripts of testimony from the hearings expose extreme shortcomings in Smith Barney's policies and practices and several examples of violators who were kept at the firm.

58. John Reagan did not respond to a registered letter from the author received by him on August 11, 2000.

59. *William S. Gray v. Smith Barney Inc., Therese Obringer, and A. George Saks,* case number 95-01185 (State of Michigan American Arbitration Association, Southfield, Michigan, December 12, 1996), testimony of James Stewart Boshart, managing director, capital markets division, Salomon Smith Barney, pages 1364–1366.

60. *William S. Gray v. Smith Barney Inc., Therese Obringer, and A. George Saks,* case number 95-01185 (State of Michigan American Arbitration Association, Southfield, Michigan, December 12, 1996), testimony of James Stewart Boshart.

61. John Larrabee, "Fugitive Playboy's Verdict Due: Jury Considers '86 High School Rape Case," *USA Today,* November 12, 1996.

62. Mary L. Schapiro, Linda D. Fienberg, and Deborah Masucci, NASD Regulation, Inc., memorandum to James Buck et al., April 2, 1997.

63. National Association of Securities Dealers, Inc., Central Registration Depository records of Lew Lieberbaum & Co.

64. *Equal Employment Opportunity Commission v. Gruntal & Co. Inc.,* 97 Civ 3275 (U.S. District Court for the Southern District of New York, May 6, 1997); EEOC Press Release, "Gruntal Agrees to Pay in Sex Harassment Suit," May 6, 1977.

CHAPTER 13
MARTENS WITHOUT MARTENS

Relying in part on the recollection of counsel for the Smith Barney plaintiffs, this chapter depicts a meeting in January 1997 between Linda Friedman, Mary Stowell, and representatives of Smith Barney and The Travelers. The reader should be aware that Smith Barney was not cooperative with the author, and thus was not available for ongoing queries. It is likely that the firm would depict the meeting differently than Friedman and Stowell did.

1. It was later argued by Linda Friedman that it would not have been appropriate for Cole to have had an office or telephone at Smith Barney, because Cole was supposed to be independent of Smith Barney.

2. Steve Fields, memo to Smith Barney Branch Managers—NY Suburban Region, August 13, 1996.

3. Pamela Martens, e-mail to Linda Friedman, February 11, 1997. Martens told Friedman that "Janie Paton, one of the sales assistants in G.C., went into the computer to check on registrations for her brokers and found that she is listed as a registered sales associate even though she is not registered … I believe they simply increased the registered number of women by data entry so that they could claim they have 10% female brokers."

4. Friedman said that her confidence was based in part on the fact that she and Smith Barney had not included any titles with the words "sales assistants" in their counts of total numbers of female brokers. However, the woman about whom Pam was concerned reported that she saw her name listed as "licensed sales associate."

5. Through his secretary, Rotman declined to comment for this book.

6. Linda Friedman, e-mail to author, May 22, 2001.

7. Mary Stowell, letter to Pamela Martens, September 24, 1996.

8. Mary Stowell and Linda Friedman, letter to author, August 25, 2000. Stowell and Friedman said that, to their best recollection, "we faxed Pam a copy of Rotman's standard mediation agreement the day after the Westbury meeting but again with the caveat that we were not certain it would even apply to the class mediation." But Friedman said in a June 20, 1997, cover letter to Pam that the agreement "was sent to us specifically for the upcoming *Martens et al. v. Smith Barney et al.* mediation July 9–10, 1997."

9. Mary Stowell and Linda Friedman, letter to author, August 25, 2000. Stowell and Friedman wrote that Friedman did not recall "yelling into the phone that the treatment was 'outrageous' or that she had never been treated so badly," which was how Martens described the incident. Stowell and Friedman pointed out that they stayed at the Westbury Hotel several times after the June meeting.

10. Mary Stowell and Linda Friedman, letter to author, August 25, 2000.

11. Pamela Martens, interview by author, May 16, 2001. Martens said that during a long telephone conversation with Friedman several days before the NOW convention, she suggested that her lawyer not attend the awards ceremony, given their differences over the confidentiality issue.

12. Pamela Martens, interviews by author, May 4 and May 16, 2001. Martens said this was an erroneous depiction of her motivation and that her relationship with Stowell and Friedman became irreparably harmed by disagreements over the signing of confidentiality documents. She also said that it would not make sense that her NOW award would lead to her becoming more rigid, particularly about the settlement talks. Pam considered Friedman's analysis to be ridiculous, considering that, ultimately, the national office of NOW wound up siding with Stowell and Friedman and supporting the settlement, while Pam was left only with the support of the New York State and New York City chapters of NOW.

13. In a letter to the author on August 31, 2000, Martin London, defamation counsel to Smith Barney, said that the author's version of what transpired at the mediation "violates the spirit of confidentiality" of the sessions in July 1997. "As much as Smith Barney would like to correct the record," he wrote, "it cannot do so without

violating the confidential nature of those proceedings."

14. Linda Friedman, interview by author, New York City, October 28, 1997. Friedman said, "Smith Barney in July walked in and said, 'We're not gonna settle for a lot of money like Texaco' ... The mediators said, 'Here's the deal. They don't want to wear a sign saying "A penny more than Texaco." But they'll pay a billion.'" The latter was a speculation about what the combination of mediations and arbitrations might ultimately cost Smith Barney.

15. Linda Friedman would later tell Patricia Clemente that the women gave up the promise of starting with a settlement figure at the arbitration phase at least as large as the last offer at mediation in exchange for unlimited punitive damages.

16. *Martens et al. v. Smith Barney et al.,* 96 Civ 3779 AGS (U.S. District Court for the Southern District of New York, October 17, 1996), second amended complaint.

17. Linda Friedman, letter to Pamela Martens, March 7, 1996.

18. Ultimately, the invitation to the media was less than met the eye. Broadcast reporters were eliminated, and only two print reporters at most would be permitted at an arbitration hearing, the first of which took place in November 2001. (As of August 2002, it was the only arbitration to have taken place.) And a plaintiff could choose to have the hearing behind closed doors, which was the stated choice of class representative Beverly Trice, who told the author at an interview in Tampa, Florida, on November 27, 2001, that she had an agent and a publisher for a book about the lawsuit against Smith Barney and thus was not inviting the press to her hearing.

19. Mary Stowell and Linda Friedman, letter to the author, August 25, 2000. Stowell and Friedman made the additional argument that Smith Barney agreed that "it would follow that ruling" if the class won a court fight against the NASD and NYSE on the issue of mandatory arbitration. Such an "agreement," however, would amount to no concession at all; a court ruling on mandatory arbitration would have forced compliance on Smith Barney. (The judge dismissed the counts against NASD and NYSE.)

Another way in which Smith Barney would have been forced to end its policy of mandatory arbitration would have been if the self-regulatory organizations—the NYSE and NASD—that adjudicate complaints either refused to hear civil rights complaints or refused to hear complaints of anyone who was forced into arbitration. NYSE wound up changing its rules such that it would not hear complaints of anyone forced into arbitration, but NASD continued to take cases where the complaining person had been forced to sign away his or her rights to court. Several brokerage firms—not including Smith Barney—in the meantime disposed of their policies that required employees to arbitrate civil rights claims. In a telephone interview on September 7, 2001, Friedman told the author that it was her belief that Smith Barney's practice of requiring employees to sign contracts in which they agreed to mandatory arbitration was a violation of the "spirit" of the July 1997 mediation. When NASD ceased to mandate arbitration of civil rights claims, Friedman said that it was her expectation that Smith Barney would cease to require its employees to sign contracts agreeing to arbitration. Friedman said that she had this expectation based on statements made by Chuck O. Prince III, Travelers's general counsel, during the July 1997 mediations between Smith Barney and the litigating women in the

Martens suit.

20. Stowell and Friedman would later be criticized for not having sought the help of a larger law firm to handle the nearly 2,000 individual claims that were later filed against Smith Barney. In defending themselves against their critics at the time, they said that they were adequately staffed to handle the assignment. In a telephone interview with the author on December 2, 2001, however, Friedman said, "We're not a large law firm" when explaining why she could not get the claim forms of all the women filed before the original deadline.

CHAPTER 14
SETTLING THE SETTLEMENT

This narrative relies in part on the recollection of the plaintiffs' counsel of the settlement negotiations with Smith Barney. From the point of view of Linda Friedman, one of the women's lawyers, there was a quid pro quo that when the settlement was announced, Smith Barney would not highlight the fact that it had put forth no settlement fund, and the women would not speculate about the amount of money that Smith Barney might ultimately pay out. The reader should be aware that Smith Barney was not cooperative with the author and may have had a different view about any quid pro quo.

1. Linda Friedman, telephone interview by author, July 17, 2000.

2. Linda Friedman, letter to Pam Martens, March 7, 1996. In the letter Friedman had, by comparison, been encouraging Pam's support on the issue. "I am sure you will agree that our fight to stay out of arbitration is important," she wrote.

3. Linda Friedman, telephone interview by author, September 7, 2001.

4. Linda Friedman, telephone interview by author, July 11, 2000.

5. Linda Friedman, telephone interview by author, October 27, 1997; Friedman subsequently said that she did not say this. Subsequent to the denial, she wrote that she "would have said that in writing a book about the Smith Barney settlement or the phenomenal change at that Firm, that Pam should not be the source of that information." In the telephone conversation, however, the author recalls, and her notes confirm, that Friedman did make the suggestion; that Friedman was speaking in a hostile tone about Martens; and that, later in the conversation, Friedman was pressing the author to take on a book project with several of her Smith Barney clients—a project the author had declined.

6. Friedman also cut the author off from most communications for long stretches of time, including more than a year during which the named plaintiffs who were aligned with her simultaneously ceased to speak to the author. After a stretch of approximately one year of lack of cooperation from Friedman or Stowell, the author wrote to them on July 12, 2000. At that point, Friedman reopened communications and wrote back to the author to respond to questions and to say that the author's research was inadequate. Friedman and Stowell in their letter suggested that in order to properly research this book, the author interview many of the same people they previously had shielded.

7. Stowell and Friedman behaved similarly with the author, although not consistently. On several occasions, Friedman raised the possibility of suing the author, including during a telephone interview with the author on September 7, 2001. Ms. Retkwa disputes having been "spooked" by the letter and having asked to be taken off the story. She maintains that once the settlement was announced she decided no longer to report on the litigation because she no longer considered it newsworthy. Ms. Retkwa did continue to report on certain aspects of the litigation even after her editor received the Stowell and Friedman letter.

8. Linda Friedman, telephone interview by author, December 2, 2001. Friedman said that several of the class representatives in fall 1998 were spending money that they anticipated receiving in their mediations even before the mediations were scheduled. One bought a red BMW, said Friedman. Another bought a house.

9. Linda Friedman, telephone interview by author, February 19, 2001.

10. Mary Stowell and Linda Friedman, letter to author, August 25, 2000.

11. Martens would not be permitted to speak at the fairness hearing.

12. Judy Mione, statement supplied to the author dated January 26, 1998, describing the December 7, 1997, visit of Lorraine Parker and Lydia Klein to the place of business of Mione's son in Rockville Centre, New York; Lorraine Parker, telephone interview by author, July 25, 2000. Parker said that she and Lydia Klein were in the neighborhood by happenstance and did not know that the establishment was owned by Mione's son.

13. Dennis Vacco, letter to the Securities and Exchange Commission, December 17, 1997.

14. Jeffrey Liddle, letter to the Securities and Exchange Commission, January 2, 1998.

15. Mary Stowell, letter to class representatives, January 14, 1998.

16. Louise F. Fitzgerald, Expert Report, *Cremin et al. v. Merrill Lynch et al.,* March 3, 2001.

17. Elizabeth Cohen and Kathy Bishop, "Still Room for Boom-Boom; Smith Barney RX in Sex-Harass Suit Is a Sham: Probe—Special Investigation," *New York Post,* February 10, 1998, page 7.

18. Depositions were taken of people chosen by Smith Barney to speak on general policies. But the specific individuals Pam Martens wanted to see held accountable were not deposed.

19. Daniel Wise, "City firms get poor grades in survey on women lawyers," *New York Law Journal,* October 27, 1997, page 1.

20. Anna Snider, "Consultant hired to aid firm's image with women," *New York Law Journal,* February 2, 1998, page 1.

21. Laura Harris, librarian at the *New York Post,* telephone interview by author, December 15, 2000; Kathy Bishop, "Smith Barney: Sex Hotline Was on Fritz; The Brokerage Firm Tries to Make Amends," *New York Post,* February 11, 1998. The article that ran on February 11 did not constitute a correction. In fact, Johnetta Cole, diversity adviser, called the reporters back for the first time after having seen the February 10 story in which it was noted that she had not returned the reporter's telephone calls. The librarian for the *Post* said that no corrections that correspond with either of the two stories exist in the newspaper's database.

22. Although the dismissals were not lacking for publicity, less than three weeks later, one of the two men had landed a job at an investment-banking firm known for its work advising brokerage houses and other financial services companies.

23. Beverly Trice, telephone interview by author, July 17, 2000. Trice said that she had made a remark about a foul smell in the ladies' room, but that it had to do with a broken toilet that was filled with excrement, not with Pam's entry into the room.

24. In an August 25, 2000, letter to the author, Friedman and Stowell denied that they told plaintiffs not to speak to Cara Beth Walker. In a sworn affidavit dated March 6, 2002, Lisa Mays said that Friedman had made disparaging remarks about Walker (that she was "drunk" or "on something") a number of times.

25. *Martens et al. v. Smith Barney et al.*, 96 Civ 3779 CBM (U.S. District Court for the Southern District of New York, August 6, 1998), consolidated stipulation of settlement, 38.7.

CHAPTER 15
PARIAH OR VISIONARY?

1. In a telephone interview by the author on September 7, 2001, Linda Friedman said she believed that Pam wanted documents in order to produce what Friedman referred to as "Pam packets" that criticized Stowell and Friedman. In another telephone interview by the author on July 17, 2000, Friedman said that she and Stowell would travel to visit with class representatives to show them drafts of the settlement—but not give them copies—in part out of fear that a copy would get to Pam, who might publicly criticize the draft.

2. Linda Friedman, telephone interview by author, August 21, 2000.

3. In a telephone interview with the author on January 17, 2002, Judy Mione said that "it wasn't an issue of the money" for her, and that she came independently to the decision to fight Smith Barney and to split off from the settling women. Mione said that she would not have received the satisfaction she now had if she had gone along with a settlement she did not believe in.

4. Linda Friedman, telephone interview by author, February 19, 2001; *Cremin et al. v. Merrill Lynch et al.*, 96 Civ 3773 (U.S. District Court for the Northern District of Illinois Eastern Division, February 27, 1997), stipulation of settlement, page 77; Marybeth Cremin, telephone interview by author, August 31, 2001.

5. In the memo to Judge Motley, Stowell and Friedman wrote: "As to Class Counsel, the following cases are only a few examples of the high regard in which Stowell & Friedman are held: *Cremin v. Merrill Lynch, No. 96 C 3773* (Castillo, J.) [*sic*] (in approving class settlement, court remarks, 'there have been no more competent counsel that I've ever had in a case than have appeared here on behalf of the plaintiff …')." Although the full text was attached as an exhibit, the main text gave the impression that the judge had singled out Stowell and Friedman. *Martens et al. v. Smith Barney et al.*, 96 Civ 3773 CBM (U.S. District Court for the Southern

District of New York, December 8, 1999), plaintiffs' memorandum in opposition to Kent Spriggs's motion to substitute, page 3.

6. Cliff Palefsky, telephone interview by author, June 8, 1999.

7. Linda Friedman, telephone interview by author, December 9, 2001.

8. A Smith Barney representative in another setting made a case that a broker cannot tie his or her success to this sort of largesse. During the November 27, 2001, arbitration hearing of *Edna Broyles v. Smith Barney*, Tom Greene, former operations manager at the Tampa branch of Smith Barney, said that a broker's success can't be contingent on getting accounts passed on from others. The reason, he said, is that brokers will not leave a firm unless they can take 75 to 80 percent of their accounts with them, leaving little of significance to be picked over.

9. Marybeth Cremin, telephone interview by author, August 1, 2000.

10. *Martens et al. v. Smith Barney et al.*, 96 Civ 3779 CBM (U.S. District Court for the Southern District of New York, December 8, 1999), plaintiffs' memorandum in opposition to Kent Spriggs's motion to substitute, page 5.

11. Initial submission of claimant Linda Atkins Smoot, pursuant to Paragraph 7.12 (1) of the Class Action Settlement; *Martens et al. v. Smith Barney et al.*, 96 Civ 3779 CBM (U.S. District Court for the Southern District of New York, May 20, 1996).

12. *Martens et al. v. Smith Barney et al.*, 96 Civ 3779 CBM (U.S. District Court for the Southern District of New York, May 20, 1996), Sondra C. Collins Maddy statement of claim.

13. Roger Shuster, telephone interview by author, August 2, 2001. Shuster said, "I left there because I wanted to," and that Smith Barney did not request he resign.

14. *William S. Gray v. Smith Barney Inc., Therese Obringer, and A. George Saks*, case number 95-01185 (State of Michigan American Arbitration Association, Southfield, Michigan, December 12, 1996), pages 1364–1366.

15. Smith Barney Shearson, letter to Deborah Masucci, director of arbitration, September 7, 1994, Re *Eileen Valentino-Condon et al. v. Smith Barney Shearson et al.* (NASD #94-01586).

16. In inspecting approximately thirty records, the only time the author found a reference to a complaint, arbitration, or firing related to civil rights, the wording was too vague for the casual reader to understand. The CRD of the securities analyst who was fired from Smith Barney for distributing pornography via the firm's e-mail system listed a "violation of firm's e-mail policy; non business related."

17. Darlene Livingston and others tell of a shell game whereby accused men are removed while attention is focused on charges against them, only to be reinstated after the worn-down accuser leaves the industry. Livingston, who prevailed in her arbitration against her firm, bumped into an old colleague years later at a pasta store on Staten Island. She learned that one of her harassers was back on the job. "It just hurt," she said, adding that she hadn't slept in the week since she'd learned the news. In the Garden City, New York, office where Pam Martens worked, one of the brokers who was named in the *Martens* complaint disappeared from the office for months during the heat of publicity, only to reappear in 2000.

18. There was, however, evidence that women who considered going into the settlement during that time frame were discouraged by branch managers. Guita Bahrampour, a former broker in Berkeley, California, testified in a July 2002 affidavit that her boss told her in 1999 that his job would be at risk if she should file a claim. She had complained since the late 1980s of discriminatory problems in the workplace. The boss added that, if Bahrampour filed a claim in the class action, her job and that of her husband, who worked with her in the branch, would also be at risk. She said that she didn't know that retaliation was illegal, and that she knew of other women who would have filed claims if they had not been intimidated. She said in her affidavit that a suicide attempt in December 2000 was connected to her job-related depression.

19. *Cremin et al. v. Merrill Lynch et al.*, 96 Civ 3773 RC (U.S. District Court for the Northern District of Illinois Eastern Division), corrected status report, page 6. The status report describes the Chairman's Club gathering at which Launny Steffens told his audience that the women who filed claims in the class-action lawsuit against Merrill were low producers.

20. Schlein said that he was on his way into the building and had not been aware that there was a demonstration.

21. Pamela Martens, memo to Kent Spriggs sent via facsimile, October 29, 1999.

22. Mary Stowell and Linda Friedman, letter to author, August 9, 2002.

23. Affidavit of Patricia A. Clemente, July 15, 2002.

24. Patricia A. Clemente, telephone interview by author, August 2, 2002. Clemente said she could only confirm that she had settled and that she was no longer permitted to discuss her previous complaints about Smith Barney. Although it is Clemente's understanding that Linda Friedman counseled her at the end of the mediation that she could say only that she was "pleased about the whole thing," Friedman said in a letter to the author on August 9, 2002, that "Ms. Clemente's Settlement Agreement does not bar her from discussing her case. Ms. Clemente did agree that she will not disclose the terms or conditions of her Settlement Agreement."

25. *Crawford et al. v. US Bancorp Piper Jaffray Inc.*, 00 Civ 1611 CRB (U.S. District Court for the Northern District of California San Francisco Division, May 8, 2000).

26. *Martens et al. v. Smith Barney et al.*, 96 Civ 3779 CBM (U.S. District Court for the Southern District of New York, May 15, 2000), hearing before Judge Motley; on November 20, 2001, the Second Circuit Court of Appeals said that the District Court had failed to give Spriggs adequate opportunity to defend himself on those charges and sent the matter back to Judge Motley.

27. On November 20, 2001, the Second Circuit Court of Appeals said that the District Court had failed to give Spriggs adequate opportunity to defend himself on those charges and sent the matter back to Judge Motley.

28. Pamela Martens, telephone interview by author, December 9, 2001.

29. Large law firms offer hundreds of jobs to young lawyers each year, making it likely that Paul, Weiss made the offers innocently. A clerk involved in the *Martens* matter who received such a job offer, though, should have been recused from the case. As for Motley's son and his Smith Barney revenues, it would be hard to imagine a banker who was not getting business from a firm Smith Barney's size.

30. Linda Friedman, telephone interview by author, July 11, 2000.

31. Linda Friedman, telephone interview by author, September 7, 2001.

32. Patrick McGeehan, "Wall Street Highflier to Outcast: A Woman's Story," *New York Times,* Sunday, February 10, 2002, Business, page 1.

33. Affidavit of Laura Sweezey, May 23, 2002.

CHAPTER 16
ARBITRATION AFTER ALL

1. These terms, which included keeping silent about their stories and about the terms of the settlement, were described in redacted pages of two Merrill Lynch settlement documents that were anonymously supplied to the author in November 2001.

2. *Martens et al. v. Smith Barney et al.,* 96 Civ 3779 JGK (U.S. District Court for the Southern District of New York, July 2002), moving plaintiffs' motion to supplement motion to enforce, page 40.

3. Kate Kelly, "Floor Governor at Big Board Claims Sex Bias at ING Barings," *Wall Street Journal,* January 11, 2001, page C1.

4. *Jennifer Solomon v. Salomon Smith Barney Inc., John B. Hoffman, and Kevin McCaffrey,* Index number 117001/01 (Supreme Court of the State of New York, County of New York, November 1, 2000), amended complaint.

5. Later that fall, the EEOC argued before the Supreme Court that Waffle House, Inc., did not have the right to prevent the EEOC from suing it on behalf of an employee who had signed a mandatory arbitration contract. Waffle House was arguing that the contract applied even to the federal government, an argument that the Supreme Court rejected in its January 15, 2002, ruling against the firm.

6. Arbitration of *Edna Broyles v. Smith Barney,* Tampa, Florida, October 31, 2001, page 21; *Martens et al. v. Smith Barney et al.,* 96 Civ 3779 CBM (U.S. District Court for the Southern District of New York, May 20, 1996). The Broyles arbitration transcript is not part of the court docket.

7. A witness for Smith Barney would later say that office scuttlebutt had it that Bladon's firing was over an "innocuous" action that she took "to facilitate something" and that the witness, Janet Nichols, was sad that Bladon had been fired because she was an honest person. Nichols said that Frank Powers, the branch manager, called a meeting in the office after Bladon left, and that he appeared to be shaken. "I mean, I thought he was going to cry in that meeting," she said. Nichols's characterization seemed at odds with Huang's line of questioning of Bladon, in which Huang portrayed the broker as a rogue.

8. Arbitration of *Edna Broyles v. Smith Barney,* Tampa, Florida, November 27, 2001, page 915.

9. Ibid., pages 148, 149.

10. Ibid., page 317.

11. Ibid., page 824.

12. Arbitration of *Edna Broyles v. Smith Barney,* Tampa, Florida, November 27, 2001, page 819; *Martens et al. v. Smith Barney et al.,* 96 Civ 3779 CBM (U.S. District Court for the Southern District of New York, May 20, 1996). The Broyles arbitration transcript is not part of the court docket.

13. Ibid., page 818.

14. Ibid., page 947, testimony of Frank Powers.

15. Ibid., page 956, testimony of Frank Powers.

16. Its author, Janice F. Madden, was hired by Stowell and Friedman as an expert to analyze statistical data.

17. Edna Broyles, telephone interview by author, January 4, 2001.

18. Tamar Lewin, "Bush May End Offices Dealing with Women's Issues, Groups Say," *New York Times,* December 19, 2001, page A23.

Index

A page number followed by n. or nn. refers to an endnote and is followed by the specific number(s) of the note(s) on that page. Page numbers in parentheses following an endnote citation refer to the text page on which the note reference occurs.